Recollections
The Life and Travels
of a Victorian Architect

Recollections
The Life and Travels of a Victorian Architect

Sir Thomas Graham Jackson Bt R.A.
HON. D.C.L. OXFORD, HON. LL.D. CAMBRIDGE
HON. FELLOW OF WADHAM COLLEGE, OXFORD
ASSOCIÉ DE L'ACADÉMIE ROYALE DE BELGIQUE
F.S.A.

1835 – 1924

Edited and arranged by
Sir Nicholas Jackson Bt,
HON. FELLOW OF HERTFORD COLLEGE, OXFORD

With an Introduction and Gazetteer of the Buildings by
James Bettley

Unicorn Press
London

Unicorn Press
76 Great Suffolk Street
London SE1 0BL

email: unicorn@tradford.demon.co.uk

First published 2003 by Unicorn Press

ISBN 0 906290 72 4

Typesetting by Ferdinand Page Design, Surrey
Printed and bound in Great Britain

Contents

List of Colour Plates   vii

Acknowledgements   viii

Foreword   ix

Preface   xi

Letter to T.G.J. from Sir Gilbert Scott   xv

Introduction   1

Chapter

1   Family History and Early Recollections   15

2   1849-54   27

3   Wadham College 1854   33

4   Oxford 1855-58   40

5   At Scott's Office 1858   50

6   1858-60   61

7   1860-64   70

8   1864-65   77

9   1867-73   92

10   First Work at Oxford 1871-75   104

11   1876   117

12   1876-79   126

13   1879-80   140

14   1881-85   150

15   1881-87   161

16   1882-85   165

17   1887-91   185

18   1891-93   199

Chapter

19	1893	208
20	1894-97	219
21	1897-1900	232
22	1901-06	241
23	1908-10	244
24	1911-14	249
25	Reflections	253
	Conclusion	255

Appendices

I	The Lambarde Family	257
II	RIBA and Registration of Architects	260
III	Winchester Cathedral	264
	Gazetteer	266
	Footnotes	301
	Bibliography	317
	Index	321

Key to modern place names

Agram	= Zagreb	Arbe	= Rab	Carlstadt	= Karlovac
Curzola	= Korčula	Fiume	= Rijeka	Lesina	= Hvar
Parenzo	= Poreč	Pola	= Pula	Ragusa	= Dubrovnik
Sebenico	= Sibenik	Spalato	= Split	Trau	= Trogir
Zara	= Zadar				

List of Colour Plates

Between pages 48 and 49

1   Examination Schools, Oxford
2   Sir Thomas Jackson Bt R.A. aged 86
3   Examination Schools – the Quad before the old buildings were demolished
4   Organ case at the Sheldonian Theatre, Oxford
5   Tenby, 1858
6   St David's Cathedral – Bishop Gower's Screen and Tomb
7   Eagle House, Wimbledon
8   Alice Jackson
9   Letter depicting a dog-cart written from Holland in 1890
10   Letter written to Hugh in 1890
11   St David's Cathedral and ruins of Bishop's palace
12   A Village in France

Between pages 144 and 145

13   Notre Dame la Grande, Poitiers
14   Laon
15   Furnes (Veurne)
16   Béthune
17   Chartres Cathedral – North Porch
18   Blois – the Staircase
19   Loches – Hôtel de Ville
20   Loches – S. Antoine
21   Nîmes
22   Como – the Broletto
23   Isola Bella – Lake Maggiore
24   Isola Piscatore – Lake Maggiore

Between pages 208 and 209

25   Siena – Cortile of the Palazzo Communale
26   S. Vitale, Ravenna
27   Ancona, 1881
28   Hvar – View of the city with the tower of S. Marco
29   Korcula
30   Hvar – Loggia and Forte Spagnuolo
31   Dubrovnik
32   Ragusa – Rector's palace
33   Rab. View of the Campanile from the sea
34   Mostar – the bridge

Acknowledgements

I would first like to acknowledge my indebtedness to Dr James Bettley for his participation in this book, which has included writing the introduction, doing extensive research in order to provide the comprehensive list of buildings and designs, compiling the bibliography, many of the footnotes and for reading the proofs.

I have to mention with particular gratitude the following: Dr Donald Buttress, LVO, Architect Emeritus to Westminster Abbey, for writing the Foreword; Mrs Philip Pilkington for photographing many of the drawings and watercolours illustrated; Mr Richard Norton, for permission to reproduce an excerpt from a diary of The Rev Henry Boyd; Lady Beresford-Peirse, for her help with matters relating to Croatia; my sister Mrs Michael Taraniuck, for permission to reproduce three watercolours in her possession; The Royal Academy of Arts; Mrs Charlotte Gere; Dr Paul Coones; Mr Roland Wilcock; my wife Nadia for her invaluable help and encouragement.

I am most grateful to the following for the generous contributions they have made towards the production of this book: The Drapers' Company, Hertford College, Oxford, Corpus Christi College, Oxford, Radley College, The Art Workers' Guild, The Surveyors' Club, Dr Donald Buttress.

Finally I must thank Hugh Tempest-Radford for agreeing to publish this revised edition of my Grandfather's 'Recollectons' with Unicorn Press and for the care and trouble he has taken over its production.

Foreword

Thomas Graham Jackson's 'Recollections', now at last re-published and expanded, are a century and more old. After the usual period of neglect, his reputation today stands high in the pantheon of great nineteenth-century architects, alongside Scott, Butterfield and Pearson. Born in the late Georgian era he lived through the whole of the Victorian period and its successive architectural fashions. Perhaps his greatest contribution was to reinvent and then popularise a long-lasting revival of English vernacular design; the term 'Anglo-Jackson' has been coined and has stuck.

His written memoirs and keenly observed watercolour and pencil drawings are a delight, as fresh today as ever, and form a valuable record of a long-vanished world of landscapes and urban scenes, undamaged by industrial development. As a one-time Master of the Art Workers' Guild, in 1886, he valued collaboration between architects, artists and craftsmen. Skilled draughtsmanship is less admired today, replaced by ephemeral computer-generated imagery; its demise surely accounts in part for the contemporary decline in taste and seemliness in design? Jackson tells us that he carefully drew out and measured details in Westminster Abbey under George Gilbert Scott's direction. He likewise surveyed and recorded the ruins of the spire of Chichester Cathedral after it had collapsed in 1861, making possible its careful reconstruction.

He was active throughout his long life in preservation and repair, rebuilding and improving old buildings. I have little doubt that he would not have found the self-important and limp dicktats of twenty-first-century conservationists much to his liking. His account of a visit to inspect the spire of Great St Mary's, Oxford in 1891, accompanied by an elderly William Morris, and his wry comments on the SPAB and the 'anti-scrapes' still have resonances today!

In 1888, the two then unfashionable renaissance churches of St. Mary-le-Strand and St. Clement Danes were threatened by road widening; with others Jackson prevented their demolition.

Today we live in a greatly changed world, lacking the certainties of Jackson's more settled times and comfortable middle-class background.

Goodness knows what he might have thought of Libeskind's crumpled-biscuit tin aesthetic, Mayor Livingstone's eccentric headquarters building across the river from the Tower of London, or the London 'Gherkin'! In his day the best buildings had ordered facades, carefully articulated plans and showed respect for their historic urban context.

Above all, Jackson was a creative artist and designer of elegant buildings guided and informed by impeccable scholarship. By enjoying this book we can savour his wit and his art – it is truly a record of an outstandingly successful and remarkable life.

Dr Donald Buttress LVO, D Litt, FSA, ARIBA

Surveyor Emeritus of Westminster Abbey,
Past-Master of the Art Workers' Guild,
Surveyor of the Fabric of Chichester Cathedral
President of the Ecclesiological Society

Preface

*Purists may disapprove of Jackson, and aesthetes may scoff, but there is a
fertility of invention, an enviable self-confidence and – most important of all –
a sheer panache about the man that takes one's breath away …
He deserves to be far better known than he is.'*

John Julius Norwich
The Architecture of Southern England (Macmillan 1985).

In 1915 Sir Thomas Graham Jackson had bound into two large volumes
what he described as his 'Recollections', which he had written on and off
during the previous ten years.

When in 1950 Oxford University Press published an edition of them,
arranged by his son Basil Jackson, it was favourably reviewed in the
Observer newspaper by Harold Nicolson, who perceptively observed, 'One
cannot help feeling that the original text of these memoirs must have been
more vivacious and illuminating than the wary abridgement which we are
now accorded,' and may have felt that my uncle Basil Jackson was too close
to the subject matter for a sufficiently objective viewpoint.

In the 1890s Harold Nicolson endured, at the same period as Basil
Jackson, a few years at a preparatory school called 'The Grange' in
Folkestone. In his book *Some People* Nicolson says 'At 'The Grange' we
were cold and underfed: we were incessantly bothered about our moral
tone … the Headmaster would kick us if we made the slightest noise. I was
puzzled by all this and spent my time dreaming about things to eat …
warm rooms.'

Like all diaries the 'Recollections' contained repetitions, which needed
editing but parts that may be found entertaining and informative have now
been included which, it is hoped, enliven these memoirs in a way that
Harold Nicolson might have approved of.

Following the visit to Croatia that my wife and I made in 2002, these additions now also include entries taken from the diaries of both T.G.J. and his wife Alice when they were exploring that part of the world in the 1880s.

I began re-editing the 'Recollections' in 1980 at which time, as Organist and Master of the Choristers at St. David's Cathedral, I was living, coincidentally (together with my wife and a small son who had recently also been christened Thomas Graham Jackson), in the same house where 85 years earlier T. G. Jackson had witnessed the signature of resignation of the 93-year-old Dean Allen from his cathedral.

Although I never met my grandfather (being born nearly a hundred years after him), as a boy at Radley I sat daily in the Chapel and Dining Hall he had designed along with a Boarding House, the Memorial Arch, the Sanatorium and the Cricket Pavilion. On days out, a regular pilgrimage was to visit his buildings in nearby Oxford, and be shown his portrait, which hung in Hall at Wadham College. As it was thought that I too might become an architect. I was taken on sketching tours in France and Italy by my uncle Basil Jackson much as he had been taken by my grandfather, even on one occasion staying at the Delphino Hotel,[1] Isola Bella, Lake Maggiore, where he had often stayed 70 years earlier.

Enthusiasm for Victorian architecture was, to some extent, due at that time to the influence of John Betjeman, whose interests embraced the works of Butterfield (particularly his streaky bacon style at Keble College, Oxford and at All Saints' Margaret Street) and of Gilbert Scott (undergraduates positively genuflected at the mention of St. Pancras Station).

T. G. Jackson, after visiting Italy in 1864, had reacted against the revival of Pure Gothic, so it was hardly surprising that despite Betjeman's walks round Oxford with Maurice Bowra, seeking out examples of what they called 'Anglo Jackson', his work remained out of fashion.

Enthusiasm is an attractive quality, and when combined with such a wit as Betjeman's, unlikely subjects such as steam engines, old iron bridges and lancet windows were all suddenly in vogue even if they sometimes fell into the category of what Americans like to call 'quaint'.

T.G.J's architecture did not come under this heading, and an all-time low in his popularity was reached when Pevsner referred to Jackson setting his 'elephantine feet' on many places in Oxford. When I arrived at Wadham in 1956 his portrait had been removed from Hall, though I did once discover it inaccessibly placed at the top of a small staircase behind the Senior Common Room.[3]

Few people are aware that more of Oxford University's buildings have been designed by T.G.J. than any other architect including the medieval ones. Much of his Oxford work tones in so well with the old buildings that they have been taken for granted. What television programme about Oxford does not now include a shot of Hertford College Bridge over New College Lane? 'So much more beautiful than its distant inspiration in

Venice' proudly claims the college publication called *Seven Hundred Years of an Oxford College.*

In 1983 Dr James Bettley, an authority on Jackson's architecture, curated an exhibition of T.G.J.'s buildings in the Examination Schools, where everyone was astounded by the extent of his Oxford work and articles and publications began to appear about him.

In 1986 I dined at Hertford College and was pleasantly surprised by the unanimous enthusiasm for his buildings, and venturing into Wadham on the following morning was delighted to find his portrait back in Hall again. In 1997 I unveiled a new portrait of T.G.J., which now hangs in the Octagon at Hertford College.

Besides being a successful architect, he was an accomplished water-colourist (considered by some to be Turner of Oxford's best pupil) and a great traveller – viz his three-volume work on Dalmatia etc. Although he wrote many books, his 'Recollections' were left in an unpublished state and 'only for the eyes of his family', to whom he devoted much time writing wonderful picture letters, *Six Ghost Stories*[4] and a beautiful set of illustrations for Bunyan's *A Pilgrim's Progress.*

Sir T. G. Jackson was still alive and working in 1924, although he had been born in the reign of King William IV and had seen unparalleled changes to a world which was, in his boyhood, much as it had been for hundreds of years. His elder son Hugh (my father) lived to be nearly 99, his younger son Basil (my uncle), who also became an architect, having died two years earlier in 1976. His daughter-in-law (my mother) attended a lecture about T. G. Jackson that I gave in Eagle House for the Wimbledon Society in 1995 and was still living in the year 2000.

In 1988 Sir Hugh Casson's delightfully illustrated book *Hugh Casson's Oxford* was published in which the author's enthusiastic assessments of Jackson's Oxford buildings are much at variance with those expressed by Nikolaus Pevsner and do perhaps now better reflect the regard in which they are held by most people today.

Wadham – 'Thomas G Jackson R.A. baronet, scholar – who during his life can be said to have changed the face of Oxford in his particularly free Jacobean style.'

Brasenose – 'New Quad confidently designed in his usual free-range style by Sir Thomas Jackson, and very nice too.'

Corpus Christi College – 'across Merton Street another handsome piece of T.G. Jackson.'

Hertford College – 'How perceptive and imaginative of him to endow Hertford College with two such postcard popular eye-catchers as the Blois-type stair tower in the quad and the 'Bridge of Sighs' over New College Lane, placed to the regular delight of tourists.'

In 2002 I was contacted by Lady Beresford-Peirse, founder of The International Trust for Croatian Monuments, who was interested in putting on an exhibition of T.G. Jackson's Dalmatian drawings and water-colours. This led to an exhibition, in 2003/2004, of his travel drawings held in the Library and Print Room of The Royal Academy of Arts, as well as a simultaneous exhibition of his Dalmatian watercolours at the Croatian Embassy which would be later taken to Croatia.

Nicholas Jackson
2003

Letter to T.G.J. from Sir Gilbert Scott

St Leonards
Nov 7. 1861

My dear Jackson,

I am quite taken aback at hearing that the term of your pupillage with me has expired. I wish very much that I could have made it more profitable to you but perhaps I may now you have mastered the preliminaries be of more use than while they were in hand, and I assure you it will give me the greatest pleasure if such be the case and will only beg you to press it upon me that my constant interruptions may not cause it to escape my memory. I am exceedingly glad that you have during your recent outing given your attention rather to the measurement of details than to picturesque sketching – not that I think lightly of that in itself, but rather that I thought that you were more in need of the study of those actual practical details of which architecture consists than of more pictorial matters – indeed that your artistic powers were considerably in advance of your acquaintance with these details.

I had been over and over intending to write to you, while out, on this subject, but always procrastinating; and I had abused you unjustly in my mind for the imagined sin of sketching mountains and waterfalls instead of architecture. What I had especially intended was to beg you to devote all the time you could to Furness Abbey and I rejoice that you did not need my advice to do so.

Now as to the future. In the first place I will say that I shall be only too glad for you to make all you can of my office in any way which you think will help you.

I think you should now consider what are the principal classes of study to be followed up and divide your time as systematically as you are able between them. I would put them as follows:

1st Artistic skill & knowledge-
2. Knowledge of actual architecture
3. Practical Knowledge
4. Literary knowledge of architecture

On the first I take a very different view from what is customary. I view picturesque drawing and watercolour painting as beautiful accomplishments indirectly aiding architecture but not strictly speaking necessary to it nor in any degree a portion of architectural art – in the stricter sense. What I mean then, by my first class of study is high art or art of a fine class as applied to actual architecture. As for example – The power of drawing and designing architectural decorations of all sorts – as foliage, figures, animal life whether natural or conventional and these all in their varied combinations <u>as actually used</u> in the highest classes of architectural decorations; the power of drawing and designing mosaics, inlayings, painted decorations, needlework, enamel, metal works etc etc. In fact those classes of artistic power which are necessary to make architecture a fine art and which have in this generation been almost wholly neglected in the education of architects.

For this you should practice at the Architectural Museum and other museums at South Kensington, at the British Museum and from books but should especially devote yourself to the figure & to animal life with a view to their <u>uses in architectural decorations.</u>

2. The knowledge of actual architecture – that of Gothic architecture can only be well obtained from actual sketching most determinedly followed up with details. I do not mean to exclude picturesque sketching of fine examples by any means, but you should always draw the details of what you have sketched, and look into its actual construction.

Classic architecture, I fear, must have its due attention; for this Sir William Chambers and Stewart's Athens are good sources.

If you would like to go and stay for a time at my house you can have constant reference to these and other books there now plenty of room. Stewart's Athens is also a good book for figure sculpture of the highest kind. <u>I am sure that every Gothic architect ought to understand classical architecture.</u>

3. Practical knowledge.

I think that this could best be obtained in the way you mention by actual residence for a time on a work in progress. Much can, however be done by constantly watching works in progress and taking notes, by reading practical books as Nicholsons, Tredgolds Carpentry or by reading & taking notes of specifications – by studying those interesting works the builders' price-books, by learning how artificers works are measured and valued etc etc etc

4. The literary knowledge of architecture.

Reference to a good architectural Library is the best for this – If you were to become an associate of the Institute you would obtain access to their Library which would be of great use. You should also, if you have not done so already, gain access to the British Museum and Manuscript room.

If you spend the winter & spring partly in my office and partly in following out these things particularly in drawing at the Architectural Museum in studying the figure and drawing figures at the British Museum and watching your opportunities of obtaining practical knowledge wherever it falls in your way I am sure you cannot go wrong. I will then see if there is any work which seems mistaken for you to go to in the way you name.

With my kind remembrances to Mr & Mrs Jackson and many thanks for your kind sympathy.

I remain faithfully yours
Geo: Gilbert Scott

As soon as ever I can get to town I will see the work at K. College. I think the best Marble for shafts will be the two or three richer kinds of Devonshire which Mr Field has by him.

The <u>bases</u> I fear will not do, I am very glad they think of going on.

Introduction

The Reputation of T.G. Jackson[1]

Pink may, double may, dead laburnum,
Shedding an Anglo-Jackson shade…[2]

Few architects have given their name to the style they practised, and to find that style slipped so evocatively into a poem is an even rarer occurrence; that the author of the poem was John Betjeman should come as no surprise, even if Betjeman did, on another occasion, consign Jackson to the category of architects whose work 'is a dead end in itself, being lost in self-conscious efforts … to parade 'scholarship'.'[3] Elsewhere, he described Jackson as 'a man of great culture, who wrote better than he practised',[4] an opinion that has come to be widely shared, not least because of the disapproving manner in which so many of his buildings are described by Nikolaus Pevsner in the *Buildings of England* volume on Oxford: the reference to Jackson's 'elephantine feet' sets the tone.[5]

When Betjeman wrote 'Myfanwy at Oxford', it must be doubtful how many readers would have understood the reference to 'Anglo-Jackson', although the man to whom the phrase refers had been dead for only fifteen years; but he suffered a fate not uncommon among architects who lived to old age of being very quickly forgotten by all but a few after, if not even before his death. The case of Jackson, however, seems particularly curious because on paper, in terms of worldly achievements, his claim to lasting fame is greater than most. During his lifetime he had an almost unrivalled reputation as an architect of collegiate and school buildings, as a sensitive restorer of historic buildings and monuments, and as a scholar and writer, and he was heaped with honours: Royal Academician, Royal Gold Medallist, fellow of the Society of Antiquaries, honorary doctor of laws at Cambridge and of civil law at Oxford, honorary fellow of Wadham College, Associé de l'Académie Royale de Belgique. He had the rare distinction of having a style of architecture, Anglo-Jackson, named after him – an epithet which was current in his own lifetime – and he received the unprecedented honour of being created a baronet, the first architect to be granted an hereditary title.[6] The rise and fall of Jackson's reputation is not the least interesting aspect of the work of this most self-effacing of architects.

The start of Jackson's career was not especially promising, but circumstances were such that he had a number of lucky breaks. He was born in 1835, the son of a solicitor who was then living at Hampstead and was a near neighbour of Sir George Gilbert Scott. Jackson was educated at Brighton College, where Scott was then building, and Jackson was later to build. In 1853 he matriculated as a commoner of Corpus Christi College, Oxford, but the following year was offered a scholarship by Wadham College and entered there instead. It is no exaggeration to say that going to Oxford was probably the most fortunate thing that ever happened to him, for without it his career would have been very different. He took a gentlemanly third in *literae humaniores* in 1858 and, things being what they were in those happily unreformed times, was able to become without much further effort a Fellow of the college in 1865. This achievement was of great immediate use to him, as it gave him an assured income: an immense help for a young man just embarking upon an uncertain career as an architect. For in the meantime he had been articled to Scott, serving in his office from 1858 to 1861, and he continued to do work for him on an informal basis for a few years after that.

This period provides a good example of what has happened to Jackson's reputation, because for many people he is best known for the fact that he worked in Scott's office and left behind what is probably the best account of that office;[7] an account which is all the more valuable because it covered that most crucial stage in the history of nineteenth-century taste, the battle of the styles of the design over the Foreign Office. What is important about this affair for us is the effect it had on the mind of the young Jackson: troubled not so much by the relative merits of Gothic and Classic as by the fact that there needed to be any debate, let alone such a dogmatic debate, at all, he began to turn against the Gothic Revival, as others were doing, although his personal revolt was not to show itself for at least ten years. Another aspect of Scott's office, the unartistic professionalism of the place where work was delegated and the master might have little idea of what was going on, also made a lasting impression upon him. Nonetheless, he continued to work for Scott for the time being, and his first success, the first occasion on which he came before the public eye, shows that he followed closely in the master's footsteps: the winning design for the Ellesmere Memorial at Walkden, Lancashire, published in the *Builder* in 1868, is very much the work of a product of Scott's office, a cross between the Martyr's Memorial and the Albert Memorial.

Ellesmere is the one moment in the 1860s when Jackson flits briefly across the public stage. For most of the decade he was, as far as one can tell, doing very little by way of building, although he was developing his career in other ways: he got his fellowship at Wadham; he travelled abroad a good deal, making his first visit to Italy, 'the land of promise', in 1864, which brought him to appreciate the glories of the Renaissance and the 'catholicity of art' and which finally made him turn his back on fanatical medievalism. [8] He also met James Powell, the stained glass maker, who remained a life-long friend and travelling companion, as well as executing many of Jackson's designs for stained glass and mosaic. Jackson was also busy at this time designing table glass for Powell, who regarded him and Philip Webb as the two most significant glass designers of the day.

1873 saw the publication of a small book that Jackson had been writing on his knees in the train as he commuted to his office in London from Sevenoaks, where his parents had been living since 1867. *Modern Gothic Architecture* was Jackson's manifesto, in which he set down what he disliked about the Gothic Revival: the rigid adherence to Gothic principles required by the 'school of purism and precedent' to which 'we are indebted for the "Gothic" lettering that we cannot read; the "Gothic" fire-places that will not draw; the "Gothic" lamps, candlesticks and salvers that look like chalices and patens in disguise; the "Gothic" furniture which fatigues us with its clumsy weight, and hurts us with its uncomfortable knobs and angles'.[9] But he also discussed the value he found in it, that of capturing the spirit of Gothic, which for him lay in good workmanship, a close relationship between the architect, the painter and the sculptor, and in buildings suited to modern requirements which made best use of up to date materials and techniques. In short, he perceived 'the advisability, nay more, the necessity of a judicious eclecticism'.[10] As regards style, he came down firmly in favour of the English Renaissance:

the architecture of the Elizabethan houses of England, by Thorpe and others... is thoroughly Gothic in treatment and sentiment whatever it may have gathered to itself of Classic details. It is, in fact, a style of Gothic architecture, in spite of the fact that it makes use of many forms of Classic origin.[11]

These ideas, as the *Builder* said at the time, 'may be new to the nonprofessional public, to whom Mr. Jackson's book is partly addressed, but they are certainly not new to architects',[12] and many of Jackson's sentiments were echoed the following year by J.T. Micklethwaite in his *Modern Parish Churches*.[13] However, the *Builder* made their review of *Modern Gothic Architecture* their leading article, devoting two whole pages to it, because 'in point of style and tone it is a thoroughly well-written book, the production of an educated and cultivated mind'; if the ideas were not new, they were said in a more readable and comprehensible manner than had been done before. Not for the last time, Jackson showed in his writing an idealistic desire to ignore the mundane aspects of the architect's business that are, for most of them, the source of their daily bread; but on the whole the reviews were favourable, and the *Architect* concluded by cordially recommending 'his little work to our readers as better worth their reading than most of those which have recently appeared'.[14]

For a short while, therefore, Jackson was probably better known as a writer than as an architect; but this was soon to change. Most of his early work was of the standard beginner's type: questionable church restorations, such as those at Binsted and Slindon,[15] a couple of private houses at Sevenoaks, a rectory at Send for C.R. Tate who had coached him for entry to Brighton; but it also included at least one remarkable church, that at Hornblotton, the inside of which is decorated from floor to ceiling with sgraffito and is probably the best, certainly the prettiest church he ever designed. He also got his first design (for the church at Annesley) hung at the Royal Academy, in 1873, which was an important step for his public reputation; his work was shown almost every year thereafter until his death.

And, of course, there was Oxford. Things started slowly, mainly in the form of minor work at Wadham, where he took an active part as Fellow and was, in 1879, elected Bursar for the coming year, and his presence in Oxford meant that he was invited, in 1874, to submit a design for the completion of Wolsey's tower, over the staircase to the Hall, at Christ Church. He did not win the competition – the prize went to Bodley and Garner, although their design, like Cardinal Wolsey's, was never completed – but his design attracted a good deal of favourable attention, and this in turn led to his being invited to compete for the most important new building in Oxford for many years: the Examination Schools on the site of the Angel Hotel in the High Street. The story of this competition is as tortuous and, in some respects, as disreputable as any number of competitions before and since; suffice it to say that Jackson won, saw his design or the greater part of it executed, and his name was made. Two questions need be answered: why did he win, and why was the building so important, not just in terms of Jackson's career but in the context of Oxford architecture as a whole? The answer to both questions is the style that he chose for the Schools. In spite of the fact that the most common criticism levelled against Jackson is that he was a bad planner, particularly when designing on a large scale, the Schools is one building where that does not apply, [16] but the basic layout of the building, with the great hall on the High Street insulating the rest of the building from traffic noise, the viva-voce rooms on the ground floor looking out on to the quiet quadrangle, and the writing schools on the first floor with tall windows on both sides and of such a shape as to allow for easy supervision, was largely determined by the brief. It was the style of the building which made it stand out from the other competitors' designs. 'My object has been to give the building a collegiate character which would not be out of harmony with the tradition of Oxford and with the majority of the buildings in the University,' Jackson wrote in the report that accompanied his design;[17] the *Architect* referred to 'that late eclectic style of Gothic of which Oxford and Cambridge contain admirable examples … The general effect is good and harmonious … and on the whole we may be content, after much that has been done in Oxford, with Mr. Jackson's designs.'[18]

'After much that has been done in Oxford …' Oxford had been in the grip of the Gothic Revival for the past thirty-five years, ever since Scott won the competition for the Martyr's Memorial, and so confident were the competitors for the new Examination Schools that Gothic was here to stay that they all, with the exception of Jackson – the others were T.N. Deane, John Oldrid Scott, G.F. Bodley, and Basil Champneys – submitted Gothic designs. Even Jackson thought he would have to, and went so far as to dissuade Bodley from sending in a Renaissance design. Bodley had already had success with his Renaissance design for the School Board Offices on the Embankment in London, 1872-3, and a year or so later had no trouble in getting the Renaissance style approved for the new Master's Lodgings at University College.

But as far as Oxford was concerned, it was Jackson who got in first, drawing for his inspiration on the Jacobean architecture to be found at the Bodleian, for example, or Wadham, but above all inspired by the building he considered to be 'in many respects the most beautiful building' in the English Renaissance style: Kirby Hall, Northamptonshire, 'now, alas! … a melancholy ruin, buried in woods, a wilderness indeed, and not easy to find'.[19] The introduction of a new style into Oxford was revolutionary, particularly as the site of the new Schools was one of the most prominent in Oxford; and the effect on Jackson's career cannot be underestimated. The Oxford Almanack for 1883, which carried a fine etching by R. Kent Thomas of the new building, lists twenty-three colleges and halls; by 1888, when the Schools were completed by the addition of the block for non-collegiate students, Jackson was working on no fewer than eleven of those colleges, not including Somerville. He had, moreover, become something like the official University architect; he did some work or other, mainly restoration work, on practically every University building, from refacing the Bodleian to building the cricket pavilion in the Parks. For, as Sir Howard Colvin has observed, 'Jackson enjoyed a unique advantage: alone among professional architects before or since, he was a Fellow of a College and a Senior Member of the University.'[20]

This is not to say that he did not have his opponents. E.A. Freeman, the Regius Professor of Modern History, complained in a lecture on Oxford architecture in 1887:

If we do go back to make a fresh start in architecture, surely we should avoid the corrupt style of James I, but in the New Schools and New Trinity that was the type selected. It is architecture gone out of its way to jumble together different styles, bad Gothic and bad classic mixed together, when we might have had good work like Magdalen and New College – the only two bodies who have not bowed the knee to Baal.[21]

John Ruskin, when Slade Professor, grumbled about having to give lectures in 'this black hole, with its nineteenth century ventilation' (he was speaking in 1884) because the University chose to spend its money 'building ball rooms rather than lecture rooms; it thought worthy of spending £150,000 for the elevation and ornature, in a style as inherently corrupt as it is unEnglish, of the rooms for the torture and shame of her scholars... whereas the only place where her art workmen can be taught to draw is the cellar of her old Taylor buildings.'[22] It is ironic that the School of Drawing and Fine Art named after Ruskin should now have its home in a part of the buildings he so detested.

To judge Jackson's success one need only consider the quantity and variety of his work at Oxford: to mention just some of the more outstanding or curious, the High School for Boys, in George Street, and for Girls, in Banbury Road; the front quad of Trinity, and the High Street front of Brasenose; practically the whole of Hertford, in a wide range of styles, including one of the most photographed structures in the city, the Bridge of Sighs; the house in Mansfield Road, called King's Mound, originally conceived as part of a proposed new hall under the auspices of Balliol; later works, such as the Radcliffe Science Library and the Electrical Laboratories; vanished frolics such as the Oriel College barge, or the wooden bridge over the Cherwell in Christ Church meadows; and the Military College at Cowley, which never really got off the ground. The sheer quantity of Jackson's work in Oxford is staggering, and one of the best things about it is that it is so unobtrusive, without being insipid. His buildings fit in well with Oxford, to the extent that they often go unnoticed, or are assumed to be much older than is the case, but are, in themselves, pleasant to look at. The extent of his acceptance can be judged by, for example, W.S. Purchon's account of 'The Architecture of Oxford' in 1912. Jackson's arrival is described as 'beginning a fresh chapter in the history of the buildings of that city', and 'of most of his work in Oxford, it can be said without exaggeration or fear of contradiction that it is at home amidst its beautiful surroundings'. Henry T. Hare's Town Hall, according to Purchon, 'is treated in the manner most characteristic of Oxford', with 'great gables reminiscent of Kirby Hall'; here Jackson seems to have become synonymous with Oxford, architecturally speaking.[23]

In 1880, Jackson married Alice Lambarde of Sevenoaks. It was a significant moment in more ways than the obvious one. It meant, for example, that he had to resign his fellowship at Wadham, so did not take up the post of Bursar (he was elected an Honorary Fellow in 1882). It signalled that his reputation was sufficiently well established for him to afford to lose the financial support which his fellowship provided and to take on the new responsibility of supporting a wife and family. He set up home in Nottingham Place, London, and their first son, Hugh, was born in 1881. But it was a change that had come none too soon. Jackson was 44 in 1880; 'it had been a hard fight,' he wrote later, 'and until three or four years before I had been almost unknown except perhaps among my brother architects'; but the Schools 'had lifted me into the front rank', and 'I seemed to have become the fashion. It became a joke, when a man said his college was going to build, to say "Jackson of course!".'[24] The hard fight – although not so hard as for many others, given his personal circumstances – was worth it, and the 1880s and 1890s saw him at the height of his reputation. His work was selected for and won prizes at a number of international exhibitions: Paris 1878, Sydney 1879, Adelaide 1887, St Louis 1904. He published in 1887 his three-volume history of Dalmatia, and in 1893 and 1896 books on Wadham and St Mary the Virgin, Oxford, all three definitive works at the time and still of real value. He was a leading figure in the campaign against the compulsory registration of architects, editing with Norman Shaw in 1892 a volume of essays entitled *Architecture – a profession or an art*; in the same year he was elected Associate of the Royal Academy, 'a foregone conclusion,' said the *Builder*; 'we have only wondered that the honour should not have been offered earlier to an architect whose claims to it were so indisputable.'[25] The *Art Journal* described him, intriguingly, as a representative 'of the advanced school of architecture', but did not go on to explain what they meant by this unusual categorisation.[26] He was made a full Academician in 1896, an honour which made him in a sense a public representative of Architecture with a capital A; and it was generally thought that 'a better representative could not have been chosen … Mr. Jackson is not only an architect of profound knowledge, but he is also – what in these days is all too rare – an artist, his profession being to him less a Profession than an Art … Architecture is the mother of all Art, and yet how disdainfully is she treated by her children. It is to such men as Mr. Jackson that we look to raise her to that high pedestal which is her right.'[27]

In one respect, it must be said that he failed. Whether from a sense of duty, or because he wished to repeat the success of the Schools, or simply because he wished to establish himself, late in life, as a designer of major public buildings, from 1881 he went in for a series of competitions. The first of these, for a memorial church to Czar Alexander II in St Petersburg, was of some merit, and reflects his familiarity with and interest in the architecture of the near east; but he thought it no good, and destroyed it. A similar fate, with more justice, was meted out to most of his other entries, which were almost unqualified disasters. There was the design for the Admiralty and War Office buildings in Whitehall in 1884; the Imperial Institute followed in 1887, of which Alfred Waterhouse, the assessor, told him: 'when my design was unpacked, he said, 'Oh that's the one!' but that my planning was inferior. I think he was right.'[28] An anonymous critic in the *British Architect* was less courteous:

> Mr. Jackson thought there was wanted a charming Oxford college with inclosed courts, Tudoresque lead-lighted windows, and a grand college hall of lofty height, to allow of the expansion of savoury effluvia. At least I presume this was the intention, for it is stated to hold 1000 persons, and as it is narrow and measures 160 ft in length, it could only do this for *eaters*, not for *hearers*.[29]

Planning, again, was the problem, although it is only fair to add that the critic dealt with all the entries in this acerbic manner. The competition for the South Kensington Museum followed in 1891, and then came the most public disaster of them all, Christ's Hospital in 1894. So badly was his entry received ('Mr. Jackson hardly appears at his best, either as regards design or drawings'[30]) that he refused to allow his design to be published, as was the normal practice, and produced a new design the following year solely for publication and for exhibition at the Academy. The critics were non-committal in their judgement on his designs for the layout of the Mall and monument to Queen Victoria, in 1901, and for County Hall, in 1908.

Among these giants was his design for a new public library at Hampstead, of 1894, of which the *Builder* had this to say:

> We regret very much to see the set of drawings to which the name of 'Thos. G. Jackson' is appended. It would have been far more dignified for an architect in Mr. Jackson's position to have declined the invitation to compete rather than to have sent in a set of drawings which are a discredit to his reputation, and a reflection upon the fame of the Royal Academy, of which he is a member, and upon the Art of architecture, of which he poses as an exponent. Mr. Jackson should remember that his position demands that he should uphold the dignity of architecture as an Art in the eyes of the world, both on its artistic and its constructive side. The plan which Mr. Jackson submits shows either an absolute ignorance or a cynical disregard of the requirements of a Free Public Library ... The exterior is treated in a picturesque but extravagantly expensive manner, whilst the design is characterised by an unsatisfactory lack of good proportion, and the insertion of coarse and eccentric detail. In fact, taking it all round, the design is quite unworthy of its author.[31]

At least it can be said that this criticism shows how generally well regarded Jackson was: the tone of the rebuke is more sorrowful than angry.

Some other criticism need perhaps not be taken too seriously; Edmund Becket, Lord Grimthorpe, for example, sniped at him in the pages of the *Nineteenth Century*, initially over the matter of the registration of architects, but then questioning his architectural skill.[32] More important were three running battles with the Society for the Protection of Ancient Buildings, all of which Jackson may be said to have won. The first was over the restoration of St Mary the Virgin, in 1892-6, at the end of which the *Builder* remarked that the SPAB 'will probably see the wisdom of letting Mr. Jackson alone for the future'[33]; but they did not, and attacked him again over his restorations of Winchester Cathedral and Christchurch Priory.

The architectural press was for the most part bound to support the architect against the preservationists, but there is little doubt that he was highly thought of by the professional critics of the day. Robert Kerr, in his new edition of Fergusson's *History of the Modern Styles of Architecture*, published in 1891, included mention of the Schools, 'particularly well worthy of illustration, as showing how one of the best opportunities has been made available for producing an ensemble of the highest order of attractive proportions. The proper name for the style of design the reader may determine for himself, with due regard for the exigencies of the day.'[34] The *Builder* had a similar problem of taxonomy when it called the Schools, in 1887, 'one of the best and most original buildings of the recent English school for which it is so difficult to find a distinctive title'[35] − hence the facetious but serviceable 'Anglo-Jackson'. In 1897, he was the subject of no fewer than three lengthy articles in architectural journals: fifteen pages in the first volume of the *Architectural Review*, twenty-seven pages in the second volume of the short-lived monthly, *Architecture*, and four pages in the *Builders' Journal and Architectural Record*, a forerunner of the *Architects' Journal*.[36]

Although, to judge from these articles, Jackson was known principally as a scholar, a fine draughtsman, the champion of artistic freedom, and above all as an Oxford architect, he was doing a large amount of work outside that city. This includes buildings for thirteen public and other schools, the most extensive being at Uppingham, his own school Brighton, and at Radley; the most curious being the Temple Speech Room at Rugby, opened in 1909, and Giggleswick School chapel, opened in 1901 − the latter a remarkable building to find anywhere, let alone on a Yorkshire fell, a Gothic building with a dome so authentic that he used a photograph of it under construction to illustrate his exposition of the technique in his *Byzantine and Romanesque Architecture*; buildings for the Drapers' and Grocers' Companies, and for the Inner Temple, in London; the Sedgwick Museum, law library, and other buildings on the Downing Street site in Cambridge, from 1899 onwards; the campanile of Zara (now Zadar) Cathedral in Croatia, and a church at Edmonton in Canada; the Church of St John the Evangelist at Northington in Hampshire, his most impressive ecclesiastical work; a host of sensitive restorations and additions to churches, country houses, and historic monuments; a street of workmen's houses, Lime Tree Walk, at Sevenoaks; even a grand piano, to go in the music room of the house he built for Athelstan Riley at Kensington Court, London.

As Jackson approached his 75th birthday, the honours started to come in thick and fast. On 14 June 1910, he was up in Cambridge to receive his honorary doctorate of laws; six days later he was back in London to receive the Royal Gold Medal, awarded by the sovereign but on the recommendation of the Royal Institute of British Architects, whom he had so strongly opposed over the matter of registration some twenty years before. Jackson was in fact the second choice for that year, the medal having previously been offered to Norman Shaw who declined the honour (he had already done so once before) because, he said, it was too great, but probably because of his past differences with the Institute, which of course he had shared with Jackson.

Ernest George, the President of the RIBA, in presenting the medal, paid tribute to 'a grand record of scholastic work which at the same time is *scholarly* work':

> Mr. Jackson has had the satisfaction of making his impress especially on one city, with which his name will always be associated. Oxford, almost unique in its survival as a mediaeval city, was bound to move with the times, and we might have feared the results of changes that must come. But, by good fortune, the modern growth of the city has been generally under wise direction; the spirit of the old has been preserved, while there is freshness, originality and beauty in most of the schools and colleges that have risen in our own time, and that harmonise happily with the works of the pious fathers, and for very much of this work Mr. Jackson is responsible.[37]

So, appropriately enough, just over a year later it was Oxford's turn to honour him, with the honorary degree of Doctor of Civil Law: an honour to which he probably attached more importance than any other, being particularly taken with the Chancellor's description of him as 'Artifex Oxoniensissime' – most Oxford of artists.[38]

At this stage of his life he was more before the public eye than ever; not, however, by reason of his new buildings or academic honours, but because of his restoration, or salving, to use the more dramatic term that Jackson chose, of Winchester Cathedral. This was a long job, lasting over six years, and the visible signs of his work there are the buttresses along the south side, part of a projected reconstruction of the old cloisters, and the Epiphany Chapel in the north transept which includes some fine stained glass made by Morris & Co.; but the aspect of the work which so caught the popular imagination, and still does (although few remember the name of the architect who directed the operations) was the underpinning of the foundations by means of substituting concrete for the old wooden piles, submerged in water, on which the cathedral rested. This hazardous work was carried out almost single-handed by a diver, William Walker, and in Winchester today he is the folk hero with whose name the preservation of the Cathedral is now connected. But at the time the honours were apportioned differently. King George V attended the Thanksgiving Service on completion of the work in 1912, personally congratulated the diver, and conferred a knighthood on the civil engineer, Francis Fox; and when it came to the architect, made him a baronet in the following New Year's Honours. Jackson's unique standing in the history of the architectural profession probably owes more to hierarchical niceties than to an objective assessment of his achievements, but there have certainly been many less deserved baronetcies.

Jackson was now 77, one of the grand old men of architecture, much respected but something of an anachronism. There is more than a touch of allowance for old age in the *Builder*'s comments on his exhibits at the Academy in 1913: he 'is to be admired for the manner in which he adheres to the type of English design which he has studied, and in which he believes he is, so to speak, a last barrier against which the tide of the later Renaissance is pressing, and such an attitude indicates both his strength and sincerity'[39] – and reading between the lines, indicates also that he is a die-hard reactionary. By 1917, in a special number on the nineteenth century, the same journal talks of him almost as if he were dead, illustrating the church at Northington, 'a characteristic example of the work of Sir Thomas Graham Jackson, to whom Oxford owes much; Sir Thomas will always be remembered as an exponent of architectural scholarship.'[40]

He designed little after 1913, although his energy remained undiminished: during the war he went off once a week to make munitions, and after it there were memorials to be designed; he alarmed his workmen by scrambling about on scaffolding, and as recently as 1908 had been on a rowing holiday with his son Basil that was more strenuous than most would undertake at any age, let alone 72.[41] Most of his intellectual energy, however, went into his monumental seven-volume series, *Byzantine and Romanesque Architecture*, *Gothic Architecture in France, England, and Italy*, and *The Renaissance of Roman Architecture*, published between 1913 and 1923; a work which sealed his reputation as a scholar and also as an implacable opponent of what he considered to be the stifling, doctrinaire principles of Vitruvius, and of the direction in which he feared modern architecture was moving.

Jackson died on 7 November 1924 at the age of 88.[42] There were, as might be expected, many fulsome obituaries; the criticisms are rarer and more telling. Beresford Pite, for example, pointed out that 'a certain lack of imagination kept him faithful to a narrow path', and spoke of 'prominent anachronisms' in some of his later work.[43] Similar sentiments may be read into Arthur T. Bolton's view that 'artists whose lives are so prolonged are bound towards the the end of their time to find themselves somewhat isolated' and he noted also, with some understatement, that 'his rare competition designs certainly did not add to his reputation; their plans led nowhere and had the involved character natural, perhaps, to a house planner'.[44] Jackson's dislike of professionalism received general praise for its sincerity, as it always had done, but general criticism for its misguided or impractical idealism.

The posthumous reputation of Jackson was largely shaped by H.S. Goodhart-Rendel, whose judgements became increasingly negative. He gave a long talk on Jackson to the RIBA in 1926,[45] and little that has been said on Jackson since cannot be found there; he followed this up with his entry in the *Dictionary of National Biography*, published in 1937, and some hard-hitting remarks in his *English Architecture since the Regency* (1953). For Goodhart-Rendel, the 'elegance of his ornament' is set against the 'ineptitude of his planning'; he was 'a competent decorator, having a great deal of what people call "good taste," and considerable sensitiveness to subtleties of form and proportion', but he was not, in the end, 'a man who understood his job'.[46]

The charge of bad planning can be fairly applied to his designs for large buildings, such as those for which he entered competitions unsuccessfully in the 1880s and 1890s, but with the conspicuous exception of the Examination Schools. Another deserved criticism is that he paid almost too much attention to ornamental detail, to the detriment of the broader picture. This was a view expressed by Reginald Blomfield in his obituary of Jackson, which is fulsome at its beginning and end ('leaves a gap not easily to be filled in the ranks of the architects of this country … A fine architect and a fine character, all architects will mourn his loss.') but is more reserved in the middle:

> he never quite shook himself free of the sketch-book habit of design, design, that is, mainly preoccupied with details. And indeed he always seemed to me to have rather misconceived the meaning of Renaissance architecture, regarding the work of the ornamentalists as architecture, when he should have ignored those ingenious tradesmen, and concentrated his attention on the real architects …[47]

Sir Howard Colvin has taken this further:

> Jackson's great weakness lay not so much in his artistic promiscuity (fully apparent only to the professional architect or architectural historian) as in not knowing where to stop. He would repeat a motif *seriatim* where it would have been more effective in isolation, or try simultaneously to

express two architectural ideas in a situation where there was room for only one.[48]

Jackson's 'artistic promiscuity' is what he himself called 'judicious eclecticism',[49] for which he had been taken to task by the *Architectural Review* in 1896: 'we are inclined to utter a gentle remonstrance to Mr. Jackson: his work seems to us varied to the verge of eclecticism'.[50] There is an air of frivolity about eclecticism that makes the results appeal to amateurs, whether clients or casual observers, but which can distress professionals, whether critics or fellow architects. It can be fun to deconstruct some of Jackson's buildings, so that one may say of the Examination Schools, for example: here is a Venetian window; here is another, but this time used as the porch; these windows are copied from Kirby; this loggia is just like the Foundling Hospital in Florence; this woodwork used to be in the old Divinity Schools, and was rescued by Jackson from the vaults of the Sheldonian; and so on.

But such buildings do not fit neatly into stylistic categories, they are outside the mainstream of architectural development, and for that reason did not appeal to Nikolaus Pevsner, who had little enthusiasm for architects whose buildings were not, in his eyes, leading anywhere. Pevsner seldom has a good word for Jackson's individual buildings – of the Examination Schools he wrote, 'What a puny image of examination such a building creates: the puny candidates and the moloch of the testing machinery' – although he has a grudging respect for his skill: 'Here was a mature man of supreme confidence handling with undeniable panache a style no longer Gothic or Tudor but licentiously fabricated out of elements from the Quattrocento to the Georgian with the main stress on the impure classical of the C17.' Similar vocabulary – 'levity and licence', 'impudent' – is used in the introduction to Oxford:

> There was a tremendous panache in the way he handled big jobs, no fear of over-ornateness, no fear of noise … That Jackson left Oxford a grosser place than it had ever been, nobody should deny, but he left it a place with a potential for architectural adventure, and for that one should be grateful to him.[51]

Popular though he was in his lifetime, it is noticeable that he had very few followers or disciples. This was to a large degree of his own choosing. He set the fashion at Oxford for a few years, where his style was taken up by Basil Champneys and Henry T. Hare, notably in the latter's Town Hall,[52] but outside Oxford it was a different matter. Emotionally Jackson was very much part of the 'Queen Anne' movement, and the High School for Girls is one of his totally 'Queen Anne' buildings, but he now earns little more than a footnote in the history of that movement: his chief value is seen to be as the chronicler of the Registration debate, and of the life in Scott's office, which provided the background of the architects who were of real influence – G.F. Bodley, E.R. Robson, G.G. Scott junior, Norman Shaw, J.J. Stevenson, and others.[53] His forte was designing medium-sized buildings for colleges and schools, a restricted field, where there was more scope for decoration than there was for planning. Equally restricting was his insistence on keeping his office small, to avoid the commercialisation he had found in Scott's office, which means that he sent into the world neither disciples nor fruitful rebels.[54] When he died, his practice died with him.

In recent years, Jackson has come to be considered more on his own terms, for what he was rather than what he was not, notably by J. Mordaunt Crook in 'T.G. Jackson and the cult of eclecticism', the only substantial review of Jackson's *oeuvre* to have been published since Goodhart-Rendel. Jackson must be judged as 'an artist and archaeologist, a scholar-architect of school and college, a doughty opponent of professional uniformity, above all as a committed eclectic'.[55] His buildings have come to be appreciated for their high quality – in this respect he was fortunate that his clients were mostly able to pay for the very best – and it is no accident that very few of them have been demolished.[56] Time has made the debate over the registration of architects, so important in the 1890s, seem tedious; much of Jackson's published work is now inevitably out of date, and his implacable opposition to pure classicism appears unreasonable. What has kept Jackson's name alive is the work he did in Oxford, and one cannot hope for more than that Jackson should have the reputation of being *the* Oxford architect *par excellence*: not an architect of national standing who happened to do work in Oxford, of which there are many; nor a provincial architect, like William Wilkinson or H.W. Moore, or Frederick Codd, who had the temerity to accuse Jackson of plagiarising his own unsuccessful design for the High School for Boys;[57] but the only Oxford architect of national standing.

James Bettley

1

Family History and Early Recollections

Duddington ~ Hambleton ~ Sir William Beechey ~ Dr. Arnold ~ Hampstead
Early Days ~ Move from Hampstead to Clapham ~ Posting to Stamford ~
Hampton Court ~ Move back to Hampstead ~ Hampstead in 1840-50
Visit to Leamington ~ School at Brighton and Clapton

Like port wine and bric-a-brac, and many other things, letters and personal reminiscences gain by mere lapse of time an adventitious value
to which originally they never could pretend.

An old diary of a hundred or even fifty years ago, maybe only the record
of an uneventful life by a dull writer, has for us an aroma and flavour quite
independent of its literary merits. As we read we are carried back into a different world which has passed away with all its differences of habit,
thought and expression, the world of Cranford and Miss Matty, even that
of Elizabeth Bennett and Mr. Collins seems familiar, a world where young
ladies were joked about their beaux and young gentlemen about their part-
ners; where the father was addressed as 'Sir' though I think the mother had
ceased to be 'Ma'am'; where railways were few and slow and coaches were
still running; where posts were infrequent and expensive, and where electric science was illustrated by such simple experiments as making a doll's
hair stand on end, or making bits of paper dance after a stick of sealing-
wax rubbed on a coat sleeve. And so, in the evening of life, I think it may
amuse those who come after me if I put together some account of their for-
bears, such as I have been able to collect from my own memory, aided by
old letters, diaries and other records, and of such events in my own life as
they are not already familiar with.

We come of a family that must, I fear, be considered undistinguished
though it can boast of a respectable measure of antiquity, having owned
and lived on the same estate for nearly three centuries. From one Nicholas
Jackson who owned lands round about Stamford, at Helpstone, Castor and
Duddington in Northamptonshire, at which last place he restored the
manor house in 1633, the estate passed to his son William who died in

Duddington Manor

1667. His son and successor, Thomas, a Justice of the Peace, was made a gentleman and received a Grant of Arms in 1689.[1] Duddington descended regularly from father to son for the best part of the next two hundred years. They and theirs mostly lie buried in Duddington Church, which is paved with their tombstones.[2]

Hambleton Manor: The Pike

My father, Hugh Jackson, was born in 1799 and was only in his second year when his father was killed by a fall from his horse, riding home from Peterborough. His mother married a retired naval officer, and went to live at Hambleton which she inherited from her father Tobias Hippisley. The house although of moderate dimensions contained some good rooms of moderate date (late 18th Century) in the middle, between two older wings dating from Jacobean times. In one of these was a gabled oriel window of a kind peculiar to that part of the world and called by the country people a 'Pike'.

For Hambleton, where he passed his boyhood, my father had a strong affection and nothing pleased him more than to take us there on foot or on horseback across the fields, past the diamond well which still sparkled and sent up its jewels at the foot of the hill, to spend a long day in the old house and to call on the principal farmer tenants. Hambleton was then only to be reached by field roads through gates, and was about as rural and primitive a village as any in England. Many were the tales he had to tell of the simplicity of the villagers of his boyhood. How a young farmer married a girl from Braunston, five miles off, and brought her home on a pillion to

Hambleton, farther from home than she had ever been before, and how she asked him, 'John, is that the same moon that shines at Braunston?' How he remembered two buxom daughters of another farmer rushing out after their brother, who was riding off to Oakham Market, screaming, 'Don't forget the boots. Remember, the largest size made for women.'

So little did the peasantry of those days move about, that long after the days we are speaking of, my grandmother's maid at Stamford, when undressing her mistress while an eclipse of the moon was in progress, begged she might go and call Tom, the footman, because he was not used to these town sights.

From Hambleton my father and his brothers used to go to the grammar school at Wisbech, of which the headmaster at that time was his uncle the Rev. Jeremiah Jackson, Fellow of St. John's, Cambridge. The journey from Hambleton was made partly by road and partly by boat along the great Fen dykes.

He could not have been more than seventeen or eighteen when he left school for London, where he was articulated to a firm of solicitors, Messrs. Fladgate & Young, 12 Essex Street, Strand, where his elder brother John was already at work. The firm in time became Fladgate, Young & Jackson.

Of his life during the next fourteen or fifteen years I know but little. He went to Corsica on business connected with General Paoli.[3] He was intimate with the family of Sir William Beechey, R.A.,[4] who lived, I think, at No. 18 Harley Street and had a large family of sons and daughters. Sir William was the favourite Court painter, and Queen Charlotte, the Prince of Wales, Lord St. Vincent and Lord Nelson stood sponsors and gave their names to many of his children. His daughter Anne married my uncle John Jackson; another daughter, Charlotte, was married to Lord Grantly; and one son, Frederick,[5] became famous as an Admiral and Arctic explorer and has given his name to some island or sound in those frozen seas.

It was at Stamford that my father met and married my mother, Elizabeth Arnold. Her parents had come to live there from Leicester where her grandfather, Dr. Thomas Arnold, practised as a physician. He was a pioneer in the rational and humane treatment of lunatics. His book on insanity is mentioned in Boswell's *Life of Johnson*. Dr. Arnold was to have been called in to George III had Dr. Willis's[6] treatment of the king's disorder been less successful. Their eldest son, my grandfather, Dr. Thomas Arnold, came to practise as a consulting physician at Stamford, where he lived in a roomy old-fashioned house with a walled garden and a mulberry tree in the middle, in St. Martin's Stamford Baron, at the corner of the road to Easton.

The Arnold household was very strictly ordered, and its rigid punctuality was the terror of my childhood and youth, that never having been one of my virtues. All were expected to form regular habits of study and self-improvement. I have a diary of William Arnold, who died young, kept when he was at Uppingham School, in which he puts down exactly what he read every day, not only at school but in the holidays; and a pretty long list it is. The occasional cricket match, with the number of 'notches' he made, makes a very different figure from that it would show in a diary of a boy nowadays, though I don't think boys now keep diaries at all.

The daughters had their choice of accomplishments, either music or drawing, but not both. My mother, who had no ear, produced some paintings from nature of birds and flowers, not perhaps showing much originality but marvels of delicate finish.

After the wedding they went straight to their new home, Dr. Beatty's cottage in Hampstead. My uncle John Jackson was already married and living at Hampstead in a nice old-fashioned house on the upper terrace. There were two gardens joined together by a tunnel under an intervening lane, the upper garden bordering on the Heath and having a fine view to Elstree and Harrow and, on a fine day, to Windsor where, with a glass, the flag might be seen waving on the round tower. This upper garden is now detached and is nearly filled with a great house in the middle of it.

The newly married pair seem to have found many new friends in Hampstead, some like themselves connected with Stamford; also Captain Beechey the explorer and his wife; and finally Sir William Beechey came to be among his married children, having just lost his wife.

If it were disputed whether the happiest marriages result from similarity or diversity of temperament, my parents would be useful witnesses in favour of the latter alternative. My mother was of a tender affectionate nature, serious and sensitive, utterly unselfish herself, but full of anxiety on behalf of those dear to her, and inclined to look rather on the dark than on the hopeful side of all that concerned them. The ordinary cares of domestic life, difficulties with servants and governesses, anxieties about income and expense were real troubles that weighed heavily on her and would not be shaken off.

Fortunately for her, this gentle pessimism was encountered by a buoyant and sanguine temperament in her husband. My father was a born optimist who met the ills of life with a cheerful optimism that robbed them of their terrors. To my mother's troubles he would reply, 'Why don't you laugh at them?' His was not a selfish optimism however, for his life was given to helping others. It led him to see good in most things and even in most men and disposed him to take an especial interest in many scamps and ne'er-do-wells whom he helped to moral and social improvement.

There never lived a more unconventional man, or one less careful of appearances than my father. He was always for going to the straightest way to his point, whether it were the usual way or not. The same impulse, which led him into disastrous shortcuts on our walks, drove him to take the readiest way of escaping from any difficulty. I have known him when penned in at the far end of a pew full of people, deliberately escape at the end of a service by stepping over into the pew behind; no doubt a natural and sensible thing to do, but one calculated to shock proprieties.

In his business, though he had a high reputation as a lawyer, he showed the same tendency to take shortcuts, which though often successful, sometimes led to difficulties, which would have been avoided by the ordinary paths. I do not think these unconventional ways distressed my mother, unlike as they were to what she had been used to: the only thing she never quite condoned was my father's unpunctuality. Brought up in a household where everything went with the regularity of clockwork, she never quite liked my father putting on his hat and setting out for a walk as the dinner bell was ringing.

My father and mother moved before the end of 1835 to the little white house in Heath Street where all their children were born and to which my earliest recollections attach themselves. It is still standing unaltered, the middle one of the three houses in the sketch.

Here I first saw the light on Monday, 21st December 1835. I can remember lying in my nursery with a Japanned lantern pierced with round holes, through which the light magnified and distorted itself into huge fantastic eyes on the wall and ceiling. Outside in the gathering gloom a dog barked – then another, then up went the doleful cry of some belated huckster of fish, fruit or green stuff – instantly rushed on my memory the nursery rhyme which always filled my childish mind with mysterious terror:

Hark! Hark! The dogs do bark,
The beggars are coming to town!

And I quaked under the bed clothes thinking they were really come, – those awful strangers.

I can remember too, sitting with my father drawing in a buff-leather covered sketch book with a clasp that he had given me, and at another time searching in vain for some secret flap in the sideboard which I hoped would lift up and disclose the black and white keys of the piano, my little musical soul longed for, but which was not to be found in a house where no one could have played it.

I also remember when I was four years old, my father taking me down to my mother's room to see a present she had got me; and how disappointed I was at being shown the little pink creature in her arms that afterwards developed into my younger sister, Emily. Had I been a girl I should have been delighted, but the mere boy has no taste for babies.

Shall I ever forget my first children's party, where there was a conjurer? Those were the days when old ladies had their doubts about conjuring, and hinted half laughing and half seriously at 'the Black Art' – 'It is very wonderful' they would say, 'are you sure it is quite – eh? – You know we are told in the bible …'

My mother's diary is full of domestic details, such as the birth of my two sisters and a brother. There were frequent visits to Stamford, a long coach journey with fractious babies. On 28th January the diary records the death

Heath Street, Hampstead

of Sir William Beechey, whose eighty-fifth birthday they had celebrated in December 1837. He died without having painted his promised picture of my mother. I think my mother was shocked by his plentiful use of 'swear-words', which was beyond the fashion of that day, when swearing was becoming less common.

Constable writes to his wife, 'Beechey was here yesterday and said "Why damn it Constable, what a damned fine picture you are making but you look damned ill and you have got a damned bad cold" so now you have evidence *on oath* of my being about a fine picture and that I am looking ill.'

For some reason in 1841 my parents were again house-hunting, and after beating up in vain the districts of Hamilton Terrace, Oxford Terrace, Kensington and Nottinghill, they finally took a house at Clapham, opposite St. James's Chapel. This proved a disastrous move. In the light of modern sanitary science it is obvious that all the family were poisoned by bad drainage. We were all ill in turns, sometimes many at once. In the autumn of 1841 my father nearly died of rheumatic fever and it was not till late August that he was fit to travel. We then went to Stamford, this time by railway to Blissworth, where we posted on through King's Cliffe and Rockingham Forest.

I can remember sitting by my father on the box as we bowled along the fine Northamptonshire roads, with a generous space of green sward on either hand, and his showing me a hawk poised in mid-air, the first I had ever seen. I seem also to see the postilion bobbing up and down in front and the sweat coming through his pipe-clayed breeches.

How well I remember my grandfather's house in St. Martin's. The wide, stone flagged hall, scrubbed spotlessly white, the spacious staircase beyond, and at its foot the pantry with its aroma of decanter washings and portlees, the sanctum of old Abbott the butler whom we used to kiss, and whom I am sorry to say, had to leave afterwards for getting tipsy. Beyond was a door leading out under a splendid magnum bonum plum tree to a long paved yard with the stables and my grandfather's favourite coach and horses. A side door led into the garden, a walled paradise of flowers mixed with vegetables, where an old mulberry stood on its own little lawn on which the ripe fruit fell and waited for us to come and eat it.

All this was very delightful to a child from Cockneydom, but I think we liked still better my uncle Tom Jackson's house in St. Mary's Street, where the discipline was more lax and where we were petted and teased by five girl cousins, of whom the eldest was engaged to Lord Exeter's chaplain, while the youngest was still in short frocks. Here also was a kennel of pointers and setters, loose in a sort of covered yard and we used to go to an open balustraded gallery and see them fed. I was not allowed to go in to them, being told they would tear me to pieces. Once, however, when I had my wish I was given quite a friendly reception.

There were nice books, too, at that house. I remember reading one called

'The Female Bluebeard'. It was about a lovely but unprincipled lady who had an ill-regulated appetite for matrimony. She lost husband after husband with amazing rapidity. Their eyes grew larger and more and more lustrous and beautiful and then they died. The hero of the story was already in her toils and the crisis was approaching when my aunt came in and said: 'How could you give the child that book to read', and she took it away. It has been a matter of lifelong regret to me that I have never seen it again.

We were no sooner back at that death-trap at Clapham than one after another fell ill. My poor little brother fell into what was called an infantile fever. He was dosed with calomel till he was salivated, convulsions followed, and he died. My dear mother never forgot him and when she died nearly forty years afterwards, we found treasured in her wardrobe, the little wooden horse he played with, and other relics, which were put in her coffin and buried with her.

On 9th April 1842 my mother's diary reads: 'Went to Hampton Court ... Graham delighted with his day.' Indeed I was. It was my first introduction to the arts. The Great Hall made an enormous impression on me, but above all things I was enraptured with a picture over a door of a woman lying down, probably a Magdalene, with a blue robe I had never seen the like of. I remember trying to reproduce it and my despair at finding no pigment in my childish paint-box that would give that celestial blue that ravished me.

In March 1843 we moved from that ill-fated house at Clapham back to Hampstead, this time to a nice old house and garden on the Upper Terrace.

Upper Terrace, Hampstead

The garden was only divided from the Judges' Walk by a fence with a gate leading onto the Heath. At Hampstead we lived for the next thirteen years and when we left my sisters were grown up and I was at college. Changed and vulgarised as it is, I love the old place still. The part where we lived is comparatively little altered externally.[7] Towards London all is new and hideous, but 'old' Hampstead on the hilltop still retains its shady groves enclosed by rails and gates leading to old world houses with nice gardens, curious little steep alleys ending in flights of steps upwards or downwards, raised paths with white handrails, and some of the tiniest little bandboxes of houses that ever were seen, with miniature gardens in proportion.

The Hampstead of my childhood was still semi-rural and open country still divided it from London. The town ended at Downshire Hill, after which was a gap as far as the group round Pond Street and the Green. Beyond the 'George' it was clear down to the bottom and on to Chalk Farm except for a few scattered houses. West End Lane was really a country lane bordered by open meadows that stretched up to Church Row and down to Swiss Cottage and the Finchley Road, on which there was not then a house. These were the 'Water-Carriers Fields'. There was, of course, no water supply in those days and but few people had a well of their own, and nearly all Hampstead was dependant on the water-carriers who came and went all day long to the Shepherd Well, under a brick archway, with a yoke and a pair of buckets which they carried round to their customers, selling the water for a halfpenny a bucketful.

Hampstead society of that day was tolerably self-centred and independent of London. It was divided into many cliques by lines of cleavage that ran partly on the social and partly on religious differences. Money, I think, then carried less weight, and the professional class looked down on the commercial. But the great dividing line was between the congregations of the two principal churches. Doctrine at St. John's and the Parish Church was mildly high in an old-fashioned way that would now be thought very inoffensive, but which to the Evangelical party then seemed the dry bones of morality. Those who held with the latter party frequented a Chapel of Ease in Well Walk which had been the Pump-room when Hampstead was a fashionable spa. It was a long lofty room with galleries, in one of which was a little organ, said once to have belonged to Handel. In the middle of one long side-wall was the pulpit with reading desk, and a pew for old Kelly the clerk, whose bald head shone like ivory. Exactly opposite was the communion table, over which were painted the Ten Commandments with the Creed and the Lord's Prayer, between two malachite pillars with gold capitals represented as supporting a splendid curtain of crimson velvet fringed and looped up with cords and tassels of gold. This composition, I think, influenced irresistibly my early conceptions of church architecture. The Clergyman who was to preach sat in a pew in his black gown till he was wanted for the communion service, when he went out for his surplice.

I remember we asked my mother: 'Why does Mr. Atkinson go out and come back to show himself in his night-gown?'

In many houses, amongst them ours, dancing was thought worldly and was not allowed, but we had many other ways of amusing ourselves, at evening parties with games and charades and acting; and we did dance too, in houses of the laxer sort, especially at my aunt's where there was always something going on as my cousins grew up.

The artists who used to frequent Hampstead had by that time mostly disappeared. Constable died a year or two after I was born and lies buried in the old churchyard. Clarkson Stanfield,[8] however, lived in the High Street and Cockerell[9] the architect at North End. I remember him as a little, alert, upright figure.

When I was eight years old, I was sent to school two doors off with the Miss Brooke's. My friend there was a little half French boy named de Vidal. Many years afterwards when he was grown up, his father the Baron de Vidal tried to murder him as they were riding together by striking him with a loaded horse whip. The Baron was arrested but nothing would induce young Alfred Vidal to give evidence against him.

In the autumn we went to Leamington while my father went to Sicily on business connected with Nelson's Brontë Estates. I remember an expedition to Kenilworth where I was broken-hearted at being made to sit in the carriage while they visited the ruins, for I was already mad about architecture and had been revelling in the Beauchamp chapel and the Confessional at Warwick.

In the autumn of 1844 I left home for the first time and went to a boarding school in the New Steyne, Brighton, kept by three Miss Hodgsons and their brother. It was recommended by Lady Grantly. We were well taught and I owe a great deal to the grounding I got there. In particular we were made to draw maps, and as I was always ready to draw I took a liking to the subject, which has served me through life.

In 1846 I was removed to a more advanced school at Clapton, which had been kept by the Rev. Charles Heathcote,[10] brother to my uncle Tom Arnold's wife. He had just given it up and his successor was the Rev. John Gilderdale[11] from Yorkshire. It was a good school, though it had the defect of mixing old and young boys together, for some of the elder ones were just going to college. We were very well taught and I was reading Horace and had begun Homer before I was twelve. For one thing I learned there, I cannot be too grateful; I was taught to sing easily at sight and have never had any trouble since in doing so.

I think Dr. Gilderdale was, however, too passionate for a schoolmaster. We learned to read disaster in his morning face, especially when he came down in a black and white bird's-eye cravat. Mrs. Gilderdale called her husband 'Mr. G', by which name he was always spoken of amongst the boys. 'Who is Mr. G?' I asked when I was fresh at the school. 'Oh, you'll jolly soon find out who Mr. G is,' was the reply. We used to be caned and whacked a good deal and I remember once when Mr. G had mislaid his weapon, he sent me into the garden to cut a stick for my own back. But I had my revenge, for I cut him a young horse-chestnut sapling and put the sticky end into his hand. He afterwards took over the Forest School at Snaresbrook and we were all transferred with him.

I stayed at Forest School till I was nearly fourteen and remember my parents coming over to see me carry off the prize for an essay on the Ministry of Moses, which I recited to the company, and the first prizes for Latin and Roman history. So I made my exit with something of credit.

2

1849-54

Entered at Brighton College ~ Tutor at West Clandon ~ Brighton College
1851 Exhibition ~ Duke of Wellington's funeral
Inclinations to Architecture ~ Trial for scholarship at Corpus
Leaving Brighton and to tutor, Mr. Tate, at Ripley
Model dwellings at Hampstead ~ Scholarship at Wadham

At the end of 1849 I was to have gone to Harrow but at the last moment my father feared the expense and I was entered at Brighton College, but as I broke out with scarlet fever in the holidays they would not take me there till Easter.

Meanwhile I went to read with the Rev. Charles Richmond Tate[1] at his curacy at West Clandon near Guildford. Here I was supremely happy. It was my first taste of life in real country; and a more remote and rural place than Clandon then was, would be hard to find.

The vicarage was a modest little cottage embowered in creeper, part of it very old, and I slept in a little room with lead lights and white dimity curtains. The church was delightful with its timber belfry, its high pews and whitewash and window traceries of chalk, and that sweet untouched look now, alas, so rare. Now it is restored and vulgarised and the people are awaking to the fact that they have spoiled it and the other day I was asked to advise them how to *un*-restore and make it an old church again, as I have already done to the sister church of East Clandon.

Brighton College had only been in existence two or three years, and had just moved when I entered it (in 1850) from its first home in Lion House at the top of Portland Place to a new building by Gilbert Scott[2] at the foot of the Downs. The boys lived in the boarding-houses, chiefly in or about Portland Place, where I was.

The first principal was the Rev. Arthur Macleane,[3] the editor of Horace, rather an awful person who frightened us a good deal; but he was somewhat at a disadvantage in being deprived of the *ultimo ratio* of a schoolmaster, corporal punishment not being allowed. The consequence was that

Brighton College, new buildings

expulsion became so common for want of an alternative that the school suffered and in the end flogging had to come in.

Macleane, under whom I was till turned fifteen, was an excellent though somewhat formidable master. I remember the scorn he would pour on the idiot editors who thought Horace's Lydia and Pyrrha and the rest were real women with whom he was really in love. But I gained most from George Long, the senior classical master, under whom I came when I turned fifteen. He was a dry, shrewd old lawyer who always wore a barrister's gown in school instead of the usual academic toga. He was caustic and intolerant of nonsense, but he had a real genius for teaching and he first made me read an ancient author as I should read a modern one. On my first going up to him we read Thucydides and Terence. Afterwards, as was natural, he took us into Cicero, his own special subject, and we hunted down that rascal Verres with as much zest as if we had had him up at Bow Street or before a judge of the Assize. Finding I could draw a bit he set me a copy and catalogue a collection of Graeco-Sicilian coins – or, I should say, sulphur casts of them – with which he would illustrate the subject as each town came up in the course of our study. All this helped us much to realise the actuality of what we were reading about, whereas at the hands of many teachers it would have remained mere dry bones of words and grammar.[4]

We had plenty of music at Brighton College, where we made acquaintance with the Messiah, the Creation, Mozart's masses and good old English madrigals innumerable. Our music master talked semi-broken English as if his native tongue were Italian, of which language I believe he knew next to nothing, as I found out when he failed to translate the Italian songs he taught me.

Of the great 1851 exhibition in Hyde Park I remember very little but the great glass roof, the two elm-trees that were enclosed in it, and the gay carpets hanging from the balconies. My mother's diary records her first visit thus: 'Went to this wonderful exhibition and was more pleased than I expected. The Queen was there. A wonderful machine for folding envelopes attracted much attention. Also one for giving flax the proportion of cotton.' Such were the wonders of those early days of machinery.

It was in that year that we went to a musical party in Frognal where a little boy in lay-down collars, a nephew of Mr. Perkins the curate, played in a marvellous way on the piano. I now know him as Sir Walter Parratt,[5] organist at Windsor and Master of the King's Musick, the greatest poet on his instrument that I have ever listened to.

The time was almost come for me to be thinking of university. One of my cousins Johnny Cairns came to London to start in his life's career. He had passed into Addiscombe, the college for cadets in the East India Company prior to which he went to the famous army crammers, at Nelson House, Wimbledon, now Eagle House in which I write these lines; for thirty five years afterwards it became mine (Plate 7).

On 17th November 1852 Johnny Cairns and I met at Hampstead to see the Duke of Wellington's funeral the next day. Sir Charles Young, Garter King of Arms, had sent us two tickets for St. Paul's, but my mother dare not use them as it was reported that she would be kept there till night and have to go before daylight. So she and my father and sisters went to see the procession start from Horse Guards Parade, which they did from the windows of the colonial office in Downing Street. The tickets for St. Paul's were given to Johnny and me and we started by Hampstead omnibus before dawn and were carried as far as Fleet Street, after which we had to go on foot, for all the traffic was stopped except for private carriages. It was wet and muddy and the crowd blocked the footways and we had to walk up the road in the wake of a carriage till our black clothes were plastered with mud. However, we didn't mind and in time found our place in the north transept with a capital view. The day was as gloomy as a London November day could be and the cathedral was lit by gas, which increased the effect. The spectacle was splendid as the area filled with gorgeous uniforms, official and military, set in the great black cloud of ordinary people like ourselves, which made an admirable foil.

I remember thinking that by far the most dignified and impressive costume was that of the judges in their scarlet and ermine. Through this sea of blazing colour wound the thin line of the choir and clergy, their white, mellowed by the gas to a creamy gold, contrasting strongly with the black pall that covered the catafalque under the centre of the Dome. The most impressive moment was when the coffin sank slowly through the floor into the crypt below to the solemn accompaniment of the Dead March in *Saul*.

It was towards the end of my school life that my tastes were more and more definitely turned towards art and especially architecture. But from my earliest days I think it had been my passion. As a boy I was always drawing imaginary cathedrals and modelling buildings in cardboard or cork. At the Forest School there was a copy of Parker's *Glossary*, over which I used to pore and make drawings from the cuts. Mr. Herbert Evans, our doctor at Hampstead, so often mentioned with affectionate regard by Constable in his letters, was a medieval enthusiast and he inspired me with a fancy for rubbing brasses, from which I learned a good deal about Gothic detail. In my holidays I used to haunt Westminster abbey, for music as well as for the building. My school friend Reginald Thompson[6] knew Dr. Turle[7] the organist, and I went to his house at 4 Upper Belgrave Street to sing quartets with him and his sisters to Dr. Turle's accompaniment. Dr. Turle told us stories of his friend Mendelssohn, and of a gentleman who wanted to know how many tunes his organ had? For it seemed to have a great many! But the architecture attracted me most. I got a sketching order and enjoyed it to the uttermost.

But the crowning delight was my first visit to Oxford at the end of my seventeenth year. I was sent up from school to sit for an open scholarship at Corpus, not that I was likely to get in at my age but because it was thought that a preliminary canter would steady me for a serious effort next year. My cousin Charles Arnold[8] was then a Commoner of Corpus and was to try for the scholarship too. I was committed to his charge and was allotted rooms in the college during the examination.

To have to conform to the routine of college life was in itself a joy, and the possession of rooms of my own, even thus casually, a delight. The glories of 'the High', the grey colleges with their comely architecture, sober yet sufficient and now and then rising to splendour, the University church and the procession of dons in scarlet with Bedells and Maces at the Sermon – all was new and enchanting. And in the evening what could be more delightfully suggestive of the life that was to be my own, than my cousin

Charley's rooms, smugly red curtained and panelled, with the kettle singing on the hob, and the booming of Tom rising and falling on the night air as he tolled his mystic hundred and one. On Sunday evening I was taken to the organ-loft at New College where I found Dr. Stephen Elvey[9] in a silk doctor's gown. He used to play Handel in a way I have never heard surpassed, although he only had one leg, the other (as tradition went) having been shot by his brother, the other organist, Sir George Elvey of Windsor.

Neither my cousin nor I got the scholarship, but he was awarded an exhibition and I was offered admission to the college as a Commoner. So ended my first Oxford experiences. As I left from the railway station, which then stood in the meadows beyond Folly Bridge which were afterwards the Christ Church cricket ground, I little thought what Oxford was to be to me in the future. To me, above most of her sons, she has indeed been an Alma Mater; she not only trained me, but employed me; and so to her I owe not only some of my best friends and some of the pleasantest incidents in my life, but also some of the most interesting and delightful opportunities for the exercise of my art that have fallen to the lot of any architect. The spell she wove round me from the first has never been broken, and nothing pleases me more than to hear that I am sometimes spoken of as 'Oxford Jackson'. At midsummer 1853 I left Brighton College, carrying off with me the prize for a Latin essay on Homer, of which I recited parts on speech-day to the edification of the ladies who formed the majority of the audience.

I spent the next year with my former tutor, the Rev. Charles Richmond Tate, who was now married and had the living of Send-cum-Ripley in Surrey. Mrs. Tate, without much voice, was a charming singer and accompanied herself with a light delicate touch that suited her voice to perfection. She made us laugh by saying; 'when a widower marries again he always says he does it because the express wish of his dear departed wife. Now Charles, if you should lose me, it is not my wish that you should marry again.' Poor woman, she did die not many years afterwards, and he married one of her closest friends.

Across the village green, which had been the nursery of more than one county cricketer, was Dunsborough House. Mrs. Trevenen lived there with her daughters who used to play duets on the piano and thus I learned to know Beethoven's symphonies.

In 1854 my father was at last able to realise a scheme, which he had long had in view. He was one of the pioneers in the matter of providing wholesome buildings for artisans and labourers at fair rents. He had not sufficient means of his own to do anything in that way, but a wealthy stockbroker and a bachelor proposed to leave him a legacy of £10,000. My father at first declined this on his own account, but it was afterwards accepted on the implied condition that it should be used for his scheme of housing for artisans and labourers. My father proceeded to buy an acre of land between Brewhouse Lane and Flask Walk, Hampstead, on which he built a block of thirty tenements in flats, and during the period of nearly fifty years that they have passed since they were built, not a single tenement has ever stood empty.

In those days, before the alterations made by the first University Commission, nearly all the scholarships at Oxford were confined to certain counties, and as I had the misfortune to be born in Middlesex, a county for which there were no scholarships, my only chance of getting one was to try for one of the few that were open. Balliol had thrown hers open and so laid the foundation of her greatness, and a Balliol scholarship was then and has always remained the blue ribbon of such prizes. There were but few others, and when three open scholarships fell vacant at Wadham my tutor thought it right to send me up to try for one of them. I had, of course, to get leave of the authorities at Corpus, where I was already enrolled as a Commoner, and I was required to reside there during the examination.

As I started from Ripley, Mr. Tate, who had thought me very idle, said, 'Well Mr. Jackson, I don't know if you will get the scholarship, but if you do I don't think you will have deserved it.' However, I disappointed his forebodings by getting it after all, and when many years later I reminded the dear old man ('Uncle Tate', as my little boy Hugh used to call him) of his speech he indignantly repudiated it. The election in those days was on 30th June and on that day in the year 1854 just as I was packing up to go home, never dreaming of success, I thought I would just go up to Wadham to see who had succeeded and to my astonishment saw my name on the list which was posted at the buttery hatch. My pleasure was a little dashed by the thought that I had to leave Corpus, but I knew how great a relief it would be to my father to whom the cost of my four years at Oxford would have been a serious matter. The other two successful candidates were Samuel Warren,[10] son of the author of *Ten Thousand a Year* and Fred Halcomb,[11] my inseparable friend during my undergraduate career and now settled in Australia. I began my residence the same year at the end of the long vacation.

3

Wadham College 1854

*Positivism at Wadham ~ Warden Symons ~ Wadham boat at Henley
Teaching at Oxford ~ Pembroke Junior Common Room ~ Rowing ~
Training, Eights in 1856 ~ Wadham head of the river ~ Campanology
~ Sunday lectures ~ Collections ~*

Wadham was then a college of eighty or ninety undergraduates, attracted by Richard Congreve[1] who had left Rugby to become a tutor in his own College. Dr. Congreve's personal influence over all with whom he came into contact throughout his life was very great. An ardent disciple of Comte[2] himself, the college through him became a nursery of positivism. Frederic Harrison[3] had just become fellow and tutor and Bridges[4] was head of the scholars' table when I took my seat at the bottom of it. The prevalent tone at Wadham was Evangelical, which was due to the personal influence of Benjamin Parsons Symons,[5] the Warden and his wife Lydia.

It is difficult to convey a correct idea of Dr. Symons to those that did not know him. In person he was tall and heavily built, with thick, hanging lips and a large nose, suggestive, like his name, of a Hebrew strain in his descent. His utterance was thick and rather indistinct, and I suppose he was short-sighted, for I never remember him without spectacles. His figure and features lent themselves readily to caricature and there were few men in college who could not put something on paper recognisable as 'Big Ben'. His whole life had been collegiate. He was elected scholar in 1803 at the age of seventeen; in 1808 he received Dr. Wills's prize for the best reader in Chapel; in 1811 he was elected probationer and in 1812 admitted a full Fellow.

In 1831 Dr. Tournay[6] resigned the Wardenship on the understanding that Symons would be elected, as he was, four years before I was born. He lived to admit me as scholar and afterwards as Fellow, and held the Wardenship for forty years, resigning in 1871 and dying in 1878. No monk ever clung more closely to his convent and identified himself more thoroughly with it than Symons did to the college, which was his home from early youth to extreme old age. It was no wonder then that his mental range was limited and his horizon rather circumscribed.

There were more stories current about 'Big Ben' than any other celebrity of his day, but many of them are calculated to give quite a false idea of the man to those who did not know him personally; for there were two Symons, Symons the man and Symons the Warden. The *man* was naturally good-natured and genial, a keen man for business, and a shrewd bargainer, not without some sense of humour in other people. The Warden was autocratic and conservative in his management of the college, defiant to his Fellows in a way that ultimately brought his regime to ruin, and utterly without a sense of humour in his dealings with that risible race, the undergraduates. He was never at a loss for an argument to counter an unwelcome proposition – a good one if it were to be had, a foolish one rather than none at all – anything to close the mouth of a petitioner. A man excused himself from cutting morning chapel on the grounds that it was too cold. 'On the contrary, the chapel is too warm,' said the Warden, who had a stove at the back of his stall. 'But, Sir, think of the candles, how they blow about in the draughts.' 'Currents of warm air,' said the Warden blandly.

A good example of his use of the reply fatuous was his answer to Arthur Thompson,[7] who came to complain that the rain came into his attic and dropped upon his bed. This touched him on the economical side, for he hated spending money. 'Really, Mr. Thompson, you surprise me. I remember your uncle living in those rooms and I never had any complaint from him.'

But he surpassed himself when Jack Prescott[8] applied for leave to go to a relation who was dying, to whom he was under obligation and who in fact left him a handsome fortune. 'What relation is he to you?' asked the Warden. 'A cousin, Sir.' 'Well, you may go, but I could have wished it had been some nearer relative.'

Many are the tales of the Warden's breakfasts, to which three or four of us used to be asked in turn and which were very formal affairs, especially in Mrs. Symons's time. The Warden had certain sayings which recurred with unfailing regularity on these occasions, and which we always anticipated with amusement. One was about the use to be made of vacation. 'The term,' he would say, 'is a signpost to show you what to do during the vacation.' 'Yes, Sir,' said a nervous freshman, anxious to please. 'I was told, Sir, you would be likely to make that remark.' An awful silence followed, but Mrs. Symons came to the rescue. 'I am glad the good Warden's sayings are so well known in the college.'

This was indeed being a crown to her husband. But the Warden himself sometimes fell under her rebuke. He had been to the Duke of Wellington's funeral and the crowd amazed him. 'I could not help wondering to myself where on earth will they all get their dinner?' This was exactly what the natural man Symons would have thought, but he caught his wife's eye and added: 'I also thought, where will they get their spiritual food?' This reflection no doubt does not ring quite true, but there is no ground for doubting his religious sincerity. Mrs. Symons was an ardent proselytiser and used to encourage any young man that shared her views. I am sorry to say some of the worst men in college imposed on her in order to gain the indulgent regard of her husband.

Smoking was an abomination to him. 'Sir,' said he to Sale,[9] 'you have been smoking tobacco. You positively stink.' Of the performances of the colleges in the cricket field and the river – football in those days was almost unheard of – he had an incurable suspicion. The only exercise he was ever known to have indulged in was riding, and he and his ponderous steed used to be known in Oxford as the Elephant and Castle.

With sport of any kind he naturally had no sympathy. Athletics indeed at that day had not received the sanction they now enjoy with the authorities, and they were treated by the dons with no sort of consideration. When the college boat was going to Henley in 1849, the crew could not get excused lectures and the boat had to be entered as the 'St. John of Malta' and the crew under pseudonyms for fear of being stopped. They kept their lectures in the mornings and reached Henley in a drag in time for the race in the evening, returning to college by 10 p.m. after winning the Ladies' plate against Trinity College, Cambridge and Oriel College. The next day they repeated their performance and carried off the Grand Challenge Cup, the latter for want of a competitor. The Warden so far condoned this perhaps unwelcome triumph as to allow a supper in Hall to which the vanquished Cantabs were invited, only stipulating that there be 'no hot lush'.

College lectures in those days were like our lessons at school, in which we were put to construe in turn. This I believe is now a thing of the past, abolished when the system of inter-collegiate lectures came in. The defect of the old plan, arising no doubt from the insufficient number of tutors, was that scholars and commoners were all lumped together into the same lectures, which if reduced to the capacity of the weakest were, of course, very little use to the more advanced students. The result was that when one began to read for Honour Schools the first thing one did was to go and ask to be excused attendance at college lectures – which was granted as a matter of course – and instead of them to put on a coach with whom the best part of one's reading was done.

Professional teaching, of which so much is now attempted to be made, was in my time a mere farce, except in the case of one or two professors who really took their office seriously. To qualify for examination we had to produce certificates from two professors that we had attended a course of their lectures, and but for this condition most of them would have lectured to empty benches.

Some of the scientific lectures were *choses pour rire*. It was excellent fun to attend those of Professor Daubeny[10] on chemistry; the men used to groan when the lights were lowered, and give little shrieks when an explosion was expected. The explosions seldom came off when they ought and often occurred when they were not expected, and the little professor used to say to his assistant, 'John, John, how is this? It went very well when we did it the other day.' There were shrewd suspicions that some of the wags among the students were in league with John to produce these fiascos. It is amusing to look back on the position of science in those days, now that she is carrying all before her and threatening to oust Greek from the examinations and put herself in its place.

The two great coaches of my day were Rawlinson[11] and Thorold Rogers[12] – rivals and naturally contemptuous of one another. Rogers spoke of Rawlinson as 'that old rascal in St. Giles's' and Rawlinson regarded Rogers as little better than a crammer. I read with Rawlinson and found him very thorough and useful, though in the end, through no fault of his, I fear I did him little credit.

I found a great many friends at Oxford, some school-fellows from Brighton College, and Mrs. Trevenen introduced me to her nephew, William Molyneux[13] of Loseley Park near Guildford, who was at Pembroke. Pembroke was almost the only college with a Junior Common Room, and there, after dining with Molyneux in Hall, we used to be entertained by John Bent,[14] the chartered humorist of the university. I cannot recall any very brilliant flashes of his wit at those gatherings, but I remember I used to think we had rather too much of him, especially at a public concert in the Town Hall, where, of course, ladies were present, his friends and admirers insisted on hoisting him onto a bench to make a speech and interrupt the performance. 'Three cheers for John Bent,' said he. 'Who's John Bent?' cried someone in the audience. 'Why, I am, you fool,' said he. The best thing I know of his was said long afterwards when he was a parson of a very poor living in Woolwich, where I believe he worked very well. A lady said to him, 'I think, Sir, you are the incumbent of this parish?' 'No, Madam,' he replied 'I am Bent without the income.'

The river at Oxford gave me the first opportunity of 'coming off', as a schoolboy would say in athletics. The short sight, which had been a trouble to me since childhood, cut me off from most games at school. Fives I could play pretty well but at cricket I was hopeless, for I could not see the ball until it was close to me. In those days it would have been a bold boy who mounted spectacles, and it was not till I left school that I took to a single eye-glass. I think due weight is not given to the effect of short sight on a boy's character. It is apt to make him shy and diffident and drive him in upon himself. Partly cut off from what goes on about him he stands on his guard and becomes reserved and stand-offish. He often gets a reputation for being unawares, and a character thus formed is not easily shaken off in after life, when assurance at last comes with greater experience. Such, I think, was the effect of short-sight on me at all events. I believe I was a reserved, shy and disagreeable child, whom some of my mother's friends thought 'Not quite right'; and at school I was a boy of few intimate friendships, though those few were close and lasting.

Boating, therefore, for which I had always had a passion but little opportunity was for me a great and sudden expansion. Short-sight did not matter, and the close society into which training brings the members of a crew was an admirable way of breaking through the crust of the reserve. I took to rowing in my first term and in the following spring was put into the Torpid and had my first experience of training. When once in training the crew was cut off from general society and had all its meals apart, turn by turn in each man's rooms. Various theories of diet were in vogue successively during my boating career, all equally empirical and absurd. At one time dried fruit was supposed to make muscle and we ate largely of figs and raisins. Another year porridge was all the fashion and we ate it until there seemed to be a cannonball under the lower part of our waistcoats. It is difficult to believe as one looks back on those days that a breakfast of underdone beef-steak with one cup of tea followed by a draught of college ale can have been good for us or likely to promote activity. But at that age a man can eat and digest anything and we survived.

Wadham was then a good boating college and, as colleges went, with its eighty or ninety men it was not amongst the smaller colleges. There were seldom more than fourteen boats on. New College then only consisted of Winchester scholars and three gentlemen commoners; Magdalen only put on a boat towards the end of my time and surprised everyone by doing it.

In the following summer term I was promoted to the college eight. We were a very promising crew, and had the stroke of the university eight, for our stroke. We started fourth on the river and bumped Christ Church the first night at the Willows, Brasenose the second night in the Gut, running right up on the canvas. There remained Balliol, the head boat, with Walter Morrison[15] stroke and Lonsdale[16] and Edmond Warre,[17] both university oars, in the crew. It was a splendid race, but we made our bump when Balliol was half-way past the winning-post[18] and so gained the headship of the river.[19]

Forty years after, Morrison and I came together over the chapel I built at his expense for Giggleswick School. I reminded him of this race: 'Ah,' said he 'that bump has rankled my mind ever since.' At about the same time I got a letter from Edmond Warre, now become headmaster of Eton, asking me to take his son Edmund as a pupil into my office, and winding up with 'Are you the same Jackson who bumped us in 1856?' We had not met for forty years and the friendship which followed has been one of the pleasantest incidents of my later life.

The same year Halcomb and I all but won the University pairs against Lonsdale and Warre, who only beat us by a few seconds. When I reminded Warre of the famous bump he replied, 'Yes, but I was *Primus inter pares.*'

When we were training there was always a dull time in the afternoon between our dinner which was from 3 to 4 o'clock and the time for going down to the river, so I used to go and ring one of the two bells, ding-dong, for New College chapel at 5 p.m. I never succeeded in setting my bell exactly when I pleased, however, and my performance must have amazed the college sometimes.

Sunday afternoon at most colleges was devoted to long walks in the country, but at Wadham an obstacle to this was opposed by the Warden's lecture on the Thirty-nine Articles from 1 to 2 o'clock, which was always resented as a grievance. He afterwards altered the time to 12 o'clock, which was a little better for us and left us free until afternoon chapel at 5; his reason for the change was that it left us more time to go to the University sermon at 2 o'clock and 'Moreover,' said he, 'one o'clock is the hour at which you take your little luncheon, such of you at least as take luncheon, as I am sure it is highly conductive to health.' It was seldom the old gentleman was so lively at Article lecture, which was generally a very dull affair, enlivened only by the tricks of irrepressible undergraduates. The Warden sat at the head of High Table and we on benches down the sides of it. One trick was for the men at the far end to sidle up and push one another nearer the top until the man next the Warden was pushed off the bench and, after retaining for a moment the sitting posture with nothing under him, lost his balance and went down on the floor. But the Warden was equal to the occasion and scored off the principal offender. Fixing him with his spectacled gaze he said, 'Twenty years ago, sir, I should have had you flogged at the buttery hatch.' 'Anybody who attends carefully to these lectures,' he would tell us, 'will acquire a sound body of Divinity.' I believe they were really very good, but I fear few of us profited much by them. Instead of making notes we were occupied in drawing Big Ben, and all I remember of them is the anecdotes with which he sometimes illustrated them and which from his entire want of humour sometimes recoiled upon himself. As an instance of providential design in creation he would stroke his own huge nether limb and say 'but for that, my leg might have been like the leg of an elephant'. There were stories, too, that proved the general untruthfulness of Roman Catholics. One was about the way in which he had been cheated by a washerwoman abroad. Another about the way he was swindled at the exhibition of some relic 'for which they charged me an enormous sum – I think it was as much as five shillings!' It does not take much to make a man of twenty laugh, and as the Warden, though very rich, was very 'near' in money matters we used to enjoy these and similar anecdotes extremely.

At the end of term we had collections: professedly a college examination in the work we had been doing, but more truly an opportunity of being seen and commended or slanged, as the case might be, by the Authorities. We went into Hall in white ties and wrote papers, which were not always looked at by the examiners. There was a good deal of whispering and subdued laughing and drawing of caricatures which the dons if good-natured tried not to see while pretending to look another way, or if severe punished by an extra paper. The Warden and Fellows sat at the High Table and had us up one by one for viva voce followed by five minutes' conversation with the Warden, who was generally in a good humour and wanted to know how many brothers you had, or recommended home as better than a reading party for work in the vacation 'unless you have troublesome sisters'. Sometimes he became quite facetious, and noticing the younger Simcoe's[20] budding moustache told him he was 'like a fierce barbarous savage beast and only fit for the North Pole'. He was very deaf and his audible asides to the tutors were sometimes rather embarrassing to the subject of them. 'Who is this young man?' he would ask the Sub-Warden sitting at his elbow. 'Mr. So-and-so, Sir.' 'Oh, I remember his father [or his uncle] who was always thought a stupid person.' This in a tone heard halfway down the Hall! The Warden, by the way, was not ignorant of the nickname by which he was popularly known. He said that Dr. Lloyd,[21] Bishop of Oxford 'slapped me on the back and said, "How do, Big Ben" – a very coarse man.' But he would have learned it, if nowhere else, at Commemoration when as curator of the Theatre he was freely addressed from the gallery.

4

Oxford 1855-58

First visit to France ~ Move to Sydenham
Fall of Wadham boat in Eights
Theatricals at Wadham ~ Lessons in painting
William Turner of Oxford ~ Visits to Hamersleys at Pyrton
County Ball ~ Reading for Greats ~ Indian Mutiny
Oxford in long vacation ~ Tried for University Eight
Schools ~ B.A. ~ Discussion on future career

Towards the end of my first long vacation (September 1855), when I
was nineteen, I made my first acquaintance with foreign parts. My
father and I went for about a fortnight across the channel and we took with
us my black-and-tan terrier, Nelly. We crossed to Boulogne and visited
Abbeville, Amiens, Beauvais, Caen and Falais returning by Le Havre and
Southampton.

I think this was a critical event in my life. The freshness and novelty of
France seen for the first time awoke the passion for drawing which had
somehow gone to sleep since my school-days, and I began to sketch vigorously everything I saw – especially architecture, towards which I think this
tour gave me the final impulse. The sketches I brought home are still in
existence, and on looking at them I find that, bad as they are as drawings,
the architecture is correctly represented and fairly well understood. (Plate
12). I had been well grounded in perspective by an old Mr. Pickersgill[1] who
was a retired lieutenant in the Navy and I remember his telling us one day
that his son was elected an Associate of the Royal Academy. This was
Frederick Richard Pickersgill, afterwards R.A. and the highly popular
Keeper of the Academy who, strangely enough, was my proposer for election to that body many years later.

My father wrote from Beauvais: 'I cannot tell you how delighted
Graham is with the cathedrals and of those you are to expect a variety of
sketches … Whilst our artist is sketching I stroll and peep about the
towns.'

Caen, Abbaye aux hommes.

At Abbeville and Amiens and the other great towns we visited, the streets were lit with the lanterns across from side to side, which had been found handy for hanging aristocrats during the Revolution. There were no side *trottoirs* for foot-passengers, and the rough pitching of the roadway was laid with fall to a central gutter down which all the slops of the town formed a fragrant rivulet. The peculiar odour that hung about an old French town, arising from these unsavoury streams, mixed with the aromatic scent of roasting coffee, may still be encountered in out-of-the-way places. It always makes me think of quaint, picturesque street-scenes and good subjects for sketching, for nasty smells may awaken pleasant memories. Viollet-le-Duc[2] tells of a visit to St. Cloud with an old lady who in her youth had been at the court of Louis XV, when the corridors even of royal palaces were polluted with all kinds of nuisance regardless of decency; and as they strolled through the now-deserted halls an evil smell they casually encountered caused the old lady to exclaim: 'Ah! Cette odeur! Comme il me rappelle un assez beau temps.'

From Beauvais to Rouen, a distance of fifty miles, we travelled all night for nine hours in a shabby diligence – a *drôle de voiture* , as a lady called it who shared the coupé with us. Diligence travelling in France has now come to an end as there are railways everywhere, but many a long journey have I made in that way in my time. Tedious and uncomfortable as they were, there is a certain pleasure in looking back to them. By day, if you had a good seat, they were not unpleasant, but to pass whole nights doubled up in a coupé, where you could hardly sit upright, rattling over the rough pavé, with the jingling of the horses' bells, the 'youp-youp' of the driver and the ceaseless 'crick-crack' of his whip, was at the time something of a penance.

At Rouen where something medieval delights the eye at every turn, we persevered in seeing all that could be seen. At the Hôtel d'Angleterre, the large dining room was turned at night into a servants' dormitory, and the oak floor was covered with dirt that you might scrape.

From Le Havre my father wrote: 'After breakfast we walked down to the port of which Graham seems to have an utter abhorrence, it being, I presume the opposite to all that is or was medieval.' I fear the fanatical medievalism from which I suffered at that time must often have been a bore to him, but he never showed it.

At Paris, where we stayed at the Hôtel du Louvre, the first of the monster hotels now so common, I need hardly say, our first point was Notre Dame where the whole interior was under repair, and then on to the Palais de Justice. A visit to the Opera to hear Auber's *Domino Noir*[3] brought this trip to a conclusion.

My father felt that he had never been treated quite fairly by his firm, and in 1857 the juxtaposition of my Uncle and his family next door became awkward.[4] After house hunting in various places the family finally settled in a semi-detached villa at Sydenham, where we stayed three years. It was a purely cockney creation of the railway and the newly opened Crystal Palace, and though we at first had the enjoyment of Laurie Park, in which our house was one of the first excrescences, houses soon began to rise around us in a mushroom growth. There were pleasant rural places within reach – Bromley, Beckenham, and Chislehurst as yet untouched by the railway, and I rode all over the country about Wickham and Hayes, where I passed the grove of old oaks from one of which Millais[5] made his picture of the concealed Royalist.

The Crystal Palace also was a great source of attraction. We had season-tickets and I could walk up through the grounds from a gate near our house. There was a Handel festival in the palace the first year of our residence at Sydenham, the first of its kind, I think, and I remember running up from Oxford for one of the performances, which impressed me greatly. At that age one is subject to megalomania and does not always distinguish quantity from quality. The oratorio was *Judas Maccabeus* and the solo singers were Clara Novello,[6] Madame Rudersdorff, Miss Dolby, Sims Reeves, Smith, Herr Formes, and Weiss.[7] The names now seem to take one back to ancient history. The Queen was there and Clara Novello sang the first verse of the National Anthem. The most affecting and overpowering incident, however, was after the last chorus, 'Hallelujah'; everyone remained standing as if in expectation of something further, and then after a single chord on the organ the whole mighty choir in unison with the band in harmony burst forth into the Old Hundredth Psalm, 'All people that on earth do dwell'. It had an indescribable effect on me and, I think, on everyone.

The summer of 1857 was as pleasant as summer terms at Oxford always are. A seductive time of lying under trees in verdant gardens with a book that does not get read, or of gliding with crash of oars on the smooth waters of the Isis and punting idly in the cool of evening up the Cherwell,

Annihilating all that's made
To a green thought in a green shade.[8]

Anything I fear but steady reading, of which the little that is done is liable to interruption by the invasion of ladies, young and old, whose claims on your attention are obvious and irresistible.

It is the term, too, of the 'Eights', marked sadly this year in the annals of the college by the descent of our boat from the proud position of Head of the River. There were several of the victorious crew of last year in the boat but the new men ruined us, and we had perhaps grown stale ourselves. Disaster followed mismanagement. Two men were changed in the race week itself, and George Pyne[9] our captain and No. 7 must needs go rook-shooting and get nabbed by Shirley,[10] the most relentless of our dons, as he was driving out of Oxford without leave, for which he was sent down in the middle of the races. Needless to say we fell, and great was the fall of us. Another thing that told to our disadvantage was the revolution that had taken place in boat-building. We rowed in the boat built for us by Hall last year, while our successful rivals had the new short boats without keels invented by Mat. Taylor of Newcastle, which steered much more easily round corners and certainly were vastly superior to the old pattern.

But if we disgraced ourselves on the river we distinguished ourselves at Wadham this term by giving some theatricals, then rather a novelty at Oxford. There was at that time no theatre open at Oxford in term time and what public dramatic performances there were, were allowed only in vacation when the men were away. Our stage was put up in the large room, No.5 one pair right, which I afterwards occupied as a Fellow. My rooms as a scholar were opposite on the same landing and were used as the Green Room of the performers. We gave two pieces, *Take That Girl Away* and *Two Heads Are Better Than One*. I acted in the latter and painted the drop-scene which, seen by friendly eyes, received much commendation.

The impetus, which my foreign trips had given to my drawing, did not fail; indeed I think it has never flagged from that day to this. I took lessons in watercolour from William Turner[11] – Turner of Oxford as he is called, to distinguish him from his greater namesake. He was then a quiet old recluse with a white tie and a gentle retiring manner, reminding one of a certain pleasant type of old clergyman that has now, alas, ceased to exist. He lived in John Street, a dull enough place, with a little plot of garden behind, where he grew a few plants, useful for foregrounds. From this hermitage it was very difficult to move him and I never succeeded in getting him to my rooms or in persuading him to go out with me sketching. He had shut himself up after the death of his wife. His retirement naturally injured his art, for though he continued to exhibit at the Old Watercolour Society, of which he was one of the oldest members, he never saw what the other men were doing and so fell behind, with an old-fashioned mannerism that robbed his work of its interest. Although he had little power of composition, a defect of which he was conscious and which I heard him bewail himself, he had been when in his prime, and when he travelled and painted from nature, a very attractive artist, and in a certain kind of sky with rolling cumulous clouds, he was, as Ruskin remarked, almost unrivalled. When he died not long after my degree, his unsold works went to Christie's and fetched very little money. I bought several, and in particular one I had always admired in his portfolio, of cattle waiting for the ferry to Skye. I gave four guineas only for it, and a few days after the sale the dealers were offering less important drawings which they had bought at similar prices for thirty guineas.

Turner's method was to paint a picture before his pupil to show how to carry it through step by step, and we copied each stage between our lessons. He used mainly transparent colours, cobalt and rose madder, cobalt and brown madder, brown madder and gamboge, for distances as they approached; raw sienna or Indian yellow with Prussian blue for trees (cyanine was yet unknown); and Smith's warm grey for rocks, a colour which was a great favourite with him.

'You have the Smith's warm grey, Sir, have you not?'

'Why no – I don't think I –'

'But you will get the Smith's warm grey, will you not?'

Some of the most original of Turner's drawings, rising to a pitch somewhat beyond his usual achievements, were in the possession of Mr. Wharton,[12] Precentor at Radley.

Among the pleasantest recollections of this time is my intimacy with the Hamersleys at Pyrton Manor in Oxfordshire. Hampden,[13] when he was wounded at Chalgrove Field a few miles away, rode first to Pyrton, which was his father-in-law's house, but being pursued had to go on to Thame where he died. Mr. Hamersley, as a hunting man, said that, though wounded, Hampden must have jumped Great Haseley brook, which is considered a creditable performance for a sound man.

Pyrton Manor, of which there is a small view in Skelton's Oxfordshire, is an interesting old Elizabethan house with the usual hall and fine old stair from it with oak balustrading leading to an oak-panelled room where Hampden is said to appear in a suit of blue velvet on Christmas eve, after driving up to the house in a coach and six.

Mr. Hamersley was the picture of a country squire – handsome, a good sportsman, and an active magistrate and chairman of the Oxfordshire quarter sessions. Mrs. Hamersley and the two grown-up daughters used to come into Oxford for the balls at Commemoration and were often my guests in college at luncheon and on the river, and I used to go over there for the county ball which was held at Watlington in order not to be swamped by the university as it would have been at Oxford. The ballroom was the upper floor of the best inn, and a bridge was thrown out through one window across a narrow street to the upper floor of the picturesque little Jacobean Town Hall, in which we had supper. To get leave to attend this ball required, I remember, a good deal of diplomacy. It was seventeen miles from Oxford, but it would have been useless to ask the Warden for permission to sleep out of college, so I only said I had an invitation to Pyrton and asked for leave to knock-in late.

'Well, Mr. Jackson,' he said, I suppose you will start back from Mr. Hamersley's by half-past ten, for you can't stay later than that you know possibly; and you will be back by half-past twelve or one.' This took me rather aback, for about half-past ten the ball would just be beginning. So I only said I would get back as soon as I could. I started at five in a dog-cart which I put up at the Hamersleys', arriving just in time to dress for dinner. After dancing till nearly 4 a.m. I returned to Pyrton, where some supper was waiting for us in the hall. Then my horse was put to and I drove back the seventeen miles to Oxford arriving about a quarter to seven, in time, had I been so disposed, to have gone to chapel. Such is the ardour – the enviable ardour – with which youth pursues its pleasures.

It is natural that the memory should throw back to these pleasant episodes but, except for the desperately idle, the times of stress come at Oxford when the schools fill the whole range of mental vision. For much of my time at the university I confess I trifled away my chances and thought too little of the serious object of my being there. My second in Moderations might, as I saw plainly afterwards, have been a first had I not put off reading till late, and then made myself ill by trying to recover lost time. And it was not until a year before 'Greats' that I began to read for them in earnest.

In October 1857 I was back at Oxford and set to work seriously to read for Greats, for which I was to go in next May. On three mornings a week I went for an hour to Rawlinson, my coach; on the three alternate mornings I had Farrar's[14] lectures on the *Ethics* in college. Beside that, the programme I drew up for myself in my new-found zeal prescribed eight hours of reading by myself, a counsel of perfection, which I found I could not live up to. But as there was less boating this term to distract me I did pretty well.

At this time I first appeared before the public as an illustrator. Metcalf,[15] a Fellow of Lincoln, who was once a master at Brighton College, had published a book called *The Oxonian in Norway* and had asked me to make some drawings from rough sketches of his own for engraving in a second edition. They were trifling affairs but I was very proud of seeing myself in print. I afterwards did some better drawings to illustrate popular Norse legends in a second book of his, *The Oxonian in Thelemarken*, which appeared some years later.[16]

1857 was the year of terror when the Indian mutiny was at its height. Every mail brought news of fresh disasters. My cousin John Cairns was at the front, with the first Bengal Fusiliers at Delhi. He got through the siege of Delhi without a scratch and was one of the first in the breach, where he took one of the enemy's guns, turned it on them and worked it himself. When it was all over he went on guard at the Cashmere Gate, was seized with cholera, and, as no doctor could be found, he was carried to the camp and died in three hours. He had been in twenty-six engagements and escaped without a single wound of any consequence. At the time it was supposed that Russia had something to do with exciting the mutiny.

I spent Christmas at home and went back to Oxford a few days afterwards to read during the rest of the vacation. The Warden, into whose bad graces I had got, made a great favour of letting me come up. 'I understand, Mr. Jackson, it is a very hazardous experiment to allow you to stay up; if I hear of you being out late at night, you know, or galloping over the country hunting – eh – eh – um – you must not be surprised at my sending you down again you know.' In my then virtuous mood I rather resented this. Besides, I never hunted and did not often ride. But the old gentleman stuck to his opinion, and when I called on my arrival he would not see me but only asked through his manservant whether he had given me leave to come up.

Oxford was empty and dismal – as Tom Hilder the doyen of the scouts said, 'Lor, Sir, don't ee look foolish? It be horfull dull.' George, the porter, met me with the cheerful news that there was nobody up but the Warden and said that I was the last gentleman he should have thought of seeing in vacation, from which it appears he shared the Warden's opinion of my frivolity. All this was depressing enough, but the dullness was what I had really come for and I got seven or eight hours a day steady reading, besides my time with Rawlinson my coach – and during the vacation a few other men came up and we had nice little dinners together, so the dullness was a little bit lessened. In the afternoon I sculled on the river and even sketched, for it was nice open weather, or went out fishing with David the water-man or drew in the Taylor Galleries, a practice I had begun the previous winter term.

My virtuous resolutions did not fail me when the men did return – I read hard all the rest of my time, dining early in my rooms instead of in Hall and refusing all invitations to wines. A few others were in like predicament to myself and we formed a small society by ourselves.

One distraction by which I was threatened fortunately for me ended in nothing. I was tried for the University Eight, and rowed bow for some time. Finally they chose another man in my place, which was a bitter disappointment to me at the moment, though really the best thing that could have happened, for had I been put into training it would have ruined what little hope I had of doing anything in the Schools. Nevertheless I have always felt an undying grudge against my supplanter, one Thomas of Balliol.[17]

My reading was begun too late. I had idled away a good deal of time after Moderations and I paid the penalty by only getting a third class in Greats. But the effect of my steady reading for the final year had a lasting effect on me. I had formed habits of study, and I knew that the Fellowship to which I looked forward would never be mine unless I continued them. I began to read more and more for pleasure and profit; the thirst for knowledge stirred within me and I can safely say that I have never been idle since.

In order to take a bachelor's degree I had to pass a second School, and had my choice of law and modern history, or mathematics, or natural science. The last-named school was to begin in a week's time after I had got my Testamur. It was a newly founded School and made easy with a view to attracting candidates, and in it I saw my way to getting my bachelor's gown that term. Rawlinson encouraged me. With the natural contempt of the classical scholar for mere science, he said: 'they are sure to be very obliging in this School. There are only fourteen men in, so they can ill afford to lose one-fourteenth of their candidates, for they wish to become popular.' So I set to work on Carpenter's *Physiology* and Fownes's *Manual of Chemistry*, of which I found the latter very 'slow' and the former very interesting. The work interested me so much that I felt half-ashamed of myself for cramming it up in such a hurry, but I wanted to get my gown on that term and there was no other way. 'Learnt such rum things about one's inside that I can't conceive how one manages to go all right for a day together.' In this I anticipated what a great surgeon once said to me: 'the more I think of it the more I wonder that anyone is alive.'

I had three clear days reading before the Schools, and I made the most of them. In the examination I came out strong in physiology with a fine drawing of a heart, and managed pretty well in mechanical philosophy, but failed in the questions about electricity, which I had not yet looked at. We were to take a special subject chosen from among several that were named and I had only time to read up my special subject on the evening of the first day's examination. At breakfast next morning I got up the subject of 'Light' from Fownes's *Chemistry* and answered two-thirds of the questions set us, which were absurdly easy. Then came viva voce by Dr. Coote,[18] a London physician, in physiology and Mr. Dale in mechanical philosophy. Coote was a most delightful examiner, laughing with you and almost apologising for asking questions you could not answer – an agreeable contrast to grim Thorold Rogers, under whom I had just suffered in the other School. I was complimented on my Physiology paper, which was pronounced 'Very Satisfactory', and when I explained that I had not seen muscles in dissection my ignorance as to the different muscular structures was excused. I was told to come back for an extra paper in the afternoon. What could this mean? Good heavens! Electricity! One precious hour intervened for this and luncheon. I flew to Fownes's *Chemistry* again and by one o'clock had primed myself with a general knowledge of the subject, and on returning to the Schools I managed to answer four questions out of five. The whole thing was rather comic, but the joke would not be complete unless I got through, and I was rejoiced when after chapel, as I was waiting in the lodge, some wild figures appeared in the direction of the Schools coursing along and waving a piece of paper, which was my Testamur. One of my friends said he would rather have floored the School like me after twenty-five hours' reading than have got a first in the Greats. I wished I had the chance of changing one for the other.

On 26th May 1858 I put on my bachelor's gown – the *toga virilis* – and my undergraduate career came to an end. The rest of the term was spent in rest and enjoyment of the lovely Summer weather. I ran up to town to hear Don Giovanni for the first time. Is there such singing now? Those were the days of the real 'bel canto', when the voice rang true as the violin. Now everything is ruined by that accursed tremolo, and tone is sacrificed to sentiment.

1 Examination Schools, Oxford

2 Sir Thomas Jackson Bt R.A. aged 86. Painted by his cousin Gerald Goddard Jackson and exhibited at the Royal Academy in 1922

3 *Examination Schools – the Quad before the old buildings were demolished*

4 *Organ case at the Sheldonian Theatre, Oxford*

5 *Tenby, 1858*

6 *St David's Cathedral – Bishop Gower's Screen and Tomb*

7 *Eagle House, Wimbledon*

8 *Alice Jackson*

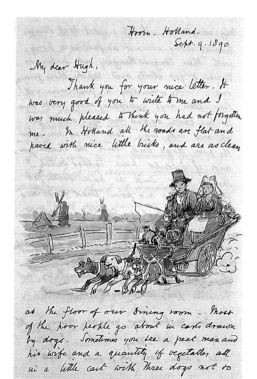

9 *Letter depicting a dog-cart written from Holland in 1890*

10 *Letter written to Hugh in 1890*

11 St David's Cathedral and ruins of Bishop's Palace

12 A Village in France

I rowed my last race and won the pewter pot in the college scratch fours as I had done in all the scratch fours but one since I took to rowing. Then came Commemoration, for which I succeeded in persuading my father to come up, and I took him into the area of the theatre where he was much amused at the little respect paid by the gallery to the university dignitaries. In the afternoon we sat in New College gardens and discussed my future career. Two openings had been offered him for me – a writership in India and a cadetship, but he had declined both. He wanted me to be an architect, a calling for which he believed me peculiarly qualified. But though I loved architecture my bent at the time was towards painting, and that seemed a hopeless profession for one who had to earn his bread. My wish was to go to the Bar, especially if I succeeded in getting a Fellowship, but he would not hear of that. He knew too much of the briefless throng to encourage my fancy in that direction. And so we came to no conclusion but adjourned to New College Chapel and heard the service, and then he dined with me in Hall before going back to town.

I left Oxford, not to see it again for some years, by water, rowing down to Reading in a four, and then going to stay at Pyrton and to Henley regatta with the Hamersleys before returning home.

5

At Scott's Office 1858

Interview with Mr. Gilbert Scott ~ Tenby and Wales ~ Letter from Scott
Architecture decided on ~ First days of office life ~ Gothic revival
Scott's Office ~ His large practice ~ Remains of old London
Hungerford Market ~ Sales and picture exhibitions ~ London antiquities

My father lost no time in pushing his views as to my profession to a decision. Mr. Gilbert Scott, then at the head of his profession, had come to be our neighbour[1] and we had made his acquaintance before we left Hampstead; my father showed him one of my sketch-books and arranged that I should go and talk the matter over with him. I went to breakfast with him and he offered to take me to the 'Brompton Boilers', as the irreverent had christened the temporary buildings in which the South Kensington Museum had its origin, and where the architectural casts with which he was concerned were temporarily housed. We walked across the Conduit Fields – now fields no more – till we took an omnibus, from the top of which I remember he disparaged Decimus Burton's arch opposite Apsley House as 'a thing one could design in ten minutes'. In his disregard of personal appearances I think he outmatched my father. His negligent dress and ill-brushed hat were counterbalanced by a certain unconscious dignity in his manner and were part of the modesty and simplicity of the man. He would stand still in the middle of the road and take out a case of pencils and a notebook and illustrate by a sketch what he was saying. I was much touched by the freedom and absence of pretension with which he discussed architecture with me, a mere tyro and a youngster with the merest smattering of knowledge on the subject. He told me how he began by travelling for a year after his articles, and then put himself with some large builders to see practical work for some months before starting for himself. He said he managed to keep himself after four years and that his success began with winning competitions for Union workhouses when the Poor Law was revised. In that way, after winning a great many, he gradually came into notice. 'Dirty disagreeable work,' he said, 'but the rule should be never to pick your subjects but go in for whatever offers whether you like it or not, for if you compete only for the subjects you like you will nearly always fail.'

I told him of my leaning rather towards painting, but he thought it late to begin at my age. 'However,' he said, 'there is Mr. Jones[2] of Exeter College who has done it.' The Pre-Raffaelites[3] nevertheless seemed not much to his taste; he said they painted like a school of madmen let loose. This roused me to defend them, for I was steeped in Ruskin[4] and mad about Hunt[5] and Millais. 'Well,' said Scott, 'bring your Pre-Raffaelitism into architecture, for it is exactly what architecture is most in need of at this present time.' After this conversation I took to drawing the statuary at the Crystal Palace, for Scott had said how all-important it was for an architect to be able to draw the figure well and not be obliged to depend on a sculptor for the statuary of his buildings. I still hesitated, however, as to the line of art I should take. Charles Arnold, who knew a little of Burne-Jones when he was at Exeter College, had sent him some of my sketches for his opinion, and we waited for that before deciding between painting and architecture.

I went off for my holiday without anything being settled and paid a round of visits in various parts of England, ending by joining the home party at Tenby (Plate 5). It was my first visit to Pembrokeshire with which country I was destined to be so familiar. Our pleasure in this and many subsequent visits to Tenby was owing largely to our intimacy with the family of Mr. Gilbert Smith,[6] Rector of Gumfreston, about two miles away. He was a remarkable man, full of fire and vigour, warm hearted and kindly, but dogmatic and violent in argument, and almost as eccentric and unconventional in his pulpit as in his parlour. His scientific acquirements were considerable, and his acquaintance was sought by all the Geologists who came to Tenby. He kept open house for all his friends who were welcome to drop in uninvited, at all hours, to breakfast, dinner or tea. His wife was a gentle old lady, a contrast in everything to her husband, and his daughters who spoiled him, were my sisters dearest friends and companions. With the Smiths we haunted the old castles in which 'Little England beyond Wales' abounds, we sailed to Caldy Island, picnicked at the Stack Rocks and explored the caverns in the inaccessible limestone cliffs beyond Giltar point which the sea never leaves. Within a very short distance we examined twenty-one of these caves – some of them were enormous, running in 200 or 250 feet and so high that the roof was lost in darkness. In one we found at the end, jammed immovably between two rocks, the stem of a large vessel with its iron bolts, jagged, bent, and rusty, standing out where it had been torn away from the wreck. It was all that was left of a French ship, we heard afterwards, which had been swept in there bodily one stormy night and had not been found for some time. In some caves we could land, as the tides were low; in others we took the boat. In one there was a second outlet high up in the cliff to which we climbed by a sort of chimney. In another an opening below the water threw up a soft, green light into the darkness of the cavern. In another, so deep that the light from the entrance was lost, as I groped along there was an offensive smell and my hand fell on something clammy and hairy, which I believed to be a drowned sailor, but which may perhaps have been the nose of my dog Smike. The sea was brilliantly phosphorescent as we rowed back in the dusk, every dash of the oars lighting up sheets of flame; and as the tide was high and the sea calm we took the boat through the cave that pierces St. Catherine's Island, which the phosphorescence lit up like an illumination. A sailor who took us to Caldy Island a day or two later was much interested in my supposed drowned sailor. He had once found one and had taken the body to Lloyd's agents who, he understood, took charge of everything found at sea, and was much surprised when they would have nothing to do with it. They were probably much surprised, too. He told us one curious nautical belief, which he held firmly, that the moment a boat gets a dead man in the net however fast she might be going she stops still in a moment. He had once had four dead men in his net and never wished for another.

The Rectory at Gumfreston was characteristic of its master. It was a long low building, like a farmhouse, with thick stone walls, whitewashed, and with a careless, ordered garden before and behind where things seemed to grow with a luxuriance unknown in the East of England. To the left of the low stoneflagged hall was the hospitable dining-room, low pitched and rather dark, the walls lined with books, and at the far end a blazing fire, which was battered down with culm at night and never went out from year's end to year's end. The moist warm atmosphere of Wales condensing on the thick walls made the house damp and mouldy, and the fire was acceptable even in summer. To the right of the Hall was a dark den, intended for a study, but devoted to a vast collection of bones from the caves, fossils, geological specimens and various odds and ends all in the most admired confusion.

I forgot when Mr. Smith died, but in 1870 he wrote me a Socratic farewell.

My dear Graham,
   The people have been working at the Vestry door all week; it will look very well. Now I want a design for a table for this vestry. It must have a deepish draw and lock up.
   I am going to die, dear friend; you are going to live – I find it pays me well to love God and man with 'all my heart'.
   Like foam on the river
   Like the bubble on the fountain
   I'm gone, and forever.
Yours ever, I trust.

Lovingly
G.N. Smith

He did not, however, die for some years after that, and I was several times at Gumfreston when at work on Narberth and Robeston Wathen churches. After his death the Rev. Gilbert Smith's collections were bought by the town of Tenby and placed in a museum there.

Tenby, when we first knew it, was still contained within its town walls and was accessible only by a drive of fourteen miles from Narberth Road station. Though there were many visitors even then, it gave itself none of the airs of a fashionable watering-place and, as most of the lodging-houses had steps of their own down to the shore, you could see as much or as little company as you pleased. The roughness of the country was of a piece with the primitive character of the people, which again was reflected in the rudeness of the local architecture. But rude as they are, there is an inde-scribable charm in the quaint little Pembrokeshire churches with their mil-itary-looking towers, vaulted in the ground story and furnished with pigeon-holes in the upper stages, in which the villagers could take refuge and find sustenance when the wild Welsh-men made a raid into the English pale.⁷ Many of them are covered with barrel-vaults from end to end, which form the exterior roof as well, without any timber at all; and the interior with its narrow arches no bigger than doorways between nave and chancel and transepts, resembles the natural caves with which the neigh-bouring limestone cliffs are freely riddled. Gumfreston Church was a very good example of the kind, and its tapering tower with a cornice of chopped corbels under the parapet is perhaps the most beautiful in the district.

Meanwhile, though the current seemed to be setting towards architec-ture, I was still at sea about my future career. Had I been allowed, I think I should still have chosen the bar, but my father was resolute on that point. The opinion of Burnes-Jones when at last it reached us was not encourag-ing, and an artist who was painting at Tenby admired my sketches of archi-tecture but thought little of the others. My father wrote again to Scott who replied as follows:

20 Spring Gardens S.W.
Aug. 12 1858
My dear Sir,

I will hold myself open in case your son should give in his adhesion to my art or 'Profession'. From what I saw of him I feel sure he would succeed if he followed it with a single heart to it.

I think his only danger is one connected with the great vice of our day in matters of art. Of old, painting and sculpture were subordinate to Architecture so far as this, that their highest object was to enrich it. In these days they have so thoroughly severed themselves that Architecture has too generally become a profession rather than an art. The aim of those whose heart is in the Cause is to put an end to this divorce and to enlist in the architectural cause those who are artists at heart. Such is the case with your son, but he seems so far influenced by the prevailing severance of the arts as hardly to feel that this is the very reason why he should be an Architect and why – being so – he would be the more likely to do his part in elevating Architecture and himself with it.

I am of opinion that as a painter alone he would hardly expect actual eminence, but his artistic power if brought to bear upon architecture especially to that of the 13th century whether in England or in France and especially to architectural sculpture, figure and animal drawing and drawing foliage from nature will be admirable accompaniment.

I remain my dear Sir,
Yours very faithfully
Geo. Gilbert Scott

And so at last I made up my mind to be an architect. I had been in a miserable state of hesitation all the summer and was much relieved when it was finally settled. On looking back I see that my friends knew me, and gauged my capacities much better than I did myself. What I should have done at the bar must remain forever unknown, but as between the other arts I feel now that my forte was rather in making things than in depicting them, and that what natural gifts I may possess as an artist have found their easiest channel of expression in architecture, for which from a child I had always shown a strong predilection.

Behold me, then, fairly launched on my life's work. I went for the first time to Mr. Scott's office, 20 Spring Gardens, on Wednesday, 20th October 1858. At the door I found myself face to face with Andrews,[8] a fellow collegian. 'Well,' I said, 'you are just in time to see me take the plunge. I am going to become a man of business in five minutes.' 'Eh, indeed, and what are you going to become?' 'An architect, Sir, and a pupil of the first architect in England, Gilbert Scott.' 'What,' said he, 'a scholar of Wadham going to be an architect! Upon my word, do you know, I think it would be just the sort of thing to suit me. I tell you what, old fellow, I'll come in with you now and talk to Mr. Scott about it, if he won't mind.'

This abrupt resolution was rather startling. However, he said the 300-guinea premium was no obstacle, and though he did not see Scott then, I believe he really did afterwards. But it came to nothing. He had no vocation for art and had never thought about it before, and next time I saw him he was a clergyman. Scott received me very warmly and said he was glad I had resolved on architecture, and I was soon introduced to his senior pupil, O'Brien, and set to work to draw out to a different scale an elevation of Tintern Abbey.

The first effect of this plunge into a sedentary life, bending all day over a drawing board, was to send me home with a sick headache for almost the first time in my life; and I lay all night dozing and waking again, and all the time drawing in imagination the west door of Tintern Abbey, ruling, circling, and finding centres and correcting, and then finding it all wrong and all to be done over again, until that doorway became nothing but a hateful nightmare. It took me three or four days to recover, and I have known pupils of my own suffer in the same way on suddenly exchanging an outdoor life with plenty of exercise for that of an office and sedentary employment.

When I entered Scott's office the fervour of the gothic revival was still at its full blast, though the movement had somewhat changed its character. The idea of the early revivalists had been to take up the discredited Gothic art at the point where it had been dropped about the middle of the sixteenth century. It was consequently mainly Tudor work that was studied, and though aberrations in an earlier direction were not wanting, the real hope of the Revivalists seems to have been fixed on the latest phase of Gothic. Tudor was the style chosen for the Houses of Parliament, and it was not till later that architects, and after them the public, began to recognise higher claims to their reverence in the earlier styles, first of the fourteenth and then of the thirteenth-century. When I made my entry as a student, the taste in England was falling back still farther and thirteenth-century work was in danger of being deposed to make way for the vigorous transitional work of the late twelfth-century date. In France the cult of Viollet-le-Duc, whose lucid literary style and clever though imaginative illustrations had an enormous influence on both sides of the channel. 'We all crib from Viollet-le-Duc', said William Burges.[9] In France the worship of the thirteenth century penetrated to a stratum of society that one would not have supposed likely to be sensible of it. I remember when in 1869 I was sketching the west front of Noyon Cathedral, a rag-and-bone man came to call for rubbish at the house against which I was sitting. He put down the sack from his back by my side and asked me very politely to mind it while he went inside. I, of course, undertook the temporary guardianship of his treasures, and an acquaintance being thus established, we got into conversation when he came out. After some critical remarks, surprising as coming from a scavenger, he concluded with a sigh of admiration for the façade: 'Mais oui, c'est du treizième, voyez-vous?' and left me wondering. In 1858, then, nothing would pass muster with the young enthusiasts among whom I found myself in Scott's office but severe Geometrical Decorated, or, better still, the severer Transitional. The five orders of classic architecture were scoffed at. We were never made as pupils to draw them, and in fact I have never in my life drawn them out as they used to be drawn. Pure Palladian Classic was regarded as mere pedantry – the cheap mechanical reproduction of orders and proportions out of pattern books. Elizabethan or Jacobean work was the accursed thing, and Perpendicular Gothic was, we thought, not much better. A certain indulgence was accorded to fourteenth-century Flowing Decorated, but everything later that that was condemned outright, was regarded with suspicion.

To say a thing was medieval was to crown it with honour. I remember one of my fellow students (Thomas Garner,[10] afterwards Bodley's partner) falling into raptures over a hansom cab. It was 'so truthful,' he said, 'so – so – so medieval!'

This temper it was that inspired Pugin's[11] *Contrasts*, a shallow performance enough, which might easily have been exposed by anyone of equally strong convictions on the other side, had there been any such person or such convictions, but the ardent spirits at the time were all in the camp of the medievalists.

It was the influence of Viollet-le-Duc, no doubt, that brought the early French Gothic to play on us. The severity of the style recommended it, and square orders and square abaci became the rage. I remember when my master Gilbert Scott, in an Academy lecture, after comparing the French square abacus with an English round one avowed his preference for the former, the sentiment was received with a round of applause by the students. Wherever we went nothing medieval escaped us. We were sure to 'spot' it, and having spotted it we never rested till we had sketched and measured it. The amount of information we garnered in this way laid a foundation of sound knowledge not to be got otherwise.

In one way the narrowing of our respect to one short-lived phase of gothic art caused mischief; it made the architects of that day treat with scant respect the work of the discredited styles when restoring or repairing ancient buildings. I don't think Scott or any of his contemporaries would have hesitated to take out a genuine piece of late tracery if they discovered evidence for an antecedent window of Early English or Norman work.[12] To this temper we owe the substitution of a good deal of modern imitative work for what, if not the original design, had at all events existed long enough to gain the respect due to antiquity. This danger has perhaps nearly ceased to exist and old work, even of the latest type, is dealt with by sensible people as tenderly as that of a superior age.

A revolt from the tyranny of Palladio[13] and the Five Orders drove us in our youth to the extreme of medievalism. Classical tradition was exploded and the revival of Gothic architecture was hailed as the opening of an era of liberty and as an escape from the fetters of precedent and prescription. But the new movement led shortly to a tyranny of its own. The superstitious reverence for the Five Orders transferred itself readily to the styles of the Middle Ages, especially the earlier examples, and imitation, pure and simple worship of authority and precedent, regard for orthodoxy and dogma, soon ruled with the same supremacy as in the days of classical architecture.

Such was the state of the School of English Gothic when my student life began. Classic architecture seemed dying or dead and all the enthusiasm of the day was enlisted on the other side. It was natural that a reaction against the state of things should take place a few years later; but I must not anticipate.

Scott's office was a very large one. Counting pupils, salaried assistants, and clerks, I think we were twenty-seven in all. I was put to work in the first-floor room at the back with six others; there were about a dozen more in two rooms on the second-floor; the ground-floor front room, which served also as the waiting-room, was the sanctum of Mr. Burlison,[14] the head man, who made the estimates and surveys. Scott's own room was the ground-floor back, and farther back still were the writing-clerk and the office-boys. The front room first floor was let to a Mr. Moriarty, a barrister, a mysterious person whom we never saw. Of Scott we saw but little. He was up to the eyes in engagements and it was hard to get him to look at our work. I have seen three or four men with drawings awaiting correction or approval grouped outside his door. The door flew open and out he came: 'No time to-day!' the cab was at the door and he was whirled away to some cathedral where he would spend a couple of hours and then fly off again to some other great work at the other end of the kingdom. Now and then the only chance of getting instructions was to go with him in the cab to the station. I see I wrote at the time, 'What a fine thing it is to be so busy'; but looking back from my present standpoint I find nothing in such a career to envy, and much to wonder at. It need hardly be said that it is an impossibility really to direct so large a staff as Scott's; but the work had of course to be done somehow. The heads of different rooms were capable men with a good knowledge of construction; Scott had a wonderful power of making rapid expressive sketches and from these his men were able to produce work which, curiously enough, did fall into something of a consistent style that passed for Gilbert Scott's and which one can always recognise wherever one meets with it as coming from that office. There are many amusing tales which show the slight acquaintance he had with what came out of his office: how he admired a new church from the railway-carriage window and was told it was one of his own; how he went into a church in process of building, sent for the clerk of works, and began finding fault with this and with that till the man said, 'You know, Mr. Scott, this is not your church; this is Mr. Street's, your church is farther down the road.'

This mode of conducting architectural work on the lines of a great professional – not to say commercial – business, though it impressed my youthful mind as something rather splendid, seems to my riper experience distasteful and hopeless. So far from managing an office of twenty-seven I have always found it hard to get through my work fast enough to keep seven or eight men employed and have often wished to reduce them to three or four. To feel that every moulding and detail down to the door furniture and finger-plates comes from one's own hand, and that nothing has been delegated to others but mechanical working out of sketches and setting out drawings for one's own correction, gives a higher pleasure than the prodigious turn-over of a year's work too vast to be digested really by a single mind.

The list of architects who came from Scott's office and have since made a name for themselves is a long one. Street[15] had left many years before I entered there and was already famous; Bodley[16] had left some time later but was beginning to establish a reputation; Crossland,[17] the architect of Holloway College, was in practice. Among the pupils of my time were Scott's two sons Gilbert and John;[18] the former a very able architect on strictly medieval lines who is now dead; the latter has been my travelling companion in many sketching tours. There were also Hodgson Fowler,[19] architect to the Dean and Chapter of Durham; J.J. Stevenson,[20] the real originator, as it is believed among architects, of the sensible and manly style of the School Board buildings in London; Johnson, who settled and died at Newcastle; and Garner who often joined Bodley as his partner. After my time were Somers Clarke,[21] later architect to the Dean and Chapter of St Paul's; Micklethwaite, who later held the similar office at Westminster; and many others more or less known to fame.

O'Brien, the senior pupil when I joined, of whom Scott expected great things, died young before he had an opportunity of doing anything. Many of these alumni of Spring Gardens afterwards diverged from the paths of strict Gothic rectitude into tracks where, in our days of pupilage, we should have thought it sinful to walk, and I fear that if our revered preceptor and master could return from the grave and see what some of us have been doing he would turn his back on us renegades and apostates.

Perhaps what did us as much good as anything in Scott's office was the sharp fire of criticism that went on and from which none escaped. Even our master's work fared badly, for the pupils never ran in the regular office grooves like the assistants, and often when sketches came up for some new 'job' we fell upon them and metaphorically tore them to pieces. The salaried assistants, in Scott's absence, were our great resource, and though they used to complain that it was not their business to teach the pupils, they were very good to us. I got Coad,[22] the head man of the lower room, to teach me how to put a building into perspective from points, to effect which, I remember, I invaded his place in his absence, and carried off his board and instruments to the to the room where I sat so that he should not escape. He grumbled but submitted. He was afterwards an enthusiastic sergeant in the Queen's Westminster Volunteers and used to give us supper at his lodgings in Lupus Street after drill. There was also an excellent John Bignold, head of the upper room, a perfect mine of information on building construction, whose whole soul was wrapped up in the office. Some of us once persuaded him to go to the theatre, where the only thing that provoked him to make a remark was the inadequacy of the doors in the scenery, which he pronounced 'a bad piece of jiner's work'. Irvine,[23] a Shetland man, full of the *Perfervidum ingenium Scotorum*, afterwards left the office to become clerk of works and established a high reputation as an antiquary. He was in charge of Wells Cathedral and afterwards of Peterborough.

Of the other assistants I have no very clear recollection except of one whose attendance was somewhat irregular, but who had some secret clue to Scott's movements and was as good as a barometer is for telling the weather, for his appearance at the office was a sure signal of Scott's approach.

And now I fell into the regular routine of a man of business. I started out at 9 a.m., generally with my father and Charles Arnold, who had come to lodge near us. The twopenny steamer took us from London Bridge to Hungerford bridge whence through Hungerford Market and Scotland Yard we found our way to our respective destinations. Charley and I generally met to lunch at 1 o'clock at Knight's oyster shop, where we had two sandwiches and a glass of ale for 6d. and sometimes a game of billiards to fill up the hour. At 5 o'clock we met again at Hungerford Pier and so back to London Bridge and home to dinner. Sometimes we varied the performance by walking and discovered strange passages and ways along Bankside past St. Saviour's Church and Market, and there I remember seeing what was probably the last relic of old Winchester House, the palace of the bishops, a melancholy fragment surrounded by dunghills and filth and doomed to speedy disappearance. Not a trace of it is now to be found.

Hungerford Market occupied the site of Charing Cross Station. It was rather a picturesque place, an open space enclosed by shops under a colonnade, which by an abuse of language was called a 'piazza'. It had an entrance from the Strand at one end, and at the other led directly to the Hungerford suspension bridge, a rather graceful structure with an enormous span between two fairly good Italian-looking towers. When the bridge had to give way to the present railway viaduct the suspending chains were used to complete the bridge over the Avon at Clifton. Below was Hungerford Wharf, and on the shelving shores of mud and gravel left at low tide by Father Thames, as yet unembanked, used to be drawn up in long ranks, like the Grecian galleys at Troy, the quaint straw-boats that came up the river from Southend and the Essex marshes. They were admirable subjects for sketching, their hulls painted gaily with red and white and emerald green and their great lugsails stained a fine reddish-brown. We often spent our Saturday afternoons drawing them, to the great delight of the watermen, who often begged to be drawn themselves, the sitter's friends helping the artist with suggestions towards a truthful portrayal – 'Mind you puts plenty of oil on his 'air, he's uncommon partikler about that.'

We used also to haunt the picture-galleries and salerooms at Christie's and elsewhere. I carried off my father to see Holman Hunt's *The Light of the World*, then being shown at Jenning's printshop in Cheapside. My taste at that time was all for Pre-Raffaelites. John Lewis's[24] *Harem Life* in which local effect is combined with the minutest finish, struck me amazingly at the Old Watercolour Society's show in, I think, 1857; and Naftel's[25] *Guernsey Lane*, which he told me in after years he had been obliged to repeat so often that he had almost lived on it for some years. Naftel was then the rising hope of the Pre-Raffaelites at that gallery, but he afterwards fell into a certain mannerism and did not realise his promise. He was ruined as a great landscapist by his large and profitable practice as a drawing-master. When urged to devote himself entirely to painting he used to say that he could not afford to give up £1,500 a year.

I remember a wonderful sale at Christie's a little later, when I again saw the *Harem Life*, which was sold together with some fine Turners. For Turner I think I had a natural affinity, for I remember being taken when quite a child to the Royal Academy and standing enchanted before a picture of a train coming through a mystery of cloud and steam, and trying my best to draw it from memory on getting home. I now know it as Turner's famous picture of the train coming over Maidenhead bridge. At the same sale were sold two pictures by Millais, one of a lady cutting off a lock of hair and the other of his *Potpourri*; there were also several Reynolds. His portrait of Mrs. Hoare fetched £2,500, then thought an enormous price, and the Millais works sold for over £100 and £195 respectively, which would not be thought much nowadays. The passion of hunting up and sketching antiquities in and near London was now strong within me, and I devoted my Saturday afternoons to poking about and exploring all remains of medieval work, occasionally with my father.

Our information was derived chiefly from *The Beauties of England and Wales*, my pet book from a child, about which I used to be laughed at a good deal; and naturally a good many of the antiquities it promised had disappeared. This was the case at Fryern Barnet, where of the old Norman church nothing was left but a doorway, and that had been taken down and rebuilt. The sexton, a grim lanky, unshorn scarecrow of a fellow, told us of some other buildings that formed part of Squire so-and-so's house, that had lately been pulled down. 'And has the squire built a new house?' 'No, no. Squire's dead – so he don't want no house. I built him a house – a good strong one too – one as he can't get out of – ' and he went away with a ghastly chuckle. It was Hamlet's gravedigger over again.

6

1858-60

Visit to Stamford ~ Parliamentary election at Stamford
University of Stamford ~ Brasenose College
Sketching at Westminster Abbey
Ruskin ~ Prospect of Fellowship at Wadham
Scott's appointment as architect for Foreign Office, design changed to Classic
Move from Sydenham to Ewell ~ Friends at Ewell
Visit to Tenby and St. David's

Office work was new to me and at first rather trying, and I was not sorry when Christmas came and I had a run down to Stamford for a fortnight. It was bitterly cold weather during this visit but I sketched industriously about the streets, now and then running in to thaw my frozen fingers at the fire in Johnson's reading-room. Coming with the fervour of my new studies upon me, Stamford appealed to me with double force. But I had always admired and loved the beautiful little town which, indeed, has few equals in the kingdom. Since I used to frequent it, I understand Stamford has struck out beyond its ancient bounds into the outskirts, and villas have sprung up where I knew only open fields. But the heart of the old town remains the same, with its picturesque stone-built streets and squares where every corner brings a fresh church into view; and the grand spire of All Saints' and the yet more glorious steeple of St. Mary's, to which Sir Walter Scott used to doff his hat as he coached it along the Great North Road. I wonder whether the people have changed as little as the place. When I first read *Cranford* it seemed to me that Cranford must have been Stamford. It was a society where everybody knew all about everybody else; where every strange arrival created a mild sensation; where you could not go out for a walk without all the street knowing it; where I could not come back late for my dear forgiving grandmother's meals, as I fear I often did, without my misdemeanours being known and commented upon by the people opposite.

Above all was the reverence for the great house of Burghley, not yet shorn of its ancient prerogatives, owning a great part of the town and returning two members to Parliament. I was once at Stamford when an election was going on, but there were no signs in the street to lead one to suppose anything unusual was happening. We strolled into the venerable Town Hall where, counting ourselves, who were not electors, there may have been twenty or five-and-twenty people assembled besides the Mayor and the two members *in posse*. To this slender audience the candidates nominated by the Marquis made their speeches with as much oratorical unction as if they had been facing a gathering of thousands. And they were worth listening to, for Lord Exeter always put in men of mark and on this occasion they were no less personages than Sir Stafford Northcote and Lord Robert Cecil, afterwards Lord Salisbury, then a youngish-looking man, slim and with black hair.

When they had perorated the Mayor asked if there were any other candidates, and as there were none, declared them duly elected.

Of the short-lived University of Stamford the memory was kept fresh by the oath of which Oxonians down almost to the present day had to take, that they would not go there to study. It originated in the feud between the northerners and the southerners before the days when colleges and university buildings had become numerous and valuable enough to chain the schools of learning to the streets of Oxford or any other place. A migration from Paris on account of some dispute is supposed to have originated the University of Oxford. A joint secession from Oxford and Cambridge at one time nearly resulted in a university at Northampton, and in 1333 and 1334 a number of scholars left Oxford in dudgeon and established themselves at Stamford.[1]

The chancellor of Oxford appealed to the king and the new university was promptly nipped in the bud, though it required the forcible interventions of the High Sheriff to close the schools and expel the students. There remains at Stamford at least one memorial to this event – the gateway of Brasenose College, though the college itself has been replaced by a modern house in which, at the time I am writing about, lived our friend Miss Hurst. She used to show us the old knocker, or brazen nose, which had been removed for safety from the door in St. Paul's Street and was then kept in a box. Many years afterwards, when I was building the new front of Brasenose College in the High Street of Oxford, I said to the Bursar, Alfred Butler,[2] 'I think I must try to get the old Brasenose knocker from Stamford and put it in the new gateway.' Till then I don't think its existence was known in Oxford. I was unsuccessful. Miss Hurst had been dead many years and the new owner would not part with it. In 1890, however, the house itself came into the market, and the knocker, which always went with the house, was included in the sale.[3]

It is now fixed to the panelling at the end of the college Hall and I had to contrive a special hinged frame to hold it that could be locked, to secure the precious head from becoming the prey of curiosity hunters. What took me by surprise in seeing it again when I knew more about such things was its age. It is a piece of eleventh – or twelfth – century work, and therefore much older than Brasenose College, Oxford, which was not founded till 1508; older, too, than the Stamford College of 1333. It probably belonged to the old Brasenose Hall at Oxford, which, with several others, was absorbed by Bishop Smyth and Sir Richard Sutton in their new foundation, and it had no doubt been carried off to Stamford by the seceders who founded the new Brasenose there. The ring of the knocker is of wrought iron but the head, which holds it is of bronze and from it the name 'Brazen nose' was no doubt given to the Hall it belonged to.

At the beginning of the year 1859, I read in my diary, 'I have now been more than two months at my "profession" and am very well satisfied with my choice. Of course there is a great deal of stiff dull work to do at first but that is the case in every profession I suppose ... Scott has been quite as good as his word in doing what he can to save me the drudgery of the beginning, for he has strongly urged me to draw a great deal from casts of architectural subjects at the Brompton Museum[4] and elsewhere and even to go and study at Westminster Abbey; advice which it is very agreeable and pleasant to follow.'

As Scott was Architect to the Abbey his pupils had the run of the building pretty much as they liked, and we used to explore the triforium and various recesses of the place, including the mysterious vaulted substructure of Edward the Confessor's work, and had full liberty of sketching and measuring what we pleased. At this time, also, Scott employed me among others to draw illustrations for his Royal Academy lectures. The ornamentation of the coronation chair in gilt gesso fell to my share – an ornamentation invisible to a chance observer, for it was not till I knelt down and examined it with a candle that I saw the brown and dull coating which still adheres in patches to the back and elbows to be tarnished gold over a thin white 'intonaco' on which are traced in punched lines charming diapers and scrolls with birds and fruit.[5] A great many of us were engaged on these illustrations. Gilbert Scott, in particular, was most indefatigable and did a great number of fine chalk drawings of capitals and cornices under his father's direction. Besides drawing in the museum I took to reading in the Art Library. Ruskin's *Seven Lamps of Architecture* appealed to me so strongly that I made an analysis of it, and illustrated it with drawings of buildings it refers to, which I hunted up elsewhere. Ruskin does not teach one practical architecture, for which I might more usefully have looked elsewhere, but he puts a student into a properly reverential and receptive frame of mind and I am not sure that my choice, at that stage of my education, could have been better directed. *The Stones of Venice*, which I read next with avidity, fed the passion for Italy and Italian Medieval art which had been fostered by a study of the Pre-Raffaelites. The land of poetry and romance, of marble and mosaic and precious inlays and sculpture, of swelling domes and basilicas with long-drawn colonnades of luscious hues, became the object of my desire, the fancied goal of my travel, which, however, I was not destined to reach for some years to come.

The interest thus awakened turned me towards the study of history, especially that of Gibbon's period. I began to read his immortal volumes for the first time. I had an additional reason for doing so in the prospect of qualifying myself for the Fellowship of which I might have a chance at Oxford. Under the old system, which preceded the first University Commission in 1854, the Scholars of Wadham had a preference when a fellowship fell vacant; that is to say, the Fellowships were not open to outsiders unless there were no scholars qualified to hold them. It did not follow that every scholar succeeded to a Fellowship. I remember at least four who were for various reasons passed over. But the system will be understood perhaps as well from the letter I received at this time from the Sub-Warden:

> … The inferences which your father drew from what passed in conversation between us are quite correct. You have a preference to a Fellowship of the old system, and there is a power of rejection. Whenever a vacancy takes place you will be summoned together with the other scholars remaining on the old system. It does not follow that you will be elected last because you stand last on the list now. This may or may not be the case. On this of course I offer no opinion. You had better keep up your reading, classical and historical. The candidates for Fellowship have always an essay to write, some translations from Latin and Greek and a few questions in History.
>
> Yours very truly,
JOHN COOPER[6]

I began upon Gibbon the very night after receiving this letter, and during the evenings of that and the following year I made a careful analysis with maps of volumes iii to viii, supplementing them with extracts from Sismondi and Guizot, and in that way I fixed the period so firmly in my mind that I have never forgotten the main outlines of it.

We were in great state of elation at the office early in 1859 over Scott's appointment as architect for the proposed new government offices in Whitehall.[7] It was a great triumph, not only for him, but also for Gothic over Classic, for which I wrote 'we must thank the present excellent Government'. But a little later our joy turned into woe by a debate in Parliament, in which the Gothic style and Lord John Manners' appointment of Scott were vehemently attacked by Lord Palmerston. He said he 'would rather have the new offices in a Grecian or Italian style; – something admitting of a gay and lively front with plenty of light and air than the barbarous Gothic of the middle ages'. Scott was in a terrible taking and rushed into print in *The Times* in defence of the style he loved.[8] He was not to succeed, however. Lord Palmerston had his way when there was a change of government, and when Scott argued with him that Gothic was more elastic, more convenient than Classic and admitted of larger windows and more light and air, Palmerston only laughed and said, 'Yes, Mr. Scott, but you know you are a Puseyite.' And so Scott had after all to build the new offices in Classic, and though he nearly broke his heart about it, I think that building is the finest thing he ever did.

I was at this time already beginning to feel a revulsion from the fanatical medievalism with which I was surrounded. I had been to hear Mendelssohn's *Oedipus Coloneus* and on my return I wrote: 'Mendelssohn and Sophocles have roused in me this evening a Classic fit which would no doubt make my gothic friends at Scott's office regard me with contempt and derision. Their bigotry makes them carry their prejudices even beyond architecture; they cannot even look at a Roman wall or antiquity of any sort with interest because it is not made by a Medieval artist and in the 12th or 13th century.'

I had now mastered the use of my instruments and from exercises in enlarging and reducing from prints had gradually been promoted to do some of the office work. My earliest efforts in designing seem to have been gargoyles and weather-cocks, and I remember designing an iron floor-grating which was made by Potter of South Molton Street and which I constantly find and recognise in churches that have been restored.

House-hunting now set in, for the inconvenience of the jerry-built house at Sydenham began to be unbearable. On the eve of quitting Sydenham I found my way to Eltham and sketched the fine roof of the old Palace Hall. It was then propped up with shoring for safety, being in a dangerous state. In that condition I found it more than forty years afterwards when I had the pleasure of putting it to rights, so that it now stands by itself and no longer needs crutches.

At Ewell we found a house to our liking. Pit House[9] was built, as its name implies, in a chalk-pit, and the first floor was level with the high road, to which the house presented nothing but a blank wall, one storey high without any windows. From the front door a wide flight of steps led down to a good large hall, a storey lower, and from this the principal rooms opened. Beyond, at this lower level, was the garden, forming the bottom of the disused chalk-pit and bounded at the far end by a thick hedge in which year by year a pair of nightingales used to build. Beyond this again, but still in the chalk-pit, was a little meadow with a pond, shaded by willows. The house and garden were altogether delightful and so was the village (as yet untouched by the building mania), with its red roofs and comely brickwork

Pit House, Ewell

warmed by the genial Surrey climate and breathing an air of repose and ancient peace.

As to the society, as I look back upon it it reminds me of one of Miss Austen's villages, where a few families living near together visited one another without ceremony and enjoyed an intimacy unknown to a larger neighbourhood. Our nearest neighbour, Sir John Reid, a baronet, had been a Governor of the Bank of England and on the opposite side of the road was his sister Mrs. Lemprière. Sir John was a courtly a old gentleman of a bygone school who wore a shirt frill and shorts with silk stockings in the evening. He was a great humorist in his way and excellent company, full of good stories and amusing recollections. I remember one curious story he had of an incident that happened when he was on the direction of the Bank of England. They had a letter laid before the Board in which the writer said they might like to know that he could get into the treasure vaults where the Bank bullion was kept, and that he would engage to meet the Governors there on a certain day at a certain hour. The Governors went at the appointed time and sure enough there they found him. It seems he was one of those strange beings who knew their way about the sewers, rat-catching or what not, and by some drain or other found his way into this El Dorado, and being an honest man wrote to warn the Governors of their danger. I hope he was well rewarded.

In our time Ewell was still a village and from our house we got almost directly on to the open Downs where I used to ride before breakfast and gallop along the outside of the Epsom racecourse, where we saw the race-horses in training out for their morning exercise.

My mother was happier at Ewell than at any of the many homes she knew. She used to say 'every dog has his day, and I am having mine here'.

In the autumn before we moved to our new house we were at Tenby and I made the first of my many pilgrimages to St. David's four of which, according to the old belief, were reckoned to be equal to one to Jerusalem. It is still perhaps the most inaccessible place in the kingdom; from the station at Haverfordwest sixteen miles and seventeen hills have to be traversed before you reach the little whitewashed village that proudly styles itself a city. Welsh is still the mother tongue of the people and the only tongue of the old folks, and there are some of them who have never been to 'town' (as they call Haverfordwest) or seen a railway. 'Dear me,' said one old lady as the first engine she had set eyes on came puffing into the station, 'how it do make the poor thing pant to be sure.'

My pilgrimage to St. David's was made on foot with a knapsack and the faithful Smike for a companion. From Pembroke we walked to Bosheston; we arrived after dark and knocked up Farmer Hitchens where we were most hospitably entertained. Next day, under Farmer Hitchens's guidance I saw the stack rocks, the haunt of Eligugs,[10] and St. Govan's chapel, hidden away half-way down a rent in the cliff. The chapel is vaulted and

T.G.J. playing chess with his mother.

retains its stone altar, and at one end a few steps lead to a natural grotto with an impression of the body of St. Govan, who was miraculously concealed there from the Danish pirates. The popular belief is that it accommodates itself to the size of anybody who lies down in it, though as Mr. Hitchens, who I fear was a sceptic, remarked, 'If it takes the big'uns of course it takes the little'uns.' In the floor is a miraculous well, the water of which will cure sore eyes, and outside is the ringing-stone on which the pirates rested the chapel bell they had stolen and which has ever since been musical. Returning to the top of the cliff we saw Bosheston Meer, a wonderful 'blow hole' which in stormy weather throws up a fountain a hundred feet in the air; and then parting from my friendly host I followed the coast, which is magnificently varied with bays and headlands and flying arches, for the rest of the day. I slept at another farmhouse near Angle on Milford Haven.

Once over the Haven in Bill Batson's boat I topped the hill and came upon a glorious view of St. Bride's Bay with the little range of Trap rock mountains beyond that ends in St. David's Head. At Newgall Sands the little brook runs into the sea which in old days divided the Welsh from the English and Flemish colony and to this day – so durable are racial differences – Welsh is spoken on the farther side and English on the nearer. A stranger finds himself in St. David's before he knows it, for it is hard to recognise the city in the humble village street of straggling whitewashed cottages, until you look over the brow of the hill at the end and see the marvellous group of cathedral (see Plate 11), college and palace in the valley below. I know nothing in the country to equal the picturesqueness and romance of its situation, which still appeals to me though the view has become so familiar from repeated visits. The beauty of the refined and delicate architecture is enhanced by contrast with the simplicity of the little village-city and the wild rough country around.

7

1860-64

Joining the Volunteers ~ Chichester Spire ~ First Commissions
Office in Salisbury Street ~ Music ~ First works
To Normandy ~ M.A. at Oxford ~ Fellowship at Wadham
'Idle' Fellowships ~ Uses and abuses

In 1860 my cousin Charley Arnold and I joined the London Scottish Volunteers, which mustered eight companies, of which the two flank companies wore the kilt. We did not feel Scotch enough for the garb of old Gaul and contented ourselves with the modest trews of the inner companies. Volunteering was then in full swing. It had sprung to life from suspicion of the designs of our ally Napoleon III.[1]

Lord Palmerston moved a resolution in the House for increasing our national defences. Portsmouth was, he said, at one time defended by one small fort; Plymouth was imperfectly defended at sea; while at Sheerness we had but one gun that could go off and were obliged to apologise to a French ship that put in there for our inability to give them a salute.

On 21st February 1861 a gale, one of the most violent I remember, did a great deal of damage all over the country and brought down the beautiful central tower and spire of Chichester Cathedral. It had been undergoing repairs at the hands of the cathedral architect,[2] and a solid screen between the two eastern piers had been removed to satisfy the mischievous craze that then prevailed for seeing all the interior of your building at a glance. This screen may have given support to the piers, and its removal may have hastened the ruin. The piers were of poor Norman masonry, built as usual with bad mortar, and they were unequal to the load of the Decorated upper portion. The shoring that was applied was very slight and the repairs seem to have been very superficial. The cracks expanded, the core began to run out, and the gale finished the matter. The builder withdrew his men and locked the doors, and at half-past one the apex of the spire inclined first one way and then another and then the whole sank in a moment into a gigantic heap on the floor, pulling with it the adjoining bays of the four arms of the building. The architect was sitting at luncheon in the inn opposite when someone at the window cried out 'There she goes', and before he could look up it was gone. Scott was sent for to advise about the rebuilding, and he took me and his son John down with him to measure the adjacent bays and recover what we could of the design. The cathedral architect was universally blamed. The little boys in the street used to say as he passed, 'That's him as let the spire down – that big 'un.' Whether he deserved it or not I cannot judge. He seems at all events to have underrated the danger. But Scott said to me: 'We ought to be very careful how we judge men in our profession. The worst of architecture is that there is always the chance of it tumbling down, and therefore if we are hasty in condemning our brother architects we may someday incur a similar condemnation ourselves.' The measuring was very interesting and capital practice for us, though it was rather dangerous, for the walls near the crossing about which we had to climb were much shaken and dilapidated. The mason who accompanied me to help in taking the dimensions said when we had finished, 'Well, Sir, thank God that's over.' I had to go down again later to finish my measurements, after the ground had been cleared of the mound of ruin; this time Gilbert Scott, the son, was with me, and from the mass of debris he and the clerk of works sorted and collected the worked stones of the belfry windows and other features of the steeple, which had suffered very little by their fall and were, I believe, all used again in the rebuilding.

When I had been two years and a half with Scott and had still half a year to spend in his office, the eventful moment came when I received my first commission. When my pupils' term of apprenticeship comes to an end their fathers sometimes ask me how they are to get work. The only answer I can give is that I don't know, but that in all probability they will get it at first from their friends. How indeed can it be otherwise? As I look back on my own career I am astonished at the way people trusted me and employed me and took my advice when I was a mere tyro and had been given no evidence whatever of my skill in my craft. One cannot expect this confidence from a stranger; it is only a friend who will take one on trust and give one the chance of making a beginning.

He is not like the painter or sculptor who can make himself known by showing his work in exhibitions: the architect can show nothing at all unless someone employs him. It is everything to him to get some work really executed; and after that one thing leads to another and unless he fails from incompetence, carelessness, or defects of manner he will find himself pretty sure to be passed on from his first employer to others. He may of course win a competition, though it is extremely unlikely till he has gained experience by actual work done, and for young men competitions are rather opportunities of practising design than openings for employment.

Nine people out of ten who employ an architect know very little about architecture and either go to some well-known man of established reputation with whom they feel safe or give their work to some personal friend of whom they feel a kindness.

My first commission came from my dear old friend and tutor Mr. Tate, who wanted to build a vicarage at Send, the parish, which he held conjointly with Ripley. I made the plans in 1861, but the building was not begun till two years later, when I was out of my pupilage. I had also several castles in the air – a great hotel at Llandrindod and a new church at Rickmansworth – but these came to nothing, though the planning did me a deal of good. Other less visionary things, however, awaited me being able to undertake them on leaving Mr. Scott, such as the chancel of Ketton Church near Stamford, of which Scott was restoring the nave.

All these matters, whether visions or substantialities, kept me very busy after my apprenticeship came to an end in the autumn of 1861.[3] I used to work in the library at home but I was also a good deal at Spring Gardens, where I continued to do work for Scott for some years. I remember doing a great perspective drawing for him of the Foreign Office design and another of Memorial Hall for the Prince Consort, which was never built. In 1862, however, I started an office at No. 7 Salisbury Street, a gloomy narrow place running down to the river from the Strand where the Cecil Hotel now stands.[4] I shared it with John Newton,[5] a fellow pupil at Scott's, and his brother, who was an engineer.

We engaged a housekeeper, a certain Mrs. Stacey, to whom we explained carefully what we expected her to do. 'And now, Mrs. Stacey, you know what we want, do you think you can manage it?' 'Oh yes, Sir,' said she, 'I am sure I can – you see I have had the care of the insane for many years.'

The next thing was to engage an office boy or, rather, someone half office boy and half draughtsman, and I took a boy in lay-down collars, Alfred Rickarby, son of one of my father's clerks, who is now, after being with me for forty-one years, a venerable grey-haired person who dresses in semi-clerical garb and is sometimes supposed to be my chaplain.

Music continued almost to rival architecture in my affections. I used to attend once a week at the Crystal Palace a singing class conducted by Henry Leslie, the great master of part-song, and in 1862 had the pleasure of being admitted by Henry Leslie to his famous choir, then at the height of its reputation, having won, in the previous year, the highest honours at Paris. The conditions of membership were a tolerable voice and the power of reading perfectly at sight. Candidates had their voices tried and were then called upon to take part in a quartet which they had not seen before. If you were found passably good you were set to sing in the choir and occasionally became aware that someone had stolen up behind you and was listening to your performance. Leslie was an admirable conductor; not a wrong note escaped him. I remember singing one of Bach's Motets for double choir, and as I sat with basses thrumming around me I felt as if I were a pipe in an organ or some instrument played upon by a master hand. We used to meet for rehearsal at Puttick & Simpson's auction room in Leicester Square, Sir Joshua Reynolds's house, though it was not certain that the big room was his studio or even of his date. The choir was then limited to eighty voices, a very manageable number, admitting of strict selection and just suited to the Hanover Square Rooms where we gave our concerts and which have long ceased to exist. There were four or five concerts there during the season, the programme consisting almost entirely of unaccompanied part-songs or choral pieces. We often had musicians of note to hear us at rehearsal, especially when we were doing any of their works. I remember Meyerbeer[6] coming one night, a slender Jewish-looking man in a black wig, and we sang him his *Pater Noster*, with which he professed himself much pleased, and after that Mendelssohn's motet 'Judge me O God' which always seemed to go like some mighty organ.

The choir consisted of a certain number of amateurs like myself, but mainly of professionals or semi-professionals, men and women from music shops, singing masters and mistresses, and some musicians of greater pretensions such as Branby, who was afterwards organist at Eton. Rather apart at the end of one row of the basses, never speaking to anyone, sat Charles Keene[7] the artist, the greatest draughtsman, in my opinion, that *Punch* has ever had.

I was now very busy with my first works. Oh, those first works! How we love and how we nurse them! How we haunt the scaffolding and seize every excuse for a visit. Nothing afterwards gives one quite the same pleasure. To feel yourself for the first time a creator – a poet – to see things you have yourself designed actually carried out in brick and stone, timber and tile, to watch the walls rise, and finally to pace the floors and climb the stairs of your own contriving, surely this is one of the purest and most innocent of earthly delights. And what is more it is one of the best of educations; one learns more from one's own handiwork than from any amount of drawing done for other people. The sense of responsibility steadies you; you feel that it will not do to make mistakes; you discover the gaps in your knowledge that need stopping and the defects in your taste that want correction. What you lack in experience you have to compensate by careful attention, and if a young architect is conscientious his employer gains in that respect what he has to do without in the other.

One danger to be guarded against by the beginner is the tendency to put too much into the design. Your mind is teeming with ideas that you long to realise and too often you let fly with them inopportunely, unable to hold them back till a legitimate occasion offers itself.

And so it was, I fear, that in some of my first efforts I did things that I should now leave undone. More commendable perhaps was the passion for truth, as inculcated by Ruskin, which made me, at Mr. Tate's vicarage, expose the brick corbel course (which carries the plate of the upper floor) in all its nakedness as a cornice round the rooms.

Send vicarage (1863), though my first commission, was not begun first. I started (in January 1863) by reseating the pretty little brick Jacobean church at Malden near Ewell and, yielding to the Gothic influence of the day, I fear I treated it not as I should now do. Ketton chancel, which I re-roofed and in which I some years later replaced the old fifteenth-century seat-ends, was begun in the spring; and a little later I restored the little church of Madehurst near Arundel in Sussex. In the autumn I had about a month's hard work sketching in Normandy, From St. Lô to St. Malo I had to travel by diligence all night, and I remember waking up in the street of Dol as the moon was breaking and finding myself all alone in the coupé in absolute stillness, not a soul to be seen, and nothing but the bare pole projecting in front without the horses. In fact we had only stopped to change horses and have coffee, but the picture to which I awoke was dramatic in the extreme; a street of gabled over-hanging houses, slated down the front and carried on pillars and arcades such as one seldom sees except on the stage of a theatre.

In the preceding June I revisited Oxford for the first time since my degree of B.A. in 1858. I was still technically a scholar of Wadham, though without emolument, and it was now intimated to me that I take my M.A. degree if I intended to stand for a Fellowship. Accordingly I went up and took my place at the table in Hall with an examination paper before me quite like old times. We had a long passage from Plato's *Phaedo* to translate – the story of the God Theuth who invented writing and recommended it to the king of Thebes as an aid to memory; to whom the king replied that on the contrary it would impair memory by superseding it.

In 1864 there were three Fellowships vacant and Warren and I were sent for. Halcomb, who had equal claims as a scholar on the old foundation, had gone to Australia and failed to present himself and so was disqualified. We had an examination of two days, and among other things had an essay to write. They considerately, and I think very properly, gave me a subject connected with my profession, on which I wrote pages and pages, copiously illustrated with sketches. Thorley, the tutor, told me afterwards that the examiners thought it very interesting but did not manage to get to the end of it. In the result we were both elected to probationary Fellowships, and in response to a telegram my father came up to dine with us in Common Room. It has been the fashion to decry non-resident Fellowships – Prize Fellowships as they are called, idle Fellowships as Lord Salisbury stigmatised them, and to represent them as mere sinecures and abuses. They are all, or nearly all, at an end now, and I suppose there never will be any more. No doubt they often were abused and wasted. I certainly remember cases where very distinguished scholars stagnated as Fellows and never produced anything afterwards. Nor can I justify K——,[8] who held besides an ordinary

Fellowship an additional Fellowship for Law, but whose only title to fame was that of a ruling spirit at the Garrick Club, and refused the only brief offered him on the ground that it was out of his line, that he was not used to it, and that it had better be taken somewhere else. But, on the other hand, if a Prize Fellowship be properly used as a means to higher study in a profession than would otherwise have been attainable, I know of no more useful form of endowment.

I can only say that to me such a Fellowship has been everything. It enabled me to wait and study my art at leisure instead of engaging at once in the struggle for bread and cheese. It let me fill up my time with work of an improving but pecuniarily unprofitable kind such as furniture, embroidery, painted glass, decoration, table-glass, and plate, all which gave me admirable training in design and was especially useful as a relief from strict architectural work which, practised by itself, is apt to stiffen a man into hardness and conventionality. It enabled me in fact to realise, though in a very imperfect way, that pattern of an all-round artist, which has always been my ideal and in the attainment of which lies, I think, the hope of English art in the future. Above all, it gave me the means to travel and study the art of other countries as well as my own.

The Senior Fellow when I was elected was Orlando Haydon Bridgeman Hyman, stepson, I think, of that queer genius, Haydon[9] the painter. He was a fine scholar but one of the most eccentric beings conceivable. He lived alone in Porchester Terrace with three greyhounds and when he died he left hardly anything behind him but these three companions. We expected to find a great library, for he was always telling us of lucky bargains of rare editions that he had picked up, but to our amazement his shelves were empty. This was partly explained by a story I have heard him tell. He found at a bookstall a valuable edition of some obscure classic author which he bought for 5s., and he told the man if ever he had another to ask a sovereign for it. He took a cab to hurry home with his prize. We asked him what followed. 'Oh,' said he, 'I cut out with scissors the notes that interested me and put them in a drawer'; as for the rest of the book, he tore the leaves out one by one as he read them by way of marking his place! Somewhat in this way I suppose his whole library disappeared; at all events it had gone somehow. One would think that much learning makes men mad, and certainly when combined with seclusion it seems to tend that way. The monk in his convent is preserved from madness by the constant occupation of routine duties and church services. But a man may live in college in as perfect retirement as a monk, without the relief of these distractions, and it is no wonder if his mind gives way. So it was with Ross,[10] another of our Fellows, a brilliant scholar of enormous knowledge even on the most unexpected subjects, but so nervous, shy, and irritable that he threw up his tutorship and all college work and lived amid his books like a hermit in his rooms, into which, so far as I remember, no one but his scout was ever admitted.

When I was first a Fellow, however, Ross used to dine with us in Hall and come to Common Room, where he generally sat in silence, now and then coming out suddenly with flashes of a curious caustic wit. The Warden, Dr Symons, published a sermon, and sent copies to most of the Fellows but not to Ross, who complained: 'Lo, these seven years have I served him and yet never gave he me a little sermon that I might make merry with my friends.' When the loving-cup goes round at the Gaudy each man as he drinks says: 'Prosperity to Wadham College, peace and good fellowship and charity to all mankind.' 'You see,' said Ross, 'we wish the virtues to all the world but keep the solid advantages to ourselves.' Poor Ross got worse and worse. He gave up Hall and Common Room and seldom exchanged a word or even a salutation with anyone. Finally, he became quite mad and died in his rooms at Wadham, if I am not mistaken.

At the beginning of 1864 Charley Arnold who had long lived almost as one of the family became really one of us by marrying my sister Annie. It was a happy alliance both for them and for us, though he could hardly be more of a brother to me than he had been for many years past since I first got to know him at Oxford.

8

1864-65

Office at Devereux Chambers ~ Tour in France and Italy ~ Venice
Conclusions from the Tour ~ Early Works including All Saints' Stamford
Full Fellowship at Wadham ~ Liberalism at Wadham and reforms

The arrangement by which I shared an office did not last long and I had to look out for an office of my own. In the end I took two rooms on the second floor in Devereux Chambers[1] entered from Devereux Court but looking into New Court, in the Temple. They were very pleasant quarters, so quiet that the chimes of St. Clement Danes, inaudible in the roar of the Strand, reached me over the house-tops distinctly, and the only sounds were the splash of the fountain under the trees below and the footfall of the passengers on the flagged court into which my windows looked. There was a little closet big enough for a bed where I sometimes slept, and at night there was a real live watchman, not the ghost of one, with a real watchbox, such as the mohawks of the Regency used to upset. He used to call the hours at night quite in the old way.

I moved into these new quarters on 28th June 1864 and there I stayed for twenty years, annexing, as time went on and my staff increased, another set of chambers on the same floor. But that was many years afterwards, and at first two rooms, one for myself and one for the clerk and office boy, were more than enough for my modest requirements.

In July my father had a severe and nearly fatal illness, which was a warning to him that the time was coming when his professional life should end, and though he got well enough to return to work it was chiefly in order to wind up with a view to retirement. This was made easier for him as I was off his hands, with a Fellowship tenable till marriage and work enough to enable me not only to make a return for income tax but even to begin a modest investment of savings. The first use I made of these easier circumstances was to make a considerable trip abroad and to realise the long-deferred dream of seeing Italy. My master, Scott, urged me strongly not to defer travel. 'Go away for six months,' he said. 'It will do you all the good in the world, and you will never be able to do it unless you do it now.' He was quite right in his conclusion, for I never have got away for so long and even then I only managed to take half the time he suggested, but those three months did do me all the good in the world, and I came back a new man as far as architecture goes. His second son, John, was to be my companion, and we had a long consultation with them at Hampstead over maps and pictures. John and I also set to work to learn Italian, and by the time we started were able to read and even talk it enough for the purpose of travel.

We started by way of Southampton and from Le Havre crossed by steamer to Honfleur, and thence went to Sées, Le Mans, and Chartres (see Plate 17), which impressed me amazingly, as was to be expected. I wrote home 'The Cathedral here is very splendid architecturally – I should say the best in France and almost the best in the world. Fancy one hundred and thirty windows of stained glass.' From Chartres we found so much to do that we stayed on some days.

We went to Bourges and Nevers and pursuing our way southwards entered the volcanic country of the Auvergne. At Riom we directed the bus to take us to the Hôtel du Palais. 'This the driver did, and we landed at a little sort of shop door, and entering found ourselves in a vaulted room of the eleventh century! Fare rough, but the rooms good. N.B. – We have never been bothered with dirty beds or vermin at the Hotels.' We found, however, that as we went southwards the garlic and the fleas became more aggressive, and after retiring from one railway journey with sixty-seven wounds I protested against the economy of travelling third class.

Near Riom is the abbey of Mozac, were I spent some days in making a careful coloured drawing of an enamel chasse of Limoges champlevé work. It is as near a facsimile of the original, polish and gold included, as I think possible, and it fixed that kind of work on my mind for ever – a thing very useful to do once, and which for purposes of study one need never repeat. The costumes of the Auvergne peasants of those days were curious, especially the *chapeau du vieillard*, a cocked hat which was worn when a man reached a certain age.

From Clermont Ferrand, our next halting-place, we ascended the Puy de Dôme. We spent some days sketching at Clermont and Brioude and then, as the railway went in those days no farther, we took diligence for Le Puy, which answered all our expectations. Indeed I don't think it can have an equal for picturesqueness and romance.

Auvergne peasants

Le Puy Cathedral

From Le Puy we had a diligence journey of seven hours, though the distance is only twenty-five miles, to Pradelle. A diligence took us to La Bastide, and thence we walked to Villefort through a splendid mountainous country, much finer than the volcano district. Next morning we started on a twenty-two mile walk to La Levade, where we were to pick up the broken thread of the railway, the other end of which we had left at Brioude. As we began to descend towards the great plain of the south and were enjoying the sight of myrtles and white mulberries and other vegetation strange to northern eyes, we were stopped by a mounted gendarme who demanded our passports. We looked, I daresay, disreputable enough.

However we assumed the dignity of the injured Briton, and said we were English and did not need a passport. 'How can that be?' said he. 'No Frenchman can go from one village to another without a passport. Is it likely you could go about without one?' *'Messieurs, vous êtes en cas d'arrestation.'* He had never heard of the international convention, in the absence of which no doubt his argument was reasonable. So he marched us back three or four miles to the last village we had passed, where we were to be taken before the Maire.

As he did not seem quite sober we tried a five-franc piece which only threw him into a state of virtuous indignation – 'a hundred thousand francs should not tempt him'. I made him rather uneasy, however, by asking his name and that of the Préfet of the Department and writing them down ceremoniously in my notebook. Fortunately we did not go before the Maire who might have been as ignorant as the gendarme, Jean Oiyac (I have never forgotten his name), but while he was gone to stable his horse we met his brigadier, who of course released us at once. On reaching Nîmes we wrote an indignant complaint to the Préfet, of which, however, he took no notice. After visiting Nîmes, Arles, and Avignon we reached Marseilles. There was then no railway along the Riviera and John Scott decided to go by diligence. I shouldered my knapsack and walked the first part of the way, sleeping a night at Monte Carlo, then deserted and out of season. It was a most lovely walk, and by a lucky chance I missed the regular track and followed a little path between the cliffs and the sea, generally about half-way up the former and passing through groves of olives, oranges, lemons, figs and stone pines. I crossed the frontier and set foot with a thrill of exultation for the first time in Italy, the land of promise. Genoa was the first Italian town I saw, and a good one to begin with. Its narrow smooth-flagged streets, accessible only to pedestrians and pack-mules, its marble palaces and stately churches, are all novel and striking to one who has crossed the Alps for the first time. In 1864 the peasant women still wore the *mezzari* of gay printed calico over their heads, and the higher classes wore the *pezzotto* of white muslin, one of the most graceful coverings for the head imaginable. I fancy this is rarely if ever to be seen now.

From Genoa we crossed by night to Leghorn. From Pisa we went to Lucca, Florence, and Siena (see Plate 25), returning to Pistoja whence we crossed the Apennines by the Porretta pass in a diligence and then to Modena, where Scott left me, in a hurry to get home.

Albergo della Porta
Parma
Oct. 30th 1864
My dear Mother,
    I think I told you that at Modena J. Scott and I should part company. The fact is that as long ago as Clermont there began to be some talk of his

going home. I did not tell you because I thought you would bother yourself to death about my going into Italy (with all its brigands and dangers of all sorts) all alone. At Claremont Mr. Scott (G. Gilbert Scott) had sent a message saying that he wanted John to return straight from Avignon as they were about to move into a new house at Ham, although the real reason was simply that they were like you, nervous about the dangers of Italian travel.

The effect of it all was that though he did not want to go at first, the accounts of the new house gave him a home fever of which the premonitory symptoms were a disposition to stand about with his hands in his pockets looking at my sketch instead of attending to his own and an abandonment of regular sketching hours.

I was sorry to lose him as we had got on capitally together, and as you know I hate my own company for more than a day or two at a time …

Yours ever,
T. Graham Jackson

Left alone I went to Parma where I remember dining with only two or three companions at the Inn, and a quartet of violinists coming into the room and playing so delightfully that I gave them a gold five franc piece. They apparently did not at first take it for more than a silver half franc, but after I had gone to my room, they found it out and came back and played a quartet outside my door which I thought very pretty and graceful of them.

From Ravenna, where I spent some time, I went to Venice, the goal of my travels. The last part of the journey from Padua to Venice was by train (this was the time of the American Civil War) and my travelling companions were two officers of the Confederate man-of-war *Rappahannock*, which the French were detaining at Calais where she had put into refit. My companions were on the whole very good fellows and gentlemen though their aversion and violence against everything Yankee quite surprised me.

If they are a fair sample of popular feeling in the confederate states I should say there is about as much chance of the two parties being reunited as there is of a union between England and France.

(A letter from John Scott was awaiting T. G. J.'s arrival in Venice)

Hotel de la Ville
Milan
My dear Jackson,

I got happily to Parma and walked into the town pursued by cabs and valets de plas.[2] I got rid of them by roaring the Italian negative at them and at length asked my way to the cathedral. I was entirely flabbergasted by the view of the W front; it is the strangest queerest looking thing you ever saw etc.

I hope you will not find it dull alone. I must say that I do already tho: I have the prospect of soon getting home to counteract it … Please let me have a description of that wonderful place (*Venice*) from you. As I shall of course be much better able to picture it from your description than from what is written by men I never saw.

Believe me.
Yours very truly,
John Scott

Albergo Barbesi

Venice
November 8th 1864
My dear Father,

Here I am at last at the goal of my wishes and of my tour. I must try and tell you what Venice is like as well as I can. But I can give you no idea of its strangeness and wonderful beauty. No photograph will do that either for they make it all black and white which is the last thing it is. Nothing but Turner's pictures will give you any idea of its poetry and its grace – I saw it first under a very peculiar aspect, but one which is perhaps as expressive of the character of the place as any that I could have chosen – it grew dark before the train had gone far from Padua and the moon was hidden by clouds so that I feared that I should see nothing of Venice. I had set my heart on entering so as to secure a favourable impression at first sight. I was not disappointed and indeed I doubt if under any circumstances Venice could fail to delight and surprise a newcomer. First of all was the novelty of finding the station opening only upon a quay, and of taking a gondola instead of a cab.

Venice. Arrival in November, 1864

82

In a few minutes we were travelling smoothly down the Grand Canal in a silence broken only by the splash of the oars. Tall palaces whose marble traceries might dimly be seen through the gloom rose up on either hand out of the water that rippled against their walls as we passed – black gondolas flitted by us that were scarcely visible; – lamps flashed in the water and multiplied themselves a thousand fold; every now and then we had mysterious peeps of the interior of the city down some narrow canal that opened out of the grand thoroughfare; a curious perspective of bridges, palaces and thronging gondolas dimly shown by the lights of the city.

So among palaces we threaded our way, the walls echoing with the splash of the oars – Suddenly the scene grew familiar; on the right and left huge piles of buildings towered above us, and high up in the air the black canal that rippled between them was spanned by a bridge – the famous Bridge of Sighs. Well did I know what to expect when a sweep of the oars took us out again into the open lagoon and in a blaze of light we saw the front of the Doge's Palace with its endless arcades and traceries, the high campanile of which the top was lost in the night, the two pillars, the piazza and beyond the strange eastern looking dome of St. Mark's – for

Venice. Palazzo Sagredo

Venice. Palazzo Dario

Venice. Palazzo Cicogna

Venice. Palazzo Bembo

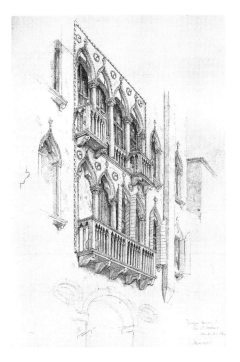

Venice. Palazzo Boelan

four or five days past I have been sketching for seven hours a day in a gondola wrapped up in a great coat … I must give you some idea of the comfort of these gondolas; fancy my half sitting, half lying, on luxurious leather cushions with a comfortably sloped back to support me and with convenient broad ledges on either hand on which to lay out my tools, pencils, knives, India rubber, perspective glass etc. ready for constant use; then fancy the boat with me and my apparatus gliding smoothly along green sea water streets under the marble walls of splendid palaces: and then if any subject tempts me into a sketch I have only to speak the word and my boat is moved in the proper place from which to take my view and then without having to move from my easy seat and without any fear of being annoyed by spectators (N.B. I am sure Nature made boys to spite us artists: I have long thought so and this autumn has convinced me of it). I work as for as long or as short a time as the occasion requires. An English lady (her name is Miss Fanny Cox) goes out sketching with me sometimes on the condition (to be *strictly observed*) that she shall not interrupt me and not expect much conversation except on her side to take place … Post time so I must finish …

Believe me,
Your affectionate son,
T. Graham Jackson

That Venice surprised and delighted me goes without saying. I found it an architectural paradise and spent all the rest of my time there. I stayed at the Hôtel Barbese on the Grand Canal, and there was a pleasant party at the table d'hôte including some Austrians, Count Mittrowski and his family. The old gentleman was something about court and the ladies spoke English perfectly having learnt it from an Irish governess who was with them.

I stayed at Venice till it was too cold to go about sketching in gondolas, even though wrapped up in a great coat and a rug, and then went home as fast as I could travel.

The Mont Cenis tunnel, though in progress, was not finished and we had to pass the mountain on sledges, for the road was deep in snow. The sledges were old coach bodies taken from their wheels and put upon runners and they bumped and bounced about so disagreeably that, as one lady said, it was worse than the *mal de mer*. I reached Paris at 7 a.m. on 1st December 1864 and arrived at home on the day following.

I came back from my grand tour with many books full of sketches and notes and my head full of new ideas. It had in fact been my renaissance. It taught me to take a wider view of my art, to recognise that in all its phases, however much they differ phenomenally in different countries and at different dates, it is right and good only so long as it obeys the same natural laws and follows the same general principles of design.

As this notion of the catholicity of art grew upon me, I saw more plainly the inadequacy from the modern point of view of studying it only from one side. To walk, as I had been trained to do, along the narrow path of medieval orthodoxy, keeping one's attention rigidly on the way and shutting one's eyes to all other attractions right and left as if they were sinful things, now seem to me irrational and unworthy of those who were 'heirs of all the ages – in the foremost files of time'. Believing as I did that art cannot really live as an anachronism, but must reflect its own age, it became clear to me that deliberately to ignore what you know, to shut your eyes to what you cannot help seeing when they are open, was no better than nursing a delusion and would never advance art a step onward.

Another catholic lesson Italy taught me was the close union of the three arts, Architecture, Sculpture, and Painting, in a fashion that of course I had never seen before. It was an object lesson that has never since lost its effect on me to find them all three commonly practised by the same man from the earliest times down to the days of Bramante and Michelangelo, after whom the arts fell apart and the divorce took place which is not yet reconciled.

I came back resolved that architecture pure and simple should not absorb all my attention, but that I would devote myself also to the decorative arts in the hope that if it were too late for me to attain any great executive skill I might at all events be qualified to contrive and direct the carved and painted work of my own buildings and in that way secure consistency and harmony instead of the failure so commonly seen when the architect either has no conception of decoration, or, having it, is unable to convey his ideas to those who collaborate with him. It was on this tour also that I first came in contact with the work of the ancient Roman world in the amphitheatres of Nîmes (see Plate 21) and Arles, the Maison Carrée, and the Baths of Diana. The first sight of the handiwork of the mighty race whose history and literature have been the study of one's boyhood and youth cannot but be of amazing interest. I remember being struck curiously with the fact that they had a sort of modernity about them and did not impress one with anything like the same sense of antiquity as the old church of St. Trophime at Arles, which is their junior by a thousand years. Italian architecture, however, appealed to me very much more than Classic and it does so still.

Perhaps nothing was stranger and more novel to meet in this tour than the free use of coloured materials, which opened up possibilities in architecture of which I never dreamed. To one used only to freestone masonry, the first sight of the ranks of great cylindrical columns of claret-coloured marble at S. Lorenzo in Genoa was fairly staggering. Not less surprising was the inlaid work of precious marbles there and elsewhere, notably at Pisa and Lucca and in S. Miniato at Florence, also the pavements of *Opus Alexandrinum* at S. Frediano Lucca and the Baptistry at Florence, and the later pavements of incised and inlaid work of Siena. Of all these I made careful drawings which have often inspired me in later years. Still more wonderful to the architectural novice was the glass mosaic work at Ravenna (see Plate 26) and Venice, and the great golden cave of St. Mark's, which one hardly criticises as the work of human hands but accepts as one does the beauties of nature. I learnt for the first time that in the use of beautiful material and colour, architecture has resources not inferior to those of form with which alone our northern habits and the natural material of our country have familiarised us. I think also that I saw for the first time how marble may be abused. It seemed to me that is proper use was in columns, and surface decoration such as wall linings, mosaics, and pavements, where its colour can have full play and be enjoyed without alloy. For architectural carving it is inferior to stone. The Italians as a rule knew this and made their chimneypieces and architectural compositions of Istrian stone, reserving marble for sculpture pure and simple of the human form. I learnt further that coloured marble must be used with restraint and with a limited palette instead of mixing up all sorts and colours in a general mess as I had seen done in England in the few cases where these precious materials had been employed, that for ordinary English architecture it is unsuitable and requires special treatment, and that marble must be used alone and should never be mixed with stone, with which it will no more unite itself than oil with water.

Thus it was that I came back from my travels cured of medievalism. I loved the ancient Gothic work, and especially English Gothic, no less than heretofore, but I regarded it henceforth as my tutor rather than a model.

For the next seven or eight years I worked on chiefly at small church restorations and an occasional parsonage house. I was very busy and had to engage an assistant now and then, and I also worked occasionally for Scott. I made, however, little or no profit, for my office expenses, rent, clerk, and assistance for many years absorbed all and more than all my earnings. But for my Fellowship I could not have kept myself, though I don't think I could have worked harder than I did. With that to keep me I was relieved from anxiety and could afford to wait, though I remember often when I made up my professional accounts at the end of the year my heart sank to find there was no balance on the right side and, so far as I could see, no prospects of things mending.

My early work fell into groups. In Sussex I restored or enlarged the churches of Binstead, Burpham, and Slindon near that of Madehurst, which was almost my maiden effort. Round about our home at Ewell I restored and twice enlarged Malden Church, added an aisle to Chessington, built a village hall at Cheam and an addition to Cheam House.

Near the vicarage I built for my old tutor at Send I enlarged Ripley chapel and restored the pretty little church at Pyrford close by. In Rutland I had Lyndon and Ketton Churches in hand and at Stamford in 1870-3 extensive repairs to All Saints' Church, which was undermined by graves and in a perilous condition. At Sevenoaks I built a chancel to the church, founded principally by old Mr. Lambarde at Sevenoaks Weald, restored Kemsing and the chancel of Sundridge Churches, built schools for Mr. Tritton[3] at Otford, and rather later (1873) two considerable houses at Sevenoaks. At one of these, a house called 'Woodlands', I contrived a curious double staircase of oak up which two people can go without ever meeting. Till then the largest work I had had was the restoration and enlargement of Dursley Church (1866) in Gloucestershire which cost from first to last £5,000, a big order for me in those days. The most hazardous task had been the repair of All Saints' Church at Stamford (1870-73), where I had to underpin the greater part of the walls, to take out the pillars and reset them on new foundations, and to bring the leaning south wall to the upright. I did this by underpinning it and leaving a wedge-shaped slit all along the top of the underpinning so that the old wall, when started by wedging the shoring, gradually sank back, pivoting itself on the outer edge, and so closed up the slit. At Hatfield Church near Doncaster I had a similar task in taking out and resetting the columns, which had crushed their bases.

I had been pestered, like most men in chambers, by impostors who got admission by saying I knew them, and who then produced bottles of furniture polish which they proceeded to try with magical effect on my mahogany desk, or steel pens or tortoise-shell combs of their own making which they were trying to sell to pay for a brother's passage to America, and I had given my clerk Rickarby strict orders to protect me from these invasions. I heard him one day in 1869 struggling with somebody at the door, and was only just in time to prevent his sending away a gentleman with a roll of drawings under his arm who turned out be Lord Normanton,[4] whose fancy it was to disregard appearances and dress as shabbily as he pleased. He came to ask me to restore Ellingham Church near his house at Somerley, at which Dame Alice Lisle, one of Judge Jeffreys' victims, lies buried. This in later years brought me a great deal of work in that part of Hampshire.

In Pembrokeshire I restored Gumfreston Church for our old friend Gilbert Smith and rebuilt the modern church of Robeston Wathen retaining the ancient tower. In those days when working at such a distance from town, I used to save time by travel at night, and I remember walking from Robeston Wathen the two-and-half miles to Narberth Road station, and getting caught in a storm of rain which turned to snow, and having to travel up to town all night wet through in the bitter cold and arriving at 4 a.m. nearly frozen.

I went in for several competitions unsuccessfully and learned how unsatisfactorily such things were often managed and how little chance the man who conforms to the conditions of expense has against one who disregards them. However, they did me good and I gained experience, and for that reason alone it is quite worth the young architect's while to incur the vexation of soul they generally provoke.

In 1865 I was admitted as a full Fellow of Wadham College and it was now my duty to attend the stated meetings of the Society and take part and the government of the college. The tone of the society, or the majority of it, was then decidedly liberal though Warden Symonds was a bulwark of conservatism and some of the clerical Fellows stood by him. Hitherto he governed the college as an autocrat. Rightly or wrongly he held that he was by statute the sole executive officer in the college. He had been known to buy estates without consulting the Fellows and to bring the conveyance to the meeting to be sealed. He maintained that every proposal or discussion must be introduced by him and not by the proposer, in order that he might first express his approval or the contrary. He declined, till compelled, to answer the questions of the first University Commission in 1854. He refused to put to the meeting a motion for admitting Non-conformists to the college, and wrote a note in the minute-book that the Warden had the sole right of admitting or removing students and that this proposal would have controlled his power. The college appealed to the Visitor, who directed that question must be put, and in the following year the proposal was carried by nine votes against five or, rather, six, for the Warden had two votes. I remember the poor old man holding up his hands in dismay when Cooper the Sub-Warden voted in favour of the resolution, and he recorded at length in the minute-book after his fashion his protest and the reasons for his objections. It was in truth the time when the old order was passing and giving way to new. The day was over for this despotic rule and the revolt began about the same time as my experience as a Fellow.

I therefore threw myself with ardour into the various Liberal measures proposed: the admission of Non-conformists, the abolition of compulsory chapel, a measure I have since regretted, the attempt to throw the Wardenship open to laymen, which the Visitor refused to sanction and which was only enacted by the last University Commission of 1879, the better organisation of the establishment so as to reduce the expenses of the undergraduates. I was on the committee appointed to deal with this last matter and though we did some good we failed, as everybody fails, to get behind the structure of custom and perquisite that prevails in all such households as clubs and colleges. We attacked in vain the 'scout's basket'. It was the custom in those days for men to give huge breakfasts. One asked half one's friends one day and half another. The tables are put together on a diagonal line across the room from corner to corner and covered with dishes of steaks and chops, fish, eggs and bacon, and kidneys, with a lavish profusion, and tea and coffee and tankards of ale to top up with. Men dropped in at all times between chapel and lecture in constant succession, but though ample justice was done to the provisions, not half was touched and the rest found its way into the scout's basket which went out of college on the scout's arm. That was his by right of custom. I remember that a man who had to leave his breakfast half-eaten in order to attend lecture, and who sat down to finish it on his return, was solemnly reproved by old Thomas his scout for taking what was not his. We did our best, but failed to find any effectual remedy. The real remedy, of course, would have been to discourage those extravagant feasts, but they could only be done away with if the men themselves gave them up, and they showed then little disposition to help us. Things are, I understand, better now and big breakfasts are out of fashion. As to the expense to the college from illegitimate profits in the kitchen, the corruption of servants, commission given by tradesmen, connivance at waste and overcharge, no one has ever devised a mode of checking them.

Now and then an exposure of gross swindling and peculation is made but as a rule it seems to be the normal state of things for clubs and colleges to submit to be cheated and to know as little about it as possible.

9

1867-73

Move from Ewell to Sevenoaks ~ Lambarde family ~ Sevenoaks hospital
Architectural work ~ Powells of Whitefriars ~ Life class
Designs for glass and decorative work ~ Sketching tour of France
First new churches ~ Thring of Uppingham
R.A. and exhibition of rejected works ~ Volunteering at Sevenoaks
Revolt from medievalism ~ First book ~ Modern Gothic Architecture published

In 1867 my father finally gave up his business. We left Ewell for a small house and settled at Sevenoaks, in Vine Cottage, which we took furnished from Samuel Lover[1] the novelist, song-writer, and artist, who afterwards transferred his lease to us.

Our little cottage faced the Vine, a green famous in cricketing annals, and at the back looked over hop gardens towards Holmesdale valley and Maram's Court hill. Sevenoaks was not as yet much changed except that the Chatham and Dover Railway had opened a branch from Swanley to the 'Bat and Ball' station at the bottom of Workhouse Lane, now euphemistically re-christened 'St. John's Hill'. This concession to gentility, however, was significant of worse things to come. The South Eastern Railway Company were making what is now their main line from New Cross through Chislehurst to Sevenoaks and to join their old line at Tonbridge. The opening of this a year or two after our arrival brought about to the reign of villadom which has completely altered the character of the place.

When we first went to live there, however, Sevenoaks was still the retired little country town with a few families living in the town itself and several great houses of noblemen and county families round about. At the head of these was Knole, loveliest of English mansions, in its unrivalled park of beech woods and glades of fern and undergrowth. There are finer and more stately palaces in the land, but I know none comparable with Knole for poetry and romance or possessed of the same homely charm mingled with an antique grace all its own.

Hospital for children with hip disease at the Cottage on the Vine, Sevenoaks, 1870

In the winter of 1862 I attended a dance where I met Alice Lambarde, which was the beginning of what eventually came to pass. I had never seen anyone like her, nor have I ever done since. The Lambarde family, which had moved to Sevenoaks in 1654 was descended from William Lambarde, keeper of the records in the tower to Queen Elizabeth I. In 1600 he left a full account of his interview with the Queen (see Appendix I).

Alice's father William Lambarde had gone straight from school at Westminster to join the Royal Regiment of Horse Guards in 1815 at Nanterre, missing the Battle of Waterloo by five weeks.

I first saw her travelling up to town with her elder sister Harriet and her niece (who was almost the same age as Alice)[2] but they did not introduce me, supposing no doubt that we were already acquainted. Nor did I meet her at the Lambarde's garden party held at their house Beechmont,[3] overlooking the Weald.

Soon after our coming to Sevenoaks my sister Emily started her work in the treatment of children suffering from hip disease. The hospital, which has now reached considerable dimensions, began in a very small and accidental way. A poor child in a cottage near us suffered from hip disease, and my sister Emily went to the hospital in Queen's Square, Bloomsbury, and learned the treatment. Other cases offered themselves and were brought to a little cottage in the Vine which Multon Lambarde kindly allowed my sister rent free, which was the first beginning of the hospital. After some thirty years or more of patient and persevering effort, I had the pleasure of building her a new hospital on a fine site, with all modern conveniences and appliances.[4]

Hospital for children with hip disease, Sevenoaks, as built in 1901

The rectory of Sevenoaks was held at that time by Mr. Sidebottom,[5] a clergyman of the old school whom we all esteemed and loved even when we did not agree with him. The parson of that generation was a friend and companion to whom one could talk with the same freedom as to other people. His successor, in nine cases out of ten, is a 'priest', one of a caste who never forgets his cloth and between whom and yourself a barrier insensibly rises up which checks perfect intimacy and communion of ideas. To take a very simple illustration, the 'parson' of my younger days used to dress for dinner like other men, the 'priest' of to-day comes down in his clerical dress of the day-time. The ever-widening difference between clerk and layman, which we cannot but lament is a double misfortune; the one loses a great part of his influence for good, and the other loses one of his best and most helpful friends.

It was in 1866 that I first became acquainted with James Powell,[6] one of the Powells of the famous Whitefriars Glassworks, with whom I have ever since kept up an intimate friendship and who has often been my fellow traveller. Our first meeting was at his works, where I went to order a window of painted glass for Lyndon Church in Rutland, which I was then restoring. From what he has since told me I seem to have struck him as a person of very positive and decided views on art which it would not be safe to trifle with. But I suppose it is at the beginning of one's career, when one knows least, that one is apt, as it seems I was, to be most cocksure of oneself and one's opinions. Perhaps it is best that it should be so. Disappointment and failure and the sense of incompetence are sure to follow before long and to knock the conceit out of a man before it has done him any irreparable harm.

Glass designed by T.G.J. for the Whitefriars Glass Works

In 1868 Powell and I made a pilgrimage to Canterbury on foot from Sevenoaks. I think it was the hottest summer I remember, we spent a week at Canterbury working hard in the Cathedral, which was the only cool place. On our way thither we went to Rochester, where my portmanteau was to meet me. But it was not at the hotel and it was not till there had been a rapid-fire of telegrams and letters that I found that I had directed it to another hotel where it lay peacefully awaiting my arrival. This piece of cleverness produced the following jeu d'esprit from my father, and I did not hear the last of it for some time:

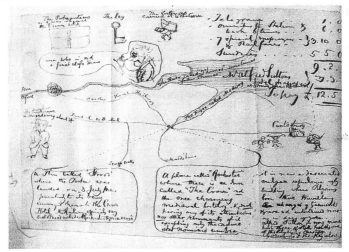

Cartoon. In a letter from Hugh Jackson (T.G.J.'s father)

One result of my travels with Powell was to turn my attention to painted glass, of which I made many studies both at Canterbury and abroad. I took also to drawing the figure. For a short time I worked at South Kensington and then in January 1870 we got up a life class, mainly among architects, in one of the galleries in Powell's works at Whitefriars. I tried to interest my old Master Scott in it, but he did not seem to care about it, though he used formally to impress on me the importance of drawing the figure. However, his son John and several of his office joined us, and we mustered fourteen to twenty, including some of Powell's own draughtsmen.

I learnt a good deal that has been of infinite use to me in designing and directing the sculpture and decoration of my buildings, and I wish it were the practice for every young architect to pass through a life school and to do it earlier in his career than I did.

I used to design windows for Powell and sometimes for my own churches. I remember doing three large lights for a church in Tasmania, and I designed a window for the Jesus Chapel in Norwich Cathedral. I used also to design a good deal of table glass for the Powells. The agreement was that I was to have one piece of everything I designed, or the value of it. This paid me very well in the larger and more expensive articles, but not in the smaller. I remember, for instance, designing a wineglass which caught the public taste, and at one time I used to see it everywhere when I dined out, together with the decanter and finger-glass that went with it, and I used to chaff Powell about the *one* wine-glass that formed my remuneration. (Plate 35). I was occupied also in designing pavements in an opaque glass that the Powells were making. With these and other decorative work such as embroidery and church plate I filled up my time in the intervals of positive architecture, and derived the greatest benefit from the habit of looking at design from many sides instead of from one only.

It was with John Scott and Powell that I started in the Autumn of 1867 for a sketching tour in France. At Auxerre wedding festivities took place at our Inn, and lasted from midday to midnight. Never shall I forget the sight of two old servants of the hotel doing a frog-dance with their hands clasped round their knees and a stick across under their hams; in which pastime, unbecoming their years, they were surprised by the sudden apparition of the maître d'hôtel, silent and grave framed in the doorway against the black night like the Commendatore in *Don Giovanni*.

From Auxerre we went to Vézelay,[7] a quaint little town perched on the top of the hill, along which the little street runs to the famous abbey at the far end. On enquiring for a conveyance, we were shown into a room where the wife of the horse-keeper was in bed. To our horror, on hearing what we wanted, she began to get up, but she emerged from the bed-clothes with all her clothes on, including shoes, proprieties were saved. I walked up the hill of Vézelay ahead of the carriage, in brilliant moonlight, not resting till I had reached the outside of the great church.

Vézelay

We lived in a simple little inn at the town gate, where to save our hats we had to dodge the joints of meat that hung in the passage. We went on to Avallon and Tonnerre and then by a long diligence journey to Troyes, whence we came home with full sketch-books.

Sept 3rd 1869. Fairly off at last for the Continent, my people having let the house for two months and going to Tenby leaving me homeless. Met James Powell and Thompson at Charing Cross, landed in due course and travelled thence to Amiens where we put up at the Hotel du Rhin. Saw the cathedral, tried to get a sketch of the organ, which has always struck

Taroiseau

me as wonderfully picturesque, but was stopped for want of permission from the architect M. Viollet-le Duc.

Amiens Cathedral, though grand and imposing in the highest degree, is not very sketchable. It is like the Alps, too vast for one thing: and also it is in that style of gothic which is so good and perfect and correct that it provokes neither curiosity, expectation, nor antagonism; and though it commands approval it fails to excite emotion and is (to me) always rather insipid.

Sept 4th. St Quentin. Of this place we expected much there being a great church and as I understood from Mr G.G. Scott, very fine. Perhaps we expected too much for certainly I was much disappointed.

Sunday Sept 5th. Noyon. Heard part of the afternoon Mass. The Great West Organ is old and very fine; though the full organ is rather rattle-trappy as many of these great French organs are for want of proper care … Got really to work at last. There being no mistake about this cathedral, whatever may have been the case with St. Quentin and the subjects for sketching seem inexhaustible. What I am particularly delighted with is the West Front, about which there is a simplicity and dignity that is very rare.

Sept 11th. Rheims. The cathedral is undeniably grand and beautiful. The first effect of the interior as one enters at the West End is magical. I have never seen anything in England or France that strikes one so well at first sight …

Sept 12th. Rheims like Amiens is rather too good to draw.

Sept 14th. Laon. Reginald Thompson and I attempted a very difficult view looking across the walls and boulevards and down onto the plain with the Palais de Justice and the cathedral on the left; a splendid subject but one that wants a Turner to deal with it. (Plate 14).

Sept 17th. Soissons. Found the cathedral here exquisitely beautiful; I was never so delighted.

Sept 17th. Drawing all day in the cathedral; Powell also at the grisaille grumbling dreadfully at the intricacy of the patterns.

Sept 18th. A large market in the town. Powell and I wandered about with sketch books in the crowd drawing old women on the sly.

Sept 20th. Started off for a completely different district of France and reached Blois at about 1 a.m. I could not resist the temptation to go, late as it was, a few steps along the bridge and see the great river swirling under the arches by the dim starlight. (Plate 18).

Sept 21st. The Château is quite as vast and impressive as my memory painted it. The great Front has a grandeur and at the same time a picturesqueness that are seldom contained in one building. It towers royally over the town … Started after lunch for Chambord some ten miles off; an interesting walk along the dyke of the south side of the river. Chambord is the sole spot of French soil, which belongs to the legitimate claimant of the French throne, Henry V, the Count of Chambord; and its owner is almost the only Frenchman who can never enjoy it because he is forbidden to enter the country. There is something melancholy in the deserted air

Soissons. Market Day, Sept 18th, 1869

which pervades the place, especially as the building is so carefully protected from the weather and preserved from decay that there seems no reason why it should not be inhabited. Everything reminds one of the absent owner; everything seems kept in a state of expectancy for his return.

Wednesday Sept 22nd. Found that leave could be obtained to sketch and do as one pleased in the château. It was very interesting wandering down deserted corridors which are never shown, pushing open doors with the Royal ciphers of François I upon the panel, that had not been opened for years, and at last fairly losing my way in the immense roof which contains within it a world of rooms; the Château is said to have 440 rooms and 60 staircases. Chambord will always remain impressed on my memory as one of the most interesting places I have ever seen.

The same diary contains an entry on December 15th 1870 after the outbreak of the Franco-Prussian war:

Only a year has passed since we were in France. Of all the places among which we spent a month so pleasantly, how many have escaped ruin or spoliation? This very day comes the news of the occupation of Blois, though the bridge (that bridge which we all sketched with its obelisk in the middle) had been broken down to intercept the enemy. The chateau of Blois and that of Chambord have served as military hospitals and their vast halls are full of wounded and dying men. Paris is hemmed in by victorious armies, cut off from the world, sending out her letters and even her Ministers by balloons, hearing from without only such news as carrier pigeons can bring her, feeding on horses, mules, cats dogs, rats, unclean animals from the Jardin des Plantes, and such vegetables as the adventurous can dig up under the fire of the Prussian sentries. It is impossible to realise all this: it seems like a dream. Only six months ago France was pretty much as we left it and now!

My first entirely new churches were (in 1872) at Annesley near Nottingham, and at Hornblotton near Castle Cary in Somerset for a man who became one of my best and most valued friends, Godfrey Thring,[8] Prebendary of Wells, well known as a hymnologist and author. He was a younger brother of the famous headmaster of Uppingham, who was almost

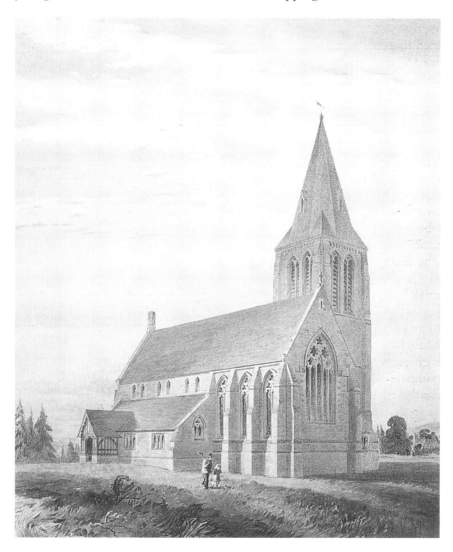

Annesley Church, Nottinghamshire, 1872

another Arnold for the influence he exercised on public school education. Under him success in examination was not the great object of school training. His care and interest extended beyond the clever boy to the average boy and the backward or stupid boy. His theory was that every boy is good for something, and he made it his business to find out what that was. It was the first school where workshops were introduced, and where a boy whose scholarship was beyond hope could develop a natural turn, if he had it, for making things with his hands. Music also played a large part in the school life, and David,[9] the music master, used to have his friend Joachim down to play to the boys, and formed a very fair orchestra and chorus among them. I only met Edward Thring[10] once, and he then struck me as a man of great power. The Uppingham townspeople regarded him as a tyrant and tried to thwart him, and resisted his demands for a better system of town drainage; whereupon he persuaded the governors to let him shift the school bodily elsewhere till the town should be made wholesome. He hired a great hotel and other houses at Borth in Wales and there they stayed till the Uppingham folk, for whom the loss of the school meant ruin, did as he wanted.

For many years I sent drawings to the Royal Academy and had them returned with either a 'D' or the fatal cross on the back. There was then an outside Architectural Exhibition Society, in Conduit Street, which generally asked for my failures and hung them. This exhibition was started not only as a consolation for the rejected but also as a rebuke to the Academy who had rejected them. It did not go on for many years, nor was the standard of works exhibited so high as to constitute a reproach to the R.A.'s who had condemned them.

Though I still made my home at Sevenoaks with my parents, I had a small bedroom at Devereux Court where I generally spent part of the week. James Powell also lived most of the week in chambers in order, like myself, to avoid a long railway journey. When I was not at the United University Club, Powell and I used to dine at the ancient hostelry 'The Cock', with high-partitioned mahogany boxes and a sanded floor and waiters – as plump as Tennyson's – chosen apparently of such a height that they could converse with the seated customers without stooping. The fare was chops or steak, with welsh rarebit to follow, and a pint of stout to wash it down with. Then we would adjourn to my rooms in Devereux Court and draw and chat and discuss art till the small hours.

At Sevenoaks I resumed my volunteering and joined the local corps. I remained a private, instead of accepting a commission, but worked up my shooting and won the marksman's badge. I used to go out at 6 o'clock in the summer mornings to practise at the butts which were then in Knole Park, a lovely place, doubly delightful in the fresh morning air with the dewdrops sparkling in the sun. Bullets, I fear, did sometimes go over into the Weald, and Multon Lambarde[11] once complained that one came and cut a hop pole in two as he was riding through his farm.

Travel and study and still more the practice of actual architecture in carrying out my own designs, had completed in my mind the overthrow of that cult of the Middle Ages in which I had been brought up. I had not been a student long, before the Neo-Gothic school, of which I had been an ardent disciple, perplexed me and shook my convictions. I could not see that the sashed window demanded by modern convenience was converted into Gothic by placing the outer half of the stone mullion in front of it, nor that we were really bringing the old art back again to life by copying the bad drawings of medieval figures.

Before I was well out of my pupilage I had begun to doubt whether in this there was any element of true modern life, whether we modern Goths were not after all pseudo-Goths – not really living characters but masquerades dressing up in bygone costumes to play a part in an imaginary drama which we should have to leave behind us when we went away into the streets of real-life. There was no revival in this – no living again.

Clearly the theories proposed by the prime movers have been to make Gothic architecture become once more a living vernacular style, to the exclusion of any other, and they had failed. They had got the old dead style on its legs and propped it up, but they could not make it walk. I concluded, the prime movers of the Gothic revival had not looked to the proper theories, which was not the revival of this or that particular style but the revival of art itself, the recovery of an artistic way of doing things, of the true artistic temper which would work unconsciously, naturally, and therefore beautifully, following its own instincts and not pulling up every moment to see whether it was treading exactly in the footsteps of precedent.

As these conclusions gradually shaped themselves in my mind I began to write them down, and the result gradually assumed the proportions of a book,[12] which, with some diffidence, I resolved to offer to the public. The moral of it was that it was not the letter but the spirit of Gothic architecture which was of use to us: its frank conformity to circumstances, its glorious liberty from the fetters or dogma that oppressed its classic sister, its ready response to the calls of construction, and its welcome acceptance of fresh ideas and principles. If we caught that spirit, I held that the revival would have served its turn; to suppose that by merely using the trefoils, the cusps and pinnacles, the arches and traceries of the Middle Ages we were reviving Gothic architecture, or doing anything for the advancement of our art, was a hollow delusion and mischievous mistake.

From condemning Gothic purism I went on to deprecate the affectation of originality for its own sake which was the antithesis of the other fault, and finally to point out the evil results of the separation of architecture from the sister arts, so that when called upon to co-operate in one building the result was inharmonious failure, the architect ignorant how to direct, and painters and sculptors unable to appreciate or understand the work they were to decorate. I urged the need of a closer association of artists of all kinds, and as far as possible the return to the practice of the Middle Ages and the earlier Renaissance, when the architect was also the decorator and decorator also the architect: 'And if those whom we call Architects have to learn to handle not only the compasses and square but the brush, the chisel and the modelling tool, those whom we call Painters and Sculptors must learn how to create as well as to decorate … Henceforth then instead of Architects, Painters and Sculptors, let us have *Artists*, men who practise not this or that form of art but *Art* itself.'

The formation of the Art Workers' Guild and the Arts and Crafts Society has done much to draw artists of all kinds together and familiarise them with each other's work. We might of course go much further, and I look forward to the day when the architect will gladly hand over the inartistic part of his work to the sanitary engineer and the surveyor and thus gain time for things more proper to his office. From the so-called architect who gives most of his time to what is probably surveyor's work, quantities, light and air, valuations and arbitrations, it is of course hopeless to expect anything good. My little book of some two hundred pages was written chiefly in the train during daily journeys from Sevenoaks to town and back again. It was finished in 1870 but I could not get a publisher until Henry King and Co. published it in the spring of 1873. Though it was not a pecuniary success, for I never got back the thirty five pounds I had to advance, it was very favourably reviewed in the principle periodicals and I think had a certain influence on architects, among whom it attracted a good deal of notice. Among others it gained the favour of Norman Shaw,[13] whose acquaintance I did not make till long afterwards, but who I knew stood my friend at the Academy exhibitions and to whose good opinion and influence I was in the end largely indebted for my election as an Associate.

10

First Work at Oxford 1871-75

Resignation of Warden Symons ~ John Griffiths new Warden
First work at Wadham ~ Competition for Tower at Christ Church
Visit to the Rhine ~ Memories of Franco-Prussian war
Italy ~ Church in Norfolk Island
Competition for Examination Schools at Oxford
Italy ~ Venice ~ Verona

The differences between Warden Symons and the Fellows became more acute as time went on. He represented the old Conservative Oxford and fought desperately for the retention of that autocratic power which, as we held, exceeded the statutory limits. Most of us, on the other hand, were Liberals, as Oxford at that time was disposed to be. Things at last came to such a pass that the poor old man resigned the Wardenship, a post which he said no gentleman could continue to hold. He retired to a villa in the new district north of Oxford, built on a ninety-nine years' lease of which he said 'three years had unfortunately expired'. He was himself then eighty-six years old. He lived, however, to enjoy seven years of this diminished term and died in 1878. On 4th November 1871 after morning chapel we elected unanimously the Rev. John Griffiths.[1] John Griffiths, whose intimate friendship I enjoyed for the remaining fourteen years of his life was in every way a contrast to his predecessor and a precisian whose scrupulous accuracy in minutiae sometimes made one smile. I remember him reproving me for finishing up with the words 'and so on' or something to that effect. He said it was a loose expression; if there was any more to be said I ought to have said it.

As a Warden his rule was not successful. He was a don of the old school, stiff, punctilious, courteous but to young men very formidable. He could not unbend to the under graduates and never invited them to his house. He said that he could not show hospitality to a man whom he might have to find fault with or punish the next day. A strange argument, which pushed to an extreme would forbid a father being intimate with his own children.

To his friends and colleagues he was the kindest of men – I personally owe much to him. He gave me my first employment in Oxford, from which so much followed. He employed me to decorate and in various ways improve the Warden's lodgings, which under Dr. Symons had been painted and upholstered in a downright philistine manner.

My work at Wadham also included designing some furniture, which Dr. Griffiths made heirlooms and attached to the house, and in building a corridor with a conservatory[2] above to connect the house and the offices. After that I was employed to heat the Hall and Chapel and to get the paint off the panelling in the Hall, and some other matters of less consequence. Griffiths had a great reputation as a man of taste in the university and my work consequently attracted a good deal of attention. Miss Smith, the great lady mathematician, sister to Henry Smith[3] of Balliol, went about asking 'Who is the unknown Mr. Jackson who has been doing up the Warden of Wadham's lodgings?'

It was in consequence of this work that in 1874 I was asked to compete with four or five other architects for completing the tower, projected by Wolsey but never built, over the great staircase leading to the Hall at Christ Church. The other competitors were my old master, Sir Gilbert Scott, Bodley, Hussey,[4] and Champneys.[5] I boldly soared aloft with a lofty tower such as I felt sure Wolsey had prepared for with his massive substructure. None of the others ventured on so ambitious a scheme. The governing body were, I think, divided for and against my design and it was lost by the casting vote of the Dean, if I am rightly informed, who did not like his

Design for the tower at Christ Church, Oxford

Cathedral spire to be challenged. And so I lost the day, but Dr. Acland[6] said 'it was the finest thing ever rejected' and the designs were bought by two of the governing body and hung in the Common Room (where perhaps they still are). It was a great disappointment to me but it bore good fruit in introducing me to greater things in Oxford afterwards.

In 1873 I went to Italy again, for the first time since John Scott and I made our Grand Tour in 1864. We started a very merry party the others being my two sisters, Charles Arnold (who was now my brother-in-law, having married my sister Annie in 1864), and James Powell. We spent a delightful fortnight on the Rhine with its vine-clad hills crowned by ruined castles.

German Gothic, which I now saw for the first time, did not interest me much. Cologne Cathedral struck me as too purely architectural, depending for effect on a bewildering mass of intricate traceries and being deficient in a complete artistic idea. The interior however was undeniably beautiful, the great height, the beautiful proportions of the section of the building, the spaciousness of the five-aisled plan, and the richness of the old glass which fills many of the windows, all combined to produce a singularly striking and satisfactory effect.

At this time the cathedral has been completed as a monument of the consolidation of Germany into one empire after the Franco-Prussian war. The two western towers were but little above the nave roof, and were massive in the extreme. When completed with their two heavy-looking spires of open masonry, the exterior gave promise of being the most disappointing and clumsy piece of architecture for its costliness and reputation that the world will contain. But if German Gothic did not appeal to me the Rhenish Romanesque did not fail to please, especially the examples at Andernach, Coblenz and Boppart.

From Boppart we made a memorable excursion over the intervening hills to the Valley of the Moselle; my two sisters on donkeys and we three walking. Through groves of walnut we climbed the plateau some 1,200 or 1,300 ft above the sea, and passing the village of Bucholz descended to the ruins of the robber castle of Ehrenburg, one of the grandest compositions of landscape and ruin that can be conceived.

It is approached by a narrow neck of land, a mere ridge of rock, that connects it with the hill behind it. The ridge was cut through at the Castle Gate, and the space had been spanned by a drawbridge, now of course wanting. The entrance to the castle, though high above the ditch, is far below the top of the pinnacle of rock on which the main towers stand, and to reach this there is a spiral roadway inside the huge round tower formed by stone vaulting with an immense central core of rubble masonry by way of newel, so that the knight and his men could ride up on horseback to the upper level. The roadway is ten ft wide and was still for the most part perfect at the time of our visit.

The whole arrangement gave me a strong impression of the lawless

Ehrenburg Castle

marauding life of a Rhenish baron in the Middle Ages. The Castle seemed really nothing but a robber stronghold, an eagle's nest, a lair of dangerous and ferocious animals of prey. In the rudest and simplest castles of Wales or England there are generally some evidences that blows and bloodshed did not make up the whole life and wholly fill the minds of those who lived there and build them. Here there was nothing of the kind. Ehrenburg was merely the stronghold of a man whose hand was against his neighbours and who lived by levying tolls and blackmail on the merchandise that passed up and down the neighbouring river highway of the Moselle. From the Schloss we went down the beautiful valley that leads to the great valley of the Moselle which we crossed, donkeys and all, by a ferry at Hatzenpost and made our way to Schloss Elz, an almost incredibly picturesque pile of bastion, tower, and steeple on a pinnacle of rock exactly like the structures in Albert Dürer's backgrounds of which it constitutes a justification.

We slept at Moselkern, in a primitive hostelry, full of tourists like our-selves, some of whom amused themselves by putting walnut shells in our boots as they stood outside the doors in the corridor. Candour compels the confession, that we had played the same trick on them overnight with lumps of a sugar from our coffee-tray!

On the 29th my sisters and Charley Arnold left for England parting from Powell and myself at Coblenz. We spent the day with the wine merchants of the place. Seated solemnly on upturned barrels, in the vast cellars of the suppressed Jesuit convent, we tasted sample after sample of the choicest Rhine and Moselle wines. Then we saw the bottling and how still wine is converted into sparkling, and I learned for the first time that white wine can be made from any grapes, red or white, and that to make red wine the skins of red grapes are left in during the early part of the fermentation. Any tinge of red or even strong yellow shows wine made from red grapes, champagne being an example. Then we drove to Ems and dined gorgeously at the Hôtel de Russie, and saw the brass plate in the pavement where King William of Prussia turned on his heel and walked away from Benedetti[7] the French ambassador, and so began the war of 1870.

It is needless to say that so soon after the event memories of the great struggle met us at every turn. The air, too, was full of menace from the new military colossus that had trampled down the French, and we in England had begun to bethink ourselves of what might be our fate. A clever little book, *The Battle of Dorking*,[8] pictured the invasion and conquest of England by this new world-power, pointing out the defects of our military preparation and especially the inefficiency of our volunteers, in a way that made me feel perfectly wretched for some days. There was not, if I remember, any ill feeling between us and Germany at that time such as has since arisen.[9] Public feeling in England during the war was, I think, pretty evenly divided between the two combatants; the upper class perhaps inclining to the Germans and the populace to the French. We used to go to the Alhambra in Leicester Square to hear the national songs. The *Wacht am Rhein* was sung by a comely well-fed Fräulein who evoked no enthusiasm. But when the French maiden came on, robed in white, with her black head down, trembling, clutching the empty air, and falling on her knees as she chanted the *Marseillaise*, our enthusiasm knew no bounds. I remember a staid elderly citizen near me tearing his hat off and flinging it madly into the air, whence if fell irrecoverably in the crowd a long way off.

At Strassburg, our next halting place, there were many traces of the bombardment. One side of the Place Kleber was roofless and gutted and a great Protestant Church was level with the ground. The old painted glass in the cathedral had been smashed and was replaced by new, and the great organ which had been knocked to pieces was also renewed. Repairs were going on where fragments of the shells had chipped and damaged the masonry in all directions.

At Lucerne I saw for the first time the snow-capped peaks of Switzerland glittering in the haze at the far end of the lake. We climbed

Pilatus and walked over the St. Gothard pass sleeping at Goxhenen, where we made friends with some engineers engaged on the great tunnel, of which about a mile at each end had already been pierced.

We had a carriage to Bellinzona where we slept and next day sent on our luggage and walked along the east shore of Lago Maggiore. The way was only a rough mountain path *'una molto cattiva via'* as the old boatman called it who rowed us across to Cannobbio in time for the steamer to Pallanza.

We tore ourselves reluctantly from the seductions of female society and the prospect of a tour around the lake with the sirens of the hotel and their Mamma, and made our way virtuously to Milan and were soon hard work sketching and measuring in churches and museums.

One evening as we were drawing into the station at Monza, near Milan, a tipsy fellow traveller opened the door and fell out and as he fell caught hold of the step and was dragged along almost under the wheels, for we were going pretty fast. I was next to the door and managed to catch him by the wrist and pull him up into the carriage, where he sat on the floor with his legs hanging out of the open doorway. He said nothing, not even a word of thanks, but clapping his hands to his bare head cried out, 'Eh il cappello!' No need, thought I, after that to talk of English sang-froid.

From Milan we went to Bergamo, Brescia, Cremona, Pavia, and Piacenze, where we met Sir Gilbert Scott travelling with no companion but a manservant. He wanted to carry us off to Ravenna, but time and work at home forbade. A visit to the Certosa of Pavia, that marvellous store-house of Italian decoration, formed a fitting finale to our tour.

I was now (1873), after more than ten years in my profession, making a modest income. My work was all of the sort I should have chosen, being of an artistic rather than a commercial kind, and independence I enjoyed through my Fellowship enabled me to wait and to choose the line of work I desired. It was evident, however, that work of this kind, carried out as I did it, leaving nothing to others but mere mechanical draughtsmanship and elaborating everything down to the smallest detail myself, must always be unremunerative except in buildings of a large scale. For small undertakings are quite as exacting in their claim on your time as large, and the labour in the lesser is out of all proportion to that of the larger. At the time most of my undertakings were on a relatively small scale, small parsonages, village church restorations, and only two or three new churches of more importance. The truth is that the art an architect puts into his work is not paid for at all. It is thrown in for nothing. The ordinary commercial architect is paid exactly the same rate as a man who brings to bear on his work a ripe artistic training in designs everything with his own hand, from main bulk of the fabric to the handles and finger-plates on the doors. So it is and so I suppose it always will be, and the artist must be content to be paid in other coin than gold and silver.

In 1875 an interesting piece of work was entrusted to me from the other side of the world. It was proposed to build a Church on Norfolk Island to commemorate Patteson, Bishop of Melanesia,[10] who had been murdered by South Sea islanders, and on the recommendation of my old friend, Robert Codrington,[11] then head of the Melanesian Mission, the work was put into my hands. And a great deal of the work had to be sent out from England. Special contrivances for shade and coolness were demanded by the tropical climate and I was rather unnecessarily cautioned to provide for earthquakes, for it appeared afterwards there were none to signify, though they were violent hurricanes to be guarded against.

The Pattesons were patriotic Devonians, so nothing would do but that the font on the pavement should be of Devonshire marble; and these, together with many of the fittings, and the painted glass by Burne-Jones and Morris, had to be sent out from England and landed with difficulty on a rock when the great Pacific swell lifted the boat for a moment to the right level. However, nothing fell into the sea and the Church, fully equipped, is the pride of the island, and Codrington says it has no rival in that hemisphere, which is saying a good deal.

For many years the University of Oxford had been considering the question of providing new schools for their examinations. The old Schools in which I had been examined were in Bodley's building, round the quadrangle of which the Bodleian Library occupied the two upper storeys. These Schools had to be supplemented by rooms in various other buildings, and the inconvenience was great. The Library, too, was in great straits from its rapid growth at the rate of 7,000 volumes a year, and cast longing eyes at the ground-floor rooms occupied by the schools. It came in fact to a struggle, which of the two – Schools or Library – should turn out to make way for the other. To move the library of over 300,000 volumes to new quarters, to rearrange it and make a new catalogue, was a task too formidable to be faced and consequently new schools were decided upon. It was to be a large undertaking, for 1,500 men were at times under examination together, and the leading architects of the day were consulted. There were several competitions in which Street, Deane[12] of Dublin, and others took part. At one time Deane's plan was chosen by the Delegacy, but upset in Convocation and a fresh competition invited. Street declined to compete, as he thought Deane entitled to have the work, but others were engaged in it and this time the Delegates chose a design by my friend John Scott. Against this, however, a strong protest was got up, pamphlets flew round to the Common Rooms, and Convocation again upset the scheme. A third competition was resolved upon; there was a suggestion made that new men should be sought for. 'There's your man Jackson,' said Thorold Rogers to Thorley[13] our Sub-Warden, 'why don't you ask him?' My design for Wolsey's tower at Christ Church had brought me into some notice at Oxford, and so to my surprise I found myself invited to compete with four more. My competitors were Deane (his third attempt), Bodley, John Scott, and Champneys, and on 1st

Examination Schools, Oxford

July we all went to Oxford to an interview with the Delegacy to receive our instructions. One or two of my competitors, I remember, lunched with me in Common room at Wadham and we had a good deal of talk together. Everybody told us it would be absolutely useless to design in any style but Gothic. Bodley had lately ventured on a kind of French Renaissance in his office for the School Board on the new Thames Embankment, and I remember well his saying as we came away in the train, 'I have half a mind after all to do it in Renaissance.' 'It's quite hopeless,' said I; 'you will only waste your time and spoil your chance.' And so I set to work on my design in Gothic and the more I did the less I liked it. The thing wouldn't come at all, and I began to despair. Before my eyes seem to come the haunting vision of Elizabethan and Jacobean work, and especially of those long mullioned and transomed windows at Kirby Hall in Northamptonshire; and finally I gave up all I had done and started afresh in a sort of Renaissance style and everything seemed to go smoothly and I got long windows in my great hall facing the High. I found the style, being more purely domestic, lent itself much better to the purpose of such a building as this.

The Gothic style suggested a collection of fine college halls for the examination rooms and the designs of my competitors naturally took that form; for all – even Bodley, whose courage failed him – made Gothic designs except myself. It seemed to me that that sort of design was eminently unsuitable for examination, where strict supervision was essential, and that what was wanted was not *halls* but *rooms*, and so in the end thought the

Venice. Palazzo Cavalli

Delegates. We had plenty of time given us so I did not lose my autumn holiday, and took my sister abroad, to Lausanne and then on by the Simplon to Stresa on Lago Maggiore, before going on to Como and Venice.

When I had been there before the Austrians were in possession and you met the white uniform at every turn. The Austrian band used to play in the piazza in the evening and the first blast of music was the signal for every Italian to get up and walk away. There were nightly disturbances in the streets and reports of men having been arrested and spirited away to the

Venice. Palazzo Giovanelli

island of S. Giorgio Maggiore, and lost to their friends who never knew what became of them.

The palaces in the canals were many of them empty or occupied by Austrian soldiers and those of which the government had not taken possession seemed falling into decay and derelict.

Now, happily, the foreign ruler was gone, and the signs of neglect were disappearing. Some of the noble families who had given Doges to the Republic still lived in their old stately homes; other palaces were occupied by dealers in

Venice. Palazzo Contarini dalle figure

bric-à-brac and some had become hotels. In one of these (the Hotel Europa), the ancient home of a Venetian noble, we were lodged, and it was a pleasure to sit under a ceiling with painted and decorated joists and look out on the Grand Canal through the marble traceries of the fifteenth century.

In the Giardino Publico, at the far end of the island, was a real horse, a wonder in Venice, which you could hire and ride up and down the alleys of the garden like the elephants and camels in the Zoological Gardens. He was a wonder to the boys, who evidently regarded him as a zoological specimen, and were never tired of following him about.

The only singing you hear in Venice is the everlasting 'Sta Lucia' which the gondoliers scream out under the hotel windows for the benefit of the 'forestieri', who take it for a touch of native romance.

In the stillness of Venice the voice travels far over the water so even this rather cockney performance has an agreeable effect when one party stops and you hear another a long way off echoing it.

Venice. Palazzo Contarini Fasan

Venice. Palazzo Tiepolo

From Venice we went to Verona. I see in my notes on S. Zenone a memorandum of the wooden-panelled ceilings, 'they are very cleverly and simply decorated. I shall certainly try my hand at it if I am successful in getting the new University Schools at Oxford!'[14] From Verona we went to Desenzano in stormy weather where the lake sent great rolling waves with a thud against the wall or the inn and covered my windows with spray. An enjoyable day on Catullus's Sirmio finished our tour.

11

1876

Schools design accepted ~ Visit to Ireland ~ Schools begun
More work at Oxford ~ Visit to Grande Chartreuse
La Bérarde ~ Lago Maggiore ~ Isola Bella

On 24th January 1876 the designs for the schools had to be sent in to the Delegates at Oxford, and on 16th February the competitors were invited one by one to meet the Delegates to explain their designs and answer any questions that were put to them.

The interview was in the upper room of the Ashmolean building where, when my turn came, I found my drawings displayed, but the designs of my competitors carefully covered up. Dr. Sewell,[1] Warden of New College, was Vice-Chancellor and among the rest I remember Dean Liddell[2] and our Sub-Warden, Thorley. I was rather nervous and felt something of the old 'Schools' fever.

March 15th was my *dies mirabilis*. It began with a blunder. I started for Oxford to attend the college spring meeting and got to Reading before I discovered I was a day too soon. On regaining my office I found an order for a new church at Lottisham in Somerset from my friend Godfrey Thring of Hornblotton, a summons to Wales to restore Lawrenny Church, and a telegram from Thorley to say my design for the Schools was chosen. I met the Delegacy on the day following and arranged certain alterations before the plans should be laid before the Convocation; for the danger still lay ahead that the third scheme should be overset like its predecessors. This time, however, there was little opposition. I attended the convocation on 15th June, in mufti, and had the pleasure of hearing the votes for the quad-rangle: *Placet* 106, *Non placet* 16; and for the Hall and Front: *Placet* 87, *Non placet* 8. I had many kind congratulations from friends, among others a very generous one from John Scott, for whose second disappointment I could not but feel compassion. Mr. Vere Bayne,[3] the Censor of Christ Church, wrote: 'I hope and believe that your work for the University will show that your design for Wolsey's Campanile would have been a worthy one for the House to have carried out.'

While my fate as to the schools was still pending I had been into Wales to the opening of my new Church at Robeston-Wathen, and to Lawrenny Castle where I first met Canon Allen,[4] afterwards Dean of St David's and a much-valued friend, with whom and his daughter I went for a few days to St David's, which I had not seen since 1866.

From thence I paid my first visit to Ireland, having been asked to design and build a small town hall at Tipperary. I stayed at Cordangan Abbey with Mr. (afterwards Sir Leopold) Cust.[5]

I sailed from Milford Haven on the 'South of Ireland,' which was grimed with coal-dust, and the decks slopped with paint and whitewash. The cook, a greasy fellow in a flannel shirt, dodged from the galley to the larder in the paddle-box with raw chops in his hands, which seemed, from colour, as if he had been helping the engineman with his stoking – luckily there are such things as eggs which cannot be soiled by dirty cooking.

The boat brought over pigs, sheep and cattle, with which pleasant companions I was to return. 'Ah! Sorr, without Oireland England would be lost entirely,' said one of the crew.

The Inn at Waterford Harbour was Irish all over. The window had no weights, the table had only three legs and the looking-glass coyly turned away when you looked at it – though looking-glasses do that even in England. My hot bath was flavoured with whisky while the water bottle was carpeted at the bottom with an illigant green moss.

After lunch I got into the omnibus for the station. A seedy old gentleman after taking a pinch of snuff and handing his box to his companion asked me if I 'indulged'. I said 'No', and by way of returning the compliment admired the river, which we were then crossing by a long bridge. He informed me in return that the Quay, which he pronounced as spelt, was the finest in the world, being an Irish mile long.

Mr. Cust's house, Cordangan Manor, was about two miles from the town in a lovely valley with a wooded hill on the opposite side of a trout stream. Within doors, barring the brogue of the servants, everything was of course English. My hosts were extremely kind and I enjoyed my visit very much.

I spent my first day entirely in Tipperary, chiefly on the building. It was petty sessions day and Mr. Cust took me to court, where he presided as Chairman and I had a seat on the bench. The room was crowded with the roughest lowest crowd you can conceive. Eighty cases were down for trial and this was the ordinary *weekly* court. Only a few were criminal, most of them for trespass or breach of agreement between master and servant and a good many for threats. The plaintiff and defendant stand on a large table in the middle of the court, with a police constable by their side and the witnesses come up and give the evidence from the table also. While the plaintiff with much eloquence expatiates on his grievance, the defendant grimaces and twists his features about into the most unearthly expressions of amusement and surprise which are intended to convey to the court what a pack of transparent lies they are having told to them.

Things were not yet so bad in Ireland as they have become since. I met Lady Cust once afterwards at dinner in London. She was then a widow, Sir Leopold having died a few years after my visit, and a Tipperary mob, headed by the priest, had tried to break into Cordangan to tear his body out of the coffin.

Work began at the new Schools almost at once. I advised the Curators, in order to save both time and money, to put in the foundations by day-work under a clerk of works, while the quantities were being taken out for the superstructure. The clerk of works I engaged was Robert Edwards, a Welshman, a very intelligent man with tastes and knowledge of geology and antiquities – far beyond his station. In digging foundations the gravel was found to be hollowed out into circular pits, many of them with hard-trodden floors, and Edwards with many others believed an ancient British village of pit dwellings was discovered. Professor Rolleston,[6] however, wouldn't have it, and in fact I found the same state of things everywhere else in and round about Oxford when digging for foundations. The pre-liminary work took over a year and the contracts were not signed for the upper part till August 1877. The building was finished and used for the first time in 1883, when it was inaugurated by the Prince of Wales at a con-cert. From first to last it cost about £100,000. (Plate 1).

The carrying out of this great building was quite an education and settled me in a style which I think has been rather my own. Jacobean work seemed to me eminently suitable to modern usage, more elastic than either Gothic or free Classic. To my mind it is really Gothic, though it made use of the Classic orders in a way of its own, and when the Gothic element dropped out of it the interest of it was gone. The defect of the work seemed to me to be the rudeness of the ornament, which is barbarous in comparison with the beauty of Gothic sculpture or the severity of Palladian detail. In particular the tire-some strapwork borrowed from the German school always, except in the Romanesque age, the least artistic in Europe, was detrimental to the English Renaissance, and the grotesque and often vulgar figure-work was often repul-sive. It seemed to me that it was possible to refine English Renaissance by avoiding its eccentricities, retaining the Gothic feeling which gave it life, and instead of imitating the gross ornamentation to which it was prone, looking rather for example to the lovely decorative work of the early or Bramantesque Renaissance in Italy. On this notion I have ever since to a great extent worked. I have never built a pure Palladian building, though I have built Gothic churches, as is still and perhaps to be expected of us.

It was a great piece of good fortune to me that this great building fell to my lot just when it did, for it steadied me, and made me look consistently on a certain definite principle and enabled me to fix to a practical purpose what had before been rather loosely floating ideas. It also afforded opportunities in design in many fields, not only masonry and joinery of oak and deal, but marble work and inlay, mosaic pavements, wrought- and cast-iron work, plaster ceilings, metal fittings of various kinds, and a good deal of furniture. The head carver I had from Messrs Farmer & Brindley was Maples, who for the following twenty or twenty-two years was almost always at work on my buildings, so that I regularly formed him and could always trust him to follow out the start I used to give him at the beginning of each work.

The Schools gave me the opportunity of illustrating what I had contended for in my book – that what concerned us in the work of the past was not the letter but the spirit of the style; and that a slavish reverence for the outward forms in which the style found expression at any particular age would be obstructive to our further progress. At the time many people thought this rank heresy, of course, for the period was not yet over when safety was sought in rigid copying only. This theory has been dying hard. Some ten years after the time I am now writing about, one of the architectural papers criticised a good design of mine as 'marked by the impurity which Mr. Jackson boldly advocates'. It was only the other day (in the year 1904) that, when showing a design I had made for a plaster ceiling, I was promptly asked by my employer, as a matter of course, where it came from.

Pupils used to amuse themselves by tracing the ideas in the designs they were set to work out to this cathedral or that. 'I think, Sir,' said one of Bodley's pupils to him, 'that comes from such and such a place.' 'I see,' said Bodley, 'the ass knoweth his master's crib.' No criticism of this kind was suffered to interfere with me at Oxford, where from first to last I was allowed a perfectly free hand, and treated, as I always have been by my Alma Mater, most generously. Of course there were many who called my work 'debased', and William Marshall,[7] then working in my office, tried in vain to persuade Ruskin to go in and see the building one day as they were passing the doorway. But I fancy the majority of the residents rather welcomed the rupture with strict Gothic precedent, which had so long ruled in Oxford. At all events they proceeded promptly after having discovered me to use me, and before the year was out I was commissioned to design the case of the new organ in the Sheldonian Theatre (Plate 4), a new military college at Cowley, and sundry repairs and alterations at the Bodleian Library. These engagements took me so often to Oxford that I used my privilege as a Fellow and took rooms in college opposite those I used to occupy as a scholar, No. 5 one pair right, in fact the rooms where we had our theatricals in 1875, and on several occasions I was able to entertain friends and give dinner parties in the Hall or the Dining room.

During the summer I paid visits to various Elizabethan and old Jacobean houses to study their style in detail. Knole of course I knew well and think it the most beautiful of all, though Kirby, were it perfect, would run it very close. Burghley is perhaps the most palatial and has fine parts, but Hardwick is full of good detail inside. Haddon had the same kind of old-world romance about it that Knole possesses, and I used to spend my day walking there and back through pleasant meadows and rambling all over the deserted rooms with the aid of a master key with which I had been obligingly furnished. Some of the rooms, which are not generally shown, have fine tapestries, and I remember well the hungry host of fleas that assailed me as I sat down to draw one of them.

In the autumn of 1876 I started off alone for a few weeks abroad, having been unable to get a companion. I went straight to Lyons, merely passing through Paris from station to station, and began with a visit to the Grande Chartreuse. Leaving the railway at Voreppe I took the diligence for St. Laurent des Ponts. The road went over a fine mountain pass that tried the strength of the rope harness with which as usual we were equipped. Of course it gave way and much rolling of *r*'s on the part of the driver followed.

'Sacr-r-r-r-ré nom de Dieu,' thundered he; exchanging it shortly for 'Sacr-r-r-r-ré nom de Diable.'

'The name,' said a passenger,' should be respected.'

'The name, Monsieur?'

'Yes, the name of God.'

'Ah, oui, sacr-r-r-r-ré nom d'un polisson d'un bougre,' said he.

We reached S. Laurent at dusk after a glorious sunset, and next morning I started with a knapsack in splendid weather for the monastery.

The desert of St. Bruno may once have been the horrible place it is said to have been in legend, but the scenery is now rather soft and pleasant. At Fourville, where the gorge narrows, is a forge, and a dependent convent at which the liqueur is made. The ravine beyond is certainly fine, especially where a great pinnacle of rock almost closes it, leaving barely room for the roaring torrent and the road, across which till sixteen or seventeen years before my visit there used to be a gate and a guard to stop further advance of womankind. The convent is an immense rambling mass of rather picturesque buildings with high-slated roofs, and still contained an establishment of forty monks called *Pères*, twenty servitors called *Frères*, and sixty servants, and it was the seat of the General of the Carthusian Order. I was lodged in a cell about 9 feet by 8 feet with whitewashed walls and tiled floor, furnished with a wooden bedstead with very clean bedding, a rather dirty deal table with a beer jug and pudding basin for the toilet, and a crucifix with a little vessel for holy water which was full of dust. A monk, exempted for the purpose from the obligation of silence which is laid on the community, took me over the building in company with other visitors, chiefly priests and seminary students with countenances of singular grossness and coarseness. From one dreary hall or chapel we were led to another, all gloomy whitewashed places with vile ornament and statuary unworthy of a waxwork show. Everything was grim and cold and whitewashed like a prison. The corridors seemed interminable, and many of them were on an incline, following the slope of the ground. The cloister seems the only part of the medieval building, the rest having been rebuilt in the seventeenth century. The only comfortable place was the library, which was well lined with books, though its chief treasures had been taken to Grenoble. Here we found the Father Librarian in white with his cowl drawn over his head and sticking up picturesquely in a point. The Chapter House is meanly panelled, and the *Chapelle des Morts* is freely adorned with skulls and crossbones and has a figure of Death on the door, joining his bony fingers in prayer. At six o'clock we dined in one of the numerous halls in which the building abounds. The Hall of France, the Hall of Germany, the Hall of Provence and Aquitaine and so on. The fare was frugal. No meat is eaten in the convent, but I dined well enough on a sort of vegetable gruel and an omelette and fried potatoes. Chartreuse, green and yellow, was handed round afterwards. I have forgotten, by the by, one course of muddy-flavoured tench.

I amused myself by wandering along the dim corridors, lit only by a petroleum lamp at each end, and found my way to the gallery of the church, guided by the monotonous chant of the monks; but there was little to be seen, though the collection of white figures dimly visible by the light of a few lamps and the movements of two monks moving up and down with tapers had a somewhat weird and mysterious effect. The awful silence of everything was oppressive. A knock at my cell door introduced a lad making strange signs with his fingers and holding my boots in his hands. He held up two fingers and I gather that for two sous he would black the boots for me. I took it for granted that he was under a vow of silence like his masters but he undeceived me by putting out his tongue and touching his ear by which I understood he was a Carthusian of nature's making. His apparition contributed something to the ghastliness of the place. Altogether the convent with its flow of visitors, its public table, its lodging for tourists, and its bill of six francs in the morning, and above all its liqueur factory with enormous profits, seemed to me rather a commonplace affair, uncomfortable but not a bit romantic, and my fellow visitors, except the priests and seminarists who dined elsewhere, made fun of the whole thing, rather in poor taste I thought. They were all Frenchmen.

From Grenoble I took the diligence for Bourg d'Oisans via Briançon, into the finest alpine scenery of Dauphiné. From Bourg I made an excursion on foot up the Val St. Christophe to La Berarde, a rude hamlet at the foot of the cul-de-sac formed by Les Ecrins, the highest mountain in France. I fancy the country is now opened up. When I was there it was only reached by rough mountain paths and mule tracks. The inns were very rude affairs and very filthy, and meat was seldom to be had. At La Berarde I slept in a loft next the hay and straw and lived on bread and eggs and tolerable wine. But the splendid scenery made up for everything. I don't think I have ever seen anything in Switzerland finer, if as fine. The natives were a simple, unsophisticated folk. The visit of a foreigner was quite an event.

Everybody down to the children wanted to know where I came from.

As an Englishman, I was asked to examine the mouth of a mule to tell its age, and I sank in the public esteem when I said I did not know how.

They seemed to know no world beyond Paris, and my bungling French, being unlike what they were used to, was generally put down to my being a Parisian. Life is very hard in those remote valleys. The hamlets are buried in snow and cut off from mankind in winter for many weeks, during which if a death occurs the corpse has to lie in the little chapel till the thaw comes and the priest can reach them from the valley and the grave can be dug.

'Ah! Monsieur,' said one villager to me, 'it is a miserable country you have come to see.' 'Why,' said I, 'I have been thinking it magnificent and beautiful.' – 'Ah, indeed, I find it ugly enough.'

Returning from La Berarde I regained the road for Italy without descending to the main valley by crossing the hills from the village of Venosc by the Col de Mont-Lans to La Dauphiné on the road to Briançon, and eventually reached Susa in Italy, and after a few days went on to Stresa on Lago Maggiore.

At the hotel at Stresa I fell in with Paul Naftel whose watercolour drawings I had long admired in the Old Society's rooms in Pall Mall.

He, with his friend and pupil, Alan Gulston,[8] moved over to the little Albergo Delphino on the Isola Bella[9] (Plate 23) after a few days, and I followed

Isola Bella. Washerwomen

Isola Bella. Livia

them, and spent the rest of my time there with them and amused myself with landscape-sketching under the eye and with the example of the Master. It was a delightful time of industrious idleness. Gulston and I used to get up at six and clamber round the corner to Count Borromeo's steps, whence we bathed, plunging into 20 feet of deep green water, tepid and delicious; and on rising to the surface at the end of our shoot we found ourselves *vis-à-vis* with the sun, just like ourselves peeping above the horizon. We breakfasted al fresco under the trees in the courtyard where Naftel was waiting our return and Teresina was there with fresh figs. By eight we were all at work before our easels, Naftel's magic pencil catching, at the first attempt, effects after which we laboured – I, at least, blunderingly. We lunched under the trees on *agogni* or *trutti del lago* sometimes with the company of ladies and others from Stresa, and then set to work again until sunset. The children, Teresina, Matilde, Romeo, Bartolomeo and the rest, who had been hanging about us all day, would carry off our stools, umbrellas, and easels to the inn, little Matilde taking my paint-box and washing it in the lake; then we would go for a row or idle about till it was time for dinner under the trees again, watching the fading light on hills and sky and the deepening shadows on the water.

'Sweetly come the chimes from distant campaniles floating over the glassy lake.'

After dinner we would sit in the piazza and talk, or tell the children fairy-tales or listen to the boys' songs, generally improvised as they went along – 'and so', as Mr. Pepys would have said, 'to bed'. It was a very happy time of which I often think. I made friends with the islanders and knew most of them, and in repeated visits kept up an acquaintance with those I had known as children. The little girls are now middle-aged women with children of their own. Omarini the landlord is dead, and so is old Giovanni Contini[10] the boatman whose craft we monopolised and whose picture I painted; and the Delphino is now (1905), I hear, managed by Omarini's daughter, the little Sylvia, who used to sit on my knee, and married an innkeeper at Cannobbio and came with him to the island when her father died.

Isola Bella. Barberina Contini

12

1876-79

Sheldonian Theatre organ ~ Church restoration ~ Work at public schools
Tour in Belgium ~ James Hooper at Thorne ~ Tour in Northern France
Death of Sir Gilbert Scott ~ Cottages at Sevenoaks ~ Henry Smith at Oxford
International exhibitions ~ Isola Bella ~ Assisi ~ Work at Oxford and elsewhere
Lectures for workmen at Wadham ~ Sevenoaks cottages completed

The new organ in the Sheldonian Theatre at Oxford was to replace a little instrument of one manual without pedals, which if not the one on which Handel produced such wonderful effects when he came, as Hearne says, with his 'crew of lousy German fiddlers' to perform his *Athalia*, at all events represented it. The new organ was to be a fine instrument, built by Henry Willis – Father Willis[1] as he came to be called – the best of organ-builders but the most aggravating of men. His only idea of the building was that it contained an organ, and he wanted, in Wren's graceful gallery, to put an organ that overhung it by four feet. This I would not consent to, but the obstinate old fellow would not give way till the Vice-Chancellor, to whom I appealed, met us in the Theatre and said, 'Mr. Willis, you must do as Mr. Jackson tells you.' So I made him keep his organ within the front of the gallery, and in recompense let him fill with pipes the two gallery windows adjoining[2] (Plate 7). The gallery of the Sheldonian Theatre, as most people know, is carried on oak pillars. These are supported on brick piers, put in to replace oak posts which had decayed in the ground and sunk, causing some slight distortion in the lines of the cornices in the gallery. It was some time after my work was done that I had a letter (in December 1878) from Dr. Moore,[3] Principal of St. Edmund Hall, and a Delegate of the Theatre, saying that he thought the gallery was giving way under the weight of the organ. It was too late to go to Oxford and I passed a wretched night and started by the earliest train next day. 'What an impostor I must be,' I thought. 'Call myself an architect and can't even construct a loft for a wretched organ!' At Oxford I rushed to a cab and was no sooner in the

Broad than I had my head out of the window, half expecting to see a crowd collected at the Theatre. It was, however, a peaceful scene; no crowd, no excitement; and when I met Dr. Moore and he showed me the distorted cornice I knew so well which had caused the alarm, I could have hugged him in my joy. I had had a terrible fright, but the relief was almost worth it.

I was now (1877) very busy. I got more work at Oxford and was engaged in restoring churches and enlarging them in various places, doing, I trust, as little harm as possible. Peper Harrow Church was reopened this year and I was at work on Iron Acton Church. Fenny Compton Church was another of my patients. It was near Edge Hill and I went with Mr. Hicks, the rector (afterwards Bishop of Lincoln), and looked down on the scene of the battle, which was very intelligible. The memory of the battle lingered among the peasantry, though one old man had his doubts as to its having been the battle of Waterloo.

In this year also I began a pretty long series of works for public schools, with a house at Harrow for Mr. Cruikshank[4] (one of the masters) next to

Harrow. House for Mr. Cruikshank (no longer standing) from a drawing by C.E. Mallows.

William Burges's speech-room, and it was in July this year, 1877, that I made the acquaintance of James Hooper,[5] a barrister in Hare Court, who had a house and property at Thorne Coffin near Yeovil.

He wanted me to enlarge and improve his house, which I did in successive instalments year by year. He was a bachelor and a Fellow of Oriel though originally a Wadham man and a great favourite of all his acquaintances. We became great friends and it was a great pleasure to me, and afterwards to my wife also, to go and stay with him from time to time while the work went on. He was excellent company and full of good stories and brimming over with humour, and he generally had a houseful of pleasant people in the autumn and use to take us about to all the fine old houses in the neighbourhood, and we went with him to tea or garden parties at Montacute, Brympton, King Ina's Palace, Coker Court, Sandford Orcas, and the rest. All the woodwork at Thorne, including an oak staircase, was done by Bennet Colley, a carpenter and joiner in the village, and better work I never saw. I remember the pains he took with his panelling; how we cut the framing and the panel different ways of the grain so as to get the contrast of the *clash* with the plain figure, a good instance of the advantage the craftsman has over the mere designer and of the need of their co-operation.

In the spring I had a short run abroad with Powell and William Marshall. We crossed to Calais and thence made our way to Bruges, stopping on the way to see Dunquerque and Furnes (Plate 15). Furnes, once a place of consequence, was sunk to insignificance and grass grew in the

Thorne House, Yeovil

streets. We stayed several days at Bruges and then went on to Ghent, where we separated. Powell went home, Marshall to Antwerp, and to Ypres, a still more deserted old-world place than any we had seen, boasting the earliest and most beautiful of all the town halls in which Belgium is so rich. No tourists seemed to find their way there, and the pleasant people at the Inn were so unsophisticated that when I ordered a dinner at four francs, they were quite perplexed, not as I supposed because it was too little, but because they did not know how to furnish forth so magnificent a repast. After an interminable number of courses I took advantage of an interval to make my escape, but before I reached the door I was spied by Madame, then engaged in preparing some further delicacy for me. 'Mais Monsieur,' cried she, 'vous n'avez pas fini', and I had to return and exhaust the menu.

In the autumn the state of my mother's health prevented my going far from home as I did not like to be beyond speedy recall; but Charley Arnold and I had a short run abroad just across the Channel, where a few hours would bring us home in case of need. Our farthest point was Abbeville, but between that and Calais we visited a number of unfrequented little towns, some of them still smothered in the tight embrace of old-fashioned and useless fortifications. From Calais we visited Guines and Ardres and walked over the Field of the Cloth of Gold. Then we went to St. Omer and Béthune, which was the most attractive place we saw. Our inn was an old fifteenth-century mansion and our windows looked on a picturesque market-place with the Spaniards' *beffroi* opposite – stern, black, and forbidding – and the church of St. Vast beyond, rose-coloured in the gleams of the sun and breathing an air of peace and kindness. I made a sketch of it which was hung in the Dudley Gallery the year following (Plate 16). We dined literally at the table d'hôte , for the landlord himself presided at the head of the table, crowned with a cloth cap like the king of Yvetot,[6] and carved all the dishes. The whole establishment was a pattern of order and good management. Every morning our host went to market in a wheel-chair, for he was old and infirm, and we saw him picking and choosing his fruit and vegetables, the tyrant of the market women. I was never better off in any inn, great or small, and when the bill came to be paid it was about half what was expected.

From Bethune we visited St. Pol, Hesdin and Doullens, places then unknown to the British tourist, where they refused the English half-sovereigns, and no-one would look at a letter of credit or a Bank of England note. We finished up at Abbeville.

At this time (1878) died my old master, Sir Gilbert Scott. He was buried in Westminster Abbey, to which he had been architect, and the funeral was attended very largely, not only by architects, but by many others. I was there with, I think, most of his old pupils. I had not seen much of Scott during the later part of his life, and for some reason or other I fancied he had taken a dislike to me; why I could not imagine, till I was told that he was under the impression that I was the author of a very slashing article in the *Quarterly Review* which made havoc of him and the school to which he belonged. My little book,[7] I suppose, convinced him of my heterodoxy, and from that he jumped on the other conclusion. That article was in fact, not written by me at all.

My father's interest in workmen's dwellings, which I fully shared, now led us to break ground at Sevenoaks. The sale of Vine Court by Multon Lambarde to a building syndicate sealed the fate of the old cottages on the Vine, and the same befell all the old cottages on sites that were attractive, and conditions were put on all the building estates prohibiting the building of anything but 'genteel' villas. The poor people were consequently pushed clean away from the town, and a new suburb of little houses sprang up below the hill near the gas fields, a district closely built round, with no garden ground and nothing to make home attractive. It was to remedy this state of things, and to do something to counteract the mischievous sorting out of classes into distinct districts for rich and poor, which always has the effect of creating as it were two hostile camps, that we now set ourselves to work. When at last we heard of a field right in the middle of the town on which no restrictions would be put we bought it and built twenty-four cottages. The result was that a great number of families were eventually well and cheaply housed on a beautiful site commanding lovely views equal to any enjoyed by their well-to-do neighbours, and that the workmen were close to their work instead of having to walk miles from home and back again twice a day.

In May I joined my Aunt Augusta Beauchamp and my cousin Alice at Aix-les-Bains, where they were staying on their way home from the Riviera. I had never seen a Southern spring, and it was almost a revelation, warm, balmy and delicious leading on without a check to full summer.

I went, one day, up to the village of Font-Couvert, for a sketch and sat on a slope fragrant with starch hyacinths. A mole-cricket came out of his hole by my side and carried off crumbs I put down for him, and returned for more. The village was 'en fête', decorated for a visit from the Bishop who came riding up under triumphal arches on a well caparisoned mule, and arrayed in violet, silk and lace. The Bishop passed through the crowd and gave his blessing: but as I went away, an old woman who had been watching me on some stairs, began to laugh – 'from your conduct it would seem that you have had enough of it' – so it appears there are sceptics even at Font-Couvert.

I meant to stay in Paris with them on my way back, to see the International Exhibition at which I was an exhibitor. But I saw by the paper that I should just be in time to vote for Henry Smith at Oxford, where he was contesting the University seat in the Liberal interest, and so I hurried home by night, breakfasted at the club, and went to Oxford to vote. Smith did not get in. He damaged his chance by a rather trimming letter in *The Times* on the Eastern question, which was then a burning one. There is a good story told of Henry Smith when Gladstone was opposed at a University election. A country parson came up and was asked whom he voted for. 'Gladst–,' said he, 'no, no, 'Eathcote and 'Ardy.' Smith promptly claimed the vote for Gladstone. 'No,' said the other side, 'he never finished the word Gladstone.' 'But he never began the others', said Smith.

I remember a man telling of two of his friends at Balliol who, coming out of the Schools after a paper on mathematics, found they had given different answers. Satisfied that both could not be right, they agreed to go and ask Smith. 'Thank you, Mr. Brown,' said Smith to the first, 'thank you for showing me your paper, very nice indeed.' Out came Brown jubilant and triumphant over Jones. But Jones was not satisfied, and he too went and showed his paper to Smith. 'Thank you,' said Smith, 'very nice, very nice, thank you for showing me your paper.' 'Well, sir,' said Jones, 'but you said Brown's paper was very nice too, though he had answered quite differently.' 'Oh yes,' said Smith calmly, 'Mr. Brown will be ploughed too.' There is something caustic about this, which is perhaps characteristic of Oxford wit and humour.

I had also missed the *Exposition Universelle* on my way out because my luggage did not arrive in Paris with me and I could not make a respectable toilet worthy of the occasion. So I spent my day sketching at St. Étienne du Mont and studying the construction of the Dome at the Pantheon. On my home I was hurrying to Oxford and so missed the exhibition again, nor did I see it when I passed through Paris once more in the autumn with Powell, for we were eager to get to Italy; while on returning, as I had a cold and was speechless, I hurried home, again without a visit and so never saw it at all – which was ungrateful, for the jury awarded me an honourable mention in the Fine Arts. But, after all, these 'Universal' exhibitions are a weariness to the flesh. Later in life I have been on Royal Commissions and Fine Art Commissions for many of them, Paris, Brussels, Chicago, and last of all St. Louis. To get a fair show such as adequately represents the current art of the day is a very uphill task. It is worst for the painters and sculptors, who have to borrow from unwilling owners the pictures and statues they need, but I have found it hard enough to get together a fairly representative selection of architectural designs. Some of the best men will not show at all and so there is an end of true representation. And when one gets a medal, one finds oneself rewarded in such strange company that one discounts the honour.

In the latter part of 1878 Powell and I made a rush for Stresa on Laggo Maggiore, which we reached in forty-three hours from Charing Cross by way of Paris and Turin. We found all our old friends on the Isola Bella well and they gave me quite a reception. Giovanni Contini had a fine new boat called *La Parigi,* which he put at our disposal and of which we made good

S. Caterina, Lake Maggiore

use. But one day, after rowing across to S. Caterina on the Milanese shore, some six miles off, we were caught in a storm and the poor *Parigi* had a hole rent on her bottom and had to be left at Reno, while we, with diffi-culty, got across in a large boat with four rowers. However, seventy francs put the *Parigi* to rights; and Giovanni, with a classic touch, which I think must have been suggested to him by the Parroco, christened her afresh *La Fenice* when she had arisen from her ashes. He took the misadventure like the gentleman that the genuine Italian peasant is, and when we said he

Assisi

should not be the loser by the accident he only said he was sorry for us and that if he were not a poor man he should say 'Niente'. We walked over the hills by Gignese to Orta and then went to Milan, Ravenna, and Bologna, where Charley Arnold met us, and we stayed some days together at Florence. Then a plague of mosquitoes and the absence of mosquito nets, and above all a sirocco which seemed to turn my bones to macaroni, drove me to a higher situation. Leaving my companions to galleries and museums I went to Assisi, where I found a cooler air.

My companion in the omnibus that slowly climbed the hill on which the city stands was one of the Franciscan brotherhood, a round, jovial rascal, quite the friar of olden time. Under each arm he had a bottle of wine, which he laid down affectionately on the seat between us. The sealing-wax on one of them attached itself to the leg of my trousers and thus served as an introduction. Praises of his convent beguiled our way alternating with ridicule of the town – 'a poor wretched place not worth a *centesimo* but for the convent of St. Francis. The noble families are ruined and the young notables gamble away everything down to the last farthing. Just look at them,' said he, pointing to a group of women washing at a public fountain; 'did you ever see such *porcheria*, washing in the public street; the commune ought to put it down.' I protested that to an artists eye the group was charming.

'Ma la porcheria, Signore!'

'Signore Frati, l'arte richiede sempre un po di porcheria.'

'Ah Signore!' said he, his fat sides shaking with laughter.

It was the *festa* of St. Francis and there was to be a grand musical service to which he was anxious I should go and promised to get me a good place. The music was to be composed by Fra Burroni, one of the brotherhood, and was to be performed by the Papal chorus from Rome and Loreto. 'Ah, Fra Burroni is a wonderful composer. He can adapt his music exactly to the words; with what expression he renders the devotional character of the psalms and the divine sentiments of the sacred offices! Ah, he is a great man! If it had not been for this [plucking the sleeve of his friar's gown] he would have written for the opera and have been a *gran maestro*; but we poor friars … ecco!' and he finished with a laugh and shrugged his shoulders. When I saw him afterwards robed in mystic garb and officiating in close attendance on the bishop, he gave me a very knowing look of recognition from the corner of his eye.

I heard afterwards another story of Fra Burroni who, it appeared, had seduced two girls (to whom he taught music), daughters of the lady in the Piazza. The brothers swore they would kill him and Fra Burroni went in terror for his life. At last he settled the matter by paying a large sum of money. Some days after, repenting of his extravagance, he got back the cheque from one of the girls, pretending it wanted some formality, and the family never saw it again.

The service of which I had been told took place in the lower church, and never have I witnessed a more dramatic scene, impressive both to eye and ear. I quote from my diary:

> The scene on entering was most impressive. The lower church, unlike the cheerful and brilliant church above it, is low and crypt-like, with vast cylindrical piers like towers dividing it into a nave and aisles and with groined ceilings of which the arches seem to spring almost from the ground. Through the great side door at the upper end, by which I entered, the afternoon sun poured with a flood of light on the floor, kindling the traceries of the marble monuments and lighting up the dim frescoed vaults with reflected brilliancy. But beyond this streak of radiance, the church melted away into a perspective of gloom and darkness. From the small stained-glass windows of the chapels that lie outside the aisles, the light hardly reaches the great cavernous nave, the darkness of which is increased by the depth of the fresco painting with which the whole church is covered on wall, pier, and roof, and which, whether in light or shade, invests the whole interior with the richest tones of colour. The pavement seems to fall gradually as you advance and the gloom grows thicker. A screen crosses the church, beyond which you catch glimpses of marble mosaic, and rich tabernacle work, lighted candles, the smoke of incense, and mysterious figures flitting about in rich vestments. Beyond is the apse, vaulted with a semi-dome, from out of which obscurity came rolling the music of voices and instruments, the

musicians themselves being invisible in the darkness. The ancient walls are ringing with the full power of the chorus, when suddenly the mood changes and the voices are silent, the instruments hushed to a soft sobbing accompaniment, and out of the distant gloom rises a single soprano voice, soft at first but rising with a grand passionate wail that fills the building. Such a voice I never heard before, so rich, so full, and musical, and yet so plaintive as to bring the tears, and withal so weird and so strange. Exquisitely beautiful as it was there was something about it almost unearthly. It was not a boy's voice, being far too powerful and too artistically managed with all the finish of an operatic singer, and it was not a woman's voice, being far richer. The truth of course flashed across me after a moment; no wonder it had seemed unnatural. It was one of the rarely successful instances of that workmanship in which the Vicar of Christ alone of all Europeans imitates the followers of Mohammed and rivals them in that manufacture of which, but for him, they have the monopoly.[8] 'Pare sempre che piange,' said a gentleman standing beside me. The next day was the *festa* and the town was filled with people from far and near, both gentle and

Assisi

simple. I went again to the church to hear the grand mass. The crowd inside was so dense that one could hardly move. Such splendid masses of colour as the peasant women formed I never saw. They wore white loose sleeves and shirts with a bodice or stays of blue or green laced at the back, skirts and aprons of homespun, and over their heads handkerchiefs of the most brilliant colours, and all of course clean and fresh for the occasion. Their arms and faces too were burned to the richest apricot colour. Perched on a ledge round the apse were the musicians, the organ and violoncellos occupying the area of the semi-circle. On high, among the tuneful choir, like old Timotheus, was the saintly Burroni in his friar's gown and tippett, beating time vigorously, and marking the accent with a sounding thwack on his desk.

The great personal beauty of the people about Assisi is very remarkable. I saw many men who might have served for the model of the Discobolus, so strongly and lightly were they put together and so easily did they move. But the beauty of the women was still more striking. During the *festa* the Teatro Metastasio was open three nights. Metastasio[9] was born at Assisi and his grateful fellow townsmen paid him the doubtful compliment of naming their rather shabby and dusty little playhouse after him. The opera was *Il matrimonio segreto* of Cimarosa;[10] a piece of good luck for me, for it is seldom to be heard nowadays. I went twice and enjoyed greatly the old courtly music that seems to suit so well the powder and pigtail of Il conte Robinson and his deaf father-in-law. There was an amusing absence of formality about the performance. The orchestra, consisting of dilettanti from the town, sat in the front part of the pit with no regular barrier between them and the audience, who in the intervals of the acts talked to the fiddlers and examined their instruments and criticised the music. Before the conductor who also thwacked his desk and shouted 'dunque' ('now then') when things went wrong – stood a worn-out old grand piano (if, indeed, it were not a veritable harpsichord) on which he accompanied the recitatives just as used to be done, if I am not mistaken, in the time of Cimarosa himself.

In country places you do sometimes have the opportunity of hearing operas that are not performed in the great capitals. I remember once hearing Paer's[11] 'Mâitre de chapelle' in the theatre at Amiens; and at Genoa 'Il Barbiere de Siviglia' with music not by Rossini but by Paesiello.[12] The libretto appeared to be the same as that used by Rossini and it was funny to hear the well-known numbers sung to the old-fashioned music, which Rossini makes Don Barolo deride and imitate satirically.

But the walk home to the hotel was much more theatrical than the theatre itself. The dark ghostly alleys between frowning walls, the glimmering lamp at the corner, the cavernous arches you had to pass under, and the mysterious corners, fit lurking places for the assassin stilletto in hand, as you stumble along over the rough paving, with nothing but the echo of your steps to break the dead stillness of the night.

I left Assisi by the midnight train on the night of the *festa*. The guests in the hotel all went to bed early, and I descended, by invitation, to the quarters of the Stoppini family. Here I found la bella Caterina, the daughter, eating her supper, and I sat and talked to her till it was time to go to the train. She confided to me all about her Dane, a visitor to the hotel, who surprised her after his departure by writing to propose. The affair was at present only in a platonic stage.

'The fact is,' she said, 'I want rest and quiet, for I have to manage all the business of the hotel, and I thought he would suit me. I think, too, that foreigners make the best husbands. Italians marry young, and then after a year – what do you expect? – they go with other women even of the lowest kind.' 'And the wives?' ... 'As a rule the wives do the same. Before marriage they very rarely misbehave, because in that case they would not find husbands – but after marriage! In this city almost every married woman has at least two lovers.' 'Every one?' 'Well, there are some who don't, but only a few.' ... 'I believe I should be a good wife – but who knows?'

I rejoined my companions of Florence and returned home on 18th October after a very enjoyable tour in which I think I saw more of genuine Italian life and manners than on any former occasion.

I was now very busy. In Wales I was rebuilding Narberth church and making a new chapel for Lampeter College, in which I remember I used some deal stall-elbows that had been turned out of the chapel of New College, Oxford. The Principal of Lampeter was Jayne,[13] now (1905) Bishop of Chester, an old Wadham man. At Oxford the schools were rising fast, the repairs at the Bodleian were in progress, also the Military College at Cowley. Mr Cruikshank's house at Harrow School, the rectory at Thornhaugh near Stamford, churches at Iron Acton, Fenny Compton, Alford, and Lottisham, Hooper's house at Thorne, the restoration of Ellingham church for Lord Normanton, and sundry other matters were in progress. Early in 1879 I was commissioned to build a High School for Boys for the City of Oxford and a little later a High School for Girls there, for the Girls' Public Day-School Company, and a block of buildings for Corpus Christi College nearly opposite their gateway.

Having now a large number of workmen engaged at Oxford (there were over a hundred at the schools alone), I got up some lectures for them in the Hall at Wadham. Among others Bonamy Price,[14] Professor of Political Economy, gave them two on that subject which were very interesting, for some of the workmen argued the point with him, and Price warmed up to the discussion and would have gone on till midnight had we let him. The new cottages at Sevenoaks were nearing completion. I had tried to make them beautiful within the proper limits of cottage building; *not* the *cottage orné*, which is detestable, but with that kind of simple grace which comes from plain sensible construction. I know nothing more difficult of attain-

Oxford. High School for Boys (first design)

ment in architecture than that, for the result ought to look as if it had come of itself, not as if it had been much designed.

They were ready for occupation in June and we gave an afternoon tea in Lime Tree Walk, as we called our new street from recollections of Well Walk and Judges Walk at Hampstead. All our friends were there and amused themselves by rambling over the new buildings; twenty-four cottages were, I think, finished by this time, some larger than others, some in flats with columns made of the local ironstone carrying the balconies.

Lime Tree Walk, Sevenoaks: new cottages built in 1879

13

1879-80

Accident and illness ~ Recovery ~ Engaged to be married ~ Work in Wales
Oxford reforms ~ Mother's death ~ Marriage
Foundation-stone of High School for Boys laid by Prince Leopold
To Rome ~ House at Nottingham Place ~ More work at Oxford
Rowing from Oxford to London ~ Architects' pupils

The year 1879 brought with it a crisis in my life, which seems to divide it into two distinct parts.

The crisis was marked by an accident that nearly cost me my life. I have never liked talking of it and I don't think I have ever told the whole story to anyone, but the experience was so strange that I wrote down some of the particulars a few years after it happened while the memory was fresh.

There had been times of weariness and depression when I asked myself whether a life of never-ending work – even the most interesting work – with nothing else to work for but the work itself, was not after all a dog's life, hardly worth living.

Matrimony had been out of the question till recently, for I could not have afforded it, and now that difficulty was removed I saw little chance of marrying as I should like.[1]

The Arnolds were at Whitby and on a sudden impulse I telegraphed to say I would join them.

The morning after my arrival I went to sketch in the harbour, but it was cold and rainy and I could not settle down to anything and so when the others went home to luncheon I started for a walk towards Robin Hood's Bay by myself. I crossed the bridge that spans the harbour at its narrowest part, threaded the narrow alleys of the picturesque old town past the market house, and climbed the steps that lead to the church and the ruined abbey. Once arrived at the top there is a pleasant path along the edge of the cliff towards Robin Hood's Bay, some 6 or 7 miles off. The cliffs descend to the sea, not quite perpendicularly, but so steeply as to be perfectly unclimbable except at a few places where they break back inland and allow a descending path.

The sea scarcely leaves the foot of the cliffs even at the low tides, though there are a few treacherous bays accessible on foot when the sea is out in which people have often been caught by the returning tide.

It is a dangerous coast and accidents are not infrequent by sea and land … I had passed the lighthouses and may have been some 3 or 4 miles from Whitby when it occurred to me that if I could climb down the cliffs to the narrow beach of boulder-rocks which the tide had exposed the physical exertion would do me good … Accordingly I began the descent. It was very steep and the foothold not very good. Once or twice I had to retrace my steps and found it not very easy, even with the help of the friendly shrub I could grasp. I became interested in my task and resolved to succeed. Arriving at the final descent I found it quite perpendicular – a sheer cliff as I imagined some 30 feet in height … Turning back I saw to the left of the way I had come, more promising scree which seemed to reach up from the foreshore, and feeling sanguine of success, I determined to try it. Leaving the brushwood fringe, I stepped out on the bare ground beyond … The rock was covered with loose shaly debris and I had not taken two steps before I found myself unable to move for fear of slipping … In another moment, how it happened I cannot tell, I found myself going. I remember a moment of wild clutching at the ground which seemed slipping away from under me – then nearing the brink – wondering in a dull way whether I was going over – then the edge of the cliff seemed to glide past me – my legs fell downwards as they cleared it, thereby throwing my head and body round in a wheel and I found myself in empty space.

All this could have taken only two or three seconds but it is wonderful that a multitude of thoughts passed through my mind in that time. I was not conscious of any fear; I remember saying to myself as I shot the edge, 'I have heard of this kind of accident to others, now I know what it is like.'

My recollection leaves me hanging in the air face downwards. I saw the rocks and beach below like a map. I thought, 'It's all over now,' and I remember no more of my fall.

Not till some days afterwards did there come back to my mind a dim recollection of being tumbled over softly as on a bed of down – of rolling and wondering when I should stop – and then, after a considerable interval, as it seemed, of my legs coming rushing down upon me from the skies to which I was looking up. All this was as indistinct as a half-remembered dream, as also the dim memory of having tried to stand up and having sunk down again into unconsciousness. From subsequent calculations I found that I lay an hour unconscious. The first thing I remember is half awaking to a nameless sensation, which was neither pain nor painlessness. Dimly I remembered I was at Whitby but what had brought me there or how I came I could not tell. I could not see anything distinctly – why I did not discover till afterwards.

As well as my clouded vision permitted me I looked up to the place whence I had fallen. It seemed a great height, how high I cannot judge for I was in no condition to think much about it. Looking round I saw how merciful had been my escape. The spot where I had fallen was almost the only one where I could have fallen without being killed. All around were large rocks on which I should have been smashed to jelly … I resolved to make my way and painfully began to descend to the beach.

For nearly two hours I scrambled slowly on, sometimes climbing a huge rock only to find I had to descend and go round it; sometimes slipping down on my side with an excruciating wrench of my back which began to feel like a mass of sprains and bruises. Once I fell headlong, within an ace of dashing out my brains against a huge rock, which fortunately I managed to reach first with my hands to break the blow. Add to this the fear of forcing my broken ribs into my lungs, which now began to occur to me and of being caught on the foreshore by the returning tide to which I began to be increasingly alive … At last I reached the nearest horn of the receding bay only to find it enclosed by a semicircle of cliffs more precipitous than the rest and actually seeming to overhang their bases.

In despair I sank down where I was on a bed of rank wet grass between two boulders of rock. Here I resolved to spend the night, sheltering myself as well from the wind and cold as I could. I was exhausted with pain and fatigue and careless of what became of me.

But shame at my want of courage again roused me; just across the narrow bay was the bluff headland which had all along bounded my view this way. Hobbling painfully as fast as I could across the bay I scrambled up a sloping scree which formed a foot to the precipice, and here I found myself suddenly on a foot-track, and following this I found myself at last on the greensward of the open down … It was now 7 o'clock and growing dark. For three hours I had been climbing in this pitiable condition over the rocks and now I knew not how far I was from Whitby, from which indeed I had been travelling away farther and farther from the point where I had fallen. No time was to be lost and I started to walk as briskly as I could along the top of the cliff. At last I reached the lighthouses and familiar ground and gained the public road. A cart passed me going towards Whitby but I shrank from the task of explaining my condition, which I should have had to do had I asked for a lift.

At last the lights of Whitby appeared. I passed the abbey ruins, the old church, and descended the ladder of stairs that leads to it, threaded the narrow streets to the drawbridge. By this time my main desire was not to attract observation but to get home as quietly and as fast as I could, and I took pains to walk as firmly and steadily as I could.

The drawbridge, to my annoyance, was just being opened as I stepped upon it. The chain was put up behind me and the usual crowd collected outside it waiting to go over. I was ready to sink with fatigue but contrived to keep up appearances, leaning my back against the handrail with my elbows behind me so as to keep my ribs well out, for I still feared they might injure the lungs. At last I reached home and passed the house a few steps before recognising it … The truth as to the injury I had received was only arrived at fully many weeks afterwards. One rib on the left side was broken at the cartilage, the breastbone was broken across near the top, and the top ribs parted from it. The left shoulder where I first felt pain was really unhurt, but a violent inflammation set in the joint of the right shoulder which lasted several months, causing the acutest agony, especially when an attack of gout was brought on which began in the shoulder and travelled down the arm to the forefinger, forming a bright red ring round the lowest joint, and then disappearing. But the most serious injury was the concussion of the brain …'

It was six weeks from the date of my accident before I could go out for a short walk. My sight still troubled me. I could see clearly with each eye separately but they would not work together and I saw double, especially when looking sideways. The local doctor forbade me using my eyes, but when I went to Brudenell-Carter, the oculist, he said the eyes were all right but the muscles were injured and the more I used them the better.

It took me a long time to get back to anything like my old health and strength; perhaps I never did quite get back to it, for it was from this time that I began to have occasional fits of gout, which has taken more and more hold of me as I grow older. The doctor prophesied that my health would be broken and my life shortened, but on the whole I have little to complain of as to physical well-being, and have managed to pass the Psalmist's limit of three-score years and ten. And the happiest part of my life was to begin soon after what had so nearly been a disastrous ending.

On 29th December I was engaged to Alice Lambarde (Plate 8).

My long absence from work, although I had been able to keep up with my correspondence and to give directions for work that was in progress, had piled up a rather formidable mass of arrears, and I had to work hard to overtake them. In January 1880 there was a great deal of travelling to do, to Oxford and Iron Acton, thence a long round to Narbeth and Tenby, and then to meet Dean Allen and his daughter at Haverfordwest and with them to St. David's. After that I went with the Dean to stay with Bishop Basil Jones[2] at Abergwili, and then on to Lampeter, where I was constructing a chapel for the college and improving the Principal's house. The Bishop, when only Basil Jones, Fellow and Tutor of University College, had been one of my examiners in the schools twenty-one years and more before my visit.

In February I attended a college meeting at Oxford as a Fellow for the last time. We had been for some months, if not a year, drafting such amendments to our statutes as the new Commission which was sitting on the University required. The main features of the proposed reform were the enrichment of the University at the expense of the colleges, which were to contribute in proportion to their means to professorships and university teaching and research, and the virtual abolition of what Lord Salisbury called 'idle Fellowships', that is non-resident Fellowships such as mine; though, as I have more than once said already, in my case the Fellowship had not made me idle, but rather helped me to work. However, whether for good or ill, the non-resident Fellow has become, after another quarter of a century, almost as extinct as the diplodocus or the ichthyosaurus, and I hear that the professors' lectures are not much better attended than they used to be in my time. The worst result of this last Commission, however, was the impoverishment of the smaller and less wealthy colleges, which could ill afford to increase their subsidy to the University. Wadham, especially, was very hard hit, for at the same time as this fresh demand came the general depression of agriculture, and this was felt worst of all in Essex where, unluckily, most of Wadham's estates lie.

We were to go to Italy and I was to have my first sight of Rome, but we could not get off until the middle of April as I had promised the Mayor of Oxford to be present at the laying of the foundation-stone of the new High School for Boys of the City of Oxford by Prince Leopold.[3]

On 5th March, when I was at Oxford, I received a telegram calling me home on account of my mother's illness and she died the following day. In accordance with the wishes of my father and all our friends it was decided that my wedding should not be postponed but should take place at the end of the month as had already been planned.

We were married quietly in Sevenoaks Church on 31st March, by my friend Dr. Griffiths, the Warden of Wadham. Thorley, the Sub-Warden, was my best man.

The following letters, which I found among my father's papers tell the story of this time.

Wadham Coll. Oxford
April 13th 1880
…We came here yesterday and are staying with the Warden, who gave a dinner-party yesterday in Alice's honour. This morning we are to go to the laying of the stone of my new High School for Boys by Prince Leopold, after which there is a luncheon in the Town Hall and then we shall at last be free to take the wing for Rome, not staying for the party in Christ Church Hall to which we have been invited to meet Prince Leopold. Tonight we hope to stay at Calais … Yesterday I had a private stone-laying of my own at the Schools. There was a lovely marble column to be set and I told Edwards[4] to have it ready about the time I was to bring Alice to see the building. So when we arrived he had everything ready, and the mortar was spread and then I said to Alice 'Now you must take the trowel and daub it about' when to my surprise, Edwards whipped out of his pocket a splendid silver trowel which Mr. Estcourt[5] the contractor had sent as a present. So we are to have an inscription put on it and to use it as a fish slice on swell occasions.

Albergo Feder, Genova
ap. 18th 1880
The fine day made it go off well, there were crowds of people, and the

13 Notre Dame la Grande, Poitiers

14 Laon

15 *Furnes (Veurne)*

16 *Béthune*

17 *Chartres Cathedral – North Porch*

18 *Blois – the Staircase*

19 Loches – Hôtel de Ville

20 Loches – S. Antoine

21 Nimes

22 Como – the Broletto

23 Isola Bella – Lake Maggiore

24 Isola Piscatore – Lake Maggiore

invited guests of whom I was one met in the courtyard of the Town Hall and then were marshalled two and two, the Doctors being in their scarlet and black velvet and the Town Councillors in scarlet and fur, into the Corn Exchange, where stood the Prince and the Mayor, who presented us in turn. After that we marched two and two, through the streets, which were lined with people to the site … The site was crowded with people. The Prince and the Mayor were on a small raised space surrounded with flowers in pots, close to the stone, which was poised in mid-air … There was a short service by the Bishop and then I handed the Prince his silver trowel, and put the bottle into its place under the stone and a bricklayer brought a board of mortar. The Prince wanted to know where he was to put it, and I said I thought anywhere, but a more sagacious bricklayer suggested that he should put a little at each corner, which he did, and walked diligently round the stone for the purpose. There was a luncheon afterwards in the Town Hall and then the speeches, which Alice and I escaped, having to run away to catch the 4.10 train … We had just time to change at my chambers and after a smooth crossing reached Calais. Alice, who had never been abroad before, found novelty in everything.

From Genoa we went to Siena (Plate 25) and thence through the most romantic scenery and found ourselves for the first time in Rome. We stayed at Rome three weeks in lovely spring weather, sometimes chilly in the evening, but always delightfully fresh and invigorating. I well remember the buoyant feeling as one came out in the early morning into the street, where the warm reflected lights illuminated the shady side of the way to which we clung, for the sun was hot enough to bake one through and through, though there was none of that sultry heaviness we get in England. We sat about while I sketched in the Forum and on the Ponte Rotto and elsewhere. The Ponte Rotto is now no more and is only represented by a melancholy ruined pier in the middle of the river. The Island, Isola Tiberina, is an island no longer but is joined to the left bank by a dry sandy bed; and the picturesque houses of the ghetto on the bank are all gone, their place now taken by an ugly embankment. All this is a result of Garibaldi's Scheme for improving the scour of the river and saving the lower part of the town from floods, which I understand it does not do, though it has irretrievably disfigured that part of Rome.

The British Ambassador Sir Augustus Paget,[6] to whom we were introduced showed us over his house, where a fine staircase had lately been put up, and introduced us to Signor Riggi the architect who designed it, and also to Commandatore Rosa, the director of the excavations in the Forum and on the Palatine. I was on the quest for fine staircases, having that at the Schools in hand, and under Signor Riggi's kind guidance we hunted Rome for good examples. But I did not find much to help me to ideas. I did, however, get hold of some useful materials from a man to whom Riggi took me. He was a mason named Stefarrori, with a yard adjoining the baths of

Rome from the Ponte Rotto, 1880

Caracalla, who in the easy times of papal rule had been allowed to pick and pilfer among the ruins at his own free will. His sheds were full of fragments of statues which he was trying to piece together, and of broken columns and plaques of coloured marbles. For £5 I bought a quantity of fragments of columns of that beautiful Africano marble, which comes from no one knows where, for the quarry has never been rediscovered. These I sent home to Farmer and Brindley, who sliced them up into thin slabs, and I inlaid them in the panels of the alabaster balustrade of my great staircase at Oxford.

We saw a great deal with comparatively little fatigue owing to Riggi's judicious guidance, and we had a very happy and restful time. From Rome we went to Perugia, and while I drew the painted ceiling in the Sala del Cambio Alice served her apprenticeship by tracing the intarsia of the panelling, which she said is very hard work. Thence we moved to Venice winding up with Verona and Milan and reaching home by way of Paris on the 2nd of June.

Our house in London was not ready, so we stayed at Sevenoaks and it was not till the latter part of the month that we took possession of our own home.

No. 11 Nottingham place, Marylebone, had Spanish mahogany doors, and the pretty Adam mouldings round the dado and door cases. Nottingham Place was an eminently unfashionable street, of which indeed I had never heard till I went there to see the house.

We lived very comfortably there all the same, and our friends from more aristocratic neighbourhoods did not disdain to visit us. Though I had reached middle life, I had never till now had a house and establishment of my own, and I felt some trepidation as to how far a modest income would stretch. But neither of us had expensive tastes, and, as my wife was an admirable housekeeper everything went smoothly.

We furnished by degrees, deliberately, picking up pretty chairs and tables in second hand shops among the Jews in Portland Street and Wardour Street; and during our engagement we had rummaged builders' yards and dealers' stores in many long delightful walks round about Sevenoaks. In that way we so far succeeded in our quest that we never admitted anything ugly, and we were rewarded when Dr. Griffiths, our Warden, the most fastidious of men, came to visit us and said there was nothing in our house that was not worth looking at. This result can only be achieved by carrying out two golden rules: first, never be in a hurry and never buy anything you don't really like; secondly, whenever you see anything you want buy it at once. The latter rule is, of course, only safe for people who know when want is real, but I have never disobeyed it without being sorry for it afterwards.

And so began my new life, a life of such happiness as falls to the lot of few men ...

Work at Oxford continued to flow in. I seemed to have become the fashion and it became the joke, when a man said his college was going to

Brasenose College Quadrangle

build, to say 'Jackson of course!' In June I was asked to build a new quad-
rangle for Brasenose and Trinity College consulted me about building a
new quadrangle next to Broad Street. The High School for Boys, the High
School for Girls, the restoration of the Bodleian, and the Examination
Schools were all in progress, as well as restoration work at Water Eaton
House on the Cherwell, refitting St. Peter's-in-the-East, and the Military
College at Cowley.

I was also engaged on a block of new buildings for Lincoln College in
what they called their Grove. In September we went to visit the Things at
Hornblotton and Hooper at Thorne. He took us to King Ina's palace, and
to garden parties at Brympton and at Montacute; after which we went to
Oxford, then in the depth of the Long Vacation, and we lived in my beautiful panelled rooms, Alice retiring to sleep at Freeman's[7] lodgings opposite. And then rather late in the year we started to row down to London.
We had lovely weather and the great crush of water-parties was over.

The first day we did twenty-one miles, lunching at Abingdon and sleeping at Wallingford. Ten miles the next day took us to Pangbourne. The
third stage was to have been Wargrave but we could not get a bed and had
to row on to Henley. The next day, as we went through Cookham Lock,
the lock-keeper disappeared into his cottage. Presently, as we sat patiently
in the boat, a photograph was pushed before my face and a hoarse voice
said, 'There, Muster Jackson, did ye ever see *that* afore?' It was a photograph of Halcomb and me in our pair-oar at the raft of Hall's boatyard at
Folly Bridge, with Morris, one of Hall's men, standing by. I looked up.
'Why,' I said, 'you are Morris.' 'Aye, Zur,' said he, 'I know'd at once it was
one of my gentlemen as I seed ye coming along. Something about that left
shoulder, never quite right.' It was quite flattering to find even one's imper-
fections not forgotten in the lapse of twenty-two years.

The row did me a great deal of good and afterwards I thought I might
fairly consider my recovery complete.

It was in this year (1880) that I received my first pupil. Since then I have
had on an average four at a time, which number I never wished to exceed
though I have occasionally been obliged to take six at once. It was only last
year (1903) that I decided to take no more and refused an offer. This system of apprenticeship which architecture has retained, though it has practically ceased with sculptors and absolutely with painters, is one which I
trust will never be swept away by the growing tendency to educate young
architects in schools instead of in the office which is really the workshop
where sooner or later they have to learn their trade. Of course, the pupils
need something more than they get in their master's office. There they are
employed in working out his designs and have no opportunity of designing for themselves. Dickens makes young Martin Chuzzlewit do his master's designs for him as soon as he enters the office; but though there may
be many Pecksniffs among us I have never found a Martin whose power of

designing at that stage would have been of use to anybody. Consequently, while it is in the office that the tyro sees how work is done and is employed in working out his master's designs, he needs a school to supplement the training of the office and to give him the opportunity of making designs of his own under competent direction and advice. There are now many admirable schools of this kind, from those of the Royal Academy downwards, and provided a man gets into a good office and sees good work there, the supplementary teaching he can have in such schools as these ought to enable him to equip himself thoroughly for the pursuit of his profession, at all events at starting. After once starting he will learn in the best of all schools, that of actual practice, in which, unless he is a useless prig, he will at once fathom his own capacity and see where he fails and what further knowledge he needs. For in art, as in most things a man is his own best master; teaching may help, but it cannot help those who don't help themselves. The great benefit of an apprenticeship as compared to school teaching is that it brings the student into touch with actual work, whereas in the schools he is only occupied with exercises. I have always noticed how rapidly my pupils got on when I was able to take them from the elementary work of copying drawings, and other exercises by which they had to learn to use their instruments and draw neatly, and turn them on to current work of the office. The feeling that their drawings were really to be used and put into workmen's hands gave them at once the interest of reality and the sense of responsibility which both steadied and inspired them.

After the autumn holidays we used generally to have a show of all the sketches we had made, and for the last eight or nine years I have been in the habit of having the pupils down once a week to my house during the winter and spring for a sort of informal lecture or talk about architecture, illustrated by books and sketches of my own. They used to take notes which I looked over if they wished it, and in this way they learned or might have learned enough to direct them in reading more deeply for themselves and studying more systematically what they saw. These talks and the preparation for them ended in my accumulating a vast amount of material in notes which I have amplified into a Comparative History of European Architecture in Post-Roman times.

Early in 1881, however, a new kind of pupil appeared in the person of our first born. A severe frost and snow storm set in, which cut off our water supply and for a fortnight all the street had to get water from a stand-pipe in the middle of the road. My dear wife and the little boy, however, fared very well and I carried her down in my arms to the Drawing Room sofa.

I had not been anxious for children, but children of one's own soon wind themselves round one's heart.

Our first boy was named Hugh Nicholas after my father and the first Jackson of whom we have any record.

14

1881-85

Examination Schools finished ~ Visit to Paris ~ Fabrique of unbreakable glass
Work at Brasenose and Trinity Colleges
Work at Wadham and Hertford Colleges ~ Public Schools
Mr. Horsley, R. A., and Mr. Frith, R. A. ~ Stratton and Northington churches
Married life ~ Hon. Fellow of Wadham ~ Visit to Cambridge

My life now ran very smoothly. I was busy and hard-worked, but I liked it and stood the wear and tear well. At Oxford I was finishing the Military College at Cowley, which, by the way, never prospered. Being neither civil nor military, under a military governor who did not teach and a headmaster who had no authority it languished and expired, and my buildings are now, I think, occupied by a factory of some sorts. The High School for Girls and the High School for Boys were finished in 1881, and the latter was formally opened by the City on 15th September. It has done good work and the son of a washer woman promptly made his way up thence to a Balliol scholarship. What has become of him since I know not. The Examination Schools were finished and inaugurated on 1st May 1883 by a concert at which the Prince of Wales was present (Plate 2). My wife and I were there and I was presented to His Royal Highness, who was very complimentary.

The restoration of the masonry at the Bodleian Library was progressing a fresh start being undertaken yearly. I was consulted about finding space for the enormous growth of the contents.

I went to the British Museum and to the Bibliothèque Nationale in Paris to consult their Chief Librarians and to see their method of storing books.

Powell was my companion in Paris and I went with him on his mission to see the *fabrique* of unbreakable glass at Choisy-le-Roi, which promised to revolutionise the art of glass making and therefore excited the Whitefriars firm to consider whether they could not introduce it into their works. The method consisted in annealing the glass in tallow fat. We saw some of the results, which were certainly surprising and could be thrown about without damage. I was given a glass beaker and invited to throw it on the stone floor. 'Je n'ose pas,' said I. 'Mais oui, Monsieur, jetez-la.' So I threw it and it smashed into a thousand pieces – which was disconcerting. We took the courteous manager back to Paris and gave him a *déjeuner*. Whether his method of hardening glass or rather toughening it is still practised I don't know. I have heard nothing of it for many years. But as Powell very justly remarked it is as well for the business at Whitefriars that glass should not be unbreakable. Dr. Warre reminded me that Tiberius had an inventor of toughened glass drowned for fear of his invention provoking disturbances among the glass-makers.

Among other buildings I carried out during these years were the new block of chambers at Lincoln College, and a new building for Somerville Hall, the ladies' college, of which Miss Shaw-Lefevre[1] was then the head. As the existing Hall had to be measured I sent Perkins,[2] my chief assistant, and another to do it. On their return I asked Perkins, who was a delightfully simple soul, how they had fared. 'Did they turn you loose among all those young ladies?' 'Oh yes,' he said, 'we went all over the place.' Then, after a pause 'I didn't think any of them good looking, and Martin didn't either.' Does the higher education of women rob them of their natural charms I wonder? It used to be said of the Blue Stockings that it unsexed them. It was finely answered by someone – I forget whom – when Mrs. Montagu[3] was depreciated: 'It matters not how blue the stocking may be provided the petticoat is long enough to hide it.' During this time I also built the University cricket pavilion in the Parks and a timber bridge over

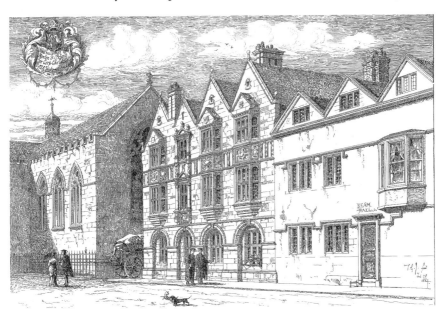

Corpus Christi College. A block of chambers

the Cherwell for Christ Church in their meadow. For Corpus I designed an organ-case for their chapel and the block of chambers on the opposite side of the street, and remodelled and added to Beam Hall, a beautiful old Jacobean house next to it. I made designs also for a new quadrangle for Merton on the north of this street, which would have almost have joined the Corpus buildings to the Schools, but this last scheme never came off. At Oriel I remodelled the interior of the chapel by extending the choir into the ante-chapel and forming an organ gallery and extra seats at the west end. I also designed some silver plate for their communion table, and engaged my friend H. E. Wooldridge,[4] afterwards Slade professor, to design stained glass for windows, which was executed by Powell. At All Souls I did some repairs in the Library and designed a monument in the chapel to Dr. Bernard.[5] Of greater consequence than these were the works I had at Trinity and Brasenose Colleges. At the latter I began with a block of chambers westward of the chapel, to make room for which I remember the old College brew-house was demolished. College ale, which was our regular drink in my youthful days, is now a thing of the past. It was wholesome stuff and really made of malt and hops. This building at Brasenose was followed by another fronting the High, thus realising what had been a dream of the college ever since the seventeenth century. Designs had been made by Hawksmoor,[6] Wren's only pupil, in Roman Classic, by Sir John Soane[7] in neo-Greek, and by Hardwick[8] in 'Carpenter's Gothic'; the last two designs monumentally dull and miserable. Finally, it has fallen to my lot – and the task was, I need hardly say, an inspiring one – to build something that should be worthy of the most important site in the most beautiful street in Europe. Part of this new front is occupied by the Principal's house. Albert Watson,[9] once of Wadham College, and a school-fellow at Rugby of my brother-in-law, Frank Lambarde, was then the Principal. He was a good scholar, and endeared to his friends by the simplicity of his manners and the genuine kindness of his heart. But he was the most reserved and reticent of men and the most difficult from whom to extract an opinion. He had, in fact, the Oxford manner in excess.

There is an amusing story of Watson saying, in an unguarded moment at a musical party, that he thought Mozart the greatest of composers. This dictum had no sooner passed his lips than he became perfectly miserable, and spent the rest of the evening in hedging his opinion: 'He did not mean to say there were not others', &c., &c. I sometimes met him at the United University Club and while his house was building I used in vain to try to find out whether he was satisfied with what I was doing. He never went into the building till near the end, when he was shown over it by my clerk of works. He made no remark till he came to the remotest attic when he pointed to a corner and asked whether there was room for a bed there. His courage failed him, however, and when the house was finished Watson resigned the Principalship rather than take up his abode in it. I made several

Brasenose College. New front to High Street

designs for this front. At one time it was proposed that the ground floor in front should contain shops. This was difficult to manage, and was given up because it appeared that there was no great demand for shops in the middle of Oxford, all the trade being attracted to the residential suburbs. Then it was proposed to have a lofty tower to add a new feature to the High Street and I designed one with a crown-steeple, and we put up poles to show where it would come in the picture, but we found it could not be made to group well with the other two steeples of St. Mary's and All Saints'. And so in the end we contented ourselves with a modest tower of the usual Oxford type.

Besides these greater works I constructed an organ-loft and designed a case for the organ in the chapel at Brasenose and built an undergraduates' library which completed the new quadrangle except in front. At Trinity College also I formed the new quadrangle next to the Broad, on the site of the President's kitchen garden, of which the old apple-trees still exist and in the spring beautifully enliven the new court with their blossoms.

My first building here was a long block of chambers with a lecture room and an undergraduates' library. This ran back from the street on a line parallel to Balliol. At right angles to this, between the end of my building and the chapel, was a rather uninteresting building containing some not very convenient chambers and known as 'Bathurst', having been built by Dr. Bathurst the President in the beginning of the eighteenth century. Inconvenient as it was and great as was the need of a better house for the President, whose lodgings consisted of various sets of rooms thrown together, there was a sentiment about Bathurst that stopped the way for some years. It was not till 1885 that I had this letter from Robinson Ellis[10]

Trinity College Quadrangle

Fellow of the College and Professor of Latin either then or shortly after-wards.

> Trin. Coll. Oxford
> March 18 1885
>
> Dear Mr. Jackson,
>   I have never been more pleased than with the result of our College meeting today. We determined by a large majority to pull down 'Bathurst' and erect a President's house on the spot, still retaining the time-honoured name. As this never could have happened without a general feeling of the beauty of your new buildings I consider the merits to lie mainly with yourself; but the President and Woods[11] and in a smaller way myself have had our share in contributing to this delightful issue.
>
> > Ever yours,
> > Robinson Ellis

The President's house which I proceeded to build, completes the new quad-rangle, nearly reaching the chapel at one end and being joined to my first building at the other end by an archway with iron gates leading to the gar-den. I think I like this quadrangle as well as anything I have done at Oxford and it found a warm admirer in Dr. Jowett,[12] the Master of Balliol. I finished the frontage of the Schools to the High by building the block containing various delegates' rooms and a library for the non-collegiate students. At my own college, besides various repairs, I designed some furniture, embroideries, and silver candlesticks for the chapel and also an organ loft at the west end and a case for an organ, besides altering and rearranging some of the painted windows. The history of the fund, which paid for this, furnishes a curious commentary on the fluctuation of tastes. Some years before I ever saw the college Dr. Griffiths, then Sub-Warden, collected a considerable sum with which he shifted several of the old painted windows in the choir from their original places and filled the ante-chapel windows with heavily matted grisaille on which were planted coats of arms in medallions. The effect of these changes was to make the ante-chapel very gloomy and to destroy the original design of the decoration of the choir. In a circular to the Society Dr. Griffiths said he had come to see his errors and that the surplus

Wadham College. Organ case in the chapel

of the original fund had been so carefully nursed that it was now enough not only to replace the windows but to pay for the organ loft and organ case. So the same fund, which had been employed in doing the mischief sufficed in the course of time to undo it! I cut out the medallions and re-glazed them in lights of white glass and made the ante-chapel once more cheerful.

Hertford College. The Stair Tower

During this same period (1880-6), I also began to build for Hertford College, and ever since that time, have been occupied in providing the college with better quarters. The new college prospered rapidly, and in 1881 got up to the proud position of Head of the River, an event which was productive of the following letter from Mr. Madden, sub-librarian of the Bodleian Library, on the restoration of which I was then engaged.

Bodleian Library, Oxford
May 26 1881

Dear Mr. Jackson,
    Last night at about 10.45 I saw out of my window a blaze of light near the Bodleian, which at once reminded me of Hertford being head of the river and of concomitant festivities, so I went out and saw that not only were rockets, bombs, and every form of firework being let off in all directions (chiefly upward) in the front quad of Hertford, but also a huge bonfire was blazing just within the great gates of the College, fed with tables and chairs by a mad set of undergraduates who were chiefly occupied in dancing insanely round it. The sparks were flying straight up to about the level of the School's tower, which, as you know, is swathed in wood-work and tarpaulins. Had there been any touch of east wind there would certainly have been showers of sparks all over the tower …
    No notice had been given to any of us of the obvious danger if the wind had blown towards the Library and the Senior Proctor (one of the curators) had, I am told specially sanctioned the fires … We stayed on the scaffolding till 2 a.m. when the men seemed to have gone to bed but it is so striking an instance of danger in a quiet summer term that you will pardon my telling you of it … I saw every part of the scaffold and can testify to the inflammable material lying about.

Very truly yours,
F. Madden

A disaster, had it occurred, to which the loss by fire of the great library at Alexandria would have been comparatively a trifle.
    I began also a series of alterations to the Powell's works at Whitefriars which continued for many years, till bit by bit I reconstructed a great part of their premises, and learned among other things how to build a glass furnace and cone. At my old school, Brighton College, I began with a cricket pavilion, which was followed by two boarding-houses and a gate-way tower some years later, the beginning of a long list of schools where I have since been employed which includes Eton, Westminster, Rugby, Harrow, Uppingham, Radley, Cranbrook, Sandwich, and Aldenham. Cranbrook, which followed first, was put into my hands by Mr. Horsley,[13] R. A., who had a country house there and was a governor of the school.

He had a great knowledge of the various private picture-galleries throughout the kingdom, and for many years he was the principal collector of works of the Old Masters on loan for the Winter Exhibition of the Academy. He lived in High Row, Kensington, and his country house at Cranbrook was an old farmhouse enlarged for him by Norman Shaw; one of his neighbours, Mr. Webster,[14] another R. A., will be remembered chiefly by his pictures of village school children, *The Smile* and *The Frown*.

He was a venerable figure with long silver hair, dressed in a black velvet coat. The early Victorian School – Webster, Horsley, and Frith[15] – is now dead and seems already to have retired into such a remote past that it is almost a surprise to find any representative of it still with us, as Frith is, though a very old man. He appears at our gatherings and votes at elections, but he finds things a great deal altered since he was in his prime. I remember once, shortly after my election as an Associate, sitting between Frith and Frampton[16] – the old school and the new – at the annual luncheon when we met to award the prizes for students' work. Frith and I walked together up the stairs from the refreshment room and I remarked what pleasant gatherings these were. 'Yes,' said old Frith, 'but they are not what they used to be; no noise then – much quieter – no Associates in those days.' This, I thought, was a little rough on me! and amused me a good deal.

In 1885 I had an interesting task in building a church for Lord Northbrook,[17] lately returned from the Viceroyalty of India. Stratton Church, a little mean damp building of brick and stucco, stood in his Park on a site which I afterwards marked by a stone cross. The new church was outside the park on the hill and by the high road. I built it with flint inlaid here and there with chequers and patterns, and used the native chalk for the ashlar and wrought-stone dressing inside.

The artist in stucco whose work I demolished at Stratton seems to have had a good innings in the neighbourhood for I was shortly afterwards invited by Lord Ashburton[18] to do what I could do for his church at Northington, which was in the same style and which I also replaced by new one. This was a more ambitious affair and was very handsomely finished with black walnut seats, richly carved, and other fittings in due proportion. 'Two things there must be,' said Lord Ashburton; 'an apse, and a pulpit reached through a hole in the wall.' At first there was to be only a low tower with a shingle spire as at Stratton, but when it was 15 or 20 ft high Lady Ashburton saw the tower of St John's, Glastonbury, and nothing would do but something of the same kind here.

As these two churches were rising at the same time there was an amusing rivalry between them. Lord Ashburton used to say, 'Now tell me in confidence, I won't tell Northbrook, which of the two do you really like best.' Before it was finished he fell into ill health, went a long sea voyage without gaining much by it, and came home to die. His widow devoted herself to completing the church as a memorial to him.

There was a third stucco church, which I also pulled down to make way for a new one, not for far off at Curdridge, near Botley. Henry Liddell, son of the late Dean of Christ Church, was the moving spirit in this work and his brother-in-law gave the tower. Liddell himself, if I remember, gave the peal of bells.

Besides these regular engagements and commissions I entered into several competitions. In 1881 there was an international competition for a memorial church at St. Petersburg in honour of the murdered Emperor Alexander II.. This kept me hard at work all through December, often past midnight. I was heartily glad on the 31st, after two cabs had refused to take the mighty case in which the strainers were packed, I saw it finally depart in my clerk Rickarby's charge to the shipping agent. I need hardly say that I was not successful and I believe a Russian got it, as might have been expected. But it was rather interesting getting up the arrangements of a Greek church, in which I was helped by Dr. Smirnoff, the Russian chaplain in Welbeck Street. I don't think mine was a good design and after it came back I destroyed it.

So passed the days. My marriage brought with it rest, contentment, and happiness unknown before, and I think I did better work afterwards than previously.

When Flaxman told Reynolds he was about to marry, Reynolds, like an old bachelor, replied that he would be ruined as an artist. Flaxman found this to be untrue. To me, at all events after so many years of solitary work, the sympathy of my wife and the interest with which she threw herself into all my engagements were as encouraging as they were novel. She had hitherto never been much in touch with art and had very little knowledge of it. But she awoke at once to the sensation of new pleasures, which it afforded, and her natural good taste, keen receptivity, and sound judgement soon made her a very apt critic. I often profited by her remarks on a design. 'So, at least, you say,' she would reply laughingly when I told her so.

I used to work a great deal at home in the quiet back room behind the dining-room where I did most of my designing, going down for half the day to my office to set the work and correct the drawings. Alice used to sit with me, and read to me when I could attend, and in the summer evenings we would walk and sit in the subscription enclosure, which ran along the South side of the water in Regents Park.

On Sunday mornings we sometimes wandered into the deserted streets of the city, where boys might be seen practising roller-skating in the solitudes of Cheapside. We would drop in on one or other of the grand old churches full of fine dark wainscotting, and lovely carving, splendid fonts, pulpits and organ-cases, and sometimes with a bevy of sweet little charity girls in snow white tippets, mob-caps, blue ribbons and yellow mittens, perched up aloft in the gallery like a choir of angels.

Many were the trips we made together in search of architecture and I remember being asked 'Do you always take Mrs. Jackson with you?' 'Yes,' said I, 'whenever I can; it was for that I married her.'

We paid a yearly visit to Alfred Stowe,[19] my old college friend and Fellow of Wadham, at Castle House, Petersfield, a charming old piece of Jacobean work with a lovely walled garden, and we were many times at Thorne with Judge Hooper, and at Oxford staying with the Warden. Once we saw the Eights and I was amused to find what ardour fired me to run and cheer the Wadham boat as it made its bump (Queen's) under the willows where I remember bumping Christ Church in 1856. At another time we had a pleasant week at Lincoln and Southwell. While at the former place a telegram reached me to say I was elected Honorary Fellow of my college. My Fellowship had, of course, ceased with my marriage. I was profoundly touched by the honour my old college had bestowed on me; and there are very few dignities that I value higher than this recognition of my humble achievements by my old colleagues. We spent a few days at Rochester and lunched with Dean Scott,[20] of *Lexicon* fame, who showed us the Liber Roffensis, which had been lost in the Medway and fished up again and which contains the terrible curse, compared with which my Uncle Toby declared the hard swearing of the soldiers in the Low Countries sank into insignificance. As in the curse in the *Ingoldsby Legends*:

> He cursed him at board, he cursed him in bed;
> From the soul of his foot to the crown of his head;
> He cursed him in sleeping, that every night
> He should dream of the devil, and wake in a fright;
> He cursed him in eating, he cursed him in drinking,
> He cursed him in coughing, in sneezing, and winking;
> He cursed him in sitting, in standing, in lying;
> He cursed him in walking, in riding, in flying,
> He cursed him in living, he cursed him in dying! –
> Never was heard such a terrible curse!

Another excursion was to Cambridge. I was engaged on the new part of Brasenose in the High Street at Oxford and went to study the gateways of the sister university, which I think are superior to those at Oxford. We lunched with Dr. Parkinson,[21] a Fellow of St. John's who was a don of the old school and a derider of the higher education of women. His house was at Newnham on the way to the college, and he complained of the young ladies of that establishment 'who,' he said, 'stand straddling across the path with their arms akimbo and shove me into the gutter opposite my own street door'. And then we went to the service at King's and as we sat under the fairy roof with that lovely organ loft on its delicately sculptured screen, pouring forth harmonies that seemed to linger in the fretted ceiling, I remember saying: 'Art can do no more than this; here you have all you can get from her.'

15

1881-87

Sales at Christie's ~ Dr. Jowett ~ Ruskin
Proposed for Royal Academy ~ Isola Bella
Competition for Imperial Institute

The year after our marriage there was some excitement in the family about the sale of the famous Bale collections. They had been formed by Mr. Charles Sackville Bale, who died a bachelor in a small house in Cambridge Terrace where he kept all his treasures packed away and only brought them out when he wished to show them to anybody capable of appreciating them. There were pictures by great masters, priceless gems, engravings, plate, books, and objects of art of all kinds. He left all his fortune, including the collections (and they alone sold for £80,000 at Christie's), to my brother-in-law Multon Lambarde who was descended, like himself, from Mr. Otway of Ash Grove, Sevenoaks, one of the daughters having married a Lambarde and another a Bale two generations back. It was not really surprising that the objects fetched very high prices, for Mr. Bale's reputation as a connoisseur was considerable. We used to go and watch the sale with interest. There was one pretty crystal locket enriched with enamels which my wife told me to buy if it went for £10. I had it in my hands to examine it, when £1,500 was bid for it. I was glad to get rid of it safely to the auctioneer's man, and it sold for £2,000. Mr. Bale had bought it in the same room for £20 some years back. I tried in vain to prompt Multon Lambarde to buy in a portrait by Reynolds of Mrs. Otway (his great-grandmother) and the little girl who afterwards became Mrs. Bale, but he stopped too soon and it was bought, for the Louvre, at £1,100.

Dr. Jowett, Master of Balliol, was Vice-Chancellor part of the time that I was busy with university work. I stayed twice in his house and have always regretted that some engagement prevented my accepting an invitation by telegram to dine and sleep there, for I learned afterwards that my fellow guests would have been Robert Browning[1] and Wendell Holmes.[2] There are many stories of Jowett that everyone knows. Here is one not so familiar. Someone was defending the naturalistic fiction of Zola and other less sincere French writers, with all its unblushing display of dirt, as being justifiable in the interest of truth. When Jowett asked: 'Do you know, Mr. So-and-so, what is written over the gate of Hell?' 'Oh yes,' was the prompt reply, 'Lasciate ogni speranza –' 'No, No!' interrupted Jowett, 'it is this, Ici on parle français.'

Never was there a man whose looks belied his nature more than did Jowett's. Behind an innocent cherubic face lay masked an iron will, and it was the common saying in Oxford that he always got his own way in the end. He consulted me about building a small college, a Balliol Hall, in the Parks, where men might live more cheaply. I built, in fact, the first part as a tutor's house, but the college could not be brought to adopt the rest of the scheme. 'Never mind,' said Jowett, 'they will come round to it by and by.' However, he died before the scheme went further, and my house, known as King's Mound, being built on part of the defences thrown up by Charles I, serves as a house for a Balliol tutor and no more.

In the intercourse I had with Jowett, more or less casual of course, I was struck with the liveliness of his mind and his acceptance of new ideas. I remember once a tolerably long talk we had about architecture, and I said that what was really wanted was an interest in the subject on the part of the public, who as a rule knew nothing and cared very little about it. Till there was a demand, and an intelligent demand, for good architecture, I said, there would never be a supply of it in amount large enough to colour the style of the day. Why could not the universities do something to spread the knowledge of true principles of design?

Jowett jumped at the idea at once, and said if I would make a scheme he had certain funds available and he would consider it. Pressure of work prevented my doing anything in this direction myself, and beyond mentioning it to some other architects I fear I let it drop and so lost the opportunity. But I have often admired the readiness with which so old a man accepted a proposal of a kind so novel to an Oxford professor.

Ruskin was living a great deal at Oxford at this time, where he had rooms at Corpus in the Fellows' building facing the garden and Christ Church meadow. I never made Ruskin's acquaintance, and indeed saw him but once, when Miss Shaw-Lefevre introduced me to him at Somerville Hall. He was standing on the hearthrug surrounded by a group of admiring girl-worshippers such as he liked, and with a shake of the hand our intercourse began and ended. He disliked my work, and called it debased, being a purist in styles, or rather in one style, Gothic. I always advise my pupils to read, as I did, *The Seven Lamps of Architecture* and *The Stones of Venice*, though I am obliged to warn them that they will not learn architecture from a fallacious and unpractical standpoint; but it puts them into a receptive and reverential mental attitude and that, as I found in my own case, is the proper one in which to approach your art.

In the Common Room at Wadham I once met Dodgson, the author of *Alice in Wonderland*. He was a cousin of the Dodgsons at Sevenoaks, one of whom married my wife's cousin, Charlotte Lambarde. He amused us with various ingenious problems – how many inches high was a man's hat; how high was an ordinary table – a question over which many bets had been lost and won; how large an object held out at arms' length would cover the sun. I think he said a large pin's head would do it, but most people generally guess half a crown or a shilling, or at least a threepenny bit.

In the autumn of every year we went abroad. In 1881 we went somewhat off the beaten track to the eastern coast of Italy. On the way we paid a visit to the Isola Bella (Plate 23), where our arrival caused a sensation. 'There is the old fisherman whose picture you painted years ago,' said Alice, and sure enough there was Giovanni, whose boat Powell and I had wrecked at S. Caterina but now repaired and rechristened *La Fenice*. Omarini, the landlord, came rushing out and conducted us with much *empressement* to my old favourite room, No. 15. Luigia, the maid, said: 'Do you know it is three years this very day since you and the other *Inglese* were wrecked at S. Caterina? I always remember it on the 21st of September.' ' Dinner as usual, I suppose,' said Omarini; and we dropped into my old habits as if it had been yesterday that I had dined under the trees in the forecourt with Naftal and Gulston (Plate 24).

On the island we were joined by James Powell and there we stayed nine happy days, sketching and rowing about in *La Fenice*. I remember on the blackest nights, wrapping Alice in a fur-cloak and rowing her out as it seemed into space, mountains, lake and sky all lost in one indistinguishable blackness. The deepest stillness reigned, we seemed suspended in void, our voices sounded strangely distinct and the soft ripple of the water seemed an interruption. From Milan we went to Pesaro, where we lodged in the Abbey of Zongo, an old ghostly palace with vast rooms and curved ceilings on which the feeble light of our solitary candle projected gigantic shadows of ourselves. We might almost as well have been sleeping under the dome of St. Paul's.

From Pesaro we went in a diligence to Urbino, the birthplace of Raphael, which was a very primitive place. The Inn was rude and dirty but the people were very civil. The cuisine was a constant surprise – a turkey was served up garnished with little round balls, which the waiter confided to us were the 'uova interne del tacchino'. The renaissance palace of Duke Federigo quite surpassed my expectations and kept us well employed. We returned to our ghostly quarters at Pesaro and then went on to Ancona (Plate 27).

From the hill above Ancona it is said that in clear weather the mountains on the other side of the Adriatic are visible. We did not see them, though we strained our eyes with a yearning look in their direction, for that strange mysterious, almost unknown shore, well outside the range of ordinary travel, had always had a fascination for me. I remember that in my school maps the long narrow islands that lie in parallel lines off the coast always interested me. Gibbon's account of the taking of Zara in the fourth Crusade, which so strangely lost its way from Palestine to Constantinople, seemed to take one into the land of romance beyond European ken. I dreamed of Zara as a city of half-ruined palaces and minsters with such distinctness that when I rose I made a watercolour drawing of it and of the boat in which, with a dog for my companion, I had made a dream voyage from Ancona. Nothing I may here say could have been less like the real Zara than my nocturnal vision of it. The country seemed almost virgin soil for an artist's exploration.

16

1882-85

Visits to Croatia

A nd so it was that in the autumn of 1882 we resolved to venture into this unvisited region, knowing but little of what we should find there, and more than doubtful what conveniences we should encounter in the way of food, lodging and entertainment.

We spent a fortnight in Germany and went by steamer up the Rhine. Alice kept a journal from which I quote:

> We sat nearly all day right in the bows and the view was splendid all the way down, particularly between St. Goar and Bingen, where the castles perched on the hills came rather close together. At Mainz we took the train to Frankfort getting there in time for dinner, after which we had a look at the place (which just round about the hotel seemed a little Paris), but we soon got into the old part where the houses have high rough-slated roofs, gables and oriel windows. We were only just in time to see the Judengasse, half of it having been pulled down but the original home of the Rothschilds was still standing. A more smelly place I never was in; every house had heaps of old clothes and rubbish outside.

At Nuremberg the town was not as picturesque as I expected, though the churches and their contents were abundantly interesting. From Nuremberg we started at 2 a.m. for Innsbruck, passing through Munich and arriving at about 2 p.m. After exploring the town in which the end of every street seemed blocked by a big mountain, we got our letters from the post office and then went off for a walk along the river.

Crossing the Brenner pass we reached Cortina and here to my joy I found my tongue again in Italian. The weather after a cold wet summer now finally broke up, and the rain came down day after day till the roads were washed away, and we found ourselves prisoners with some other English people in like case. The worst of it was the Dolomites, which we had come to see, were invisible through the mist and rain, except now and then a snow peak through a hole in the clouds, which promptly closed up again. The peasants were in despair: the rain flooded the valley, every little runlet grew while you looked at it into a roaring torrent which covered the fields with stones and mud, sweeping away mills, dams and under-mining banks. The cottagers near any of these torrents brought out their furniture and laid it on the ground, fearing the houses would give way. I offered my services to the 'Podesta' as being 'un poco injegnere', which were gratefully accepted. 'Ah Signor,' said he, pointing to a cottage which was in danger, and then clasping his hands in entreaty, 'Salvi quella casa'. I did my best by cutting down trees and chaining them together along the banks so as to divert the stream from the foundations, but as soon as this had been done a cottager lower down came to say I was throwing the water against his house; so we had to do the same there. We heard afterwards that my performance got into the local press, and that Signor Jackson when urged to go and take refreshments replied nobly, 'This is not the time to think of that.'(Though I do not remember saying anything of the kind.)

At last after a captivity of eight days we managed to break bounds and get away in a little Einspänner[1] with a good horse. The weather cleared before we reached Pieve di Cadore, where we stopped to do honour to Titian's birthplace, and for the first time saw Monte Cristello and the other giant mountains among which we had been so long confined. We had constantly to leave the main road which was either washed away or covered with a monstrous fan of scree, and to travel by old mountain tracks with men sometimes hanging on to the carriage or holding it up.

At Trieste we came down to a bright coffee-room looking across the road upon the harbour, and just opposite lay a ship from Spalato, which seemed to marshal us the way that we were going. Going out to get our letters before breakfast, we saw many other boats gaily painted, with fantastic prows and stern posts, hailing from Dalmatian ports which seemed to bring our day-dream in touch with reality.

We stayed a few days at Trieste, to draw money and make the acquaintance of the Greenhams, English merchants settled in Trieste, to whom we had introductions. We found a real Hungarian 'Caffe' where we drank Turkish coffee and listened to a Hungarian band. They worked themselves up into a frenzy of passion that was most exciting and made the strangest impression. As for the leader, Alice said, one seemed to look for sparks to come out of him.

As a gale was blowing we went to Pola by railway instead of by sea, travelling through a wild waste of stony desert. At Pola there was no decent hotel accommodation; so we decided to push on by the night boat to Zara. We could not get berths, but it was a lovely moonlight night and we sat on deck enjoying the play of the moonlight on the water and the stillness scarcely broken by the throbbing of the screw. There was a pleasant feeling of mild adventure about our plunge into unknown lands, and a mystery about the ghostly islands among which we glided after clearing the point of Istria. Behind us lay the familiar shores of Italy, before us the Dalmatian borderland of European civilisation fringed along the sea with relics of Roman colonies and traces of Venetian and Hungarian domination, but inhabited otherwise by a rude, primitive, Slav population behind whom lay the hands of Turkish conquest, still nominally subject to Ottoman rule and only within the last years taken under the protection of the Austrian emperor and Hungarian king.

Alice continues,

Zara was a very pleasant change from Pola; it did not look much from the sea, but once inside the town everything was delightful and we spent the day seeing all the churches, looking at the shops and buying some peasant jewellery. Signor Drioli the great manufacturer of maraschino, asked us to go over his manufactory and also to drive out to his country place. After dinner the Military band played in the Piazza where we sat and had our coffee, and really it was not a bad imitation of Florians at Venice, though instead of St. Mark's there was only a small church and bell-tower, and on the other side of the square a handsome old building, Venetian in style; but with the moon shining brightly on it, it was all very nice.

Zadar. A Venetian window

Signor Drioli came and saw us off giving us letters of introduction at
both Sebenico and Spalato. The entrance to Sebenico harbour was narrow
but after threading about with land close on each side one gets into a
splendid great harbour, with the town piled up on the hill opposite. The
streets are narrower than at Zara, but in every direction there are nice
Venetian doorways, windows and balconies and the Duomo promised
Graham much work. We had our dinner at the restaurant under the
Albergo, a rough place, but the food good and very cheap. Then to bed,
but not to sleep, for the room was full of mosquitoes, and the beds had no
curtains, so the only thing was to tie up one's face in a handkerchief as best
one could.

I spent the last morning at Sebenico in the Duomo and was surprised
by the canons in purple tippits coming in for a service so I gathered up my
traps to beat a retreat, but one dear old Canon grasped me by the hand and
begged I would not move. 'If we shall not disturb you, you will not disturb
us.' So I continued with a pair of reverend Canons behind me, one looking
at the sketch over each of my shoulders, mouthing out their Gregorians at
my ears. This was indeed complaisance.

Split. Interior of the Duomo

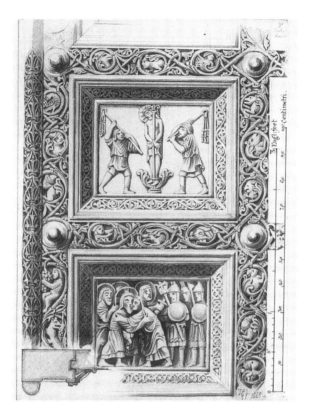

Split Duomo. Panels of the great doors

I continue from Alice's diary:

Sebenico is a queer little town of most cut-throat looking streets or alleys, but the inn is quite a smart place and we are hoping to have a night free from mosquitoes. The boat left Spalato at 4 a.m., so we were up before 3, but the porter was late in fetching the luggage, and we as near possible missed the boat, the planks having been partially removed, and I had to make an uncommon jump to get on board; luckily for me, my skirts were full, and I had not strings to tie me in, or I should not have done it.

The novelty of the country and the people, the interest of the architecture, the silversmiths' work, the embroideries, and the splendour of the native costume and ornaments surpassed all we had expected. There was also a pleasant element of exploration and discovery in our researches, for there were no guide-books of any use and Eitelberger[2] only touched upon the principal objects of interest, while Freeman[3] had no eyes for anything later than the eleventh century. The people themselves were deeply interested in their local history and monuments, almost every town and island

Sibenik. The Duomo

had its local historian and antiquary, not always to be trusted when dealing with the dates of buildings but invaluable as a guide to the archives and other sources of original documentary authority. I was well furnished with introductions, and without them I should have seen but little, for the people themselves were not always aware of the treasures they possessed and sometimes they were shy of letting them be seen and studied, especially when an object of superstitious reverence was concerned. I wanted particularly to examine at Ragusa a sacred figure of S. Biagio, which is adored in his church, where it is placed on high over the altar. The *parroco* (or parson) of the church refused to let me have it down, till I got an order in spite of him from the bishop, who made very light of his scruples. 'I believe,' said he, 'the good man thinks of his saint all day, and dreams of him at night.' I was told that the people would rise at the sacrilege I meditated, and the doors of the church were closed. The sacristan mounted the altar and tried

Sibenik. View of west end and companile

LAMP.   PETOHLJEBNICA.

Castelnuovo. Silver plate at the Convent of Savina

Istrian peasants

to take the image down. Something prevented it. 'He won't come – he won't come,' almost cried the poor *parroco*. I suggested that the string that held him could be cut; and when St. Blaise was in his hands the poor priest wiped him carefully with his pocket handkerchief and kissed him repeatedly before trusting him to my profane examination. My intermediary with the bishop, had, I found, fibbed shamelessly about us. He said the bishop asked whether I was a Catholic, and he told him I was.

The acquaintances we made in every place we visited added greatly to our interest and pleasure. Travelling difficulties were often smoothed over by our friends' kind assistance. Lodgings were got for us where there were no inns, and where there were, word would be sent beforehand to have the rooms cleaned out and made nicer for us than we should otherwise have found them.

The inns were only upper floors over shops, and between one of our visits and another they generally ceased to exist and were replaced by others. On the islands and in country places there was generally somebody who let a room, and, on landing, the boatman took our things as a matter of course to the house of *La Fiumana* – the woman from Fiume – or the woman from somewhere else as the case might be. It would seem that we were only just in time to have Dalmatia to ourselves and to see it in its unsophisticated state. It was, perhaps, the last bit of Europe to be explored in which there were any important treasures of art and I was very fortunate in the opportunity of being the explorer.

On our way back we spent a night at Pola and thoroughly looked round the Amphitheatre, both inside and out, which is in many ways the most interesting example of that class of building which has come down to us from the Roman world. We also saw the museum, which is in one of the Roman Temples, which stand side by side of each other, and one faced the Forum.

The only place we could get any food was a restaurant of the dirtiest and commonest description, where a loud talking waitress reigned. This was the only really nasty place we found on our travels.[4]

After a hasty peep at Peranzo and a day at Trieste we went to Aquileja and visited Grado which seemed never to have been visited by an Englishman before, and 'I had it quite all to myself,' as Freeman said in his review of my account of it.

We saw Padua on our way to Milan, and in Paris I had to go and see Mazzioli in the Rue de Grenelle, who was doing the mosaic pavement for the Hall of the Schools at Oxford, after which we went to the Café d'Orléans in the Palais Royale where they gave us a most sumptuous little spread. We finished the day with a turn in the Palais Royale to buy some tin soldiers for Hugh, and reached home the following day.

This peep at Dalmatia (in 1882), for it was little more, was only of the nature of a reconnaissance, but it sufficed to show what treasures of art the country contained of which the world knew nothing, and I determined to see it more thoroughly and to write a book about it. So on my return I set to work to write out my notes and to search for all available sources of information about the country and its history. I read Lucio and all the old Dalmatian historians from Thomas Archidiaconus in the thirteenth century downwards. I rather knocked myself up by working at this late into the night, for my days were otherwise occupied. One thing I learned was that the strain on one's eyes by reading foreign languages was surprisingly severe if long-continued, and I think mine have never recovered completely from the tax of so many months' work on the crabbed Middle Ages, the Byzantine Greek of Constantine Porphyrogenitus, the archaic French of Jeffroi de Villehardouin,[5] the Italian of a score of local historians, and worst of all the German of Eitelberger.[6]

We did not go to Dalmatia in 1883 but had a holiday on the Isola Bella in Lago Maggiore and at Como (Plate 22).

In the autumn of 1884, however, we made a serious attack on Dalmatia, spending nearly ten weeks there and seeing it from end to end. We went down the Danube by steamer from Passau to Vienna, a wild romantic, rather desolate river, contrasting strongly with the Rhine, which has

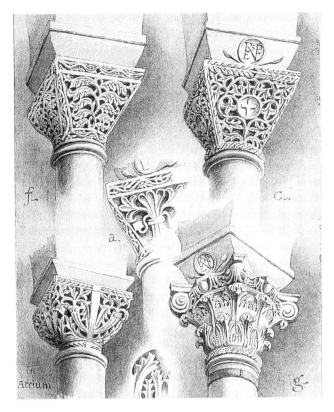

Poreč. Capitals

become a great highway or, rather, waterway and is peopled thickly along the banks. From Vienna we went into Hungary to see some of the architecture, which bore on the subject of work done in Dalmatia under Hungarian rule, especially at Trau. Thence we went to Agram and Carlstadt in Croatia and to Fiume, and thence to the islands of Quarnero, to Zara and all the principal towns and islands as far as Ragusa and Cattaro and up to Cettigne in Montenegro. We made a great number of friends, who introduced us onwards from place to place. Without these friendly offices we should have fared badly and missed seeing much that was important. The local antiquaries to whom we were introduced took an infinite amount of trouble to open up all the sources of information in their power, and gained access for me to the convent libraries in which I found many records and old authorities of the greatest value.

We found a special fascination in the wild scenery of the Gulf of Quarnero, that branch of the forked Adriatic which runs up to Fiume, with its interesting and little-known islands. It is a dangerous gulf swept by the cruel *bora*, which has destroyed nearly all vegetation and reduced the shores to something like a desert in many places. Trained amid the difficulties and

Poreč

perils of these waters the sailors of the Quarnero are extremely expert and we had some experience of their courage and skill in handling small boats during our visits to the islands. When we were off Neresine at the foot of Monte Ossero we were almost becalmed. Suddenly, however, without the least warning a gale of wind swooped down upon us, and in a few minutes we were tearing along in an angry sea and running nearly gunwale under. The waves broke over us and it became plain that the boat was too small for such rough weather, and that we were in considerable peril. The gale increased in violence and the temporary bowsprit threatened to break under the strain of the jib. The skipper resolved to try and pass the point and as the water was deep enough we did to our joy just shoot by with only a few fathoms to spare between us and the frightful rocks on which the waves were dashing themselves into foam that rose far above our heads.

Of all the mountains we had ever seen, we agreed that for beauty of colour and firmness of ragged outline none will compare with these savage hills of the Quarnero. Their absolute bareness in the upper part gives them the most exquisite tints, varying from silver-grey at noontide, when they are brighter than the sky against which they stand up, to all kinds of rosy

Karlovac. Star i Most

Tergatto, near Rijeka

and mellow orange hues, shaded with pure purple in the evening light. Their whiteness and bareness is not to be believed without being seen.

Our friends at Zara had thought proper to record our plans and movements in the local press and it was amusing at each stage to find ourselves expected. It was rather useful, for the custom-house officers who had to pass our luggage at every place – one of the results of Trieste's being a free port – often let us through without examination on hearing who we were. Thus we tasted the fruits of celebrity.

Trogir. The Loggia

Trogir. West doorway of the Duomo

Rab. Campanile (which may have inspired T.G.J.'s design for Zadar Cathedral)

Rab. View of the Campanile from the sea

On the island of Lesina, at Stari Grad, everyone told us that the town of Lesina was a poor decaying place full of priests – there was the Duomo and an old church or two but nothing to make it worth our while to go there. Undaunted by this, however, we determined to see Lesina and judge for ourselves. The way of getting there involved crossing the hills by a mountain footpath, and so dropping down on Lesina on the other shore avoiding the long circuit round the western end of the island.

Warned by these poor accounts we had been preparing ourselves for the beatitude of those who expect nothing. But the composure with which we followed the steep staircase of a pathway that led downwards was soon dispelled as one graceful white marble shafted campanile after another appeared, the turns of the pathway bringing constantly fresh charms into view and was finally converted into enthusiasm when we reached the

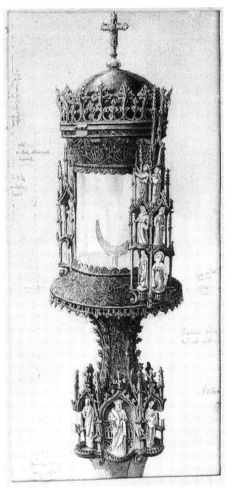

Ossero. Ostensorio in the treasury of the Duomo

shore and turning the corner of a ruined Venetian palace found ourselves close to the little port with the splendid loggia of San Michele to our left, the old Venetian arsenal to our right and a spacious piazza smooth flagged like that of St. Mark, stretching away between ancient Venetian buildings to the façade of the Duomo which with its lofty campanile closed the view. (Plate 28).

At Lesina I was shown the plan of an enormous 'Stabilmento di bagni', part of the apparatus for making a kind of Austrian and German Madeira for which its mild climate specially qualified it. But by a monstrous piece of perversity when there were charming sites vacant for the new building, the promoters chose one which involved the destruction of two of the picturesque towers which group so charmingly with the loggia of San Michele, and bear on their front the Lion of St Mark. The beautiful loggia itself and the clock tower would be dwarfed by the vast hundred-windowed

Zadar. S. Donato

factory, which it is proposed to build behind giving the poor loggia the look of a conservatory or porch to a modern hotel. I exploded rather strongly when the plans were shown me and after getting to Ragusa I explained to Professor Gelcich what was intended. He wrote at once to the Government and said he believed the scheme would not be allowed – I hope he may succeed in saving what is one of the loveliest groups of buildings in all Dalmatia.[7] (Plate 30).

On the evening of October 6th we embarked on the Austrian Lloyd steamer for Curzola, the next island on our route. We supped on board while the rain, alas, came down pitilessly making it impossible to leave the cabin and it was 11.30 p.m. before the steamer hove to in the narrow channel that divides the town of Curzola from the mainland. We could see the lights flashing in the water and the lanterns of the little boats that came out like glow-worms through the darkness to fetch us off. At any time of day and in any weather landing in little boats is a nuisance, but when it is pitch dark and the sky seems falling in solid sheets of water! However at last we got into the boat, which was half full of rainwater, and were rowed to land.

Following our train of porters past the huge town walls we came to the Sea gate over which the Lion of St Mark seemed to greet us as a familiar friend and we plunged into the interior of the town through the entrance tower. Here, after a few twists and turns in narrow alleys, we finally reached the humble hostelry of Leon d'Oro and soon our three porters and ourselves, together with our luggage, were standing and making a puddle on the floor of a very tolerable room which was to be our quarters (Plate 29).

Thursday October 7th. Though not actually raining, the morning was damp and the streets very sloppy so Alice left me to explore the town alone before breakfast. Following the steep alley in which the door of Leon d'Oro

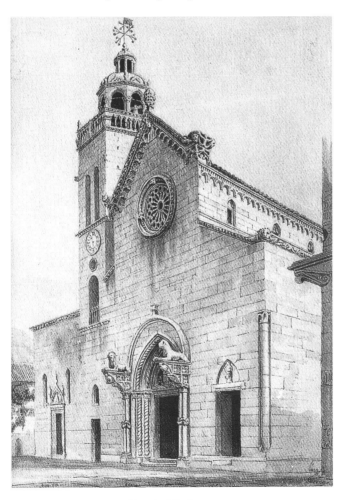

Korčula. The Duomo

Venice. Palazzo Falconi alla Fava

opens I reached the Piazza del Duomo, which as is often the case in walled towns, is so small that it is difficulty to get a satisfactory view of the façade. This like the whole building is very interesting and without exaggeration may be called beautiful, and there is a true artistic feeling in the gradual increase in richness towards the upper part which is splendid with cornices and finials in the great gable while the Campanile, plain and almost featureless till near the top, bursts suddenly into magnificence with a crowning parapet of colonnettes carrying trefoiled arches upon which rises a rich and graceful lantern.

The town is full of charming pieces of Venetian architecture in the style of the 15th century. A ruined house in a street that runs eastward from the church has a splendid window with carvings of birds and serpents in the capitals – once it had balconies on carved brackets, but the owner had sold

Venice. 'Saw this cottage 1880, (at Pantalione) vilely restored to death'

them to some American who has taken them to New York. The house is unhappily ruined, and the curiosity dealers, Jew or Greek are even now haggling with the owner for the whole of this lovely window. I suggested to the Canonica Alibranti that instead of planning their intended museum in the uninteresting church they had chosen, they ought to buy this house and place it there – I also promised to give them £5 towards the purchase of it and as the whole house was valued at only £30 I had every hope the scheme might be successful.

Our tour ended with a few uneventful but delightful days at Venice. On my return my book occupied me fully in my spare time till the year came round again (1885) and we once more started for Dalmatia, to review all we had seen and verify or correct what I had written on the spot.

I continue from Alice's diary.

At Zara Graham had special permission from the Archbishop to go to the Benedictine convent, but the permission only extended to him, and there appeared to be a greater difficulty for a woman to gain entrance than a man. These poor ladies, from never going outside the convent have a bloodless pearly white complexion and talk in a subdued far away sort of manner. At Salona Graham wanted to make a measurement of the Basilica, so inspite of the heat which had now become intense, he pounded about these ruins in full blaze of the sun, and when he had done I never saw a warmer specimen of humanity. The wonder is it did not make him ill. After lunch I went to bed for two hours, but such was Graham's enthusiasm that he sat down and worked it all out on paper, and by the time he had finished it was time for him to keep an engagement at the museum.

Sept 21 Lesina … Last year there was scarcely anything to be called an Inn, but now a very tidy one has started and we were glad to find ourselves in a very clean room and a nice room close by for dinner etc … We walked as far as the Franciscan Convent before dinner and sat outside in the moonlight, everything so quiet and lovely. Lesina is in every way delightful.

At Curzola we took a boat and went to the Badia, a Franciscan convent. It was about half an hour's sail and a very lovely one … The boatmen rowed us back as the wind was rather strong. It was a full moon, and with the moonlight on one side, and the afterglow of the sunset on the other there were the most beautiful effects. The Canonico Don Alibranti met us on the quay and came back with us to the inn. He had to explain to Graham his difficulties about starting the museum for which Graham had subscribed £5 in order to try and save a beautiful house with Venetian windows. However they took his money but he did not get the house he had stipulated upon. [8]

My book had grown to considerable dimensions and the illustrations, which were very numerous, promised to cost a good deal. On 12th June the Clarendon Press accepted the book and undertook to publish it at their expense. This book and two others of mine which the Clarendon Press afterwards published have entailed a loss, thus far, of many hundreds of pounds to the University Press; but when I once replied, to their annual statement of sales, that I was sorry my books should be so expensive to them, they said that they did not in the least regret it. This, I think, is the highest compliment I have ever received. [9]

On 1st January 1887 I finished the last of the illustrations and everything but the preface and index.

Key to modern place names

Agram	= Zagreb	Arbe	= Rab	Carlstadt	= Karlovac
Curzola	= Korčula	Fiume	= Rijeka	Lesina	= Hvar
Parenzo	= Poreč	Pola	= Pula	Ragusa	= Dubrovnik
Sebenico	= Sibenik	Spalato	= Split	Trau	= Trogir
Zara	= Zadar				

17

1887-91

Purchase and restoration of Eagle House, Wimbledon ~
Book on Dalmatia published in three volumes
The Royal Institute of British Architects
Work at Uppingham ~ Blenheim ~ Design of a piano
Widening of the Strand ~ Competition for Imperial Institute
The Art Workers' Guild ~ Visit to Holland

The year 1887, memorable for the Jubilee of Queen Victoria's reign, was also eventful for us little people. On 4th February our second boy was born, and on 12th March he was christened in the little parish chapel, once the parish church, of Marylebone. The font there is a large silver cup in which Byron was baptised, and we named him Basil after my little brother who died.

In the summer another great event was a change of residence from London to the outskirts. It was seven years since we had left the country for town, and though there was much to attract us in London we both felt we had enough of living there.

In August 1886, when we were staying with the Arnolds at Wimbledon in a house on the common which I had enlarged for them, Charley Arnold said at breakfast: 'There is an old house across the green which I am going to sell for Dr. Huntingford who used to keep a school there; it has a nice panelled room which I think you night like to see.' Thither my wife and I made our way, and found the room with fine Georgian panelling and marble window-slabs, from which we wandered to other rooms ceiled to our amazement with splendid Jacobean plaster fretwork, as fine as I have ever seen. The house was smothered with accretions added for the purposes of a school, and all the best rooms were fitted up as boys' dormitories; but all that admitted of being swept away and rectified, as a practised eye could easily see, though to the inexperienced the house looked gloomy and dismal enough.

I spent the rest of the day drawing the ceilings and the housekeeper brought us mulberries from an ancient tree in the old-fashioned garden, which seemed old enough to have been planted when the house was built in the reign of James I. In the following February I met Dr. Huntingford by appointment on the spot. The local jerry-builder had it in his mind to buy and pull down the old house and run a road through the site with villas right and left. Dr. Huntingford, I think, had a sort of lingering love for the place and a wish to save it form this desecration, so I became the possessor for £3,700 and the jerry-builder was left tearing his hair because he had not offered £4,000.

The next thing was to reduce the house to habitable proportions. The original Jacobean house of ten gables had received, about the middle of the eighteenth century, the addition of a Georgian wing in which was the oak-panelled dining room, the first lure held out to us.

I set to work to pull down a great drawing room, a pile of dormitories and a large dining hall, the removal of which restored the proper light to several of the old rooms.

This and a picturesque wooden wing at one side was more than enough for us. I had the work done without a contract under the direction of Edwin Long, my old clerk of works, who looked after my work at Winchester Cathedral. Estcourt of Gloucester, who had built the Schools at Oxford, was the builder and he insisted on charging me only cost price. On completion I gave him a silver cup with a commemorative inscription.

The work was begun on 25th March 1887 and we slept in our new home for the first time on 25th July. Eagle House, Wimbledon,[1] is a well-preserved example of the private residence of a London merchant in the reign of James I. All round the capital the little country towns and villages contained mansions with gardens, orchards, and meadow-land, to which wealthy citizens repaired to exchange the narrow and unwholesome lanes of the City for green trees and sweet country air (Plate 7).

Robert Bell, the builder of Eagle House (in about 1613), was born in 1564. He was a member of the Girdlers' Company, a Deputy Alderman, an original member of the East India Company with a factor in Amsterdam and a partner in London.

In spite of our reductions the house was so much larger than our numbers required that we were able to keep most of the handsomest rooms as sitting rooms. The hall – the old living room of the original building – with its restored oriel opened pleasantly into the garden. The great room above, with its splendid fretwork ceiling in which are the arms of Robert Bell and Alice his wife, became the library. Another room opening out of this with a good ceiling, was the drawing-room; and one (traditionally Pitt's room) with still another fine ceiling, opening into the library, was our room. Above were several rambling attics with a little hidden place, which led still upward to a sort of hidden chamber in the hollow of the roof, which in the days of the school was known as the 'murder chamber', and supposed to be haunted and caused many a thrill to the boys who slept near it. At one time

Eagle House, Wimbledon, 1810

The Library at Eagle House, Wimbledon

Pitt's Room at Eagle House,
Wimbledon

The Garden at Eagle
House, Wimbledon

I used to look forward to building myself a house, but on the whole I am glad I did not, for I think I should never have been contented with it and should have wanted to sell it and build a better. And there is a wonderful interest about owning and living in an ancient house with a history. From the old deeds and other sources I made out almost everybody who had lived in it. Pitt had often drunk his port wine at Grenville's[2] table in the oak panelled dining room. Nelson and Lady Hamilton had sat in the yellow parlour with the fine ceiling, of which I found a replica at Audley End. We were very happy in our beautiful old house, and the garden grew more and more lovely year by year. Often after having travelled abroad or in England, as we stood on the terrace and looked back along the lawn to the mellow old brick walls hung with cluster creepers we would say: 'We have seen nothing prettier than this since we left it.'

Among our pleasantest new acquaintances were the Richmond Ritchies;[3] she, the daughter of Thackeray and herself famous in literature. A great number of Americans used to come with introductions to Thackeray's daughter and she often brought them to see our house. To commemorate the Queen's Jubilee the Prince of Wales devised the establishment of an Imperial Institute to serve as a central office for the use of all parts of the Empire and as a meeting-place for all imperial purposes.

Six architects, of whom I was one, were asked to make designs in competition at an adequate remuneration. Among others were Deane of Dublin, Rowand Anderson[4] of Edinburgh, Aston Webb,[5] Bell,[6] and Collcutt[7] of London. The competition was won by Collcutt, who carried out his design as we see it. Alfred Waterhouse,[8] who was the assessor, told

Eagle House, Wimbledon. Alice Jackson in the vegetable garden

me that when my design was unpacked he said, 'Oh, that's the one!' but that my planning was inferior. I think he was right.

My book on Dalmatia in three substantial volumes was published on 20th June 1887. I had every reason to be satisfied with its reception and with the reviews. The *Edinburgh Review* gave it a long article and pleased me much by its appreciation of my wife's courageous encounter with the difficulties and dangers we had undergone.

A few days before the book appeared I read a paper by invitation before the Royal Institute of British Architects, and chose Dalmatia as my subject. My sketches were all put into frames and hung around the room. Before the meeting I dined with the council. Charles Barry[9] was in the Chair and as the guest of the evening I was placed next to him. In an interval of the dinner he turned to me and to my surprise asked me 'Why don't you join the Institute?' It seemed to me hardly a fair question to put to a guest, especially as he must have known well enough the reason, which prevented Norman Shaw, Bodley, and a score of well-known leading men as well as myself from belonging to it. So I said 'That is too long a story to go into here.' 'Well,' said he, 'make it a short one.' Of course I said no more, but I was rather put out by it. That I had not joined the Institute at the beginning of my career was partly due to accident. I think none, or very few of us, did from Spring Gardens. With the insolence and ignorance of youth we used to deride it – I dare say quite unfairly – as an assembly of old fogies. I now think that the Institute of those days fulfilled a very useful purpose. It was a learned society where architects could meet and discuss and hear papers read, and make use of a fine library. It also did good work in regulating and formulating the professional side of an architect's practice and settling the terms of his remuneration. In fact it was to the architect somewhat as the Royal Institution is to the man of science, a society open for the use of every member of the craft who could get proposed and seconded and pay his footing, with this difference that the members bound themselves by certain rules of professional conduct.

But this innocent and useful character underwent a change when the pernicious notion of making architecture a close profession hedged in by barriers of diploma and privilege began to make way. It started, I well remember, with some correspondence in the building papers – I think the *Building News* began it – about the social status of the architect. Why was it that architects were looked down upon and denied the same social rank as the lawyer and the doctor? Clearly, because they had no diploma to show, like the men of those professions. This shocking state of things must be remedied. Architects must be put on the same footing as they, and be made gentleman by Act of Parliament; and then I suppose their wives might go down to dinner before the attorney and apothecary. I think I am not exaggerating the stupid and vulgar arguments of the first movement towards what is now called Registration. Of course they could not be used seriously if it came to legislation, and so the promoters began to talk of the dignity of the profession and the protection of the public by offering them duly certified professors of architecture. The notion spread, though legislation was only a distant prospect; but in an evil hour the Institute resolved to exact qualifications from its members and to admit them only by examination. This was admittedly the first step towards putting the Institute into a position like the Law Society and closing the profession against all who were not Institute men.

Against this purely *professional* view of architecture those of us protested strongly to whom it stands primarily as an *art*, rather than as a *profession*. We held that artistic qualifications did not admit of test by examination; that not half the members of the Institute itself were really architects, the majority being surveyors who dabbled in architecture with the assistance of 'ghosts'; that no examination that could be framed would exclude such men in the future; and that to issue them to the world hall-marked as architects – that is, artists in building – would be lying and ridiculous imposture. Nothing, we held, would do more to damage the position and quench the hope of our art than to legalise an unworthy standard of proficiency, and nothing would do more to widen the breach between architecture and the sister arts of painting and sculpture than this proposed scheme to shut it within the barriers of a close profession.

With these views, of course, it was impossible for us to enter the ranks of the Institute. I personally have always been friendly with its members and have often attended their meetings and read papers at their invitation, and they have more than once done me the honour to nominate me, though not a member of their body, for public competitions. But to the typical Institute man – like Charles Barry, for instance, whose attack on me I have mentioned – it was gall and wormwood to see men practising prosperously outside their gates. All sorts of promises were held out to us. 'Come in,' they said. 'You will find many supporters and you may be able to bring the Institute round to your views.' I remember on one occasion when I had been reading a paper their Secretary, Mr. White,[10] pointed to the presidential throne and said: 'Ah, Mr. Jackson, you have great influence, but how much greater it would be from that chair.' Street actually did induce Norman Shaw by arguments such as these to join for a short time, but he found himself hopelessly out of sympathy with their policy and quite helpless, and so he speedily withdrew.

But the great fight took place later, and I must not anticipate. (See Appendix II.)

In January 1888 there was an election of an Associate at the Royal Academy and I was very nearly successful. It lay between Arthur Blomfield[11] and myself, and in the final ballot Blomfield beat me by a neck. As for Alice, she vowed she would go to no more private views or soirées till she went by right, as the wife of a member. I wrote to congratulate

Blomfield, which pleased him, for, as he said in his reply, it might so easily have been the other way.

Several new and interesting works came in the year. In August I went to stay with Sir Henry Fludyer[12] at Ayston in Rutland to meet the Governors of Uppingham School about some new buildings, which resulted in a new house for the headmaster, with class-rooms adjoining, and afterwards the conversion of the old house, which had been formed in the original hospital, into a school library with other class-rooms and common rooms for masters. In Uppingham School I had a sort of family interest, for my three uncles had been boys there, and somewhere about the end of the eighteenth century the Rev. Jeremiah Jackson, formerly Fellow of St. John's Cambridge, was headmaster. Sir Henry Fludyer says Jackson got the school up to ninety-nine boys but never could get the hundredth; and this number was never reached again till Edward Thring came and made a great school of it.

Early in 1895 I was commissioned to design some more buildings for Uppingham School. Hitherto the school had been hidden from the High Street by houses which it was now proposed to pull down so as to give the school at last a frontage to the street with a gateway tower – to do in fact what I had done for Brasenose at Oxford.

I was sent for to refit the chapel at Blenheim. The chapel had been mauled by some bungler, whose work I did not succeed in ejecting, and so I did not do quite all I should have liked.[13] The house, which I had never seen before, struck me as amazingly fine; and the whole thing, with the approach through successive courts and the men in a sort of antique costume at the gate, had a superb effect. The great central hall is disappointing and fails for want of detail, but the great rooms where the family live are grand, almost too grand for comfort. They are all vaulted in stone, and one I remember has the vault beautifully arabesqued in colour in an earlier style than Vanbrugh's. The Duchess's bedroom, which she showed me, is on the same floor as the living-rooms, and has a vast bed as big as a house, with a canopy of blue silk hangings that looks 20 feet high. One would be lost in it. The whole of the basement, into which the Duke took me, is vaulted in stone. The great room which contained the Sunderland Library reaches from end to end of one side wing and is lined with book-cases, now, alas! empty and screened with curtains to mask their emptiness. The great Duke has a monument in the chapel, and I remember the Duke showing me in some gallery or lumber-room his great ancestor's campaigning trunks.

Another and to me delightful piece of work was the designing of a grand pianoforte for Athelstan Riley[14] whose house at Kensington Court[15] I had built some years before. And now the grand piano was to give the finishing touch to the house. The piano was by Broadwood, who made the case in the rough. I decorated it with inlays of satinwood and ebony, tortoiseshell and mother of pearl, and lined the inside with gesso of scrolls of foliage in gold

Blenheim Palace: Design for an Organ Case in the Chapel

Grand Piano designed by T.G.J. and made by Broadwood & Sons

House at Kensington Court (now part of the Milestone Hotel)

on a ruby ground. There were novelties in the stand, the legs, and the brac-
ing that some critics said would revolutionise pianoforte construction in the
future. The keys were inlaid, and the hinges, lock-plates, and other furniture elaborately designed. This piano has often been illustrated and exhibited and has become almost as famous as the Burne-Jones one belonging to
the Horners of Mells. For the inlaying I employed Mr. Bessant,[16] whom the
Duke of Marlborough had introduced to me and who made the fittings for

the chapel at Blenheim. I drew the whole of the ornament full size myself, for it was not a matter in which anyone could help me.

Athelstan Riley gave a fancy dress ball which we attended. I went in Jacobean dress and Alice in contemporary style, her dress being my design and made by Madame Oliver Holmes of Bond Street.

In 1888 schemes began to be propounded for widening the Strand and taking other methods for making the traffic easier. It was perhaps natural that the first idea should be to clear away the two fine churches of St. Mary-le-Strand and St. Clement Danes, which stood in the middle of the street. The obvious thing to the ordinary civic mind, and no doubt the simplest way out of the difficulty, was to blunder on in a straight line from Charing Cross to Temple Bar, knocking down all that stood in the way. I wrote a letter to *The Times* pleading for the preservation of these two churches, which might easily be managed with a little contrivance. Others took the matter up and the London County Council consented to receive a deputation and to hear what we had to say. We were very well received and found that the council were unfeignedly surprised to find we laid such store by these buildings. It did not seem to have occurred to them that they were of any architectural interest. They asked us what style they were in, what degree of merit we attached to them, and they seemed both impressed and astonished to find we thought so highly of them. It is only fair to say that the Council altered its views after this enlightenment and that every subsequent scheme has not only respected the churches but made the most of them.

I think it was on this deputation that I first met Philip Webb,[17] the architect. Webb had never mixed with other architects nor joined any of the societies. He had been associated with the early Pre-Raffaelites and with William Morris and his companions, and shared, though I know not to what extent, their somewhat aesthetic Socialist opinions. Needless to say he never cared for a large practice or for more than he could do by himself. In his office of two or three small rooms in Gray's Inn you found perhaps two assistants. Consequently his works are few; but his influence on the architecture of his day was very great. If I were asked to name the two men whose work has most profoundly affected the current of modern architecture in England I should unhesitatingly say Philip Webb and Norman Shaw.

It was chiefly among Norman Shaw's pupils that the idea originated of the Art Workers' Guild, a fraternity which unites in a common brotherhood artists of all kinds – architects, painters, sculptors, designers, stained-glass men, printers, book-binders, cabinet-makers, paper-hangers, and still others. They meet once a fortnight, and someone reads a paper on his own craft, which is followed by others and by a brisk discussion in which all join at their pleasure, whatever their own pursuit may be. It is understood that everyone freely reveals all he knows and keeps back no secrets. The usefulness of this interchange of information is beyond price. Whatever one might want to know about any process one was pretty sure to be able to learn from a brother worker in that craft, and the methods of the different arts so freely discussed could not but have a harmonising result, bringing together those decorative arts, which had been so long sundered.

James Powell belonged to it and among others were several members of the Academy – Brett,[18] Dicksee,[19] Murray, Richmond,[20] Onslow Ford,[21] and most of the leading decorative artists, Walter Crane,[22] Heywood Sumner, Howard Mee, Selwyn Image,[23] and above all, William Morris. I remember Morris once giving us an evening on paper-making, and bringing his paper-maker, Batchelor,[24] who made a sheet for us in the room, showing how by a dextrous handshake, difficult to acquire and sometimes, strange to say, lost again, the workman secures that interlacing of the linen fibres which makes the durable hand-made article. Many years afterwards, when I was staying with Sir William Portal[25] at Laverstoke, he took me over his mills, where all the bank-note paper is made by hand and over the purest linen without any chemical adulteration. Trout play about in the millstream under the windows. There I found that the man in charge was the son of Morris's friend, Batchelor. I remember that on the evening of Morris's lecture Batchelor produced a sheet of Double Elephant paper and told us that if it were fairly suspended two men might hang by it. The great feature of these evenings, were the demonstrations by which the papers were illustrated. When enamelling was the subject there was a gas-stove in the room and enamels were prepared and burned. When plasterwork was under discussion modelling and casting were going on before our eyes. I remember reading a paper on Intarsiatura, which was afterwards published, and showing a large number of tracings from old examples and also having one of Bessant's men cutting out and mounting veneers in the room. We also had exhibitions of all kinds of art and for some years an annual display of the members' own work in various crafts. This was superseded by the Arts and Crafts Exhibitions, which grew out of the Guild.

In the beginning of 1889 I received a letter from the Fabbriceria of Zara in Dalmatia saying that the city was desirous of completing the Campanile of their cathedral, which had been left imperfect by Archbishop Valaresso in the fifteenth century. They said further that in Dalmatia there was a *mancanza d'architetti* and they wanted to know whether I was willing to undertake the work. I wrote to tell them what they wanted to know about our professional terms, but when they pleaded poverty I offered to do the work for nothing if they would repay me expenses incurred. This produced a very grateful acceptance and so I made a design and sent it out for approval. They were pleased with it and decided to carry it out, but first of all they had to get the consent of the Commission of Ancient Monuments at Vienna, and here difficulties began. The government apparently disliked the work being done by the Zaratini at their own expense instead of applying to the government to do it for them; but of course they could not very well object on that ground. The employment of a foreign architect naturally put them out vastly, and for a time there seemed little chance of the deadlock coming to an end, for neither side would give way. I had in the previous year corresponded with Herr Kupka, engineer of the Northern Railway of Austria, who had been introduced to me by a Major Chamberlain and who wanted to translate my book on Dalmatia into German. I now wrote to him and asked his assistance, and in the autumn my wife and I went to Vienna ourselves to see what could be done personally.

After crossing at Calais, we went by Brussels and Cologne on to the Hotel Wasum at Bacharach. We caught the Danube steamer at Passau, slept at Linz and reached Vienna the following day.

I had written to the British Ambassador, Sir Augustus Paget, who had befriended me when he was at Rome in 1880, and told him what had passed between the people of Zara and myself and what difficulties were being raised by the Central Commission in Vienna. Sir Augustus was away, but he recommended me to the Chargé d'affaires, who was very kind in introducing me to Baron Helfurt, the President of the Central Commission of Ancient Monuments.

They all professed to be quite satisfied with the design and one would have imagined all difficulties were at an end. Professor Hansen, the architect in charge of Dalmatian monuments, called and was very friendly, which was good of him, for I suppose he would have liked to do the tower himself.

I left all the designs with Hansen for consideration and we left Vienna for the Semmering fondly believing everything to be settled. It was, however, nearly a year more before the Campanile affair was decided.

Shortly after our return, I had the unpleasant experience of serving on the Grand Jury at the Old Bailey. We sat for two days listening to stories of crime, violence and filth that haunted me for days afterwards. When our work was done we were invited as a great treat to be taken over Newgate. This, it seems, is one of the privileges of the Grand Jury. I had the curiosity to go, but was sorry for it afterwards. We were shown all the sordid horrors of the place, the condemned cell, the apparatus of death, and the flagged passage under which the murderers are buried, each with a single letter cut into the wall opposite. This passage was the way by which prisoners passed to the court for trial, so that those on whom the shadow of the gallows was already falling walked over the bones of their predecessors in crime and the spot where their own were shortly to be laid beside them.

In 1889 I shifted my office to 14 Buckingham Street, Strand, overlooking the river and Embankment Gardens. The house is on the site of that where Pepys lived and it is also said that Etty the painter lived there. My rooms were on the second floor. On the opposite side of the street was, till

1907, a house with fine panelling and handsome plaster ceilings, where Peter the Great once lived.

In 1890 I went by myself to Hoorn in North Holland, a most delightful place, full of good sketching. There I found myself at dinner next to an English painter who turned out to be Hook,[26] R.A., who was painting there. I said to him that Hoorn was an ideal place for artists, for I had been guarded all day by a policeman with a stick who drove away the boys and ragamuffins who would have otherwise have plagued me to death. 'All that,' said Hook, 'you owe to me. Yesterday I was painting on the Quay and Mrs. Hook was sitting by me, when a nice woman came out of a cottage and offered us some tea. We were just saying what a pleasant civilised people the Dutch were, when some lads came by and threw handfuls of sand all over my picture. I went to the police-office to complain. They were very civil and apologetic and said they would do what they could and would send a policeman to keep guard the next day, but that there were only two policemen in Hoorn and they were afraid they could not always be occupied in protecting artists.' (Plate 9).

Alice joined me at Flushing and we made our way to Ziericksee, the place which Mondragon, the Spanish Captain, stormed by wading across the shallow channel that makes an island of it. This was the most picturesque place we saw and we spent several days there. But the worst of both Holland and Belgium for sketchers is the boys and, for the matter of that, the girls too, who make it unbearable, so that your only chance of quiet is during school time. I had my revenge at Bruges. A crowd of odious urchins had been leaping and grimacing all round while I was trying to paint a sunset. When I had done and began to pack up, the excitement became intense, and they all pressed in to see the shutting up of the paint-box. I had my can of water, filthy with dregs of vermilion and all sorts of colours, and as the biggest of my tormentors, a great lout of seventeen, poked his nose over the box I discharged all this dirty water in his face. It ran all down his shirt and waistcoat and got into his eyes and quite overcame him. The current of public opinion instantly veered round and all their jeers and ridicule were diverted from us to him. Such is human nature!

We came home from Ostend, the Brighton of Belgium, but then out of season and in a melancholy state of desertion. The crossing of two and a half or three hours was so smooth that a poor, delicate lady sitting with us, who gave herself up for lost as soon she came on board, asked us just as we were nearing Dover harbour why we were so long in starting, and was much pleased to find she had got over safely without knowing it.

18

1891-93

History of Wadham College Published
Elected an ARA ~ Work at Cambridge
Restoration of St. Mary's Church spire, Oxford ~ William Morris

In 1891 I was busy with another book, nothing less than the history of my own college and of Nicholas and Dorothy Wadham, the Founder and Foundress. With this object I had transcribed all the building accounts and read and made extracts from the minute books, from the date of the foundation to the present day, together with much other matter, including the Foundress's letters and those of her steward and factotum, John Arnold. These original documents threw a good deal of light on the mode of building and of designing buildings in the sixteenth and seventeenth centuries, and I discovered the real architect of Wadham is one William Arnold,[1] who worked on it himself with his son or brother and employed workmen under him. He was, in fact, one of the last of the craftsmen architects, soon to be extinguished by the learned professional architect who designed but did not put his hand to the hammer and chisel.

In the autumn my wife and I went into Devon to visit the old homes of the Wadhams and their tombs at Ilminster. We hired a pony-trap and drove to Ilton to see the Wadham Almshouses and what was left of Merifield, the mansion where Nicholas Wadham kept up such hospitality that, as old Fuller quaintly says, 'His hospital house was an inn at all times, a court at Christmas.'

We then moved on to Seaton, on the Devonshire coast, to see Branscombe church, where there are other Wadham tombs and the old manor house at Edge, the Dower house of the Wadhams, where Dorothy died.

On 4th April 1893 the book was published by the Clarendon Press. It had been a laborious but a pious task and I had determined that the college to which I owed so much should be the most completely illustrated of any in either University.

We made an expedition to Exeter and back; the interior of its cathedral, I can't tell why, always delights me more than that of any other in the kingdom. The season was late but the weather was warm and pleasant, and we finished our holiday by going back to Oxford and rowing up to town, or at least as far as Molesey, where the rain stopped us and we got home wet to the skin.

In 1892 we were surprised by a visit from our friend Salghetti Drioli of Zara. He came down to Wimbledon and was astonished to see no rocks, whereas in Dalmatia you see little else. Our little Hugh wanted to know whether there were savages in his country, which tickled him a good deal, thinking of the Croats, his political enemies, and he heartily affirmed that there were plenty of them.

Hugh was now at school at Temple Grove, East Sheen, under my old college friend Edgar.[2] Temple Grove was a fine old house with large grounds, and had traditions of William Temple[3] and Swift.

Hugh was being worked up for Winchester where he was to go. As a scholar I fear his performances were not very brilliant, but he showed promise as a cricketer, and when he came home Smithers the gardener had to bowl to him all afternoon on the lawn.

Cartoons of schoolboys done for the amusement of Hugh and Basil Jackson

Temple Grove – East Sheen

Dear Father

I hope you are quite well. My hamper has not yet come, or else they have not yet had me to unpack it. There is a rumour about the school that there is an angel in the chapel, and several chaps say they have seen it, but I do not believe in it one bit. I hope you will come and see me next Sunday.

Ever your loving son

Hugh Jackson

Temple Grove was near enough for a Sunday afternoon walk, and I often went over to see Hugh. It was five miles across the common and I hardly touched a road the whole way.

Changes were taking place around us in Wimbledon. The old school cricket field that had belonged to Eagle House was being cut up for building, and in order to protect ourselves I had to buy ½(?) of an acre – but we have had our money's worth by the pleasure that it has given. We planted it with apple trees, made a tennis court, and at the lower end a rock garden, which was Alice's special favourite and which year by year is a blaze of colour from April to June, full of alyssum, aubretia and saxifrage and all

Bookplate. Designed by T.G.J. for the library of St. David's Cathedral

sorts backed up with the peonies and oriental poppies and later on phloxes and michaelmas daisies which prepare the way for an overpowering burst of Autumn asters, the haunt of red admiral butterflies and painted ladies.

Of course we surrounded it with a wall on which we grew peaches and plums, apricots and nectarines and these with the orchard trees made a brave show when in blossom which were valued almost as much as the fruit.

Our holiday in August was unambitious; a real domestic affair for the first time; children and all with a maid to St. David's. Dean Allen although ninety was as young as ever and as enthusiastic about his beautiful Cathedral; he commissioned me to design an altar cross which I had made by Mr. Krall[4] of Langham Place, a brother of the Art Workers' Guild, and also a bookplate for the library.

When the weather was bad there was always the Cathedral in which to work, full of good subjects, and I made a sketch of the choir with the Dean and old Morgan the stone-mason standing in it, and Morgan was so delighted that I gave him a copy of it which amazed him: 'Is it all done by hand, Sir?'

There was an election of three associates to the R.A. pending in 1892 and several of my friends were doing their best for me. Norman Shaw wrote:

I don't attempt to conceal from myself or from you that elections are gloriously uncertain, often comically so, and of course they may elect three

Dean Allen and Morgan, the stonemason, at St. David's Cathedral, 1892

painters. We architects generally come off second best and often nowhere *but we shall try.*

However, I was at last safely landed within the doors of the Royal Academy, and on 23rd February I attended the Council in the evening to receive my diploma. The pleasant part of my election perhaps was the flood of congratulations that poured in from all my friends and acquaintances. Case[5] of Corpus Christi College wrote from Oxford that the election is 'to the University of Wren a happy event'. My college was pleased and the headmaster of Brighton College gave the boys a half-holiday.

It is customary for the newly elected members to call on the R.A.s and I spent two or three afternoons in that way. Most of them were out, some were engaged with models or sittings, and those that I did see were unfeignedly bored by the interruption during the precious hours of day-light. I never finished my visiting but had to give it up half-completed. A wider introduction is afforded just before the opening of the Summer Exhibition, when nearly every one of the seventy members is present at the varnishing days when we all lunch together, and on the first day the health of the new members is drunk. In my reply I said that in the happy triple election of a painter, a sculptor, and an architect one might hope to see the earnest of that reconciliation of the three arts so long sundered from one another, to which very many of us were hopefully looking forward. With my first Academy dinner, the first election, and the first course of visiting in the schools, my initiation as an Associate member may be considered complete. Beyond these functions the part played by the Associates does not reach; and till they become Academicians, which many of them never do, they know no more of the inner working of the institution than they did when they were outsiders.

Though I had done so much at Oxford in building, both for the University and a great many colleges, Cambridge apparently had never thought of me. This year (1892), however, I was sent for to design the new Geological Museum which was to be built with the aid of a fund raised to commemorate Professor Sedgwick[6] and to bear his name.

It was proposed the University should augment with half as much again to build an adequate museum with class-rooms and laboratories on the south side of Downing Street, where once was the Botanic Garden, now nearly covered with university laboratories.

I went down for the first time on 10th March and was the guest of Professor Hughes[7] the geologist, whose the Museum was to be. I went with him to dine at Trinity and made many acquaintances.

It was interesting to me to compare the two Universities, both buildings and men, and to notice how very much they differed. In the Cambridge colleges there is much less of the quasi-conventual look of our Oxford ones; the gardens are more like those of a great country-house, which, indeed, the buildings themselves somewhat resemble. The street views at Cambridge will not bear comparison with those at Oxford, but they have some things that surpass ours. There is nothing at our University to equal the Chapel at King's and the great Court at Trinity. You must go to Venice to find anything to compare with the scene as you row up the Cam at the backs of the colleges, passing along now a green lawn at the foot of some stately pile, now the ancient walls of a famous college that rise directly from the water, and threading one after another a succession of beautiful bridges with sumptuous gates of ironwork that lead from garden to garden over-hung by fine trees and embosomed in luxuriant shrubs.

As for the men at the two places, they differ, I think, almost as much as their buildings. At Cambridge there is much more open fire of criticism and discussion than with us, and I have been present at very acrimonious skirmishes which in Oxford would have been represented by a reserved silence, not perhaps less expressive.

But to compare Oxford and Cambridge is unnecessary; they are two beautiful sisters whose charms are so different that they do not conflict. My task there was not very easy. There was a good deal of contentious feeling about the extent and character of the Museum. This and shortness of money made the scheme hang fire. I made my design and it was generally approved, but many things happened and some years went by before it was realised; and when, after all, it came into being it had little resemblance to its original conception and was, indeed, on another site.

I was still busy at Oxford, adding to the Boys' High School, designing a barge for Oriel, my first attempt at boat-building, the tutors' house for Balliol, and an organ loft, organ case, and other work in the Brasenose Chapel. In June I was asked to examine the tower and spire of St. Mary's Church, as the face of one of the statues had fallen to the ground close to the door by which the Vice-Chancellor enters the church, and it was feared more might follow. I found that a great deal of the new masonry – put in when the restoration by Mr. Buckler[8] took place – was in a very dangerous state, one part in particular threatened a fall of some tons of stone. I obtained leave to scaffold the tower at once, and put some protection at this point to secure it from immediate catastrophe, and the repairs began before the end of the year. As might have been expected, it did not pass without provoking an attack from 'Anti-scrape', to use the familiar nickname of the

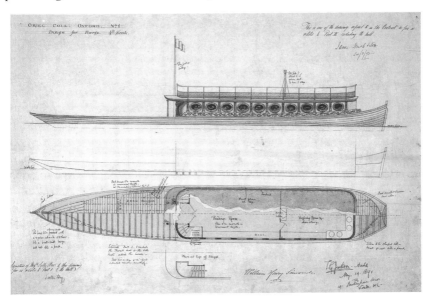

Oriel Barge. Contract drawing

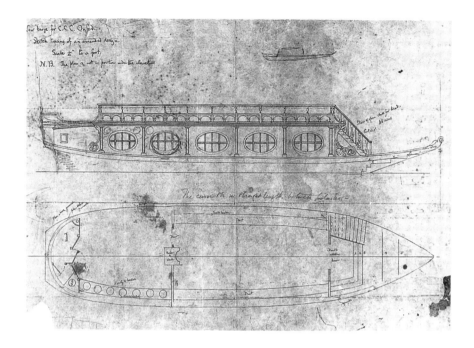

Corpus Christi Barge. Design

Society for the Protection of Ancient Buildings. In May William Morris took it up. He came to see me about the statues, and I explained to him the defects which, in my opinion, made it dangerous to replace them where they could not be approached, where the decay that was bringing them to ruin could not be watched, and where they constituted a danger both to the church and to the passers by. There was a meeting of Convocation to consider the matter of St. Mary's, and I suggested that Morris and Sir William Richmond[9] should come down and attend, after having made a thorough examination of the fabric and the figures. Accordingly we met at Paddington and went down by the morning express. Morris was delightful and told us old stories he had been unearthing and we had a very pleasant journey. When we got to St. Mary's we scaled the tower and then had to get out on to the scaffolding and walk around the outside so as to examine the statues. Richmond declined to come out and clung to the ladder, saying it was like to give him gout as it was. Morris was bolder and came round with me. He was, I think, surprised to find how much modern work there was in the statues. Richmond said, 'I'll tell you what I should do, I should whip them all round with copper wire'; but old Axtell the mason said, 'But you know, sir, if the wire broke in one place all the rest would be useless.' Richmond then said he thought there was nothing to be done with them. Morris said they ought to be banded with iron to hold them together. I pointed to a piece, as big as my hand, which was cracked and nearly ready to come off, and asked him what he would do to prevent pieces such as that falling through his iron cage; for such a lump as that I showed him was enough to settle the business of a passer-by. 'I should put something below,' said he, 'to catch the pieces.' 'What would you put?' I ventured to inquire. 'Oh,' said he in a hurry,' that I leave to you.' These suggestions did not seem to be very helpful, but no others were forthcoming. We adjourned to luncheon at Wadham, where the Warden was to entertain us before Convocation, which met at 2 o'clock. I was curious to know whether Morris intended to suggest to the University his iron cage with baskets below to catch the falling fragments. He confined himself, however, to pleading for the 'ragged regiment' (as he called it) generally. But at this meeting I had to defend not only my opinion about the statues but also my design for the completion of the pinnacles. Case, the Professor of Moral Philosophy, was bitten by some architectural tarantula which sent him all agog to design the pinnacles himself, and he produced his scheme and seriously urged its adoption in preference to mine. No decision on this point, however, was come to that day, but Case carried his scheme so far as to induce the University to have full-size models both of his design and mine, put up on the tower. I don't think anyone was in favour of his scheme, except himself, from first to last. The model, at all events, was fatal to it and the decision of the University was promptly made against it. Altogether, what with gratuitous interference of amateurs and faddists, I was considerably bored in the matter of St. Mary's, though the work itself interested me much.

1893 was the hottest year since 1868 and the thermometer in our garden went up to 131° in the sun. Alice and the boys escaped to Eastbourne, where I paid them flying visits.

On one of these occasions Basil then six and a half years old frightened us by going all alone to the top of Beachy Head. We thought he was lost and started off in all directions to find him. We set the police to work, imagining all sorts of disasters – falls over the cliff – being caught by the tide, or whatever else might befall his little inexperienced self.

But when we returned to our lodgings in despair, there sat the gentleman on the sofa as cool as a cucumber and wandering why we were making such a fuss. So much savoir-faire at that early age, we thought, promised well for the future, but it had given us a bad turn.

19

1893

Visit to see the completed Campanile at Zara ~ Mostar and Sarajevo

I had been astounded at receiving an Address from the Fabbriceria of Zara, expressive of their gratitude for what I had done for them, and with it a gold medal struck in my honour and four copies in aluminium,[1] and at the beginning of 1893 I received a letter from Dr. Faccini, one of the Canons of the Cathedral of Zara, written on behalf of the Fabbriceria, to report the progress of the Campanile. He said they had hung and rung their bells and wished to send me a telegraphic message of compliment on the occasion, but were not sure how to address it. It was, therefore, high time for me to go and see the work if I was to be of any use, though the whole direction of the building (subject of course to my instructions) had been entrusted to a local architect named Gillhüber. We had also a kind of longing to revisit our old hunting-ground. So on 23rd September we once more set off for Dalmatia.

The hot weather had gone in England and we had a chilly journey till we had passed the St. Gothard and reached Milan where it was hot enough. At Trieste where we dined with the Greenhams, they had had a spell of cold, which luckily had disposed of the mosquitoes, which are an awful plague, especially near the harbour in Trieste.

We sailed or rather steamed in the afternoon for Zara. The Austrian Lloyd boats were very good, the officers pleasant fellows and the company at dinner sociable.

We reached Zara on the morning of the 28th and expected anxiously the first view of the new Campanile, which towered above anything else in a way that surprised me and had an imposing effect, though the *guglia* or spire was still two-thirds incomplete.

As the ship was being warped to the quay in the harbour, where the French and Venetians burst the boom and assailed the city in 1204, we saw Salghetti Drioli waiting to receive us, and when we landed we were welcomed by several members of the Fabbriceria who escorted us to the inn, Canonico Faccini, my correspondent, Signor Filippi, the Chairman of the

25 Siena – Cortile of the Palazzo Communale

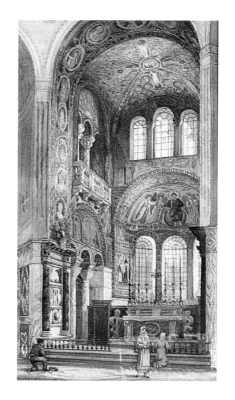

26 S. Vitale, Ravenna

27 Ancona, 1881

28 Hvar – View of the city with the tower of
S. Marco

29 *Korcula*

30 *Hvar – Loggia and Forte Spagnuolo*

31 Dubrovnik

32 Ragusa. Rector's Palace

33 Rab. View of the Campanile from the sea

34 Mostar – the bridge

New Campanile, Zadar Cathedral

Board and Signor Gillhüber, the local architect-in-charge. The inn was an improvement on our former experience. The new inn – Grand Hotel di Zara – was in an old palace and had commodious apartments, and here they had prepared for us a very large room with the conventional oval table on an island of carpet, a sofa against the wall, and half a dozen chairs of monumental weight upholstered in red velvet placed in a circle ready for a reception.

At eleven o'clock, after we had tidied ourselves, we went to the Campanile, where Signor Filippi, Gillhüber, and several other gentlemen met us.

First we visited Gillhüber's office, where all my drawings were laid out, and he explained how the work had been done strictly he said, according to my instructions, though I found afterwards that that was not so. Then we went up and I made a brief examination stage by stage. In the top storey were the great bells, and there was the mechanician, who had contrived a keyboard by which tunes could be played on five bells, so far as five bells would serve. A flag was run up in our honour and 'God Save the Queen' was played on the bells in a queer fashion, and altogether we had a very flattering reception. Shortly after noon Signor Filippi took me to call on the Archbishop. The nice, kind, refined old man whom I remembered – Monsignor Maupas – was no more. His Successor appointed by the government, as a supporter of the Slav party – much to the disgust of the Zaratini who were opposed to it – was Monsignor Raicevich, a Ragusan. Salghetti Drioli said Raicevich commanded no respect in Zara and Gelcich, our Ragusan friend, said he was 'una vera penitenza per Zara'. So high do feelings run between Latin and Slav. The Archbishop, a tall, imposing personage between sixty and seventy, received me very courteously, and led us to a room where we sat continental fashion against the wall in a corner. He then made a long speech about the Campanile, to which I had little occasion to reply, as he was a great talker and liked a good listener. Before separating he engaged us to dine with him on Saturday. Filippi, who clearly did not like him, excused himself on the ground of being in the doctor's hands.

We spent the rest of the day in seeing Drioli's new house and factory of maraschino and in buying a complete Dalmatian costume.[2] Zara was as full of variety and gorgeous dresses as ever, and the delightful little open shops where you see tailors and silversmiths at work were just as we remembered them.

I continue from my wife's diary:

Much disturbed in the early morning before we were dressed, by people coming to our door. First the photographer wishing to take Graham's likeness, and then a man saying at twelve o'clock a deputation was coming from the Fabbriceria. When our visit to the photographer came off he made such an easy business of it that it encouraged me to have mine done as well, but for those we shall have to pay; Graham gets his done for nothing as he apparently stands in the light of a public character … By this time it was necessary to get back to our room and put the table and chairs in the correct circle for the reception of the deputation, and at one o'clock we were to dine at the Archbishop's. At twelve o'clock punctually they arrived, seven of them, including Signor Filippi, who seems to be the chairman, Canonico Faccini, a nice little priest, Ballerin, who acts as secretary, Conte Lantana, a gentleman of property on the island of Ugliano, and three more whose names I did not catch. Signor Filippi made a very complimentary address, expressing the thanks of the Fabbriceria to Graham for his trouble and their satisfaction with the result of his design, and also requesting that he would allow his name to be recorded as the architect of the new Campanile by an inscription to be placed upon it ….

The Archbishop had made himself very beautiful in all his best clothes, a purple cassock with a very thick gold chain round his neck and an enormous jewelled cross, and massive rings on his fingers. He was very gracious and conducted us through several rooms into a small one next to the oratory. Dinner was announced by a man-servant in a very long great coat with silver buttons, and after quite a long walk through rooms and passages we arrived at the dining-room. The secretary and the lady who takes charge of the house made up the company, five in all. The dinner was a very good one and, as usual, a good deal of it. The Archbishop declared he ate and drank very little, but for all that seemed to do nicely and plied his little jokes, of which he was very fond, even more freely after a glass or two of champagne. One was asking me if I did not find Graham a good fellow. He said he liked the look of him and was rarely deceived in people's looks. The pudding was supposed to be an English plum-pudding but consisted of custard and sponge cake and was quite free from plums, so that the resemblance was not great. At this course we were sorely put to it, for only knives were given us to eat it with. However, fortunately some peaches were handed round at the same time, so Graham expressed a wish for a spoon, as he said steel spoilt the taste of the fruit. This elegant way of putting it did not hurt their feelings and we were saved from cutting our own throats ....

At the end of Dinner I was again armed back to the sitting room. The Archbishop being a large man, and clothed in a garment so nearly resembling a woman's dress, it was like taking the arm of a stout female without stays.

Before leaving Zara I made a careful examination of the Campanile, which I regret to say was not built as I should like. The beautiful marble-like stone from Curzola with which it is faced is not properly bonded to the backing, and the bells are hung in a way that will, I fear, shake the tower. After leaving, I wrote a strongly worded letter to the Fabbriceria, urging that at all events the bells should be lowered to the belfry floor, as my plan showed them, and be put in a frame that was independent of the walls. If left as they were I declined all responsibility of the consequences. Nothing was done, however. In Austria, and I believe most continental countries, there are various grades of architects who divide the responsibility. There is first the *Capo-ingeniere*, in this case myself, who makes the design and specification. Then the provincial architect – here a Conte Begna whom I never saw – and lastly Gillhüber, who was the sort of clerk of works, with more authority than usual owing to my absence. To make any alteration would have reflected on Conte Begna, so at least I gathered, and nothing came of my remonstrance I regretted not having visited the work while in progress but I had no idea Gillhüber was such an idiot.

On 3rd October we left Zara for Ragusa, where we were welcomed by our old friend Signor Gelcich, who appeared looking rather older than when we met last but in other respects the same good little soul, with a cigarette never out of his mouth.

Alice's diary continues:

We went to the Duomo to see an old picture, – a Madonna – covered with the exception of the face and hands with rather good silver work, which is carried in processions and they wanted Graham to do a design for a frame for these occasions. Then we walked up the hill and Graham got a sketch looking back on Ragusa. We came back by the old road and looked at the Convent of S.Giacomo where oleanders were flowering in the most lovely way. (Plate 31).

Dubrovnik. The Sponza

Unfortunately this pleasant beginning of our visit was interrupted by a worse fit of gout in my foot than I had ever had before. Gelcich fetched a young Dr. Misetic who prescribed a patent medicine by which he promised to work a speedy cure. It is called 'Liqueur du Dr. De Ville'. He prescribed also a French oil – 'des Marons Indiens' – to be rubbed into the foot when painful.

It is very trying being shut up here with the lovely sunshine outside and the mosquitoes are awful. By burning little cones of Chrysanthemum powder with the windows open and no lights burning one manages to some extent to drive them out, then one is obliged to shut the windows before lighting the candles, or they would all be in again and we have to pass the night in a temperature of a hot English summer. Even then we did not escape being bitten, though we covered our faces with net-like buns in a pastry-cook's shop. After a day we got a better fine large room with a view of the harbour and I made a sketch from the window.

The diary continues:

Oct 10th. Gelcich had asked for a note in the course of the morning saying how Graham was, but instead of writing he sent him a pen-and-ink sketch of his foot in two stages, one with a little devil attacking the joint with tooth and claw, and with a sting in his tail; the other with the little devil starting up in alarm at the sight of the 'Siroppo de Ville' though still

Dubrovnik. Aesculapius capital, the Rector's Palace

holding on by his claws. The motto of the first was '*In possessione*', that of the second '*Sta in forse*'.[3] This pleased immensely and the fame of it has gone all through Ragusa. For all his kindness a sketch of the harbour was also given to Gelcich.

We planned to go to Bosnia and Herzegovina, but were told that no one is allowed to enter without a special passport and that even with that it is certain no sketching would be allowed. So I telegraphed to the British Ambassador at Vienna, asking him to procure a passport and for leave to make drawings of objects of art and costume, and to send permission by telegraph to the Capitano Distrettuale at Ragusa. At last on 11th October I managed to get out for a drive, and on our return the Capitano Distrettuale sent word that leave had come from Vienna for me to go into

Bosnia and sketch as I liked. This was very prompt and courteous on the part both of our Ambassador and of the Austrian Minister, Count Kallay.
The diary continues:

Wed Oct. 12th. Really better and got into the Piazza to breakfast, where I met Baron di Ghetaldi-Gondola, the Podestà of Ragusa. He is really a Ghetaldi, descended from the famous philosopher and mathematician, whose cave in which he conducted his experiments is still shown here.

He was very polite and offered us an introduction to his friend Baron Benko, the Governor of Herzegovina at Mostar. He had heard I had been ill and also of the 'bello scherzo'[4] of the two sketches sent to Gelcich by

Dubrovnik. Dominican Convent

Dubrovnik. Franciscan Convent

way of a bulletin. The fame of this trifling has filled Ragusa, and I am not sure that I shall not in future be remembered in Dalmatia by it rather than by my three volumes or even the Campanile at Zara.

'At the time that your Queen Elizabeth was making laws for regulating the slave trade,' said Baron Gondola, 'the republic of Ragusa made traffic in human flesh illegal. Every Ragusan who had sold a man into slavery was allowed a certain time to find and redeem him. If he succeeded he was still punished with the loss of an eye. But if he failed he was hanged.' This was certainly humanity enforced at the sword's point; but it shows an enlightened view of the evils of slavery at a time when nobody else had got so far as to condemn it.

As we sat under the orange trees in the pretty Franciscan Cloister reading our letters from home, we were suddenly hailed by a loud 'Signor Yakson' and found our friend the Archbishop of Zara, arrayed in purple with his best chain and cross, who was on visit to his native city and lodged in the convent. Gelcich said, 'What is he come for? He is up to something,' and whispered, 'His excellency is a "bestione", an ambitious intriguer and nobody's friend.' The intrigue Gelcich referred to concerned the Bishopric of Ragusa, which was vacant at this time.

We took an affectionate farewell to Gelcich in the evening, for we were to leave early the next morning. We found our carriage in the Piazza at 4.30 a.m. It was just light enough for us to see the Arcade of the Rector's Palace with its grandly sculptured capitals, and the two convents with their graceful Campaniles (Plate 32).

It was still dark when we went on board at Gravosa. We touched Guippana, an island where there are jackals and had a tantalising glimpse of Melida – one of the claimants for St. Paul's shipwreck. We steamed up the Canale della Narenta, a magnificent inlet of the sea and reached Metcovich whence a narrow-guage railway took us to Mostar.

Our special passport saved us all trouble with the police, who had been forewarned of our visit. Here to our surprise we found ourselves in a really good hotel, full of Austrian officers and their ladies, instead of plunging as we expected into semi-barbarism.

We were up early, anxious for our first peep into an Oriental town, for the East was new to both of us. Two minarets met our eyes from our bed-room windows, and we heard the rush of the Narenta over its rocky bed close by. By nine o'clock we were out on a tour of inspection. The position of the town is splendid and bursting with minarets. There are thirty mosques in all and in the Bazaar the owners sat cross-legged smoking and drinking coffee.

We came upon the old Roman bridge[5] and went down to the river to get a good view of it. I made a sketch while we sat on a rock – rather hard after a time – but nice and clean and strange to say we weren't poisoned by bad smells (Plate 34).

After dinner we went to Blagaj where there were ruins of an old mosque, which is now the Miller's house, and he was also the keeper of two bodies of Mohometan Saints, much thought of by the local inhabitants.

The miller's wife who was a Turkish girl showed us the house and made us coffee. We were shown upstairs where there were no beds; a raised divan covered with rugs for the man and the woman slept on the floor which was also covered with bright covered Eastern rugs. Through the sleeping room was a round place that looked like a chapel; it had a dome pierced with stars. However we were told it was not a chapel but a bath. There were some embroidered towels hanging up, and water in a jug as it is said the saints come out of their tombs every evening to wash and pray.

The costumes at Mostar were very varied and we saw some lovely ladies

Venice. Palazzo al Traghetio di S.S. Apostoli

in purple and red velvet jackets short to the waist, with loose sleeves heavily embroidered with gold. Almost all the women wore trousers, so baggy that they looked like skirts. We saw one girl who was lovely. A symphony in yellow, dark orange trousers and a bodice many shades lighter, and over this a dark maroon jacket with gold embroidery. The girls all wear their hair in one plait hanging down behind, and a little biretta on the head like a Turk's cap with a tassel.

The narrow-guage railway that brought us from Metrovich ran to Sarajevo, through a wild mountainous country, winding along narrow ravines, and gradually climbing the Iran Planina, a high table-land. Thence we descended to a great plain, at the far end of which appeared the white houses and sparkling minarets of Sarajevo.

Nothing more Oriental can be conceived than the market at Sarajevo, and if you were brought there blindfolded, you might imagine when your eyes were uncovered that you were in Constantinople.

After returning to Mostar we took a steamer from Metrovich which touched at every town and island on the way to take on wine; but when we arrived at Zara we found the Drioli family on the quay. We were quite sentimental about leaving Zara, sitting on the deck and watching till the dusk hid it; however for an hour and a half we kept it in sight, the new Campanile making a fine landmark.

At Trieste we dined with the Greenhams, and crossed the sea by night to Venice which we reached just as the morning sun was drawing up the mists, and revealing the wondrous city all cream-colour tinted with rose – an effect worthy of Turner.

Here we stayed for a few days, and after a halt of one night at Milan, reached home on the last day of October.

On the completion of the Campanile I received a very kind letter from the Fabbriceria. It concluded: 'La lapide marmorea collocata nel 1º piano del Campanile e della quale ci onoriamo d'incrare a sua signoria 6 copiè fotografiche, tramanderà ai posteri la venerata memoria dell' intelligente e generoso Architetto che la ideò e diresse, ed il nome del Britanno Sign. T.G. Jackson sara sempre da questa cittadinanza ricordato con stima, venerazione e riconoscenza …'[6]

I could not help being much touched by the kindness and gratitude shown by these good people for what I had done for them.

20

1894-97

History of St. Mary the Virgin, Oxford ~ Westminster ~ Winchester
Uppingham ~ All Saint's, Oxford ~ Radley College ~ Cambridge
Visit to William Morris ~ Leighton ~ Death of Millais ~ St. Mary's spire (Oxford)
Rugby ~ Election as R.A. ~ Rome ~ Monument to Archbishop Benson
Drapers' Company ~ Walter Morrison and Giggleswick School ~ R.A. Diploma
Duties of R.A. ~ Dotheboys Hall, Yorkshire
Giggleswick Chapel dedicated ~ Funeral of Pearson

My work at St. Mary's, Oxford, in 1894, suggested a book. I am never quite content unless I have some writing on hand. It is always pleasant to have an occupation different from one's regular work – something voluntary and not merely professional. And so I undertook the History of St. Mary the Virgin at Oxford and the Clarendon Press engaged to publish it. The subject involved a great deal of reading, because the history of the church in its earlier days is really the history of the University. Till comparatively modern times St. Mary's was the scene of almost every academic function, the University having no buildings of its own, so that the first library it possessed had to be housed within the precincts of the University church, where also Convocations were held, disputations and examinations conducted, degrees conferred, and the Vice-Chancellor's *Curia* installed.

I was engaged at this time in repairing at Westminster School the famous long dormitory where the play was and is performed. Nowhere did I find the worship of tradition so strong. Nothing would induce them to let me clean the walls, which are black with age, and dirt rather than age, because the names which are written all over it might perhaps be lost, though I think the danger could have been avoided.

The old families whose sons went there generation after generation now send their boys to Eton or Winchester, if not to Harrow or Rugby, where they live in the country air. Yet when Westminster was in its prime no school in the kingdom could compare with it, and its roll of worthies, till quite modern times, is unrivalled. It had now come to my turn to choose a public school for my son Hugh. He was nearly fourteen, and instead of having to let him beat me at squash racquets in our court I had now enough to hold my own, but it was a disappointment to me that he showed no inclination towards art of any kind, as it would have been an advantage for him to have succeeded me, and made his start in life easier (Plate 10).

We had settled on Winchester and in the autumn of 1894 I took him there to be examined and left him in Mr. Hawkin's[1] house. About Winchester, the mother of public schools, there is an antique character that distinguishes it from any other. Eton has it also, but not so strongly. The College Hall with its bare severity, the Chamber Court, the brewery wing, even the little 'queristers' in their funny grey suits, who not only sing in chapel but wait on the scholars in college where no women servants intrude, all seem to have stepped out of the Middle Ages. This historical atmosphere, in which the boys live for four or five years, cannot but exert an influence on them. No boy of fair intelligence can go through either of these splendid and ancient foundations and live in their hoary and beautiful buildings without receiving impressions that never wear out. It is the same, of course, with Oxford and Cambridge, but the influences of school life are even more lasting than those that follow later.

At Oxford I refitted All Saints' Church, reseating it throughout and providing seats for the Mayor and Corporation who were to use it as the City Church, the old civic church of St. Martin, Carfax, being condemned to be pulled down to widen the street. On taking up the floor we found a most horrible mess of vaults, graves, and lead coffins, the worst I think I ever saw. Mockford, my clerk of works, was taken ill and it is a wonder the workmen were not all laid up too. I was heartily glad when we had cleared it all out and concreted the floor over.

I met Mrs. Liddell[2] and Mrs. Max Müller[3] about building a nursing-home and institute between the Banbury and Woodstock roads to commemorate Sir Henry Acland's wife.[4]

In 1893 I had begun for Radley College a new chapel of which the foundation-stone was laid on 3 November that year by Bishop Stubbs[5] of Oxford. This was an undertaking quite after my own heart; attached to the chapel were cloisters with a dormitory above. Previously I had built for the school an infirmary; the plan was rather unusual and I was made happy when Sir James Paget,[6] the great surgeon, said it was the best school infirmary in England. Now, on St. Peter's Day, 1895, their titular festival, my new chapel was dedicated.[7] I think there were four bishops there, though except him of Oxford I forget who they were. Sir James Paget was there and I think all or nearly all the governing body.[8] The chapel at Radley was followed by a boarding house[9] and Dining Hall (1909).[10]

In August 1895 we went again to St. David's, taking with us the two boys, my niece May Arnold, Foster my wife's maid and the dog, Twist. We

Radley College Chapel, showing the organ case (later removed)

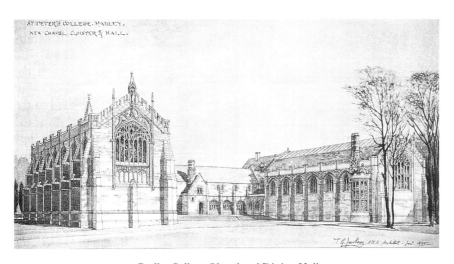

Radley College. Chapel and Dining Hall

were lodged in the same little prebendal house in the close, which we occupied in 1892. The morning after our arrival my old friend Dean Allen came to see me. He was now in his ninety-fourth year, feebler but quite bright and in good spirits. A few days later he asked me to go to him after breakfast, when he told me he was going to resign the Deanery and he wished me to witness his deed of resignation. I signed my name with regret, for the love of his Cathedral and his care in its upkeep, largely at his own expense for so many years, seemed to attach him to it with bonds that should not be broken (Plate 6).

We stayed at St. David's till September 12th – a very happy time sketching, picnicking and living as much as we could out of doors. The boys had a donkey to ride and drive, and used to bring our luncheon to the various bays in the neighbourhood. The donkey had the run of a paddock behind the house and conducted itself like an estimable animal till we got a second donkey of a less well-regulated disposition, which escaped constantly by night and persuaded the first donkey to break bounds also. Consequently we had to scour the country like Saul in a similar predicament in search of the strayed asses, Hugh and I one way, Alice, May and Basil another without finding them.

The owner of the first donkey complained that the other donkey had corrupted his. For that his donkey never used to play such tricks.

Picture letter from St. David's

I know no place where you command such an extensive and varied coast line at a short distance, for being on a promontory it has sea on three sides with a succession of bays and headlands all different and all beautiful. Westward you look out to the Atlantic beyond Ramsey Island, between which and you is a roaring and dangerous race, perilous to cross though it is so narrow that Basil distinctly heard sheep neighing on the island.

The autumn this year was one of the loveliest I remember and the hot summer weather lasted quite into October. We took advantage of it to make a trip up the Thames above Oxford. I was busy then finishing the drawings to illustrate my History of St. Mary's Church and my wife and I stayed in Cook's lodgings, the end house in Oriel Lane, looking across an open space towards Corpus and Canterbury Gate. I got my sketches done in spite of numerous interruptions by clerks of works and people on business, and at last we embarked one blazing morning early at Folly Bridge.

At Kelmscott, just within the Gloucestershire border, one of the quietest and sleepiest of all places we passed, we got luncheon at the little village inn and then invaded William Morris, whose country quarters were the beautiful old manor house of the place. We found him bare feet in slippers trying to keep cool in a charming barely furnished and whitened room partly hung with old tapestry. Only his youngest daughter was at home. 'Jenny! Jenny!' he called out of the window, 'friends from London.' We spent an hour or more seeing the house and garden which he loved dearly. This I think was almost the last time I ever saw him. It would be difficult to over-estimate the influence he has had on English decorative art. That it is as easy now as it used to be hard to get beautiful wall-papers, chintzes, and hangings for our houses is due entirely to the impulses given by Morris. He complained, I believe, that other men imitated his work and copied his designs, though it is not easy to see why he as a Socialist should have minded it. But the imitation is really the sincerest flattery and the greatest tribute to his genius. He was the pioneer of the revival of beautiful printing and now there are a dozen or more presses where fine work is turned out such as was never dreamed of fifty years ago. He and his paper-maker, Batchelor, brought good handmade paper again into vogue, and now anyone can be served with it. And in the higher field of painted glass and woven tapestries everyone knows what we owe to him and his friend Burne-Jones, who first dared to break through the wretched conventions of the pseudo-Goth and to give us designs that, while still breathing the spirit of romance of the Middle Ages, are distinctly original and modern in conception and treatment. For though Gothic art was for him the only art worth anything, he had grasped the truth which the new Gothic school ignored – that what is really of value to us moderns in the bygone styles is not their letter but their spirit. Consequently Morris's Gothic work lives, while that of the mock-medievalist is as dull as ditch-water and as dead as door-nail.

I was now turned sixty, and began to find I was outliving many of my oldest friends, but had every reason to be thankful for my measure of health and strength. I could still beat most of our friends in our squash racquet court though Hugh was getting too good for me. The secret of not growing old is to forget that you are not as young as you were, and not give in to the advancing years.

In December I was elected Master of the Art Workers' Guild and it occurred to me to signalise my year by starting a Junior Guild which has since firmly established itself.

We still had Sevenoaks as a resort, though my sister-in-law, Harriet Lambarde, had gone to live with her brother Charles who had been ordained and taken the family living of Ash seven or eight miles away on the North Downs.

Leighton had been ailing for some time but he was about again and at work as usual during 1895. On 2nd January 1896 I saw him at the Old Masters Exhibition and was able to congratulate him on his peerage. He looked worn and ill but was better and I was to have dined with him about a week or ten days later. Something prevented my doing so , I forget what, and on 26th January he died. He was buried on 3rd February in St. Paul's. The coffin lay in state in the Academy Octagon hall, draped with a Spanish hanging of crimson and gold, with Brock's[11] bronze bust of him placed at the head. We all followed in procession to the Cathedral by way of the Embankment and Fleet Street. I drove with Sargent[12] and North.[13] The streets were lined with people. The service was fine and impressive but I found it all very sad and depressing.

Millais was, of course, elected President. There could be no question about that. But he was already suffering from the ailment, which brought him to his grave before the year was out. The previous year, when Leighton was ill, Millais had presided at the annual dinner and spoke with difficulty and huskiness, though I remember the Prince of Wales made some complimentary remark as if it added new grace to his oratory. How far Millais was able to discharge the duties of his office as President I do not know. There was no banquet that year, either the Queen or the Prince, I forget which, having expressed a wish that Leighton's memory should be honoured in that way.

The Royal Academy never had more loyal sons than these two Presidents. Almost the last words of Leighton were 'Love to the Academy and all its members', and I remember Millais in his speech at the dinner bursting out with, 'I love the Academy, its boards, its easels, and everything about it.'

St. Mary's spire was at last finished. I find a note in my pocket diary on 15th August: 'To-day helped to set the vane rod at St. Mary's, Oxford, and put on the newly-gilt cock with my own hands', and in February (1896) I saw it for the first time since the removal of the enveloping scaffolding and was not a little nervous. However, I found it was all as I wished and the outline manifestly improved. The new pinnacles are six feet less in height than Buckler's (which I removed) and are gathered in closer to the central spire by a little ingenious trick in planning. The outline is new to those who only knew the spire as Buckler left it, but it is more like that which preceded his restoration and which those who remembered it in that state regretted.

A new and pleasant piece of work was brought me by my appointment as Architect to Rugby School and the commission to complete the chapel, which Butterfield[14] had left imperfect by building a new nave with aisles. This was to be a memorial to Mr. Bowden Smith, one of the masters. Butterfield was now an old man and retiring from practice, and he wrote very kindly to say he was pleased with my appointment as his successor.

At Whitsun we went for a short run abroad and spent time at Amiens, Beauvais and Abbeville. Beauvais struck me as statelier and more severe than Amiens. Norman Shaw in reply to a letter from me said:

> I am so glad you like Beauvais as I like it myself !! (delightful simplicity about this) I have not seen it for some 15 or 16 years but I know how the outside fetched me immensely. And why is it so fine and why is Cologne so hideous – is not easy to say – except that it is all right at Beauvais and all wrong at Cologne. Street said it was not to be compared with Amiens – and shut me up sharp.

Later in the year when the boys had gone back to school Alice and I set off for Rome where we had not been since our wedding.

I continue from Alice's diary:

> The drive across Paris was very pleasant, for it was a warm evening. It looked so bright with the gay shops, and the air refreshed us after the railway.
>
> When it was light we found ourselves getting into the mountains, white with fresh-fallen snow. We arrived at Genoa in pouring rain; under our window ran an electric omnibus which made a nasty buzzing sound, and I also saw a motor-carriage, but it caused no wish on my part to see them become general.

At this time the plague of motors was only just beginning.

At Rome we chose the Hotel Minerva. The overpowering associations of the place, the almost superhuman scale and majesty of the monuments, the incredible wealth of art and precious materials, conspire to separate Rome from every other place in the world, and to enthrone her in the imagination as too great and wonderful for comparison.

But to me the effect of greater familiarity with Rome was to bring out more and more into prominence view Ancient rather than Modern Rome. There is hardly anything Medieval to be seen – the monuments pass at a bound from the early Christian churches to the Rococo of Bernini, to which you can shut your eyes. But even the early Christian seem comparatively uninteresting beside the remains of antiquity. The old pagan Rome seemed to grow daily larger and larger, and to fill more completely the field of the imagination, while the Pope far away in the Vatican receded into oblivion.

While we were at Rome in the autumn of 1896 poor Millais had died. It was rather a relief to me to have escaped the funeral, since that of Leighton had been so depressing. On 4th November a new President had to be elected and it did not seem a certainty for anyone. There was also to be an election of an Academician to fill the vacancy caused by Millais's death, and it was on the cards that I should be the lucky man. At an election in March I had got five votes in the first scratching and nine in the second. At an election in July Ernest Crofts[15] and I got twenty-three votes each in the final ballot, and Calderon,[16] who was in the Chair, gave the casting vote for Crofts, who had been an Associate for eighteen years to my four.

Alice wrote:

A telegram reached us next morning with congratulations to Graham on being made a full R.A. It was a great joy, and made us long for news as to how the election had gone.

Later intelligence brought news that Poynter[17] had been elected President the same evening.

On this trip we also visited Naples, Vesuvius, and Pompeii. Pompeii itself was the principal object of our coming and we went there by train. The line skirts the base of Vesuvius passing villages, which Vesuvius has swept into the sea, or covered them with ashes time after time, the inhabitants never fail to return with unabated confidence. Signor Cozzi, the architect in charge of the excavations met us at the entrance of the ruins and most kindly acted as out guide.

Pompeii exceeded our expectations; the streets of shops reminded us of Dalmatia where there are the same open fronts with a halfway counter and a low door. But how the people lived in these houses all the year round is a puzzle. In summer nothing could be better – it would have been like living in a summerhouse, but in winter how did they manage in these unenclosed and unheated apartments? I asked Cozzi, but he only shrugged his shoulders and said 'Vivevano miseramente'.

As you stand in the Forum of the deserted city, you see in the distance Vesuvius, still smoking as he has done since that disastrous day, still ripe for mischief a sleeping or half waking giant that may break out again at any moment in fire and smoke, showers of ashes, streams of lava and boiling water.

It was dark when we got back to Naples, and from our window, which looked towards Vesuvius we saw up in the sky two dull red blotches on the darkness, which showed where the monster lay waiting his time.

Naples. 1896

We left Naples without regret. A viler city of touts, beggars, impostors and human nuisances generally exists nowhere else in Europe. Everyone begs of you, even quite decently dressed people, and everyone who catches your eye holds out his hand. A visit to Naples affords an admirable exercise of the temper, for you are in danger of losing it every five minutes. It was the greatest relief to get back to Rome where but for the beggars about the church doors there is no mendicancy, and in spite of dreadful poverty and distress – no degradation.

On 15th November we drove to Albano. Our route lay along the Via Appia Nuova, for the old Roman road is not passable for the latter part of the way. It lay parallel to us, about half a mile or less away, fringed with ruined tombs quite as far as Albano. To reach the lake you climb the hill above the town till you reach the edge of the old volcanic crater and get an enchanting view of the still lake far below in its rock cup, Castel Gandolfo and the Pope's villa perched picturesquely on the rim, while beyond lies the Campagna with the mountains on one hand, the glittering sea on the other, and in the middle distance a yellowish-white splash on the grey-green of the plain which we knew to be the eternal city. It would be from this point the travellers Rome-ward from the south would get their first view of the city. His companions would have pointed it out to St. Paul as he reached the very spot where we were standing. We had a lovely walk through the woods, where we met two mounted carabinieri who put us in the way to L'Ariccia, which we might have missed. Presently we met two more on foot and before we got out of the wood a third pair. This display of police made us wonder whether we had been overconfident in the security of the neighbourhood. On inquiring at the inn we learned that a foreigner had been stopped and robbed shortly before at Rocca di Papa. The waiter said it was all *fatto in burla*, but the fun seemed to have been all on one side. In Rome, however, our friends thought we had been imprudent, which surprised us considering how near Albano is to Rome. Elsewhere, there is still brigandage within the old Papal States. While we have been abroad two brigands have been shot near Orbetello in the Tuscan Maremma. One, a famous outlaw named Tiburzi, had some fifteen years ruled that country like a king, taking blackmail of the proprietors and peasants and in return protecting them from other depredations. Any refusal to pay was punished by rick-burning or worse, and any attempt to inform the carabinieri was followed by assassination. He boasted of seventeen murders. His income was £600 or £700 a year, and he used to visit Rome and Paris and enjoy himself like a gentleman. He was at last tracked to a house – together with his nephew and lieutenant Fioravanti – and shot as he tried to escape. Some say Fioravanti shot his uncle who, being elderly and gouty, used to make his nephew carry him. Since then another brigand has been shot in the same district, and as the Italians are too humane – *Messieurs les assassins* excepted – to inflict capital punishment, it is only in the field and from the police that these rascals get their deserts. The papers at our hotel in Rome had pictures of Tiburzi, who was propped up and photographed after death, and the surgeons were busy examining his brain to see how he did it! Most of the illustrated English papers had my picture, and the *Graphic* also had one of the illustrious Tiburzi, with whom I divided the honours of celebrity. I think I answered 110 congratulatory letters from Rome, astounding the hall porter with the extent of my correspondence and exhausting his supply of postage stamps.

On our return the boys were at school, but we were greeted by our dog Twist who nearly wriggled out of his skin with pleasure.

The year 1897 was the Queen's Diamond Jubilee, which brought me in a flood of work. In May the Prince of Wales opened my new Acland Nursing Home in Oxford. In the autumn the Duchess of Albany inaugurated the new Museum and Science Schools I had built for Uppingham School. In February a committee of which the Prince of Wales was chairman appointed me to design a monument to Archbishop Benson[18] in Canterbury Cathedral, Brock doing the effigy.

The City Companies, at last awaking to the fact that their surveyors, though excellent men of business and invaluable in managing their estates, are not necessarily artists, have begun to employ architects, and this year I was commissioned to make a new staircase, entrance corridor and gateway, and other interior alterations for the Hall of the Drapers' Company. I found at Brindleys a number of charming Renaissance capitals, which I used and supplemented to make a collonade and the head of my marble staircase. There had been a marble staircase of surveyor's work before, which I had

Drapers' Hall. The Staircase

the pleasure of destroying: I never saw marble worse abused than it was in that instance. At Grocers' Hall, too, I made some alterations and designed ceilings, gates, heraldic glass, &c., but, as I told them, it was too late to do much to improve things there. They had spent £180,000 on their buildings and when they had got them they did not like them. The Drapers' Company also appointed me their Architect for the new Radcliffe Library they were to build for the University of Oxford, at the instance of the Principal of Hertford College,[19] who was Master of the Company that year – a splendid gift costing about £22,000. At Oxford I was also busy at All Saints' Church and Carfax Tower (where I restored to use the old quarter-jacks that had lain idle for a long while in the Town Hall). In the spring Mr. Walter Morrison called on me to ask whether I was disposed to try an architectural experiment. I looked at him and said: 'I remember a Walter Morrison who rowed stroke of the Balliol boat in 1856 when the Wadham boat, *quorum pars parva fui*, bumped it and became head of the river.' He said: 'Yes, that bump has always rankled in my mind.' As to the architectural experiment, it was this. Morrison, who was much interested in the exploration of Palestine, wished as a memorial of the Queen's Diamond Jubilee to give a chapel to Giggleswick School in Yorkshire, of which he was one of the Governors. Palestine suggested a dome, and the chapel was to have a dome. This delighted me. I had never built a dome (very few architects have) and I jumped at the offer. The site, which I visited a few days later, was on a rocky spur of the fells in Ribblesdale, a magnificent situation, commanding the valley for several miles. I had *carte blanche*, Morrison's only wish being that there should be nothing left for anyone else to do.

I was determined to show that domes and gothic architecture are not incompatible and, though I shocked all the purists, I am not dissatisfied with the result. The dome was lined with mosaics executed by my friend James Powell, who had been doing these at St. Paul's in London; the windows are filled with painted glass by Burlison and Grylls,[20] the west window being designed by myself for them and the figures elsewhere drawn by James Linton.[21] The stalls and seats were of cedar specially imported by Morrison from Tucuman in the Argentine Republic; the organ was by Father Willis, as he liked to be called, almost his last work, and the *sgraffito* decoration was cut and scraped by two of my pupils, William Nicholls[22] of Hertford College and Douglas Stewart[23] of Oriel, who put on linen blouses and worked at plasterers' wages. All the fittings were in keeping. Few architects have had such a chance of carrying out a design so complete and consistent in all its parts. We had no builder but did it by day-work

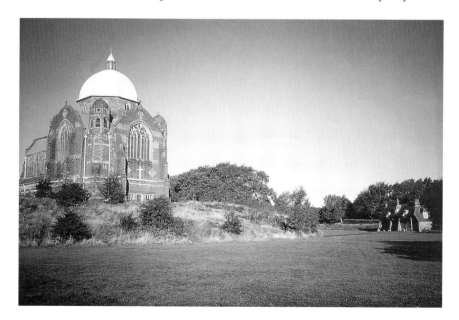

Giggleswick School Chapel

under my clerk of works, Evans, the woodwork being done admirably by Brassington, a local joiner, although it was of a most elaborate character.

The stone was laid by the Duke of Devonshire in the autumn, after the walls had risen to a considerable height, but the chapel was not finished till 1901. The dome puzzled the Yorkshire dalesmen terribly. One of them said he 'understood that thing Morrison was putting up yon was to be a kind of heathen temple'. And as 'the heathen temple' Morrison talks of it to this day.[24]

At the end of the year we had a pleasant visit to Durham to visit the Dean and Mrs. Kitchin.[25]

Leaving Alice at the Deanery, I went across by way of Barnard Castle and Kirby Stephen to Giggleswick to look after the 'heathen temple'. The journey lies all across the most desolate moorland country and you hardly see a house the whole way. The level is high and the rivers cut down into the plateau with deep channels, forming narrow valleys where the few towns and villages are buried out of sight. Among the few houses you do see is the original of Dotheboys Hall where, as we all know, 'at the delightful village of Dotheboys, near Greta Bridge in Yorkshire, youth are boarded, clothed, booked, washed, etc., etc., etc. Terms twenty guineas per annum, no extras, no vacations, and diet unparalleled.' By the way, Mr. Squeers, like many atrocious characters in history, for the Emperor Tiberius downwards, has in his turn come to be whitewashed. Some old pupils of Mr. Simpson's Academy, near Greta Bridge, Yorkshire, the original of Dickens's school in *Nicholas Nickleby*, have been writing to the papers to say they were well treated and very happy there.

On 16th December I attended Pearson's[26] funeral in Westminster Abbey, where he was buried, like his predecessors who had been architects to the building – an accomplished and original architect.

21

1897-1900

Council at R.A ~ Herkomer's picture of R.A. Council. ~ Dr. Warre and Eton
R.A. club at Sevenoaks ~ Wadham College dinner
R.A. Club dinner at Greenwich ~ Monument to Millais
Sedgwick Museum, Cambridge ~ Family holiday, 1899
Death of Alice Jackson, 1900 ~ Entrance hall at the R.A.
Council for Art ~ Death of Alice

On 17th November 1897 I received my diploma as Royal Academician with the sign manual of Queen Victoria. This ceremony takes place at a general assembly of the forty R.A.s. The R.A. elect is conducted to the room by the two junior members, set down at the table opposite the President, and after hearing the declaration read by the Secretary he signs the roll below the signatures of all his illustrious predecessors. The new R.A. comes at once on the Council, which meets fortnightly, and is plunged at once into the business of the institution.

The Council of the R.A. takes a good deal of one's time but I found it interesting and at all events it was something novel, though it reminded me a little of the college meetings of former days. In April I went through the selection of works for the annual Exhibition. The Council sit in a semicircle with the President in the middle at the end of the large room, with a great red screen behind them. A regiment of men bring up the pictures, which are then marked with a X if rejected, or a D if reserved as doubtful for the choice of the hangers. Now and then one is accepted straight away and put against the wall in the room where we sit, but this only happens very rarely. If there is a difference of opinion the majority carries it. We lunch together daily during the selection, and Eaton,[1] our Secretary, has the secret of a salad, to taste which for the first time marks an epoch in your life.

As the new member I had to 'hang' the Architectural Room – which I enjoyed, especially as I induced the Council for the first time to admit only

Royal Academy Council, 1907

Selection of works for Exhibition.
E Crofts · T G Jackson · S J Solomon · H W Leader · S Lucas · S J Sargent   B Riviere · Sir E J Poynter B! W W Ouless ·   D Murray ·   J M Swan · H von Herkomer · F A Eaton Sec!   T Brock
P.R.A.

designs and not drawings of old buildings, which should go to the water-colour or the black-and-white room. In our small gallery there is little enough room for the original designs of the year.

Herkomer[2] asked the Council of the Academy to sit for a great picture of us all – life size – sitting at the selection of works for exhibition. It was hung in the Academy in 1908 and after wandering about Europe to various shows it has at last in 1910 found a resting place in the Gallery of British Art at Millbank.[3]

Every year in the summer the Academy Club has an outing to some place within reach of London. In this way during my membership we had visited Oxford and Cambridge, Chatham and Rochester, where we saw the Dockyard under the guidance of Lord Charles Beresford,[4] who sent us down the river in a torpedo-boat. This year we went to Sevenoaks, an excursion for which I was able to help for a visit to Knole, we walked up through the park to Knole, which we saw thoroughly and had tea in the private rooms.

In May I heard from Dr. Warre, headmaster of Eton, to know if I could take his son Edmond.[5] We had been acquainted, though not intimately, as undergraduates at Oxford, and his letter concluded with the question 'Are you the same Jackson who bumped us in 1856?' The intimacy that followed this renewal of our acquaintance has been one of the great pleasures of my later years.

On 4th June my wife and I went to Eton, lunched with the Warres, where we met Sir Walter Parratt,[6] another old friend, who carried us off to Windsor and showed us the chapel before dinner.

In August 1898 I took Basil, then aged eleven, abroad with me for a fortnight on the Rhine, in the hope of awakening his artistic sense. It answered admirably and encouraged me to hope I might have one artistic son to step into my shoes when I have done with them.

I quote from a letter to my wife:

Basil is very ambitious and wants to draw everything. His appetite for castles is insatiable and says 'I can't sleep for thinking of those castles tomorrow.' He refuses to look at anything that is not old, which means he has caught the romantic fever, and will never lose the effects of it. Of course he has already lost his sketchbook, and now works in mine, which as it lives in my pocket has a better chance of survival. He is bitten by the thirst for travel and I am already at my wits end how to avoid engaging myself to take him to York, Cairo, Rome and Switzerland.

I was reminded of my father's experience when he took me abroad for the first time in 1856.

(On the Rhine they met up with Henry Boyd, Principal of Hertford College, Oxford, an accomplished watercolourist, whose diaries contain references to the days they spent sketching together.)

… We set out for a walk over the hills to where there is a most wonderful castle. I was sketching outside when I heard a tremendous voice, like a giant blunderbore, shouting at me from the castle. It was Mr. Jackson, with a speaking trumpet, from one of the windows … We went up onto the roof and in one turret found some figures that had puzzled us from below. They were wooden dummies formally clad in armour and put up to draw the arrows and shots of the enemy.

… There was an amusing incident before starting for Interlachen. We were, as usual beset by guides and porters all eager to bleed us. I left Mr. Jackson in charge of the luggage which when the diligence came round the corner, had to be carried to it. A man from the Bureau was taking it by degrees, when another man laid hold of Mr. Jackson's trunk and was bringing it with a prospective demand on our purse. Mr. Jackson saw him and looking unutterably fierce, he made a dash at him. The effect was instantaneous; in awful fright the man ran back with the portmanteau and deposited it in its old place. It was ludicrous and I could not help screaming with laughter.

The drive was most lovely and Mr. Jackson was in transports of delight all the way. It is most charming to see the way in which he enjoys everything. After some dinner at the hotel we went and sketched vigorously. Mr. Jackson was successful with his, but I am sorry to say mine was far from what I wished.

In the summer I took the chair at the Wadham College dinner in London. The survivors of the famous crew which won three cups at Henley in 1849 had put their medals and silver oars together to form a trophy which was presented on this occasion to the College Boat Club. Five of the crew were present, two more were still living, and of the two who had died one was killed by an accident. Rowing would seem to promote health and longevity.

In May I attended a Royal Academy Club dinner at Greenwich; the following is an extract from a letter.

Eagle House, Wimbledon
May 2nd. 1898

… Just back from the Greenwich dinner, it was very pleasant and I am glad I went. Being carried off to Drapers' Hall, I did not go down by boat but by train. Yeames[7] who is in charge of the Picture Gallery showed us over and took us down into the crypt which is part of the substructure of the Gothic palace. It looks like mid-15th century and is all of brick, which is curious. What a splendid thing the Palace is! I know nothing finer than the two blocks facing one another with those magnificent colonnades, and the domes at the end.

Tadema[8] was in the chair and did it well. I sat between Gow[9] and Solomon.[10] They kept sending up menus to Phil May,[11] who was very good-natured and drew absurd faces on them. But perhaps the most delightful part was the voyage back by steamer. The moon was up and the irregular line of the warehouses and the shipping half seen in the mysterious light, and the track of the moon on the broken water while every minute some great sailing barge went slipping by like a ghost, or a great steamer with flashing lights and rolling smoke – all made a most splendid vision. In the bows our quartet stationed itself and sang us half-a-dozen part-songs …

In February 1899 I was put upon a Committee for a monument to Sir John Millais. The Prince of Wales was Chairman and we met in his dining room at Marlborough House, sitting round the largest mahogany dinner table I ever saw, with His Royal Highness in the Chair. There were difficulties. The Dean of St. Paul's refused to allow a monument. 'To say the truth,' said the Prince, 'he is not over civil, and if we press the point we may get a snub.' So finally we decided that Brock should make a statue and place it somewhere in the Tate Gallery grounds at Chelsea. We all met again in the Gallery another day and I pleaded for a place on one of two pedestals outside the entrance. Sculpture, in my opinion, gains much by association with architecture. Poynter supported me, but the others and Brock himself wanted to be independent, and so Millais now stands forlorn on a pedestal with no relation to anything, and looks as if he had lost his way to the front door.

Cambridge at last! This year I really began to build the Sedgwick Museum and was consulted about a Law Library and Law School to adjoin, for which a Miss Squire had left £20,000. I also arranged the lighting and designed the fittings in the Senate House and enlarged the Hall at King's College by throwing in a passage and glorifying the new end with panelling and a canopy behind the high table. At Oxford I was still building the Radcliffe Library and was also building for the Radcliffe trustees an observatory to receive the best telescope money could buy. It was to be made by Sir Howard Grubb[12] of Dublin and to cost £5,000. He was making, he told me, another just like it, which was going to the Grand Shereef of Mecca (of all people in the world) who is, I suppose an astrologer. I finished Archbishop Benson's tomb at Canterbury and had the pleasure of restoring our Founder's tomb at Ilminster for the college. At the Royal Academy I altered and in various ways improved the Keeper's house and remodelled the great entrance hall with marble columns, oak panelling, in which is some excellent wood carving by Childs, Farmer & Brindley's head man, who has worked for me for many long years, and a plaster ceiling into which I fitted paintings by Angelica Kauffmann that had lain forgotten in the basement since the Academy moved from Trafalgar Square.

Among other incidents, this year I sat for my picture to Solomon, for the Art Workers' Guild, and also to Hugh Riviere[13] for a portrait to hang in the Hall of Wadham College, a great honour.

The great event in our home circle was the decision we came to, not without reluctance on our part, to let our elder boy Hugh become a soldier.

Our autumn holiday was suggested by the desirability of his learning French, and we took him for a month's teaching to reside with a Professor Minssen,[13] while we and Basil toured about the West of France.

Alice wrote:

Hugh and I left home on August 1st, Graham having left separately to pick up Basil from his school at Folkestone, and we met aboard the boat for Boulogne.

On the train to Paris the carriage shook us nearly to a jelly and Hugh compared French railways most unfavourably with the English. Another slow railway journey brought us to Versailles.

On the following day after breakfast, Basil and his father went off to the Gardens of the Palace where they made a sketch, and we all went to déjeuner with the Minssens who were most kind. There were two daughters (not very young) and Hugh was to be shown about by them and to hire a bicycle as they rode.'

The next day we went on to Chartres[14] which I had not seen since John Scott and I were sketching there in 1864, when I little dreamed of revisiting it with a wife and child. The interior of the Cathedral and the North porch (Plate 17) where I sat and sketched, were the only tolerably cool places we could find, and Basil was knocked up by the heat and had to be revived by a tonic, which the Chemist described as a 'vin fort

T.G. Jackson. From a Portrait by Hugh Riviere at Wadham College

agréable', but which Basil ungratefully pronounced as 'nasty'.
    Alice continues:

> At Blois, our first move was to the Château, and Graham embarked on a
> sketch of the staircase of François I. (Plate 18).
>   Some people staying in the Hôtel had come from Paris in two large
> motor cars like omnibuses with their luggage packed on top. They looked
> very happy and seemed to be having a lark, but preserve me from the like.
> The machines made the most hideous noise so that talking would have
> been impossible, and the men who worked the engines had to protect their
> eyes with large blue goggles.
>   In the afternoon Graham went off on a sketch he had marked down on
> the opposite side of the river, and I could see from the balcony where
> Graham was sitting by his white umbrella.

We drove to Chambord and stayed a few days at the little Inn where I put up many years ago, and lived mostly out of doors, reading and sketching under the trees by the little river.

At Loches (Plate 20) we spent more than a week at the Hôtel de la Promenade. The castle is a splendid piece of work covering the whole hill top, and as big as a small town. At the Post Office letters from Hugh awaited our arrival, from which I quote:

> I have hired a very good violin and Madamoiselle Marie, who is rather good looking, plays the piano absolutely splendidly. I have been up to Paris with the Madamoiselles Minssen on bikes by the Bois de Boulogne, and as far as the Place de la Concorde. The roads are not good and the automobiles are awful and such a quantity too.
>
> There is a Mlle Petit who lives next door. Rather a pretty girl – has been much prettier, but is rapidly going off. I am getting along nicely with the lingo, but should do so better if I had more tête-à-tête with Mlle Petit.
>
> The Minssens keep fairly well, especially as regards their appetites are concerned.
>
> Yours affectionately
Hugh

Basil and I began a sketch of the town gates and the Hôtel de Ville, and took up our positions outside a Grocers' shop (Plate 19). A party of American tourists who were bicycling through France came and looked over us. 'How delightful it must be,' said they, 'to be able to sit here quietly and not go away.' There was nothing, so far as I could gather, to prevent them taking their time and avoiding hurry, except that they possessed bicycles – or rather ought not we to say they were possessed by bicycles which moved them on when they wanted to stay. For I have observed that the owners of bicycles, still more of motorcars can never rest, but are always in a hurry to get on.

From Loches, a slow and tedious train journey in appalling heat brought us to Poitiers where we stayed four or five days.

Alice wrote:

> Graham and Basil took a look round by moonlight and so prepared me for the glories in the way of Romanesque churches, but no description could give an idea of the richness and quaintness of the West front of Notre Dame which Graham and Basil sketched. (Plate 13). They got a good point outside what appeared to be an empty house. But the front door belonged to a laundress and baskets of linen kept being passed in and out, to the inconvenience of the sketchers.

At the Hôtel du Palais we found Mr. Hill[15] the organ builder with two friends who were bicycling back from the Auvergne. Electric light rather destroyed the comfort in our room, as it was impossible to work by it.

On her (Alice's) birthday I gave her a pretty paste brooch I had bought at Loches. How little did I think then that this birthday was her last and that we were never again to travel in this world. The extracts from her diary show how completely she associated herself with my pursuits, acquiring a knowledge of architecture far beyond any woman I ever met.

Hugh joined us in Paris, and he and Basil amused themselves by listening to the Opera on the telephone at the St. James and Albany Hotel. We came home together and Alice concluded Wimbledon looked as if we had not been away for a day.

In 1900 a Council for Art was appointed at the suggestion of Sir William Richmond, and it has been the instrument not only of entirely remodelling the Royal College but also of improving to a lesser extent the whole art teaching of the country.

The Royal College of Art at South Kensington was founded principally for training masters and mistresses to teach in the art schools throughout the country, and its curriculum included Architecture, Sculpture, Painting, and the Decorative (or as they are called for want of a better name, the Applied) Arts. The college had sunk into a very formal and lifeless state, bound by cast-iron rules and tied fast with red tape. In the annual national competitions we had long found – in architecture at all events – that the work sent up by the Royal College was below the average of the rest of the country. A vast amount of time and labour, which should have been spent in cultivating design, was spent on elaborate mechanical drawings of no value in training for architecture and of no use to anyone. Year by year, as Examiners, we had reported their uselessness, but in vain. The teachers knew no better, and continued to send up elevations tinted and shaded like pictures on the one hand, and ill-planned and ill-proportioned designs on the other, in spite of our remonstrances. The same deadly dullness had spread over the art-teaching of the whole country which centred in South Kensington, and its lifeless condition had become a proverb. It was in order to inspire it with new life that the Council for Art was appointed.

Our first concern was with the Royal College, and here we said at once: 'Let us have no more examinations.' Instead of judging the students' merit by works specially made and exhibited for prizes, we decided to review the whole of what each man had done during the session and to award the prizes and scholarships according to the general quality of his output. We appointed a Master or Professor in each of the four Schools, with a good salary and an assistant, and we took care that he should have a studio of his own where he could continue his private practice. Mere teaching without doing, we felt, would soon make any man stale and useless as a master. We looked also to his giving the students opportunities of seeing his work, and possibly of giving them a hand in it. Spencer,[16] the Principal, had the General Superintendence. In Architecture we appointed Gerald Moira,[17] and in design, Lethaby,[18] a former pupil and assistant of Norman Shaw. We four had the charge of our respective Schools as Visitors: Richmond that of Painting, Ford of Sculpture, Crane of Design, while I had Architecture. But in awarding prizes and scholarships we all met and voted in common in all four sections, thus hoping as far as possible to bring all the arts into union and harmony and to rescue them from the isolation and discord which had so long kept them asunder. Another part of our work was to advise on the purchase of objects for the Museum.

It was arranged that we four should meet fortnightly in alternate pairs to see things offered for purchase, and report and advise whether to buy or not. I used to enjoy this work and learned a good deal by doing it. The question of authenticity came up, of course, for forgery of works of art has become a profession, and the professors of it are become so expert that nobody can always be sure of detecting it.

Sometimes, of course, there is no doubt, and then one said so; but generally I used to confine myself to saying whether the thing was beautiful and likely to be of use to students or not. Whether it were genuine or a fraud was a matter between the dealer and the Department. After all, as a matter of art it should be not the age but the merit of the work that it signifies; its authenticity or the reverse is a matter not of art but of history. If it is beautiful it deserves to be admired and possessed, whether it be old or new. If it be poor or ugly, no amount of antiquity can redeem it on the score of art, though it may interest us as a matter of history and to appeal to us on grounds that are other than artistic. If collectors were guided by this rule it would knock the forgers' trade on the head, for at present, prices paid for works of art are based on historical rather than artistic considerations.

When the Italian Government passed a law to prevent works of ancient art going out of the country, it is said that a deputation waited on the Minister to point out that a thousand men would be deprived of their living who now got it by manufacturing antiques. One has heard of a woman who wanted help for her husband who was out of work. He was, she said, a 'worm borer' to make new furniture look old. I am told that sham wormholes can be detected by putting a wire down them. The sham holes are, of course, straight but the real ones crooked or spiral.

With the new century came the great sorrow of my life. We celebrated our twentieth Wedding day on March 31st. I can see her bright face now as we pledged each other from opposite ends of the dinner table.

On April 10th she went to St. Mary's, Wimbledon, which was not warmed and she caught a chill. The doctor made light of it till the last, and I shall never forgive myself for listening to him. She died on April 21st and I laid her in the grass at Sevenoaks next my parents. It was like the end of all real life to me and the recollection of my loss still goes like a knife to my heart.

I thank God for those twenty years of perfect and unclouded happiness with her and I humbly hope in God's providence to be permitted to rejoin her.

22

1901-06

Queen Victoria Memorial ~ Visit to Berlin
Giggleswick Chapel dedicated ~ Switzerland
Visit to Dr. Warre at Eton ~ Holman Hunt ~ Winchester Cathedral

In March 1901 I was invited, with four more, to make a design in competition for the national memorial to Queen Victoria. Our work was to be a setting to Brock's monument, about which we knew nothing for it was not yet designed. Before beginning I went to Berlin to see the way in which the Sieges-Allee and other formal laying out of streets and monumental work had been done.

I dined at Berlin with Sir Frank Lascelles[1] the Ambassador and lunched with his secretary, Lord Gough.[2] On my way back I saw Hildesheim and Hanover but I had no stomach for travel and sight-seeing and no relish for anything. The successful design was Aston Webb's, which I did not admire. Mine was very favourably received.

On 3rd September Giggleswick Chapel was dedicated and formally opened by Dr. Warre, Morrison's old college friend and fellow oarsman. In December I was elected Treasurer of the Royal Academy.

In 1902 Hugh sailed to join the 2nd Battalion Durham Light Infantry in the Madras Presidency and in 1904, to his great joy, changed into the Indian Cavalry.

In 1903 Basil had come home from Winchester quite run down so in the Autumn I took him to Switzerland for three weeks keeping him from 4000 to 5000 feet above the sea, which put him to rights. We went to Berne, Thun and up to Frutigen. We shouldered our knapsacks and walked the six miles to Kandersteg – it was hot and I thought, 'What is the use of thinking of Swiss walking with the boy at my age.' But such was the wondrous effect of the mountain air that next day I was up with him at the Aschinen See and on the glaciers of the Blumliss Alp above.

Here we met an Irish barrister who was a great Alpine climber. He told us a capital bar story:

A farmer was to try his case before a very particular Judge, and said to his lawyer, 'Now, I've a nice pair of fat ducks and I'm thinking it would be a good thing to send them to his Honour.' – 'On no account,' said the lawyer, 'he would certainly take offence and decide against you.' – 'Do you think so?' 'I'm sure of it,' said the lawyer. So the case came on and he won the day. 'There now,' said the lawyer, 'you've won your case, but if you had sent those ducks you'd have lost it.' – 'But I did send them' said the man. 'You did?' gasped the lawyer – 'Yes, but I sent them in my opponent's name.'

Basil made his first ascent, climbing the Pigni d'Arolla, with guides and ropes all en règle.

The year 1904 was one of warning to me that my time is getting short. After a life of wonderfully good health I seemed to be giving way in several directions. Consequently I was unable to go to Cambridge when the King and Queen opened my new buildings in March. Three weeks at Bath put me to rights again in a manner, but what quite set me up was ten days on the river when I sculled Basil from Oxford to London.

Sometimes I used to dine with the Holman Hunts in Melbury Road, and at a dinner in 1904 the only guests were Lord Carlisle, one of the Lord Justices, Mrs. Richmond Ritchie (née Thackeray) and myself. The old man was full of anecdotes and gave us a long story of his voyage by sea from Palestine to Constantinople when there was a mutiny on board the Turkish ship. No public honours had ever been bestowed on Holman Hunt, and I found he had never had an honoury degree. At the Academy dinner I met the Vice-Chancellor and suggested a D.C.L. for Holman Hunt and the thing was done in 1905. About this time Hunt received a greater honour – that of the Order of Merit. Thus the mouse helped the lion.

My old friend Halcomb from Australia and his wife paid me a visit in the summer of 1905. I took him with the R.A. Club to Windsor Castle and Eton where Warre gave us a garden party and we dined in the college hall. To revive old associations Halcomb and I donned our flannels and carried Warre off to the river and rowed him to Datchet and back. Halcomb bow and I stroke as in the old days, Warre steering, not as before *primus inter pares*. Quite a frolic of Ancient Mariners!

I began the year 1906 as a painful cripple at Bath, trying to get rid of neuritis. I got home on 13th January, but a long day's climbing about the cathedral at Winchester on 3rd February brought my trouble back. The professorship of Architecture at the Academy being vacant I was asked to lecture this year, though I refused to stand for the professorship; and though hardly able to walk I drove up from my sofa to town and got through my course of four lectures. They were afterwards published by Murray under the title *Reason in Architecture*.

In 1899, on the death of Sir Arthur Blomfield, I had been appointed Consulting Architect to the Diocese of Winchester.

Winchester Cathedral[3] now occupied a great deal of my time and

T.G. Jackson at Winchester Cathedral, 1910

thoughts. Built on a bog it had settled in all directions and there was nothing to be done but to grout and bond the cracks, reset the crushed and sunk vault-ing of the eastern part, and practically underpin the greater part of the fabric, going down to the gravel 16 or 17 feet below ground. The difficulty of this was very great, as the last 10 feet were under water. This being beyond the ordinary experience of an architect I had recourse, with the consent of the Dean and Chapter, to the advice of Mr. Francis Fox,[4] the civil engineer, who suggested employing a diver, and all the subaqueous work was done by him to the height of 3 or 4 feet after which we could pump the hole dry without danger. But it was very anxious and distressing work and enormously costly.

For all the tens of thousands of pounds buried underground there is nothing to show. The only works of mine that are visible at Winchester Cathedral are the buttresses on the South side, a coal house in the angle of the choir and North transept which I made as inconspicuous as possible, and a little stair of which I am rather proud, to the South door of the pres-bytery. I also made a chapel with some rich screen-work in the West aisle of the North transept and refitted the Chapter Room.

23

1908-10

Hertford College chapel and other works
Rugby speech-room opened by the King ~ Radley dining hall
B.N.C. ~ Hon. Degree at Cambridge ~ R.I.B.A. Gold Medal
Electrical Laboratory at Oxford opened
Constantinople ~ France ~ Italy

I had become used to an annual illness in the winter, which in 1908 took the agonising and disgusting form of a severe attack of shingles in the face and head, and laid me up for some weeks in the spring.

However, I managed to struggle up to a meeting at the Mansion House for Winchester Cathedral, and to speak. The Archbishop of Canterbury, the Lord Mayor, the Bishop of Winchester and the Dean, and the Marquis of Winchester were there and spoke, but it was a miserable failure for I doubt if there were thirty people to listen to us in that great Egyptian Hall. However, it got into the papers and was well reported. I met the Archbishop shortly afterwards and condoled with him. He said that once, on a similar occasion, he asked a reporter how he should describe the meeting: 'Shall you call it a crowded and enthusiastic gathering?' 'No,' said the reporter, 'I shall say "important and influential".'

My chapel at Hertford College, Oxford, was finished this year and I am told is generally liked. Among other work were the new Speech Room at Rugby School, repairs at Greenwich Hospital, Wolvesey Palace chapel, a new Archaeological Museum at Cambridge adjoining my other buildings, and the Music School at Eton left half done and now to be completed. When a Latin motto was talked of for the Music School, Warre said, 'How would this do? – *Cave canem* – which a lower boy the other day translated as "Look out, I'm going to sing".'[1]

On 3rd July 1909 the King opened the new Rugby Speech Room, and I began a new dining-hall for Radley College, which was planned many years ago. I also began new buildings for Brasenose College to complete my new quadrangle and the front to the High, which was interrupted twenty years ago at the tower. I never expected to finish it. The memorial stone was set by the Bishop of Lincoln, their Visitor, exactly 400 years to a day – 1st June – since the original foundation-stone of the college was laid. It was a wet day but there was a good gathering and a luncheon in Hall at which the Chancellor, Lord Curzon,[2] the Vice-Chancellor, the Bishops of Lincoln and Salisbury, and many old B.N.C. men of mark were present.

On 13th June 1910 I went to Cambridge to receive my Hon. LL.D. degree the following day. I stayed with the Master of St. John's, Dr. Scott.[3] The ceremony next day in the Senate House was very dignified and impressive. Curiously unlike those at Oxford, but so is everything at Cambridge. The other LL.D.s were Lord Selborne,[4] the Speaker, and Mr. Ameer Ali.[5] The day finished with a banquet at Pembroke College of which the Vice-Chancellor, Canon Mason,[6] was Master.

On 20th June I received the Gold Medal of the R.I.B.A. Henderson,[7] the Warden of my college, and Dr. Warre, Provost of Eton, were with me and dined first with the Institute. A good many other academicians also, including Alma-Tadema and Sargent.

I said in returning thanks after my investiture that I valued the honour all the more because it was bestowed on one who was not a member of their society, but even at times 'I almost tremble to say it – an opponent of your policy'. On 21st June my new Electrical Laboratory, given to the University of Oxford by the Drapers' Company, was opened on completion by Lord Curzon. I came back to town with him, also alas! with preliminary twinges of gout in my foot, which prevented my being present at the tercentenary of Wadham College on the 23rd which was a great disappointment to me.

During the spring and summer I had, at leisure moments, been putting into shape materials for a History of Architecture. As I was writing on the Byzantine period I said to myself, 'This won't do; you write about things you know only from books', and so a sudden resolve took me to Constantinople in September.[8]

A stout porter carried my small portmanteau and a Gladstone bag by a strap over his shoulder from the Gare du Nord to the Gare de l'Est in Paris, and then on by the Orient Express. I had a good berth in a compartment for two. My companion was an Italian travelling in the carpet trade just back from Buenos Aires, Canada and New York on his way to Constantinople, Cairo and perhaps India.

At Vienna I was persuaded to break my journey by my friend Herr Kupka, engineer of the Northern Austrian Railway, but to my dismay I forfeited my berth to Constantinople and alas, as no berth was to be had on the next Orient Express, I went on by conventional train.

Kupka took me to Schönbrunn, the Austrian Versailles, a great yellow-washed palace of no architectural pretensions a little way out of Vienna.

While we were standing in front of the palace we were asked to move a little way aside, and the Emperor drove up in his carriage and pair; the coachman and footman on the box had gorgeous cocked hats, but there were no outriders nor was there any ceremony. My friend said 'There are only two sovereigns in Europe who could go about in this simple way, yours and ours.' The carriage was shut so I failed to see the most pathetic figure among European monarchs. Little could we have anticipated what lay in store for him; the murder of his heir, his own death and the universal crash of empires and the downfall of the Habsburg dynasty.

No place, not even Rome itself, delighted me like Constantinople. The whole thing was quite fresh, quite unlike any other place. About Stamboul there hangs a peculiar charm, not wholly of association but of character. It has no metropolitan airs, but seems rather like an overgrown village with its hilly, rough paved streets, its wooden houses mixed with trees and gardens, and its open spaces devoted to market gardening. And then, in the midst of all this irregularity, one comes at every turn on some ancient church of the Greek Empire or some great marble mosque of the conquering Turk; and all round are the bluest of seas – Marmora on one side, the Golden Horn on the other, and the Bosphorus beyond with the blue mountains of Asia in the distance and now and then a glimpse of the Homeric Olympus.

I was let in for giving a lecture on the history of the University of Oxford at the American Girls College. The girls are of all creeds and of all races, Turk, Greek, Armenian, Bulgar, Albanian and here and there a stray English Miss. At every fresh arrival I was introduced as 'Mr. Jackson – our distinguished lecturer'. The Americans seem always at full stretch – I asked Dr. Patrick, the Principal, by whom I sat at lunch, where she had spent her holiday, expecting her to say Italy or Switzerland. But no; she had spent it working out the connection between Pyrrhonism with the Greek Empire – I promptly turned the conversation. Her great relaxation of late has been to write an article on the philosophy of Anaxagoras. Here too I was out of my depth. The lady next to me on the other side, a very nice quiet person had been a great traveller and was going alone with a dragoman, through Armenia, Asia Minor, Baghdad and the Persian Gulf: she had been on the borders of Tibet and many other wild places for a woman. I wish I could remember her name.

Except for S. Sophia, Salonica has more to show an architect than Constantinople. We spent over a week there and made many friends. Here the Moslem, though dominant, is in a minority. Half the population of 150,000 is Jewish, descended from the Spanish Jews driven out by Ferdinand and Isabella and still speaking old fashioned Castilian. Greeks and Armenians constitute a large proportion of the other half of the population, which is very much mixed. I dined with a M. Lazzari, a Greek merchant, in a fine villa outside the town. We all talked French, though among the party of, I think, eighteen or twenty it was not the language of any one of us. There were Greeks, Jews, Russians, English, and the American Consul-General, whom I had met in the train on the way out. At Constantinople I was asked by the Ministry of the Efkaf, the Turkish Ecclesiastical Commission, or something like it, to report on S. Sophia, which is in a bad way. I wrote my report in the Orient Express on my way back, after having examined the building as well as I could on so short a notice.

In this train, which is very comfortable, one has one's meals regularly, goes to bed and it's like living in a moving hotel.

On reaching Paris we went to the Hôtel St. James in the Rue St. Honoré and spent the afternoon in the Louvre trying to find the Byzantine department to which no one could direct us. But I know it exists somewhere.

Lucca

Thus ends a most novel and enjoyable excursion, not without much profit and acquisition of knowledge.

Extracts from my report on S. Sophia appeared in my book on Byzantine and Romanesque Architecture and in 1911 Basil and I went on two sketching tours, to provide the illustrations.

In May we saw Tours, Poitiers, Chauvigny, Polignac, Clermont-Ferrand where I made sketches in 1864, 47 years ago, Issoire, Brioude, Le Puy, Lyons and St. Denis. We were away eighteen days, and I never spoilt so much paper in so short a time.

In September we crossed to Ostende and went via Cologne, Worms, Strasbourg, Lucerne and Milan to Florence. Thence we continued our route to Lucca where something or other set us wrong. I recovered in a day, but I had Dr. Francesconi to Basil. Afterwards a lady we met at tea in Rome said – 'Lucca, oh! That's where they killed the Doctor.' It appeared that after the patient of a Lucchese doctor had died, his friends tried some of the medicine he had been taking on the dog, who also died, upon which they killed the doctor.

I observed that Dr. Francesconi had treated Basil without any Physic.

24

1911-14

Hon. Degree at Oxford ~ Balliol College
Winchester Cathedral thanksgiving service ~ Offer of Baronetcy
Hertford College Bridge ~ World War I

In June 1911 I received my Hon. D.C.L. degree at Oxford. How little did I think on 15th June 1858 when my father and I saw the ceremony that my turn would ever come to play a part in it. I was addressed as follows:

Artifex Oxoniensissime, qui omnia genera architecturae concinnando venustam novitatis speciem huic saeculo ostendisti, Ego, &c.[1]

I enjoyed being called 'Artifex Oxoniensissime' by Lord Curzon the Chancellor, who conferred the degrees and was very complimentary.

On August 4th I went to stay with the Master of Balliol on a very curious matter. Some half-century ago Butterfield pulled down the old chapel, which I remember when I was an undergraduate and built the present one in what the youth of the day irreverently called 'the streaky bacon style'. The old glass was shifted about and rearranged and lately it has been proposed to put it into better order. This was announced at the Gaudy, and some old member got up and bewailed the loss of the old chapel. This met with applause from the older men who remembered it, and next day Walter Morrison sent a cheque for £20,000 for the purpose of rebuilding it on the old lines. He recommended me for the purpose. It was rather awkward. I began to wonder how long my new chapel at Hertford would be allowed to stand! However, I found the new college resolved on accepting Morrison's gift and rebuilding, and so I said that being so I was ready to meet their wishes. The matter, however, passed beyond the college walls. Norman Shaw and Basil Champneys wrote to *The Times* to protest against the destruction of Butterfield's work, and finally, after I had made a design which the college admired in the rough, the residents thought they ought to fortify themselves by taking a poll of outside members, and it turned out that ex-members who voted against rebuilding were in the majority.

Morrison was much amused and came to see me about it. He said he did not want the money back and I am not sure what it was eventually used for.

Winchester Cathedral was finished and opened in the summer of 1912. The last piece of work was the worst, the underpinning of the South Transept, 120 ft. high and 4 ft. 6 in. out of upright. The King and Queen attended the thanksgiving service on 15th July.

The following announcement appeared in *The Times* next day: 'The King has been pleased to confer the honour of Knighthood upon Mr. Francis Fox, M.I.C.E. Mr. Fox is the engineer who assisted Mr. T. G. Jackson in the preservation of Winchester Cathedral.' It was supposed that I too would be knighted, and I remember sitting with Hugh at the end of our terrace on a summer night and deciding that it would be refused. But on 23rd December 1912 I received a letter from the Prime Minister, Mr. Asquith,[2] proposing 'with the King's approval' that I should receive the honour of a Baronetcy at the New Year. On New Year's Eve I was asked to dine with the incoming and outgoing Council at the usual dinner at the Academy, but I did not prepare them for my appearance in the list of New Year honours next morning. I received shoals of congratulatory letters. I think I counted 320, and answered them all. If only this could have happened thirteen years ago! There is little pleasure in these things if one has to enjoy them alone. The best part of it is the pleasure it gives one's friends.

I remember the time when a Baronet seemed to be a very exalted being, figuring largely in novels as the bad man and tyrant of the story. Having attained that exalted rank, without I trust any of the odium so often directed upon it fiction, it does not seem much after one has got used to the novel address.

There is an amusing story of Millais after he was made a baronet. He arrived late one night at an hotel and was shown to a very poor bedroom. He complained to the manager, but was told in an indifferent manner, that there was no other. He asked for some supper. 'Oh no' it was too late for serving anything. 'So when they asked for my name,' said Millais, 'I sat down and wrote at full length "Sir John Everett Millais Bart P.R.A." At once a better bedroom was found for me, and as for supper, oh yes "of course you shall be served directly Sir." – and so you see it is a jolly good thing to be a baronet.'

I think however, very likely the name 'Millais' was what worked the spell rather than the Baronetcy. The unkindest thing was said about baronets after the great Tichborne trial. The claimant's friends bewailed the lot of the 'unfortunate nobleman languishing in jail', which provoked a controversy as to whether a baronet was noble or not, and one writer said a baronet was in a curious position, because he was neither a nobleman nor a gentleman!

Hugh and Basil in uniform went with me to the levee, which I thought a very dull and tedious ceremony.

In September I had a run round the great French churches of the North before finishing those chapters of my book – *Gothic Architecture*.

Hugh and Basil joined me in Paris, where at the Carnavalet Museum we met Mr. John Burns very hot on making as good a thing of the London Museum. Basil and I went on to Italy visiting Pisa, Siena and Rome. We then took flight to Naples and then by sea to Palermo. I was rather the worse for a seventeen mile walk over rough roads and so came home leaving Basil to go on to Venice.

This disastrous year (1914) began pleasantly enough. In January, Lady St. Helier[3] opened my new bridge at Hertford College, which she had

Hertford College. Bridge over New College Lane (as designed in 1899)

Ischia, 1912

given in memory of her husband. In June I had a short run to Normandy and visited Amiens, Rouen, Bayeux, Coutances and Abbeville to make sketches for my book. The weather was lovely and the roses wonderful.

My new Physiological School at Cambridge and that of Psychology adjoining it were opened by Prince Arthur of Connaught, and I attended a Grand Luncheon at Kings' and a banquet at Trinity. Basil, with capital I advanced him, built his first house and made a very nice thing of it at 23 Mulberry Walk, Chelsea. After his military career began I finished it for him.

On August 4th war was declared and Hugh went out to France where he was in the trenches. Basil got a commission in the West Riding Horse Artillery, and I received at Eagle House till the end of the war an old Belgian gentleman and his daughter.

I volunteered to help in a munitions factory at Shepherds Bush on Sundays. It was rather amusing helping in tent-making, but any child could do what I did.

Hugh wrote home:

I don't wonder you are somewhat wearisome of Monsieur and Mlle. I am afraid you will never get them to do anything. How do they like being in the Smoking Room? I dare say the arrangement suits them quite well as they were always afraid of getting frost-bitten during the journey from the Morning Room to their Bedrooms. – Tents are about the only sort of dwellings you have never dealt with so now you will be able to include even them. – Rather a change from bricks and mortar to canvas!

25

Reflections

Looking back from the standpoint of an octogenarian one asks oneself in what way the world has changed since one first knew it.

The period seems much vaster to young people than to oneself, and from the questions my boys put to me, I gather that I am to them, a sort of historical monument, and have some trouble in convincing them that in my boyhood ı travelled by railway and was not altogether ignorant of many modern conveniences.

There is certainly a greater freedom of etiquette and ceremony and young women go about by themselves in a way that in our youth would have been thought improper – though not quite yet in the American fashion where chaperonage seems an exploded superstition.

People travel more because it is easier. Instead of scrambling from the carriage and fighting in a crowd for a bason of scalding soup, which you had to leave half finished when the bell rang for departure, you now dine at ease in a refreshment car and there is no need for the rugs and wraps of years ago, when you got half frozen in winter.

You can converse by telephone with a friend at the other end of the country as though you were in the same room, and yet though we use electricity for light, motion, heat and a hundred other purposes, we are as far from knowing what it is, or anything about it but the way of using it.

December 18th 1918. This is my birthday, and I have some difficulty in realising that I am 84 years old. This morning my dear son Basil and I took the sacrament, and I thanked God for all the blessings of my long life, and above all for the measure of health and strength I continue to enjoy far beyond the usual condition, and especially that my wits are not impaired by old age. Except that I cannot take long walks, I can do all I could do ten or fifteen years ago, including splitting logs with a 13 pound sledge-hammer for firewood.

The war is happily over; at all events for the present. Germany however is impertinent and still causes disquiet, and the persistent success of Bolshevism in Russia is a source of danger to the great European Society.

Both my sons are happily safe – Hugh invalided home from France with Rheumatism. Basil won the Military Cross and a mention in despatches, and as a Major commanded the Leicester R.H.A. in Allenby's great drive which finished the annihilation of the Turkish army in that part of the world.

I gave up my London office during the war and have since done all my work at home with only one assistant, thus realising my ideal of being self-dependant.

I trust I may be spared to be able to work, and to be of some use in the world to the end.

Conclusion

After the war there was a great deal of work for war memorials, among which was the 'Memorial Arch' at Radley College.[1]

Sir Maurice Bowra,[2] when a young don at Wadham, remembered T.G.J. at about this time sometimes nodding off during Fellows' meetings – a tendency that caused some amusement when there was a ceremony to place an urn containing the ashes of a Fellow called Frederic Harrison[3] in the antechapel.

Lord Birkenhead, who had enjoyed a good lunch at the Randolph beforehand, was doing the eulogy. When the moment arrived, he said, 'Today we have come to pay homage to a great Wadham man and a great Oxford man – Sir Thomas Jackson.' Maurice Bowra said that 'at that moment, Jackson who had been asleep, woke up with a jolt and wondered where he was!'

During the war years, one of his most important works had been the restoration of Holy Trinity Church at Coventry, where the tower and transepts were underpinned as is recorded on a bronze plate in the church. His history of architecture was continued, the two volumes on *Byzantine and Romanesque Architecture* which had been published in 1913, being followed in 1915 by two more on *Gothic Architecture in France, England and Italy*, while the third volume of *The Renaissance of Roman Architecture* was published in 1923. His last book, *Architecture*, written at the request of Messrs. Macmillan, was published by them in 1925, having been finished by Basil Jackson.

Sir Thomas Jackson died six weeks before his 89th birthday on the 9th November 1924. The words of the Professor of Poetry, spoken thirteen years earlier at the ceremony when he received his Hon. D.C.L. degree at Oxford make a fitting epilogue to his career:

Restat, Domine Cancellarie, ut virum ingeniosissimum tibi praesentem, Architectum, si quis alius, nobis notissimum. Nescio an nemini plus debeamus, quippe qui Oxoniae antiquae repostor Oxoniae autem novea creator, eo iure quo qui optimo, sit nominandus. Quot ecclesias reparavit, quot collegia auxit vel ornavit, quot bibliothecas et officinas, quot scholas seu puerorum sive puellarum, quot remigum vel pilariorum papiliones ut vocant, apud nos erexit! Neque apud nos tantum. Eandem artificis scientiam et artem Abbatiae, Cathedrales, Collegia, Scholae, Sodalitates, Londinii, Cantabrigiae, hic illic per totam Britanniam sparsae confitentur! Neque graphide solum, et circino callet Vitruvius noster; calamo non minus apte utitur, quo littus Illyricum, qui ecclesiam S. Mariae Virginis, qui Collegium suum Wadhami et delineavit scitissime et descripsit. Nempe vir e collegio illo pulcherrimo ortus, matris exemplar, doctrinam matris, semper felicissime est secutus.

Adduco virum doctum, versatilem, amabilem, Thomam Graham Jackson.

[It remains, My Lord Chancellor, for me to present to you a man of genius, an architect familiar to us beyond all others. I doubt whether there is anyone to whom we owe more; he might most rightly be called the restorer of old Oxford and the creator of new Oxford. How many churches has he restored, how many colleges extended or adorned, how many libraries or laboratories, both boys' and girls' schools, pavilions for cricketers and oarsmen has he built in Oxford – and not in Oxford only – his architectural knowledge and artistry is witnessed to by Abbeys, Cathedrals, Schools, Institutions in London, in Cambridge and scattered up and down the whole of England. Nor is the skill of our Vitruvius confined to pencil and compasses – he wealds the pen with no less success and accuracy in drawing and describing the shores of Illyria, the Church of St. Mary the Virgin, and his own college of Wadham. As a son of that beautiful mother, I present to you this learned, versatile, and loveable man Thomas Graham Jackson.]

N.F.St G.J.

Appendix I

The Lambarde family

The family was descended from William Lambarde, the antiquary and author of *Perambulations of Kent*, whose father had come from Hereford and bought the Manor of Westcombe in East Greenwich in 1544.

William Lambarde was made Keeper of the Records in the Tower to Queen Elizabeth in 1600 and has left the following account of his interview with the Queen on the occasion of his presenting her with a book of those records which he called Pandecta Potulorum.

That which passed from the excellent Majestie of Queen Elizabeth, in her private chamber at East Greenwich, 4° Augusti 1601, 43°reg. Sui, towards William Lambarde.

He presented her Majestie with his Pandecta of all her rolls, bundells, membranes, and parcells, that he reposed in her Majestie's Tower at London; whereof she had given to him the charge 21st January last past.

Her majestie chearfullie received the same into her hands saying 'You intended to present this book unto me by the Countesse of Warwicke; but I will none of that; for if any subject of mine do me a service, I will thankfully accept it from his own hands'; then opening the book said 'You shall see that I can read' and so, with an audible voice, read over the epistle, and the title, so readily, and distinctly pointed, that it might perfectly appear, that she well understood, and conceived the same. Then she descended from the beginning of King John, till the end of Richard III, that is 64 pages, serving XI kings, containing 286 years: in the 1st page she demanded the meaning of *oblata, cartae, litterae clausae, et litterae patentes.*

W. L. He severally expounded the right meaning, and laid out the true differences of every of them; her Majestie seeming well satisfied, and said 'that she would be a scholar in her age, and thought it no scorn to learn during her life, being of the mind of that philosopher, who in his last years began with the Greek alphabet.' Then she proceeded to further pages, and asked, where she found cause of stay, as what *ordinationes, parliamenta, rotulus cambii, rediseisnes.*

W. L. He likewise expounded these all according to their original diversities, which she took in gracious and full satisfaction; so her Majestie fell upon the reign of King Richard II saying 'I am Richard II know ye not that?'

W. L. 'Such a wicked imagination was determined and attempted by a most unkind gent. the most adorned creature that ever your Majestie made.'

Her Majestie. 'He that will forget God, will also forget his benefactors; this tragedy was played 40tie times in open streets and houses.'

Her Majestie demanded what was *praestita*?

W. L. he expounded it to be 'monies lent by her progenitors to her subjects for their good, but with assurance of good bond for repayment'.

Her Majestie. 'So did my grandfather King Henry VII sparing to dissipate his treasure or lands.' Then returning to Richard II she demanded 'Whether I had seen any true picture, or lively representation of his countenance and person?'

W. L. 'None but such as be in common hands.'

Her Majestie. 'The Lord Lumley, a lover of antiquities, discovered it fastened on the backside of a door of a base room; which he presented unto me, praying, with my good leave, that I might put it in order with the ancestors and successors; I will command Tho. Kneavet, Keeper of my house and gallery at Westminster, to show it unto thee.'

Then she proceeded to the Rolls – *Romae, Vascon, Acquitaniae, Franciae, Scotiae, Walliae et Hiberniae.*

W. L. He expounded these to be records of estate, and negotiations with foreign princes or countries.

Her Majestie demanded again, 'if *rediseisnes* were unlawful and forcible throwing of men out of their lawful possessions?'

W. L. 'Yea, and therefore these be the rolls of fines assessed and levied upon such wrong doers, as well for the great and wilful contempt of the crown and royal dignity, as disturbance of common justice.'

Her Majestie. 'In those days force and arms did prevail; but now the wit of the fox is everywhere on foot, so as hardly a faithful and vertuouse man may be found.' Then came she to the whole total of the membranes and parcels aforesaid, amounting to ...; commending the work; 'not only for the pains therein taken, but also for that she had not received since her first coming to the crown any one thing that brought therewith so great declaration unto her;' and so being called away to prayer, she put the book in her bosom, having forbidden me from the first to the last to fall upon my knee before her; concluding 'Farewell, good and honest Lambarde!'

William Lambarde died a fortnight after this interview. The Queen's remark, 'I am Richard II', refers (as J. E. Neale, who quotes this in his

Queen Elizabeth, points out) to the Essex plot when the conspirators drew a parallel between Richard II and the Queen and had Shakespeare's play acted as propaganda for their cause. The picture referred to is undoubtedly the portrait of Richard II in Westminster Abbey. In a good light the mark of the lock and keyhole are clearly visible where it was 'fastened on the backside of a door of a base room'.

The portraits of the Lambarde family, which died out in 1974, now hang in the entrance corridor of Drapers' Hall. The Drapers' Company still oversee the administration of the Queen Elizabeth College, the Almshouses which William Lambarde founded in Greenwich and the Standing Cup he gave them always has pride of place on the dining table in front of the Master.

Appendix II

R.I.B.A. and Registration of Architects

On pp. 190-1 mention was made of the ambition of a certain class among architects to make architecture a close profession, hedged round by barriers of certificate and diploma like law and medicine, to which professions, by a false analogy they compared it.

From time to time attempts were made towards realising their object. A Bill was introduced in 1888 which led some of us to think a protest should be made by those architects to whom such a measure seemed to put the whole conception of architecture on a false ground. I wrote to Norman Shaw, whom I did not know, and received this reply:

6 Ellerdale Road,
Hampstead NW.
February 22nd 1888

My dear Sir,

I really think the Bill to which you refer has such a very slender chance of becoming law that it is hardly worth troubling about. Not that I should not be quite willing to sign any letter protesting against it. I have no doubt you saw a letter from the Institute some 10 days ago in *The Times* ignoring this Bill. I could easily call on you any morning on my way to town if you carry out your intention of writing a letter. Of course one sees perfectly well what these people are aiming at. They look on Architecture as a trade, or perhaps to put it more politely as a profession. I confess from this side I do not take the smallest interest in it one way or another. To me it is an art – or nothing; but all the same I am painfully alive to the fact that this is not the side from which the public regard it. The 'profession' and the 'public' – these are the two favourite expressions especially alas! from the R.I.B.A.

I am yours faithfully,
R. Norman Shaw

In 1891 a fresh move was made at the instance of the Society of Architects, a newly formed body, anxious to justify its existence by a show of energy. They got Mr. Noble, M.P., to bring in a Bill for the Registration of Architects and this time Norman Shaw took it up hot. This Bill was to be opposed by the Institute, but their motive, which was scarcely disguised, was to prevent anything that would anticipate themselves and prevent their making the Institute a ruling body through which alone admission could be had to the profession, just as lawyers are admitted to the Incorporated Law Society. At Shaw's instance a few architects met at Mervyn Macartney's house at the corner of Berkeley Square to consider what should be done. I was invited and there I met Norman Shaw for the first time. It was decided to send a protest to the Institute stating our views, and to get it signed as widely as possible by artists of all kinds who sympathised with us. I remember drafting the protest, writing on my knee; additions were made by some of the others and it finally took this form. It was also published in *The Times* with the following introduction.

To the Editor of The Times

Sir,

On the 4th inst a Bill is to be presented to Parliament for making Architecture a close profession like Law, Physic, and Divinity, instead of allowing it to remain as Art in its present state. The scheme has been brought forward in Parliament on former occasions but has never reached the stage of a division. Most probably it will meet the same fate this time. It is, however, no secret that some of those who now join in opposing it are doing so in the hope of substituting another measure of their own.

On the other hand there is a large number of Architects and members of the kindred arts to whom it appears that any alteration in this direction, from whatever body it may proceed, would be disastrous to the prospects of our art and we beg to enclose a protest which has been sent to the Royal Institute of British Architects and for which we hope you will find a place in your columns.

We are your obedient servants,
A. W. Blomfield, A.R.A.
John D. Sedding
T. G. Jackson
R. Norman Shaw, R.A.
L. Alma-Tadema, R.A.
E. Burne-Jones, A.R.A.

To the President and Council of the Royal Institute of British Architects

We, the undersigned, desire to record our opinion that the attempt to make Architecture a close profession, either by the Bill now introduced into Parliament or by any similar measure, is opposed to the interest of Architecture as a fine art.

We believe that, while it is possible to examine students in construction and matters of sanitation, their artistic qualifications (which really make the Architect) cannot be brought to the test of examination, and that a diploma of architecture obtained by such means would be a fallacious distinction, equally useless as a guide to the public and misleading as an object for the efforts of the student.

Architecture has for some time been less constantly associated with the sister arts of painting and sculpture than, in our opinion, is desirable and we think that examinations and diplomas, by raising up artificial barriers, would have a tendency still further to alienate these branches of art.

We think that no legislation can protect the public against bad design; nor could legislation help to prevent bad construction unless builders were required to pass the test of examination as well as Architects, inasmuch as Architects are not employed in the majority of cases.

Members of the Institute

Sir A. W. Blomfield, A.R.A.	*E. J. May
*Reginald T. Blomfield	*Mervyn Macartney
J. M. Brydon	*Ernest Newton
W. D. Caroë	A. Beresford Pite
John Douglas	*Edward S. Prior
W. M. Fawcett	John Oldrid Scott
Charles Ferguson	J. D. Sedding
C. Hodgson Fowler	George Sherrin
Charles Hadfield	*F. M. Simpson
*G. C. Horsley	R. Phene Spiers
Edmund Kirby	A. E. Street
William Leiper	John J. Stevenson

[* These seven at this time resigned their membership of the Institute.]

Not Members of the Institute

R. Rowand Anderson	A.H. Mackmurdo
John Bentley	Wm. C. Marshall
Geo. Bodley, A.R.A.	J. T. Micklethwaite
W. Butterfield	J. Hen. Middleton
Basil Champneys	Sidney Mitchell
Somers Clarke	H. Ricardo

Horace Field	G. Gilbert Scott
Thomas Garner	R. Norman Shaw, R.A.
T. G. Jackson	E. Prioleau Warren
W. R. Lethaby	Philip Webb

The following who are not architects desire to add their signatures.

L. Alma-Tadema, R.A.	Hubert Herkomer, R.A.
H. Armstead, R.A.	Holman Hunt
John Brett, A.R.A.	Selwyn Image
Thomas Brock, R.A.	Stirling Lee
Ford Maddox Brown	Herbert Marshall
E. Burne-Jones, A.R.A.	William Morris
J. B. Burgess, R.A.	James Powell
John R. Clayton	W. B. Richmond, A.R.A.
Walter Crane	Briton Riviere, R.A.
E. Onslow Ford	George Simonds
F. Garrard	Heywood Sumner
Alfred Gilbert, A.R.A.	Hamo Thornycroft, R.A.

The publication of our protest and letter to the Institute in *The Times* produced a reply in the same journal signed by Aston Webb, Hon. Sec., and William H. White, secretary, disclaiming on the part of the Institute any such ulterior object in their opposition to the Bill as we had implied. To this we replied by quoting passages by Alfred Waterhouse and Professor Roger Smith, distinctly anticipating what we supposed but saying that the time was not yet come for applying for statutory powers.

Lord Grimthorpe joined in the fray and wrote that he 'was glad to see an action brought and damages recovered against an Architect for designing and superintending his work so ill that damages ensued. That will do more than 50 Registration Bills'.

A conference between the Institute and ourselves was suggested and we agreed to meet them, provided the question of a qualifying examination and diploma was to be treated as an open one. This they declined to do, and said the Council regretted that our condition made any discussion in the proposed conference 'futile', and so for the present the matter ended. The Bill never reached a second reading. [The Registration Bill was again introduced in the House of Commons in 1927 and was passed in 1931.] Much as I differed with the Institute, I am happy to say I never quarrelled with them, or they with me and this year they did me, though not a member, the honour of nominating me to take part in the select competition for the new building of the South Kensington Museum, which was won by Aston Webb.

Appendix III

Winchester Cathedral

In 1907 T. G. Jackson wrote the following letter to the Editor of *The Times*:

Sir,

Your leading article last Wednesday about the needs of Winchester Cathedral encourages me to think it might be useful and might interest your readers to know more exactly what has happened to the building, and what repairs are necessary.

The site on which the Cathedral stands is at the foot of the declivity that falls to the valley of the Itchen. In primeval days the bottom of the valley was a bog, and when in the 11th century Bishop Walkelyn began to build, it was covered with a layer of peat 7 ft. thick, on which rested a bed of chalky marl, washed down from the surrounding elevation. The Norman church was built on the edge of this soft ground. Coming to water at the depth of about 10 feet the builders were unable to go further, and they drove in some short and ineffectual piles of oak on which they laid their foundation. It is curious that some of these piles have been used before and contain mortices, being no doubt relics of old Saxon buildings. These foundations have yielded to the weight placed upon them, but not so badly as what follows. When at the end of the 12th century Bishop Godfrey de Lucy built the Presbytery and the first Lady Chapel, the builders had to advance further into the bog than Bishop Walkelyn had done. Coming, like their predecessors, to water 10 feet below the surface, just when they reached the bed of marly chalk mentioned above, they were at a non plus; and as the best they could do, they cut down a wood of great beech trees, laid them flat, and on them Bishop de Lucy raised that building which is one of the gems of Early English art. I have no doubt that the trouble which followed and which has nearly brought this part of the building to ruin, began as soon as it was built. The tree trunks did not decay, but they were pressed down into the soft ground as much as 2 ft. 3 inches, the vaults became disturbed and pushed the walls out, and the whole building split off from the Norman part west of it and slid eastwards, leaving gaping cracks at the point of separation and in several other places. The dislocation of the vaults was so great that curves which should have been concave became convex, their arch construction was lost and they would have fallen long ago but for the iron bolts and straps by which they were hung up to the roof. This was the situation when I was called in to undertake the repair. The foundation being mainly at fault, the obvious remedy was to underpin the walls on the compact gravel that underlies the peat at 16 ft. And here the difficulty of the water which lies at the level of 9 ft. or 10 ft. below the surface presented itself. I am indebted to my friend Mr. Francis Fox, the famous engineer, for the suggestion to employ divers, of whose services he has availed himself in underpinning bridges and other works of pure engineering, which lie beyond the ordinary experience of an architect. This plan has answered perfectly. The greater part of the Lady Chapel and the Presbytery now rests on solid rock of cement concrete which itself bears on the hard gravel bed; the vaulting has been repaired and the ribs are restored to their shape; the walls have been grouted with cement and bonded; and it is probable that this part of the church will be cleared of scaffolding and restored to use by the end of the year.

The condition of the Norman transepts and the choir aisles next invited attention. The latter are now being underpinned like the Presbytery, but the transepts present greater difficulties. Partly owing to bad foundation, partly perhaps owing to injury when the Norman tower fell, as Norman towers often did, soon after it was built, by which the adjoining arches and walls would be forced outwards, the gables of the transepts overhang the base, that of the South Transept as much as 4 ft., and the side walls are shattered and dislocated to an alarming extent. Daylight could be seen through the fissures in the North Transept, and into one corner of that part no less than 25 tons of liquid cement have been injected. Both transepts need underpinning and tying back by an elaborate system of iron rods and cramps. They are now being shored to prevent disaster, and here for the present the works must stop till funds come in to enable us to proceed. Were the dangerous condition of the Cathedral more generally known, I cannot believe that it would for long be left leaning on crutches. In our great English Cathedrals we have an inestimable heritage from our forefathers, not only monuments of their piety, but treasures of art which may well challenge comparison with those of any country. It is for us to preserve them for those who come after.

The £60,00 for which the Dean and Chapter asks, is not much more than the sum given not so long ago for a single picture; and who would maintain that if Velasquez's 'Venus and Cupid' had found a house in Berlin instead of at Trafalgar Square the National loss would be comparable to that involved in the ruin of a Cathedral which stands pre-eminently in the foremost rank of those which Englishmen are justly proud?

Your obedient servant,
T. G. Jackson

The Athenaeum. Oct. 17th 1907.

Gazetteer

ABBREVIATIONS:

BoE, BoW: the current edition of the relevant volume of the Buildings of England and Buildings of Wales series (Pevsner Architectural Guides); further details given only where the title is not obvious from the location or an earlier edition is cited

Exhib: exhibited

ICBS: Incorporated Church Building Society (files in Lambeth Palace Library, London)

MS Recollections: the original manuscript of Recollections, usually cited only where it provides information not included in the published editions

RA: Royal Academy of Arts, London

RCHM: Royal Commission on Historical Monuments

Recollections: 1950 edition (*see* **BIBLIOGRAPHY**); for current edition, *see* **INDEX**

RIBA: Royal Institute of British Architects, London

VCH: Victoria County History

I. OXFORD

Recollections, 18-9, 178-9, 271-2 etc; *Architect*, XXXVIII (1887), 363; *Architect & Building News*, CXLIV (1935), 348-9; *Architectural Review*, I (1897), 154; *Architecture*, II (1897), 10; *Builder*, LIX (1890), 100-3; *Builders' Journal and Architectural Record* (IV), 1897, 355-7; *Building*, CCXLV (1983 Dec 9), 30; *Building Design*, no. 665 (1983 Nov 11), 10; *Oxford Times* (4 Nov 1983), 11; *RIBA Journal*, XIX (1912), 698-701; XXXIII (1926), 472

BoE, 59-60; J. Bettley, *Sir Thomas Graham Jackson, Bart., R.A. 1835-1924: an Exhibition of his Oxford Buildings* (1983); H. Colvin, *Unbuilt Oxford* (1983), 135-57; P. Howell, 'Oxford Architecture, 1800-1914', in M.G. Brock and M.C. Curthoys (ed.), *The History of the University of Oxford: Nineteenth-century Oxford*, part 2 (2000), 729-777; A. Martin, 'Oxford Jackson', *Oxoniensia*, XLIII (1978), 216-21; C. Tilbury, *Gothic and Classical: Sir Thomas Graham Jackson and the Traditions of Oxford building* (1983); G. Tyack, *Oxford: an architectural guide* (1998), 248-55; W. Whyte, 'Anglo-Jackson Attitudes: reform and the rebuilding of Oxford', *The Victorian*, no. 12 (2003), 4-9

ACLAND HOME, Banbury Road

Opened 1897; to commemorate the wife of Sir Henry Acland. Now part of the Acland Hospital, and obscured by façade of 1937.

Recollections, 245, 251; correspondence with Sir Henry Acland in Bodleian Library, Dept of Western MSS; *Architectural Review*, I (1897), 146, 160; BoE, 317

ALL SOULS' COLLEGE

Monuments in chapel to Mountague Bernard, 1883 (carving by Farmer & Brindley), and Thomas Lucas, 1918; repairs in library.

Recollections, 185; drawings at RA

BALLIOL COLLEGE
see also **KING'S MOUND**

Proposed rebuilding of Butterfield's chapel, 1911. One of the supporters of the scheme was Walter Morrison, the donor of the chapel at Giggleswick (q.v.).

Recollections, 273; TGJ's report and drawings, Balliol College Archive; *Architecture*, II (1897), 14; P. Howell, 'Oxford Architecture, 1800-1914', 738; P. Howell, '"The Disastrous Deformation of Butterfield": Balliol College in the Twentieth Century', *Architectural History*, XLIV (2001), 283-92

BODLEIAN LIBRARY

Restoration and refacing, 1877-84

Recollections, 143, 162, 178, 183; *Architect*, XVI (1876), 229; XVIII (1877), 247; XXVIII (1882), 252-3; XXX (1883), 244; XXVI (1881), 273; *Architectural Review*, I (1897), 154; *Architecture*, II (1897), 14; *Builders' Journal and Architectural Record* (IV), 1897, 358; BoE, 263; P. Howell, 'Oxford Architecture, 1800-1914', 749, 770

BOTANIC GARDEN

Restoration of gateway, 1891; proposed professor's house.

University Archives, UC/FF/305/2/1; *Architecture*, II (1897), 92

BRASENOSE COLLEGE
see also **FREWEN HALL**

New quadrangle, with façade to High Street, 1880-9, 1907-11; monument to E.H. Craddock, 1887; binder's stamp for book covers, 1890; chapel screen, organ loft and case, 1892-3; restoration of chapel, 1894-5

Clerk of works, Mockford. Carving by Farmer & Brindley. Lighting in undergraduates' reading room by Benson.

Exhib: RA, 1882, 1887, 1888, 1890. International Exhibition, Chicago, 1893

Recollections, 69, 178, 185, 187, 194, 233-4, 268, 270; drawings at Brasenose, RA, and RIBA; metalwork designs at RA; *Academy Architecture*, II (1890), 21; *Architect*, XL (1888), 223; XLIV (1890), 59; *Architect and Building News*, CXLIV (1935), 349; *Architects' Journal*, LX (1924), 759, 761; *Architectural Review*, I (1897), 151-4; *Architecture*, II (1897), 14, 17-8, 21; *British Architect*, XXIX (1888), 228; *Builder*, LII (1887), 832, 835; LV (1888), 84; LVIII (1890), 416-7; *Builders' Journal and Architectural Record*, IV (1897), 356-8; *Building News*, XLII (1882), 540; LIV (1888), 684; *Magazine of Art*, VIII (1889), 332-40; *RIBA Journal*, XXXIII (1926), 466, 473, 478; BoE, 107-8; P. Howell, 'Oxford Architecture, 1800-1914', 752-3, 755, 771-4, 776

CHRIST CHURCH

Competition design for Wolsey's Tower, 1874. Winning design by Bodley & Garner partially executed.

Wooden bridge over the Cherwell, 1881, since replaced.
Exhib: RA, 1875
Recollections, 127, 134, 138, 185; drawings and minutes of Belfry Committee at Christ Church; *Architect*, XIV (1875), 160; *Building News*, XXXVI (1879), 720; E.G.W. Bill, *Christ Church Meadow* (1965), 14; P. Howell, 'Oxford Architecture, 1800-1914', 747, 770

CHURCH OF ALL SAINTS, High Street
Restoration and refitting, 1896-7, to provide a new City church following the demolition of St Martin, Carfax (q.v.). Now the library of Lincoln College (q.v.); pews re-used in St Philip and St James, Woodstock Road.
Recollections, 245, 252; *Architecture*, II (1897), 14; BoE, 287, 298

CHURCH OF ST MARTIN, Carfax
Restoration of tower, 1896-7, following demolition of the church, including addition of stair turret.
Recollections, 245, 252; *RIBA Journal*, XIX (1912), 661-76; BoE, 307

CHURCH OF ST MARY THE VIRGIN, High Street
Restoration of spire, 1892-6. New statues (copies of old) by George Frampton. Internal restoration of choir, 1901, and proposed organ loft and screen, 1902.
Exhib: RA, 1893, 1902
MS Recollections, 1901; *Recollections*, 234-5, 243, 245, 249; Bodleian Library, Dept of Western MSS; TGJ, *The Church of St Mary the Virgin Oxford* (1897); *Architect*, XLVIII (1892), 431-2; XLIX (1893), 22, 28, 106, 373; L (1893), 341-2; LV (1896), 157-8; LXXXIV (1910), 88; *Architectural Review*, IV (1898), 1-8, 50-3, 109-114; XXIII (1908), 104-7; *Architecture*, II (1897), 14; *Builder*, LXIII (1892), 516 (quoting letter by TGJ to *The Times*, 28 Dec 1892); LXIV (1893), 346; LXX (1896), 493; *Builders' Journal and Architectural Record*, XVI (1902-3), 398; *Building News*, LXXIII (1897), 391-2; BoE, 283; P. Howell, 'Oxford Architecture, 1800-1914', 773

CHURCH OF ST-MARY-AT-THE-WALL *see under* HERTFORD COLLEGE

CHURCH OF ST PETER-IN-THE-EAST, Queen's Lane
Refitting, 1880. Part now the library of St Edmund Hall.
Recollections, 179; metalwork designs at RA

CLARENDON LABORATORY *see* ELECTRICAL LABORATORY

CLARENDON PRESS
Possibly the restoration of the Old Clarendon Building, Broad Street, 1909.
TGJ designed two press marks for the Press, one of which was used for his history of Wadham College (1893) and re-used for *The Church of St Mary the Virgin, Oxford* (1897).
RIBA Journal, XXXII (1924), 49; RCHM, *The City of Oxford* (1939), 13

CORPUS CHRISTI COLLEGE
Organ case in chapel, *c.* 1881.
New building on the corner of Merton Street and Magpie Lane, 1884-5. Clerk of works, Edwin Long.
Alterations and additions to Beam Hall, 1885.

Barge, 1886.
Exhib: RA, 1885, 1886
College archive, B/4/1/8; *Recollections*, 163, 185; Architect, XXXII (1884), 268; *British Architect*, XXIV (1885), 158; XXVI (1886), 176; *Builder*, XLVI (1884), 782; LIX (1890), 108; *Builders' Journal and Architectural Record*, IV (1897), 359; *Building News*, L (1886), 906; RCHM, *The City of Oxford* (1939), 166; BoE, 131; P. Howell, 'Oxford Architecture, 1800-1914', 753, 756, 771; C. Sherriff, *The Oxford College Barges: their History and Architecture* (2003)

CRICKET PAVILION, University Parks
1880-1. Clerk of works, Edwin Long. Unexecuted design for extension, 1886.
Recollections, 185; *Building News*, XLI (1881), 72; drawings in private collection; BoE, 282; P. Howell, 'Oxford Architecture, 1800-1914', 756, 770

ELECTRICAL LABORATORY, Parks Road
1908-10. Donated by the Drapers' Co. Carving by Farmer & Brindley. Now the Townsend Laboratory.
Exhib: RA, 1909
Recollections, 267, 269 *Builder*, XCVI (1909), 556; BoE, 278; P. Howell, 'Oxford Architecture, 1800-1914', 757, 776

EXAMINATION SCHOOLS, High Street
1876-83, won in competition. Clerk of works, Robert Edwards. Carving by Maples of Farmer & Brindley. Delegacy for Non-Collegiate students (now the Ruskin School of Drawing), 1886-8; Local Examinations Delegacy (Merton Street), 1895-7.
Exhib: RA, 1877, 1886, 1898 (Diploma Work); International Exhibition, Paris, 1878; Adelaide, 1887 (1st Order of Merit); Chicago, 1893
University Almanack: 1883 ('New Examination Schools', drawn by TGJ, etched by R. Kent Thomas, 1882); 1932 ('The Examination Schools', drawn by Muirhead Bone, 1931)
MS Recollections; *Recollections*, 133-142, 162, 175-6, 178, 183, 188; drawings at Bodleian Library, Dept of Western MSS, RA, and RIBA; minute book and out-letter book of the Delegacy for the New Schools etc, Bodleian Library, University Archives; metalwork designs at RA
Architect, IX (1873), 246, 291; X (1873), 56; XIII (1875), 250, 289, 374; XV (1876), 364, 408; XVI (1876), 229; XVIII (1878), 211; XXII (1879), 223; XXVI (1881), 273; XXVII (1882), 362-3; XXXVIII (1887), 254, 363; XL (1888), 223; *Architect & Building News*, CXLIV (1935), 348-9; *Architectural Review*, I (1897), 146; III (1898), supplement; *Architecture*, II (1897), 8-13; *British Architect*, XVII (1882), 102; XXV (1886), 461-6; XXVI (1886), 176; XXIX (1888), 210, 264, 354; XXXIV (1890), 190; *Builder*, XXXI (1873), 452; XLII (1882), 719-20; LI (1886), 533, 535; LII (1887), 460; LIII (1887), 906; LIX (1890), 108-113; *Builders' Journal and Architectural Record*, IV (1897), 358; *Building News*, XXX (1876), 418; XXXI (1876), 204, 230, 492, 622; XXXVI (1879), 720; L (1886), 906; *RIBA Journal*, XVII (1910), 621-9; XXXIII (1926), 472; *The Times* (3 June 1882); *University Gazette* (30 May 1876), 406-9
J. Fergusson, *History of the Modern Styles of Architecture* (3rd edn, rev. R. Kerr, 1891), II, 158, 169; Cook & Wedderburn, *Works of John Ruskin* (1908), XXXIII, 363, 476, and XXXVII, 477; H.S. Goodhart-Rendel, *English Architecture since the Regency* (1953),

176-7; BoE, 264-6; R. Wilcock, *The Building of the Oxford University Examination Schools 1876-1882* (1983); J. Bettley, 'T.G. Jackson and the Examination Schools', *Oxford Art Journal*, VI (1983), 57-66; R. Wilcock, 'Around Oxford – The Schools', *The Ashmolean* (Summer 1983), 10-1; M.W. Brooks, *John Ruskin and Victorian Architecture* (1987), 261-3; P. Howell, 'Oxford Architecture, 1800-1914', 748-9, 753-4, 770, 772, 774; W. Whyte, '"Rooms for the torture and shame of scholars"': the new Examination Schools and the architecture of reform', *Oxoniensia*, LXVI (2001), 85-103

FREWEN HALL, New Inn Hall Street
Alterations, for Brasenose College, 1888, 1893
MS Recollections, 1893; drawings at Brasenose; *Architecture*, II (1897), 92; BoE, 323

HERTFORD COLLEGE
Rebuilding, 1884-1916: front to Catte Street, 1887-9; front quadrangle, 1895; N quadrangle, 1901-16; chapel, 1903-8; bridge, 1913-4; dining hall ceiling, 1921; war memorial tablet and reredos in chapel, *c.* 1921; monument to Henry Boyd, 1922; restoration of St Mary-at-the-Wall, 1923-6.
The college was refounded in 1874, the principal benefactor being T.C. Baring; rebuilding was started by the new college's second Master, Henry Boyd. Clerk of works, Edwin Long. Carving by Farmer & Brindley.
Exhib: RA 1890, 1903, 1904, 1907, 1913, 1916
University Almanack: 1889 ('The New Hall of Hertford College', etched by Robert Farren, 1888); 1973 ('Hertford College from the South West', from a painting by Alfred Daniels, 1972)
Recollections, 189, 267, 275; drawings and photographs at Hertford; drawings at RA; metalwork designs at RA; *Academy Architecture*, II (1890), 25; *Architect*, XL (1888), 223; *Architect & Building News*, CXLIV (1935), 348-9; *Architects' Journal*, LX (1924), 762; *Architectural Review*, XVI (1904), 77-80; *Architecture*, II (1897), 14; *British Architect*, LXXIX (1913), 414-5, 422; *Builder*, LXXXIV (1903), 540; LXXXVII (1904), 274; XCII (1907), 572; *Building News*, LVIII (1890), 686; CIV (1913), 608; CXI (1916), 358 ff.; *Hertford College Magazine* (May 1910); (June 1912), 127; (May 1913), 188; (Jan 1914), 44-5; (April 1921), 9; (April 1923), 4, 7; (April 1926); (Spring 1981), 7-8; *RIBA Journal*, XVII (1910), 621-9; XIX (1912), 702; XXXII (1924), 49; XXXIII (1926), 470-2; RCHM, *The City of Oxford* (1939), 59; BoE, 138-41; P. Howell, 'Oxford Architecture, 1800-1914', 753, 772, 775-7; W. Whyte, 'Unbuilt Hertford: T.G. Jackson's Contextual Dilemmas', *Architectural History*, XLV (2002), 347-62

HIGH SCHOOL FOR BOYS, George Street
1879-81, additions 1892-4. Commissioned following competition. Clerk of works, Mockford. Now the Dept of Politics and International Relations, University of Oxford.
Recollections, 162, 174, 178, 183, 233; volume of drawings in Oxford Library; *Architecture*, II (1897), 21-3; *Building News*, XXXVIII (1880), 190, 237, 264, 340

HIGH SCHOOL FOR GIRLS, Banbury Road
1879-81, following the High School for Boys. Clerk of works, Edwin Long. Terracotta decoration by Doulton. Now part of the Dept of Materials, University of Oxford.
Recollections, 163, 178, 183; *Architectural Review*, I (1897), 146, 154; *Architecture*, II (1897), 14; *Building News*, XL (1881), 484; *RIBA Journal*, XXXIII (1926), 467

KING'S MOUND, Mansfield Road
Tutor's house for Balliol College, 1892-3. Clerk of works, Edwin Long. Intended by Benjamin Jowett, Master of Balliol, as part of a larger scheme that was not carried out. Now the Master's Lodgings.
Exhib: RA, 1893
Recollections, 233; *Architect and Building News*, CXLV (1936), 284; *Architectural Review*, I (1897), 139-41; *Architecture*, II (1897), 84-5; *Builder*, LXV (1893), 176-7; *Builders' Journal and Architectural Record*, IX (1899), 88; *RIBA Journal*, XVII (1910), 621; XIX (1912), 693; BoE, 330; P. Howell, 'Oxford Architecture, 1800-1914', 754, 773

LINCOLN COLLEGE
see also **CHURCH OF ALL SAINTS**
Grove Building, 1880-3; restoration of Hall roof, 1889, and new fireplace, 1891. Clerk of works, Mockford.
Exhib: RA, 1891
Recollections, 184; drawing at RA; metalwork designs at RA; *Academy Architecture*, III (1891), 45; *Architect*, XXVI (1881), 273; XXVIII (1882), 252-3; *Architecture*, II (1897), 14, 18-21 *Building News*, XLII (1882), 790, 794; LX (1891), 804; LXI (1891), 29; RCHM, *The City of Oxford*, 66; BoE, 147; P. Howell, 'Oxford Architecture, 1800-1914', 752, 770, 773

MAGDALEN COLLEGE SCHOOL, Cowley Place
Competition design, 1893; built by Sir Arthur Blomfield, 1893-4.
MS Recollections, 1893; BoE, 304

MERTON COLLEGE
Proposed additions to form new quad E of existing college buildings, 1877; proposed new quad on N side of Merton Street, 1878; restoration of sacristy and exterior of chapel, 1886-8; monument to Rev. G.N. Freeling, 1892 (carving by Farmer & Brindley); miscellaneous repairs, *c*. 1901.
Exhib: RA, 1879
MS Recollections, 1901; *Recollections*, 185; report and drawings in Merton archives; drawing at RA; metalwork designs at RA; *Architecture*, II (1897), 14; *Builder*, LXXXI (1901), 247; *Building News*, LVIII (1890), 221; RCHM, *The City of Oxford* (1939), 81; P. Howell, 'Oxford Architecture, 1800-1914', 772

MILITARY COLLEGE, Hollow Way, Cowley
1877-81. Clerk of works, Walter Scott. Only part executed. Taken over by the Morris Motor Works and now flats.
Recollections, 143, 162, 179, 183; *Architect*, XVIII, 1877, 72; XX (1878), 211; *Architecture*, II (1897), 22; *Builder*, LXXXIX (1905), 570; *Building News*, XLVI (1884), 1023; BoE, 343; J. Wilding, *Nuffield Press: a Jubilee History* (1985)

OLD ASHMOLEAN MUSEUM
Restoration, 1896-8.
University Archives, UC/FF/304/1/2-3

ORIEL COLLEGE
Alterations to chapel, 1883-4, including extension of choir into ante-chapel and W organ gallery; communion plate; stained glass, designed by H.E. Wooldridge, made by Powell.

College barge, 1891-2; broken up 1954, but pieces of lead decoration preserved in the college. Hull made by Salter Bros, superstructure by James Smith & Sons.
Recollections, 185, 233; drawings for barge at RA, and photographs in Oxford Public Library (OCL 4180, 4182, 76/2209; see also pamphlet OXFU 57 BOAT); *Architect*, XXXII (1884), 268; *Architectural Review*, CXX (1956), 36-42; *Architecture*, II (1897), 14; *Building News*, XLVI (1884), 552; *Country Life*, CXLI (1967), 6-8, 659; RCHM, *The City of Oxford* (1939), 93; BoE, 64, 178-9; P. Howell, 'Oxford Architecture, 1800-1914', 756, 759, 771, 773; C. Sherriff, *The Oxford College Barges: their History and Architecture* (2003)

QUEEN'S COLLEGE
Chemical laboratory, 1900, and other repairs, 1901.
MS Recollections, 1901; *RIBA Journal*, XXXII (1924), 49 (list of works); P. Howell, 'Oxford Architecture, 1800-1914', 775

RADCLIFFE CAMERA
Restoration, 1880
University Archives, UC/FF/197/2; *RIBA Journal*, XXXII (1924), 49 (list of works)

RADCLIFFE INFIRMARY, Woodstock Road
Unidentified work
RIBA Journal, XXXII (1924), 49 (list of works)

RADCLIFFE OBSERVATORY, Woodstock Road
Restoration and additions, 1900, and / or additional observatory, *c.* 1899-1903.
Recollections, 259; *Country Life*, LXVII (1930), 681; BoE, 272; P. Howell, 'Oxford Architecture, 1800-1914', 757, 775

RADCLIFFE SCIENCE LIBRARY, South Parks Road
1897-1901. Commissioned by the Drapers' Co. Clerk of works, Edwin Long. Exhib: RA, 1899
Recollections, 252, 259; correspondence in Radcliffe Science Library; metalwork designs at RA; *Architectural Record*, XIII (1901), pl. cccxxxviii; *Builder*, LXXVII (1899), 200; LXXX (1901), 641; *Builders' Journal and Architectural Record*, XVII (1903), 3; *RIBA Journal*, XVII (1910), 626-7; P. Howell, 'Oxford Architecture, 1800-1914', 774

ST BASIL'S HOME, Iffley Road
Unexecuted design, for the Sisters of the Community of St John the Baptist, 1913
Exhib: RA, 1913
British Architect, LXXXI (1914), 265, 270-1; *Builder*, CIV (1913), 596-7

SCHOOLS OF RURAL ECONOMY AND FORESTRY, Parks Road
Incorrectly attributed to TGJ by H.S. Goodhart-Rendel in *DNB*; by N.W. & G.A. Harrison, 1906-8 (now part of St John's College).
BoE, 276

SHELDONIAN THEATRE
Organ case, 1876-7; restoration, including enlargement of basement windows, 1890, 1909-10. Organ made by Willis; carving by Farmer & Brindley.
MS Recollections, 1910; *Recollections*, 143, 149-50; MSS in Bodleian Library, University Archives; drawing at RIBA; *Architect*, XLIV (1890), 230; *Architecture*,

II (1897), 14; *Building News*, XXXIII (1877), 379; RCHM, *The City of Oxford* (1939), 10; P. Howell, 'Oxford Architecture, 1800-1914', 770

SOMERVILLE COLLEGE
New quadrangle, 1881-2. Clerk of works, Edwin Long.
Recollections, 184; *Architecture*, II (1897), 14; *Building News*, XLIV (1883), 10; LII (1887), 302, 340; BoE, 251; *Victorian Society Annual* (1992), 17; P. Howell, 'Oxford Architecture, 1800-1914', 751, 771

TRINITY COLLEGE
Front quad, including President's Lodgings, 1883-8; alterations and additions to old bursary and hall, 1897; organ case in chapel (since replaced). Clerk of works, Mockford.
Exhib: RA, 1885, 1887
University Almanack: 1892 ('The New Quadrangle, Trinity College', etched by A. Ernest Smith, 1891)
Recollections, 179, 187-8; drawings at Trinity and RA; *Architect*, XXXII (1884), 268; XXXVIII (1887), 254, 363; XL (1888), 223; *Architectural Review*, I (1897), 142, 155-6; *Architecture*, II (1897), 3-4, 14; *British Architect*, XXIX (1888), 392; *Builders' Journal and Architectural Record*, IV (1897), 358; *Building News*, XLIX (1885), 488; LIII (1887), 10; *RIBA Journal*, XXXIII (1926), 472; BoE, 203-4; P. Howell, 'Oxford Architecture, 1800-1914', 753, 771

WADHAM COLLEGE
see also BOURTON-ON-THE-WATER (Glos); HAMPTON GAY (Oxon); ILMINSTER (Som); LITTLE BROMLEY (Essex)
Restoration and alterations to front quad and Warden's Lodgings, including new conservatory, 1871-6; improvements to back quad, 1874; monument to J.R. Griffith, 1882; repairs to chapel, new organ gallery and case, rearrangement of stained glass, new altar cloth and dossal, 1885-8; candlesticks, 1889; repairs to tower, 1889; pedestal for bust of Lord Westbury; binder's stamp for book covers, 1890; bookplate, 1894; monument to John Griffiths, 1901; cover design for *Wadham College Gazette*, 1904; unexecuted design for tutor's house in the garden of 35 Holywell Street, 1908; alterations to hall, executed by Basil Jackson, 1924-5.
Organ by Willis & Son; carving of case by Childs of Farmer & Brindley, modelling by Mr. George; altar cloth and dossal made by Watts & Co.
TGJ was elected a scholar of Wadham, 1854, BA 1858, MA 1863; probationary fellow 1864, fellow 1865; elected bursar 1879 but resigned fellowship on marriage in 1880 before taking up the post; honorary fellow 1882. Wrote a history of the college, published 1893. Portrait for the college by Briton Riviere, 1899.
MS Recollections, 1901; *Recollections*, 21, 46, 71-2, 90-2, 104, 124-7, 163, 173-4, 188, 193, 197, 228-9, 260, 269; drawings at Wadham, RA, and RIBA; Wadham College, Convention Book; *Architecture*, II (1897), 14; *Building News*, LVIII (1890), 221; *Wadham College Gazette*, no. 76 (1924), 154-7; no. 77 (1925), 161-2; RCHM, *The City of Oxford* (1939), 118; BoE, 215; P. Howell, 'Oxford Architecture, 1800-1914', 747, 769, 771
Architectural Review, CXX (1956), 36-42, attributes to TGJ the Wadham College barge, 1897, but there is no further evidence for this (cf. Oriel, Corpus Christi, and *Oxford Mail* (29 Jul 1975), 7)

II GREAT BRITAIN

ALDENHAM (Herts): Aldenham School
Dormitory block, 1905
MS Recollections, 1905; *Recollections*, 190; drawings at RIBA

ALDERSHOT (Hants): Church of St Augustine
New mission church, 1906-8
Incomplete.
Exhib: RA, 1907
ICBS file 10683; *Builder*, XCII (1907), 572; BoE, 76

ALDERSHOT (Hants): Church of St Michael
New nave and N aisle, 1910-11
Exhib: RA, 1907
Recollections, 270; ICBS file 10956; *Builder*, XCII (1907), 572; BoE, 74

ALFORD (Som): Church of All Saints
Unidentified work, 1877
Reredos and chancel paving may be TGJ's work. Alford House was the seat of the Thrings (cf. Hornblotton and Lottisham).
Recollections, 151

ANNESLEY (Notts): Church of All Saints
New church for colliery village, 1872-4; partially rebuilt after fire, 1907-8
TGJ's first entirely new church, for Reginald Prance, whose brother Clement was vicar. Chancel S windows and pavement by Powell.
Exhib: RA, 1873
Recollections, 117; *Architectural Review*, I (1897), 144-5; *RIBA Journal*, XXXIII (1926), 475; BoE, 27

ASH (Kent): Church of St Peter & St Paul
Restoration, 1901-4; memorial to the Revd Charles James Lambarde (died 1909). Fittings include bench ends in memory of his wife Alice, altar rail, stalls, pulpit, lectern and pews. Alice was C.J. Lambarde's brother.
Drawing at RA (lectern); BoE, *Weald*, 132; J. Newman, *The Church of St Peter and St Paul …* (1982)

ASHBOURNE (Derbys): Church of St Oswald
Restoration of tower and spire, 1912-13
MS Recollections, 1912; Church of England Record Centre 51630; *RIBA Journal*, XXXII (1924), 49-50 (list of works)

BADSEY (Worcs): Church of St James
Restoration, 1884-5; churchyard cross, 1910
MS Recollections, 1885; drawing at RA; BoE, 74

BANBURY (Oxon): Banbury Cross
Statues of Queen Victoria, King Edward VII and King George V, 1914
Carved by Boulton & Sons.
BoE, 437

BARNET (Herts): Library, Church Passage, High Street

Library for the Hyde Institute, 1903-4
Built by the Misses Paget of Handley; now Barnet Library.
MS Recollections, 1903; *Builder*, LXXXVI (1904), 614; *RIBA Journal*, XXXII (1924), 49 (list of works); BoE, *London 4* (1998), 171

BARTON ST DAVID (Som): Church of St David
Restoration, 1879-81
ICBS file 7527

BASINGSTOKE (Hants): Church of St Mary, Eastrop Lane
Addition of nave to existing chapel, 1909-12
Clerk of works, Edwin Long.
MS Recollections, 1910, 1912; Edwin Long, Notebooks (Winchester Cathedral Library, Jackson Collection D-H); ICBS file 11118; *RIBA Journal*, XXXIII, 1926, 475; BoE, 91

BATH (Som): Abbey
Restoration of W front, 1899-1904; repairs to central tower, 1904-6; organ loft and case in N transept, 1911-12; mace and sword rests, 1915; monument to A. St Reilly, 1918; War Memorial cloister on S side of nave, 1921-4; fitting out of memorial chapel in S choir aisle, 1922-4
Clerk of works, Edwin Long.
Exhib: RA, 1913, 1921, 1924
MS Recollections, 1902; drawings at RA; Edwin Long, Notebooks (Winchester Cathedral Library, Jackson Collection D-H); *Recollections*, 270; *Builders' Journal and Architectural Record*, XX (1904, supplement, Dec 28), 6; XXI (1905, supplement, Dec 27), 18; *Builder*, CIV (1913), 596-7; CXXIII (1922), 733; *RIBA Journal*, XXXII (1924), 50; BoE, *Somerset N*, 101-2; Neil Jackson, *Nineteenth Century Bath Architects and Architecture* (1991), 170-81

BATH (Som): Church of St Stephen, Lansdown
Monument to Rev. Hilton Bothamley, 1921
Drawing at RA

BILLINGE (Lancs): Church of St Aidan
Addition of transepts and apse, 1905-8; war memorial tablet, 1920
Exhib: RA, 1906
MS Recollections, 1905; drawing at RA; BoE, *Lancs S*, 75

BINSTED (W Sussex): Church of St Mary
Restoration, 1867; E window (panels by Henry Holiday, grisaille background by TGJ, made by Powell), 1869
Recollections, 114; BoE, 105

BISHOPS WALTHAM (Hants): Church of St Peter
Restoration, 1894-7
ICBS file 9921; BoE, 104

BLENHEIM PALACE (Oxon)
Remodelling of interior of chapel, including new gallery, organ, stalls and other fittings, 1888-9
Only partially executed. Fittings made by C.H. Bessant.

Recollections, 215-7; drawing and metalwork designs at RA; *Academy Architecture*, I (1889), 61; *Architect*, XLI (1889), 281; *Architecture*, II (1897), 23; BoE, 472

BOTLEY (Hants): Church of All Saints
N aisle, 1892, and narthex, 1895-6
Metalwork designs at RA; BoE, 114

BOTTISHAM (Cambs): Church of the Holy Trinity
Restoration, 1905-6
MS Recollections, 1906; ICBS file 10613; RCHM, *County of Cambridge*, II (1972), 1

BOURNEMOUTH (Hants): Church of All Saints, Castlemain Avenue, West Southbourne
New church by J.O. and C.M.O. Scott with C.T. Miles & Son, 1913-5, but working drawing at RIBA signed by TGJ, 1913.

BOURNEMOUTH (Hants): Church of St Michael
War memorial chapel (S chancel), 1920, including statue of Fortitude by George Frampton
Drawing at RA; BoE, 124

BOURNEMOUTH (Hants): Church of St Peter
Screen between S transept and S aisle, 1905-6
MS Recollections, 1905 ('additions'); BoE, 119

BOURTON-ON-THE-WATER (Glos): Church of St Lawrence
Rebuilding, keeping C14 chancel and C18 tower: N aisle and vestry, 1872-8, S porch 1890, nave 1889-91
The work of 1872-8 also included restoration and refitting of the chancel, and reseating the nave; font, 1875; pulpit, 1888. The patron of the living was Wadham College, whose Convention Book, 6 Dec 1872, records TGJ's report and grant of £200.
ICBS file 7580; *Architecture*, II (1897), 93; *Building News*, L (1886), 356; BoE, *Gloucestershire 1* (1999), 188-9

BRIGHTON (E Sussex): Brighton College
Memorials in chapel, *c.* 1880-1902; cricket pavilion, 1882-3, and levelling of playing fields; binder's stamps for book covers, and bookplates, 1882, 1886; new buildings, including gateway and three boarding houses, 1884-7; enlargement of chapel as war memorial, 1922
Clerk of works, Mockford. Some of the memorials carved by Farmer & Brindley. Proposals for a fourth boarding house, sanatorium, and great school room were not carried out. The pavilion has been demolished.
TGJ was a pupil at the school, 1850-3.
Exhib: RA, 1885, 1922
Recollections, 14-5, 190, 230; drawings, correspondence and other MSS (including TGJ's *Report on Brighton College*, 1882) at Brighton College; drawings at RA and RIBA; metalwork designs at RA; *Architecture*, II (1897), 21-2, 24; *Brightonian* (Sept 1985), 79-80; *British Architect*, XXIV (1885), 86, 96; XXVIII (1887), 156; *Builder*, XLVIII (1885), 794-6; CXXII (1922), 720; *Builders' Journal and Architectural Record*, IV (1897), 355; *Building News*, XLVII (1884), 976; *RIBA*

Journal, XXXIII (1926), 473; BoE, 443; D. Braithwaite, *Building in the Blood* (1981), 134; M.D.W. Jones, 'Gothic enriched: Thomas Jackson's mural tablets in Brighton College Chapel', *Church Monuments*, VI (1991), 54-66

BRIGHTON (E Sussex): Church of St Augustine
New church by G.E.S. Streatfeild, 1913, with TGJ as consultant. Streatfeild was TGJ's assistant, 1891-3.
BoE, 443

BROMLEY (Kent): Church of St Peter & St Paul
New chancel and S chancel aisle, N vestry with organ chamber over, 1882-5
The rector was A.G. Hellicar, father of TGJ's first pupil, Evelyn Hellicar. Destroyed by bombing (all but tower), 1941.
Exhib: RA, 1883
MS Recollections, *c.* 1885; ICBS file 8827; *British Architect*, XX (1883), 6; *Building News*, XLV (1883), 166; BoE, *London 2* (1983), 166

BROMLEY (Kent): Plonck's Hill *see* SHAMLEY GREEN

BURPHAM (W Sussex): Church of St Mary
Restoration, including new chancel arch, S transept and S aisle walls, 1869
Recollections, 114; BoE, 121

CAMBRIDGE: King's College
Enlargement of hall, with new panelling and canopy behind high table, 1899
Recollections, 259; RCHM, *City of Cambridge* (1959), pt 1, 133; BoE, 81

CAMBRIDGE: Senate House
Alterations, 1898-1909, including new lighting and other fittings by Benson of Bond Street.
MS Recollections, 1898; *Recollections*, 259

CAMBRIDGE: University Buildings, Downing Street, Downing Place and Tennis Court Road
Sedgwick Memorial Museum of Geology, Squire Law Library, and Law School, 1899-1904. Clerk of works, Robert Edwards; carving by Farmer & Brindley. Statue of Adam Sedgwick by Onslow Ford; figure of Justice on Squire Law Library by Henry Pegram.
Museum of Archaeology and Ethnology, 1910-5. Incorporates part of Inigo Jones' choir screen from Winchester Cathedral (q.v.).
Physiological Laboratory and Psychological Laboratory, 1913. Gift of the Drapers' Co.
Also on the site is the Botanical School and Museum by W.C. Marshall, who had worked as an improver in TGJ's office.
Exhib: RA, 1900, 1901, 1903, 1909, 1910, 1913, 1915, 1918
Recollections, 232, 233, 246, 259, 268, 270; drawings in Cambridge University Archives; metalwork designs at RA; TGJ, *The Renaissance of Roman Architecture*, pt. II, 164-6; *Academy Architecture* (1900/2), 24; *Architect*, LXXXI (1909), 320, 336; *Architectural Review*, XVI (1904), 117-21, 174-8; *British Architect* (1904/1), 168-9; *Builder*, LXXVIII (1900), 468; LXXXIV (1903), 488; LXXXVI (1904), 241, 286; XCVII (1909), 130; XCVIII (1910), 512, 524, 696; CIV (1913), 596-7; CVIII (1915), 436; *Builders' Journal and Architectural Record*, XX (1904, suppl., 28

Dec), 7; *Building News*, LXXXII (1902), 8; LXXXVI (1904), 341; CX (1916), 150; *Architects' Journal*, LX (1924), 762; RCHM, *City of Cambridge* (1959), pt 2, 303b; BoE, 32, 168

CANTERBURY (Kent): Cathedral
Monument to Archbishop Benson (died 1896), 1897-9, including effigy by Thomas Brock.
Recollections, 252, 259; drawing at RA; BoE, *Kent NE*, 211

CASTLE ASHBY (Northants)
Remodelling of chapel and Long Gallery, 1880; perhaps also Hall, 1884, and Dutch Wedding Room
M. Girouard, *The Victorian Country House* (1971), 177; BoE, 142; *Country Life*, CLXXIX (1986), 310-5

CATERHAM (Surrey): Church of St John
N aisle chapel, addition to church of 1881
BoE, 138

CATTON HALL (Derbys)
Addition of wing, 1907-8
MS Recollections, 1908; *Country Life*, CXXVII (1960), 569; BoE, 124

CHEAM (Surrey): Cheam House
Additions, for Spencer Wilde, *c.* 1870
Recollections, 114

CHEAM (Surrey): village hall
c. 1870
Recollections, 114

CHERTSEY (Surrey): Church of St Peter
Restoration, 1907-8
MS Recollections, 1908; BoE, 129

CHESHUNT (Herts): Bishop's College
Library furniture, 1915
Drawings at RA

CHESSINGTON (Surrey): Church of St Mary
Restoration of S aisle, 1870
Recollections, 114; BoE, *London 2*, 311

CHRISTCHURCH (Hants): Priory
Restoration, *c.* 1908-12
MS Recollections, 1906, 1910 (also 1884); *Recollections*, 270; drawing at RA (mace stand); *Architects' and Builders' Journal*, XXXVI (1912), 661; XXXVII (1913), 52; *RIBA Journal*, XV (1908), 209, 581; XVII (1910), 627; XXXII (1924), 50

CLEWER (Berks): Church of St Andrew
Memorial to G.F. Henson, 1918
Drawing at RA

COMPTON MARTIN (Som): Church of St Michael
Repairs, 1900-2
ICBS file 10237

CORHAMPTON (Hants): Church
Restoration, 1905-6
Clerk of works, Edwin Long. Used to try out the Greathead Grouting Machine, subsequently used on the restoration of Winchester Cathedral (q.v.).
MS Recollections, 1905; Edwin Long, Notebooks (Winchester Cathedral Library, Jackson Collection D-H); ICBS file 10251; *Builder*, LXXXIX (1905), 303; *RIBA Journal*, XV (1908), 249-71 (article by Francis Fox); *Transactions of the St Paul's Ecclesiological Society*, VI (1906-10), 216-36

COVENTRY (Warwicks): Church of the Holy Trinity
Restoration, including underpinning of tower and transepts, during the First World War
Recollections, 275

COWLEY (Oxon): *see under* **OXFORD**

CRANBROOK (Kent): Church of St Dunstan
Restoration
C. Miele, 'The Gothic Revival and Gothic Architecture: the restoration of medieval churches in Victorian Britain' (PhD thesis, New York, 1992)

CRANBROOK (Kent): Cranbrook School
Big School, 1883-4
Addition to existing group of buildings, to form quadrangle.
Recollections, 190; *Architecture*, II (1897), 22; *Building News*, XLVI (1884), 14; BoE, *Weald*, 244

CURDRIDGE (Hants): Church of St Peter
New church, 1887-8; tower, 1894
Recollections, 192; drawing at RA (lectern); *Architecture*, II (1897), 23, 93; *Building News*, LIV (1888), 392, 396; *RIBA Journal*, XXXIII (1926), 475; BoE, 188

DANBY HALL (Yorks NR)
New entrance etc, 1905-8
Exhib: RA 1906
MS Recollections, 1905, 1908

DEDHAM (Essex): Church of St Mary
Restoration of chancel, 1906-9, including opening up of four windows subsequently filled with glass by C.E. Kempe & Co.
MS Recollections, 1906; *Builder*, XCVII (1909), 393; *Building News*, (1909), 475

DORKING (Surrey): St Mary's Cottage Hospital
1870-1
Horace Swete, *Handy Book of Cottage Hospitals* (1870)

DUDDINGTON (Northants): Church of St Mary
Restoration of tower, 1911-3
Many members of the Jackson family are commemorated in the church, and the

monument to William Goddard Jackson (1835-1906) is by TGJ: cf. *Recollections*, 2 MS Recollections, 1911; drawings and specification at RIBA; *RIBA Journal*, XXXII (1924), 50 (list of works)

DURHAM: castle
Unidentified restoration work
RIBA Journal, XXXII (1924), 50 (list of works)

DURSLEY (Glos): Church of St James
Restoration, 1866-8
Chancel rebuilt and extended, vestry and organ chamber added, nave roof raised and clerestory inserted.
Exhib: Architectural Exhibition Society, 1867
Recollections, 114; *RIBA Journal*, XXXIII (1926), 474; J.H. Blunt, *Dursley and its neighbourhood* (1877), 73; BoE, *Gloucestershire 1* (1999), 334

EARL SOHAM (Suffolk): Church of St Mary
Restoration, 1899-1900, including removal of gallery (materials re-used for tower screen) and opening up W window; candelabra, 1906
MS Recollections, *c.* 1885; ICBS file 9351; drawing at RA; *Builder*, LXXVI (1899), 21; Brown, Haward & Kindred, *Dictionary of Architects of Suffolk Buildings* (1991), 130 (refs to *Ipswich Journal* (25 Apr 1891), and Suffolk Record Office, Ipswich, FC119/A3/1)

EAST BERGHOLT (Suffolk): Church of St Mary
Rood screen, reredos and stalls,1904-6; W window, 1905; ? lectern, 1909; First World War memorial, S aisle, 1919; chancel screen, 1920
MS Recollections, 1905, 1906; drawing at RA; BoE, 196; Brown, Haward & Kindred, *Dictionary of Architects of Suffolk Buildings* (1991), 130

EAST CLANDON (Surrey): Church of St Thomas
Addition of aisle and bell tower, 1900
MS Recollections, 1900 ('restoration'); BoE, 203

EASTHAMPSTEAD (Berks): Church of St Mary Magdalene
Chancel N window and mosaic pavement in sanctuary, as memorial to Revd Osborne Gordon (died 1883)
Glass painted by Morris & Co. to design by Burne-Jones; pavement designed by TGJ, made by Farmer & Brindley. Tablet with epitaph by John Ruskin.
Cook & Wedderburn, *Works of John Ruskin*, XXXIV (1908), 647-8, 'Ruskiniana' (first published 1890)

EAST STRATTON (Hants): Church of All Saints
New church, 1885-90
For the Baring family, commissioned by Lord Northbrook. Clerk of works, R. Evans.
Monument to 1st Earl of Northbrook, 1906
Exhib: RA, 1887
Drawing at RA; *Builder*, LIII (1887), 362, 368 (reproduction of drawing now at RIBA); *Building News*, LIII (1887), 206; *Architecture*, II (1897), 22, 93; BoE, 202

EASTROP (Hants) *see* BASINGSTOKE: Church of St Mary

ELLINGHAM (Hants): Church of St Mary
Restoration, including screen and organ case, 1869-*c*. 1880
For Lord Normanton, whose seat was nearby at Somerley.
Recollections, 115, 162; *Builder*, LI (1886), 802, 823; *Country Life* (16 Jan 1958),
111; BoE, 209

ELSTOW (Beds): Church of St Mary & St Helen
Rebuilding and restoration, 1881, attributed in BoE, 83, but actually by T.J.
Jackson
Bedfordshire County Record Office, 120/100

ELTHAM PALACE (Kent)
Restoration of Hall roof, 1901
MS Recollections, 1901; *Recollections*, 75

ESHER (Surrey)
War memorial cross, 1919
Drawing at RA; Ian D. Stevens, *The Story of Esher* (1966), 42

ETON (Berks): Eton College
Underpinning and repair of Lower Chapel and Queen's Schools, 1900; cricket
pavilion, Agar's Plough, and club house, Queen's Eyot, 1900-2; racquets courts and
science school, 1902; museum (Lawson memorial), 1903-5; completion of music
school, 1908; buttressing of Lupton's Tower, 1910; ? memorial to Sir R.T. Ritchie
(died 1912)
MS Recollections, 1900, 1902, 1903, 1908, 1910; *Recollections*, 190, 268; metalwork designs at RA; *RIBA Journal*, XXXII (1924), 49 (list of works); BoE,
Buckinghamshire (1994), 314

EVERCREECH HOUSE (Som)
Entrance hall
BoE, *Somerset SW*, 168

EXETER (Devon): Church of St Leonard
Baring family monument, 1912-13
Drawing at RA

FAIRTHORN HOUSE (Hants)
Alterations, for Mr. Burrell, *c*. 1885, 1893
MS Recollections, 1885, 1893

FARNHAM (Surrey): Castle
Decoration of chapel
RIBA Journal, XXXII (1924), 50 (list of works)

FARNHAM (Surrey): Church of St Andrew
Restoration of tower, 1906
Draft report in TGJ's notebook, Winchester Cathedral Library (Jackson
Collection, C)

FENNY COMPTON (Warwicks): Church of St Peter and St Clare
S arcade and S aisle, 1877-9
Recollections, 150, 162; BoE, 293

FLORE (Northants): Church of All Saints
Reseating, 1876-7
ICBS file 7939

FRAMLINGHAM (Suffolk): Framlingham College
War memorial tablet, 1920
Drawing at RA
Collins Guide to Parish Churches (1980) attributes to TGJ the altar and reredos in St Michael, Framlingham

GIGGLESWICK (Yorks WR): Giggleswick School
Chapel, gatehouse, and pavilion, 1897-1901
Donated by Walter Morrison. Clerk of works, R. Evans. Stained glass by Burlison & Grylls, with figures drawn by Sir James Linton. Mosaic designed by George Murray, made by Powell. Figures for stall ends modelled by T. Carter. Statues of King Edward VI and Queen Victoria by George Frampton. Sgraffito decoration by two of TGJ's pupils, W.H. Nicholls and D. Stewart.
Exhib: RA, 1898, 1901 (Frampton), 1902, 1906; International Exhibition, St Louis, 1904
Recollections, 252-4, 263; drawings at RA; metalwork designs at RA; *Academy Architecture*, XX (1901), 74; *Architect*, LXXXI (1909), 29; *Architects' Journal*, CCXI (2000 Apr 27), 22; *Architectural Review*, XI (1902), 94, 99-103, 106; *British Architect*, XLVIII (1897), 253, 256, 424; *Builder*, LXXV (1898), 230; *Builders' Journal and Architectural Record*, XIV (1901-2), 74-5; XV (1902), 102; *Building News*, LXXIII (1897), 578; *RIBA Journal*, XXXIII (1926), 475-7; TGJ, *Byzantine and Romanesque Architecture*, I (1913), pl. 1; C. Nicholson and C. Spooner, *Recent English Ecclesiastical Architecture* (n.d.), 146-50; I. Spielmann, [Report of the British Section at the International Exhibition, St Louis] (1906), 231; BoE, *Yorkshire W*, 218; J. Thomas, 'Sir Thomas Graham Jackson and the church of Hagia Sophia', *Architectural History*, XXV (1982), 98-101

GREAT MALVERN (Worcs) *see* MALVERN

GRESFORD (Denbigh): Church of All Saints
N porch, 1920-1, as war memorial
BoW, *Clwyd*, 169

GRIMSBY (Lincs): Church of St James
Restoration, including reroofing of aisles, new windows and buttresses, and pulpit, 1908-10
MS Recollections, 1908; *RIBA Journal*, XXXII (1924), 50 (list of works); BoE (1989), 337-8

GROVE PLACE (Hants)
Proposed enlargement, 1918
Exhib: RA, 1918
Building News, CXIX (1918), 344

GUMFRESTON (Pembroke): Church
Restoration, 1867-9, 'for our old friend Gilbert Smith'
MS Recollections, 1867, 1870; TGJ's report in Haverfordwest Record Office; information from T. Lloyd

HAGLEY (Worcs): Church of St John the Baptist
Wrought-iron chancel screen, 1918
Metalwork designs at RA

HAMPSTEAD *see under* LONDON

HAMPTON GAY (Oxon): Manor House
Proposed rebuilding, for Wadham College, 1901
The house was gutted by fire in 1887; TGJ's scheme for rebuilding turned down in 1901.
Wadham College Convention Book; BoE, 630

HARPENDEN (Herts): Rothamsted Manor
Internal remodelling and decoration, for Sir Charles Lawes-Wittewronge, 1900-3
MS Recollections, 1902-3; *Recollections*, 269; metalwork designs at RA; BoE, 159-60

HARROW (Middx): Harrow School
Additions to boarding house (Church Hill), for the Revd J.A. Cruikshank, 1877-8
His first school job; demolished *c.* 1921.
Exhib: RA, 1878
Recollections, 150, 162, 190; *Architect*, XLIV (1890), 303; *Architectural Review*, I (1897), 140, 146-7; *Architecture*, II (1897), 22, 91-2, 95, 96; *British Architect*, XXV (1886), 548; *Building News*, XXXV (1878), 8; A.W. Ball, *Paintings Prints and Drawings of Harrow on the Hill 1562-1899* (1978), 141, 144

HATFIELD (Yorks WR): Church of St Laurence
Restoration, *c.* 1870-2
MS Recollections, 1872; *Recollections*, 114

HAYES (Kent): Church of St Mary the Virgin
Remodelling of sanctuary, 1905
H. Thompson, *A History of Hayes in the County of Kent* (1935), 66; BoE, *London 2*, 185

HELLESDON (Norfolk): Church of St Katherine, Upper Hellesdon
Mission church, 1903; demolished
RIBA Journal, XXXIII (1926), 475

HEREFORD: Cathedral
Unidentified restoration or additions
RIBA Journal, XXXII (1924), 50 (list of works)

HERSHAM (Surrey): Church of St Peter
Monument in churchyard to J.H. Edgar, 1899
Drawing at RA

HORNBLOTTON (Som): Church of St Peter
New church, 1872-4
For Godfrey Thring. Includes sgraffito decoration, stained glass and mosaic pavement by Powell. TGJ may also have enlarged the rectory, now Hornblotton Manor.
Recollections, 117; *Architect*, XI (1874), 125; *Architecture*, II (1897), 23, 93; *RIBA Journal*, XXXIII (1926), 473-4; BoE, *Somerset SW*, 199

HORSHAM (Sussex): Christ's Hospital
Competition design for new school buildings, 1894
Exhib: RA, 1895
Academy Architecture, VIII (1895), 23; *Builder*, LXVI (1894), 457; LXVIII (1895), 376; CXXVII (1924), 753; *Building News*, LXVI (1894), 805, 834, 849, 884; LXVII (1894), 7-8, 40, 72; LXXIII (1897), 582

HUNTON (Kent): Church of St Mary
Restoration, 1900
MS Recollections, 1900

HYDE (Hants): Church of the Holy Ascension
Enlargement, 1900
Hampshire County Record Office, 55M81W/PWZ1

ILMINSTER (Som): Church of St Mary
Restoration of monument to Nicholas Wadham, 1899
Recollections, 228, 259; Wadham College, Convention Book (7 Dec 1891; note by TGJ of report on tomb in 1871); BoE, *Somerset SW*, 208

IPSDEN (Oxon): Church of St Mary
Monument, 1917
Drawing at RA

IRON ACTON (Glos): Church of St James
Restoration, 1877-80
Fittings include font with attached stone reading desk, and C15 glass reset by Powell.
Recollections, 150, 162, 173; BoE, *Gloucs 2* (2002), 546-7

KEMSING (Kent): Church of St Mary
Restoration, *c.* 1870; new N aisle, with reset windows, 1890-1
Window of 1893 by Powell, perhaps also by TGJ.
Recollections, 114; BoE, *Weald*, 348

KETTON (Rutland): Church of St Mary the Virgin
Restoration of chancel and tower, 1863-6; reseating of chancel, *c.* 1878
E window designed by the incumbent, Rev. F.H. Sutton. The rest of the church had been restored by G.G. Scott, 1860-2.
Recollections, 85, 90, 114; *Builder*, XXII (1864), 138; VCH, *Rutland*, II (1935), 262; BoE, *Leicestershire and Rutland* (1984), 476; G. Dickinson, *Rutland Churches before Restoration* (1983), 62-3; G.K. Brandwood, *Bringing them to their knees: church-building and restoration in Leicestershire and Rutland 1800-1914* (2002), 96

KIPPINGTON (Kent): Church of St Mary
Restoration, 1913; war memorial cross, 1919
Drawing at RA; H.W. Standon, *Kippington in Kent* (1958), 25, 31

LAMPETER (Cardigan): St David's College
Enlargement and remodelling of chapel, 1877-80; improvements to principal's house
The chapel had been built by C.R. Cockerell. TGJ's new stalls reused woodwork from New College, Oxford.
Exhib: RA, 1879

Recollections, 162, 173; drawing at RA; *Builder*, XXXVII (1879), 504; Beazley & Howell, *Companion Guide to South Wales* (1977), 76; D.T.W. Price, *A Short History of St David's University College Lampeter. Vol 1: to 1898* (1977), 138-9

LAVERSTOKE (Hants): Church of St Mary the Virgin
War memorial chapel (panelling and pew) in tower, 1919-20
Drawing at RA; *RIBA Journal*, XXXII (1924), 50 (list of works)

LAVERSTOKE HOUSE (Hants)
Alterations and additions, 1908
MS Recollections, 1908; *RIBA Journal*, XXXII (1924), 50 (list of works)

LAWRENNY (Pembroke): Church of St Caradoc
Restoration, 1876
Apparently not executed (and not under his supervision) until 1885-6
Recollections, 137

LITTLE BROMLEY (Essex): Church of St Mary
Restoration, 1884-5
The patron of the living was Wadham College.
ICBS file 8982; Essex Record Office D/C/F24/2; *Church Builder*, V (1885), 66

LLANDRINDOD WELLS (Radnor): hotel
Unexecuted scheme, 1861
Recollections, 85

LONDON: *see also* BARNET (Herts); BROMLEY (Kent), CHEAM (Surrey), CHESSINGTON (Surrey), ELTHAM PALACE (Kent), HARROW (Middlesex), HAYES (Kent), MALDEN (Surrey), WIMBLEDON (Surrey)

LONDON: Admiralty and War Office buildings, Whitehall
Competition design, 1884
Builder, XLVII (1884), 388-405

LONDON: No. 50 Albemarle Street
Alterations to business premises for John Murray, *c*.1893
Architecture, II (1897), 92

LONDON: public library, Arkwright Road and Finchley Road, Hampstead
Competition design, 1894
Builder, LXVII (1894), 386-7; *Building News*, LXVII (1894), 740

LONDON: No. 14 Buckingham Street, Strand
TGJ's office address, 1889-1915

LONDON: Burlington House, Piccadilly
Redecoration of entrance hall, for the Royal Academy, 1899-1900, with carving by Childs of Farmer & Brindley. Some plasterwork removed during alterations by Raymond Erith, 1962-3. Also alterations and improvements to the Keeper's House; inscription for inside of Joshua Reynolds' tea caddy, presented to the RA by the Academicians, 1898
Exhibited 1873-1924; elected ARA 1892, RA 1896, Treasurer 1901-12.
Recollections, 259; metalwork designs at RA; *Survey of London*, XXXII (1963), 421;

S.C. Hutchinson, *The History of the Royal Academy 1768-1968* (1968); BoE, *London 1* (1973), 624

LONDON: Church of St Barnabas, Addison Road, Kensington
Chancel, 1909-10
Including mosaic pavement in sanctuary, new glass by Morris & Co. in sanctuary windows, reconstruction of chancel arch, reredos and communion table.
B.F.L. Clarke, *Parish Churches of London* (1966), 102

LONDON: Church of St John the Baptist, Hampstead
Altar and reredos, *c.* 1878; refitting, including choir stalls, organ case, altar and reredos, and painted decoration, 1881-7
Mural painting in chancel aisle and glass (made by Powell) by H.E. Wooldridge; other painted decoration by E. Page Turner; carving and inlay by Farmer & Brindley.
Exhib: RA, 1887
Architectural Review, I (1897), 146; *Architecture*, II (1897), 23; *Builders' Journal and Architectural Record*, V (1897), 17, 251; *Building News*, LI (1886), 966; LII (1887), 236, 474; BoE, *London 4* (1998), 202

LONDON: County Hall
Competition design, 1908
Builder, XCIV (1908), 308; A. Koch (ed.), *British Competitions in Architecture* (1908), 26-9

LONDON: Devereux Court, Temple
TGJ's office address, 1864-83

LONDON: Dover Street
Alterations to business premises for John Murray, *c.* 1893
Demolished *c.* 1906 to make way for Underground station.
MS Recollections, 1893; *Architecture*, II (1897), 92

LONDON: Drapers' Hall, Throgmorton Street
Rebuilding of street front, 1898-9 (with Charles Reilly Sen.)
Includes entrance with turbaned atlantes by Henry Pegram, staircase with original C15 Italian work and additional carving by Farmer & Brindley, and gallery with carving by I. Carter; glass by Grylls. Intended plaster frieze by George Frampton. Henry Boyd, principal of Hertford College, Oxford (q.v.) was a past Master.
Recollections, 252; metalwork designs at RA; *Architectural Review*, XI (1902), 139-45; *Builder*, CX (1916), 353-5; BoE, *London 1*, 382-4

LONDON: No. 49 Evelyn Gardens
TGJ's private address, 1922-4

LONDON: Grocers' Hall, Prince's Street
Miscellaneous alterations, including ceilings, gates, and heraldic glass, 1897
Destroyed by fire, 1965.
Recollections, 252; BoE, *London 1* (1973), 277 (although the frieze by E. Roscoe Mullins mentioned there predates TGJ's work: see *Building News*, LXIX (1895), 152)

LONDON: Nos 2-3 Hare Court, Inner Temple
1893-4
TGJ also made alterations to the Bencher's Stairs etc, 1895-7; designed a piece of

silver plate presented to the Inner Temple by A.G. Marten Q.C., 1893, head and tail pieces for the Inner Temple Records, 1895, 1898, and electric light wall bracket, 1897; and illustrated 'Mr. Indewick's book of the Parliaments of the Inner Temple', 1898 (*see below*, ILLUSTRATIONS)
MS Recollections, 1895, 1898; *Recollections*, 151; drawings at RA and RIBA; metalwork designs at RA; BoE, *London 1*, 347

LONDON: Imperial Institute
Competition design, 1887
Recollections, 210; *Architect*, XXXVIII (1887), 65; *British Architect*, XXVIII (1887), 5, 24; *Builder*, LIII (1887), 92, 94, 99-100, 168; CXXVII (1924), 753; *Building News*, LIII (1887), 90

LONDON: No. 2 Kensington Court
New house, for Athelstan Riley, 1883-5, and fittings, *c.* 1889-93
Clerk of works, Robert Edwards. Carving by Farmer & Brindley, including modelling of terracotta made by Doulton. Plaster relief in music room by George Frampton, 1893. Now part of the Milestone Hotel.
Included piano, 1890-2, made by John Broadwood & Sons, cabinet maker, C.H. Bessant (said in *Builder*, CXXVII (1924), 753, to have been painted by Burne-Jones, but probably confused with Broadwood's 'Graham' piano); now at Trinity Manor, Jersey
Exhib: RA, 1885; Art & Crafts Exhibition Society, 1890
Recollections, 216-7; metalwork designs at RA; *Architect*, XLVI (1891), 101; *Architect & Building News*, CXV (1926), 620; *Architectural Review*, I (1897), 142, 146, 159; *Architecture*, II (1897), 85-91; *British Architect*, XXXVIII (1892), 404; *Builder*, XLVI (1884), 761; XLVIII (1885), 898, 909; LXIV (1893), 12-3, 15; *Building News*, XLIV (1883), 901, 908; LXIV (1893), 52; *Country Life*, CLXXX (1986), 424-5; *RIBA Journal*, XXXIII (1926), 469, 473; BoE, *London 2*, 265; S. Beattie, *The New Sculpture* (1983), 85; *Survey of London*, XLII (1986), 69, 70-2, 74; BoE, *London 3* (1991), 515

LONDON: King's College Hospital, Clare Market
Redecoration of chapel, *c.* 1884
MS Recollections, 1884

LONDON: Little Dean's Yard *see* Westminster School

LONDON: New Court, Streatley Place, Hampstead
Block of model dwellings, 1871-2
Original building erected by TGJ's father, 1854; between Brewhouse Lane and Flask Walk. Cf. Lime Tree Walk, Sevenoaks.
MS Recollections, *c.* 1905; *Architecture*, II (1897), 92; *Building News*, LVIII (1890), 221; *Victorian Society Annual* (1985-6), 21; BoE, *London 4* (1991), 224

LONDON: No. 4 Nottingham Place
TGJ's office address, 1883-9

LONDON: No. 11 Nottingham Place
TGJ's private address, 1880-7

LONDON: Queen Victoria Memorial, The Mall
Competition design, 1901, including triumphal arch and gates

Exhib: St Louis International Exhibition, 1904
Recollections, 263; drawings at RIBA; *Architectural Review*, X (1901), 199-211; *Builder*, LXXXI (1901), 438; *Builders' Journal and Architectural Record*, XIV (1901-2), 206; *Building News*, LXXXI (1901), 621, 763

LONDON: Royal Marines Memorial, The Mall
Consulting architect for memorial, 1902-3, to Royal Marines who died in South Africa and China, 1899-1900. Sculpture by Adrian Jones.
A. Jones, *Memoirs of a Soldier Artist* (1933), 109-10; BoE, *London 1* (1973), 596

LONDON: Royal Naval Hospital, Greenwich
Repairs, *c.* 1906-10, including restoration of ceiling of the Painted Hall
MS Recollections, 1906, 1910; *Recollections*, 268

LONDON: No. 7 Salisbury Street, Strand
TGJ's first office address, 1861-4 (shared with John Newton, a fellow pupil from Scott's office)

LONDON: South Kensington Museum
Competition design, 1891
Recollections, 227; *Architecture*, II (1897), 23; *Builder*, LXI (1891), 322

LONDON: Strand
Suggested street improvements, 1889
Recollections, 217; *Builder*, LVI (1889), 275, 320

LONDON: Westminster School
Alterations to dormitory, 1894-5, and bursary, *c.* 1895; boarding houses, Little Dean's Yard and Great College Street, 1896-7
Exhib: RA, 1897
Recollections, 243; metalwork designs at RA; *Architecture*, II (1897), 92; *British Architect*, XLVII (1897), 328; *Builder*, LXXIII (1897), 89; LXXXII (1902), 559-63; *Builders' Journal and Architectural Record*, V (1897), 318-9; XII (1900), 214; L.E. Tanner, *Westminster School, its buildings and their associations* (1923), 63; BoE, *London 1* (1973), 478-9

LONDON: Whitefriars Glassworks, Whitefriars Street
Alterations, for James Powell & Sons, *c.* 1882-5
Recollections, 190; *Architecture*, II (1897), 92; *British Architect*, XXXII (1889), 231, 236; W. Evans, C. Ross and A. Werner, *Whitefriars Glass: James Powell & Sons of London* (1995), 57-8, 374

LONGLEAT (Wilts)
Restoration, including repairs to roof of Great Hall, 1910-11
MS Recollections, 1910; *Recollections*, 270; *RIBA Journal*, XXXII (1924), 50 (list of works)

LOTTISHAM (Som): Church of St Mary
New church, 1876
For Godfrey Thring, as chapel of ease to Hornblotton (q.v.).
Recollections, 137, 151, 162; ICBS file 8011; *RIBA Journal*, XXXIII (1926), 474; BoE, *Somerset SW*, 222

LYNDHURST (Hants): Church of St Michael
Memorial tablets to A.K. and L.R. Hargreaves, 1919-20
Drawings at RA

LYNDON (Rutland): Church of St Martin
Restoration, including addition of organ chamber and vestry, 1863-6
Includes glass by Powell, his first order from the firm; carving by W. Farmer
Recollections, 90, 114-5; *Builder*, XXIV (1866), 392; VCH, *Rutland*, II (1935), 75-6; BoE, *Leicestershire and Rutland* (1984), 484; G. Dickinson, *Rutland Churches before Restoration* (1983), 72-3; G.K. Brandwood, *Bringing them to their knees: church-building and restoration in Leicestershire and Rutland 1800-1914* (2002), 108

MADEHURST (W Sussex): Church of St Mary Magdalene
Restoration, amounting to rebuilding, 1863-4
For the Revd Henry Nicholls, a school and college friend. Included glass by Burne-Jones, mostly destroyed in 1944.
Recollections, 90; ICBS file 6119; BoE, 268

MALDEN (Surrey): Church of St John
Restoration, 1863; new nave and chancel, 1875, reducing existing to S aisle and S chapel
His first job, started Jan 1863.
Recollections, 85, 90, 114; BoE, *London 2* (1983), 322

MALVERN (Worcs): Priory
Repairs, following a gale, 1895
MS Recollections, 1895; *RIBA Journal*, XVII (1910), 627; XXXII, 1924, 50 (list of works)

MARDEN (Kent): St Michael & All Angels
Restoration, *c.* 1883-5, possibly unexecuted
MS Recollections, 1885; offprint of design (1883) (private collection)

MILTON-UNDER-WYCHWOOD (Oxon): vicarage
1898
BoE, 705

MOLD (Flint): Church of St Mary
NE chapel fittings, including reredos and flooring, as war memorial, 1921; organ cases in chancel and W end, 1923
Drawings at RA; Beazley & Howell, *Companion Guide to North Wales* (1975), 39; BoW, *Clwyd*, 391

MONTACUTE HOUSE (Som)
Restoration work, including library ceiling
RIBA Journal, XXXII (1924), 50 (list of works); cf. *Recollections*, 152, 179; *Building News*, XLV (1883), 288; Pevsner, *S & W Som*, 247 and pl. 50a

NARBERTH (Pembroke): Church
Rebuilding, 1878-81
MS Recollections, 1913; *Recollections*, 162, 173; ICBS file 8396; *Architecture*, II (1897), 23; *RIBA Journal*, XXXIII (1926), 475

NORTHAMPTONSHIRE
Appointment as Diocesan Surveyor of South Northants (Diocese of Peterborough), 1871, resulted in 'one or two' church restorations and 'two or three' parsonages
MS Recollections, 1871; *Builder*, XXIX (1871), 843

NORTHINGTON (Hants): Church of St John the Evangelist
New church, 1887-80
For the Baring family, commissioned by Lord Ashburton. Glass by Powell, from cartoons by H.E. Wooldridge; carving by Farmer & Brindley; altar cloth by Watts & Co.
Exhib: RA, 1887, 1889, 1890
Recollections, 192; drawing at RIBA; metalwork designs at RA; *Academy Architecture*, I (1889), 19; II (1890), 21, 29; *Architect*, XLI (1889), 281; *Architectural Review*, I (1897), 142-3; *Architecture*, II (1897), 23, 93-4; *British Architect*, XXVIII (1887), 156; *Builder*, LIII (1887), 362, 369; LVIII (1890), 453; CXII (1917), 25; *Building News*, LVIII (1890), 64; *RIBA Journal*, XVII (1910), 623; XXXIII (1926), 475; BoE, 356

NORWICH: Cathedral
W window of Jesus Chapel, 1873, made by Powell
Recollections, 116; BoE, *Norfolk 1*, 214

NOTTINGHAM CASTLE
Adaptation of gateway for museum, 1902-9
Exhib: RA, 1903
MS Recollections, 1909; *Builder*, LXXXIV (1903), 540

OCKHAM (Surrey): Church of All Saints
E window, 1875, made by Powell
BoE, 393

OTFORD (Kent): school
For Rev. R.B. Tritton, 1872
Recollections, 114; BoE, *Weald*, 429

OVERTON (Hants): Church of St Mary
War memorial cross, 1919
Drawing at RA

OXFORD: *see* separate sequence, above

PEPER HARROW (Surrey): Church of St Nicholas
Restoration, 1876-7
Recollections, 150; BoE, 407, 599

PETERBOROUGH *see* **NORTHAMPTONSHIRE**

PORTSMOUTH (Hants): Church of St Thomas
Restoration, 1902-4
MS Recollections, 1902, 1904; *Recollections*, 37; *Builders' Journal and Architectural Record*, XX (1904, supplement, 28 Dec), 6

PURTON (Wilts): Church of St Mary
Monument to A.M.S. Maskelyne, 1902
Drawing at RA

PYRFORD (Surrey): Church of St Nicholas
Restoration, 1869
Recollections, 114; BoE, 419

RADLEY (Berks): Radley College (St Peter's College)
Infirmary and cloisters, 1891; chapel, 1893-5; boarding house, 1895; South African War memorial, 1903-4; dining hall, 1909-10; First World War memorial gateway, 1921-2
Clerk of works, Edwin Long. Chapel E window by Burlison & Grylls. Carving on gateway by Farmer & Brindley. Statue (St George) for South Africa War memorial by George Frampton. Scheme for music school not carried out; design for seal not accepted. In the churchyard is a tombstone put up by TGJ and the contractor, Estcourt of Gloucester, to their foreman, Hingston, who died while the chapel was being built.
Exhib: RA, 1893, 1894, 1895, 1904 (Frampton), 1921
Recollections, 190, 209, 245-6, 268, 275; drawings at Radley, RA, and RIBA; metalwork designs at RA; *AA Notes*, VIII (1893-4), 42; *Academy Architecture*, IV (1892), 51; VI (1894), 18; VIII (1895), 16; XXVI (1904), 80; *Architect*, XLVII (1892), 381; *Architecture*, II (1897), 18, 21, 96; *British Architect*, XLIII (1895), 346; *Builder*, LXII (1892), 340; LXVI (1894), 352; LXVIII (1895), 332; CXXI (1921), 285; *Builders' Journal and Architectural Record*, IV (1897), 357; *Country Life*, XL (1916), 664-7; *RIBA Journal*, XXXIII (1926), 476; A.K. Boyd, *The History of Radley College 1847-1947* (1948), 229, 233, 254, 264, 279, 307, 315; BoE, 197

RICKMANSWORTH (Herts): Church
Planned, but never built, 1861
Recollections, 85

RIPLEY (Surrey): Church of St Mary
Addition of aisle, 1867-9
Living held by the Revd C.R. Tate (cf. Send).
Recollections, 114; ICBS file 6707; BoE, 443

RIPON (Yorks WR): Cathedral
Memorial to Lt Col R.H. Sanderson, 1918
Drawing at RA

ROBESTON WATHEN (Pembroke): Church
Rebuilding, incorporating old tower, 1876
MS Recollections, 1876; *Recollections*, 138

ROTHAMSTED MANOR *see* **HARPENDEN** (Herts)

ROUSDON (Devon): Church of St Pancras
Monument to Sir Cuthbert Edgar Peek, Bt, 1901
Drawing at RA

RUGBY (Warwicks): Rugby School
Completion of Butterfield's chapel, 1896-7; Temple Speech Room, 1906-9
Exhib: RA, 1907
MS Recollections, 1905; *Recollections*, 190, 249, 267-8; metalwork designs at RA; *Architecture*, II (1897), 22; *Builder*, XCII (1907), 540; *Building News*, XCVII (1909), 47; *RIBA Journal*, XVII (1910), 622; BoE, 388, 390

RUSHTON HALL (Northants)
Internal remodelling and decoration, for J.J. Van Alen, 1905
MS Recollections, 1905; metalwork designs at RA; *Architects' Journal*, LX (1924), 761; *Architectural Review*, XXIII (1908), xiii

RYE (E Sussex): Church of St Mary
Unidentified work, 1908
MS Recollections, 1908

ST DAVID'S (Pembroke): Cathedral
Bookplate for library, 1892; plate, including cross, 1893, and crucifix, 1903; choir screen, 1895
Exhib: RA, 1895
Design for bookplate at RIBA; MS Recollections, 1893; Howell & Beazley, *Companion Guide to South Wales* (1977), 110. Cf. *Recollections*, 77-80, 173; *Builder*, LXIII (1892), 442; LXIX (1895), 378

SALISBURY (Wilts): Church of St Thomas
Restoration, 1902
MS Recollections, 1902

SANDWICH (Kent): Sir Roger Manwood's School
New buildings, including headmaster's house, laboratories and workshops, 1894-5
Recollections, 190; metalwork designs at RA; *Architecture*, II (1897), 23; BoE, *NE Kent*, 446; Cavell & Kennet, *A History of Sir Roger Manwood's School 1563-1963* (1963), 70, 72

SEND (Surrey): rectory
New rectory, for Revd C.R. Tate, 1863-4
His first commission, 1861, although not his first executed building. Tate had been (as curate of West Clandon, q.v.) TGJ's tutor, 1849-50. The living of Send included Ripley, q.v.
Recollections, 14, 19, 36, 85, 89-90; BoE, 450, 599

SEVENOAKS (Kent): Board School, Cobden Road
Probably *c.* 1875, the date of his design for the Board's seal
Design for seal at RIBA; *Building News*, LXXI (1896), 721

SEVENOAKS (Kent): Church of St Nicholas
Addition of choir vestry, 1908-9; memorial to his sister Emily (died 1916)
The church also has a memorial to TGJ, probably designed by his son Basil, as well as a number of older Lambarde memorials.
MS Recollections, 1908; BoE, *Weald*, 510

SEVENOAKS (Kent): Cottage Hospital
Invited to compete, but did not, 1872
Builder, XXX (1872), 462

SEVENOAKS (Kent): Emily Jackson Wing Hospital
Children's hospital, 1901
Begun by his sister Emily, *c.* 1870, as a hospital for the treatment of hip diseases.
Recollections, 112; BoE, *Weald*, 516

SEVENOAKS (Kent): Granville Road
Plan for laying out land fronting Granville Road
Possibly connected with Lime Tree Walk (see below).
Undated drawing at RA

SEVENOAKS (Kent): Lime Tree Walk
Street of 24 cottages, 1878-9, and coffee house, *c.* 1882; additional cottages, 1892
Built by TGJ and his father (cf. New Court, Streatley Place, Hampstead). Clerk of
works, Edwin Long.
Recollections, 153; *Academy Architecture*, II (1890), 50; *Architectural Review*, I
(1897), 146, 149; *Architecture*, II (1897), 92; *Builders' Journal and Architectural
Record*, XIV (1901-2), 189; *Building News*, LIX (1890), 144; BoE, *Weald*, 516

SEVENOAKS (Kent): Maywood House
New house, for Major German, 1873-4
Clerk of works, R. Swain.
Exhib: RA, 1874
Architect, XII (1874), 30; *Architecture*, II (1897), 92

SEVENOAKS (Kent): St Julian's
Addition to private house
Architecture, II (1897), 92

SEVENOAKS (Kent): Woodlands
New house, for S.S. Slater, 1873
Recollections, 114; *Architecture*, II (1897), 92; *Building News*, LVI (1889), 899

SEVENOAKS WEALD (Kent): Church of St George
Chancel and organ chamber, 1872
E window and mosaic pavement by Powell, carving by Farmer & Brindley, floor
tiling by Godwin of Lugwardine. Organ by Willis & Son.
Recollections, 114; *Builder*, XXX (1872), 309; BoE, *Weald*, 518

SHAMLEY GREEN (Surrey): Plonck's Hill
New house, for Godfrey Thring, 1893
Now called The Manor House. Cf. Hornblotton.
MS Recollections, 1893; metalwork designs at RA; *Architecture*, II (1897), 92
(incorrectly said to be in Bromley)

SHEERING (Essex): Church of St Mary
Restoration of tower, 1906
MS Recollections, 1906

SLINDON (W Sussex): Church of St Mary
Restoration, 1866-7
Stained glass by Powell.
Exhib: Architectural Exhibition Society, 1867
Recollections, 114; *Ecclesiologist*, XXIV (1866), 127; *Sussex Archaeological Collections*,
XIX (1867), 126-33; BoE, 326

STAMFORD (Lincs): Browne's Hospital
Monument in chapel to W.J. Williams, 1920
Drawing at RA

STAMFORD (Lincs): Church of All Saints
Restoration, 1870-3, including underpinning, buttresses to W front, and rebuilding W wall of S chapel
Recollections, 114; RCHM, *The Town of Stamford* (1977), 8; BoE (1989), 689

STAMFORD (Lincs): Church of St Mary
Restoration, 1870-3, including structural repairs to S side
TGJ also acted as consultant for repairs to tower and spire by H.F. Traylen, 1911-13
BoE (1989), 694

STAPLEFORD (Notts): Church of St Helen
Restoration, 1878; new nave and chancel, 1913; memorial chapel, 1923-5 (completed by Basil Jackson)
Exhib: RA, 1924
ICBS file 11378; drawings in private collection; drawing at RA (prayer desk); BoE, 336

SUNDRIDGE (Kent): Church
Restoration of chancel, *c.* 1870
Recollections, 114

TENBY (Pembroke): Church of St Mary
Proposed restoration, 1879
Nothing came of this, and restoration was carried out by J.P. Seddon in 1882
Tenby Observer (24 Jul 1879); information from T. Lloyd

THORNE (Som): Thorne House
Alterations and additions, for James Hooper, *c.* 1878-88
The work, which was carried out gradually over a number of years, amounted to rebuilding.
Exhib: RA, 1883, 1888
Recollections, 151, 162; *Architectural Review*, I (1897), 146, 158; *Architecture*, II (1897), 85, 92-3; *British Architect*, XX (1883), 18; *Builder*, LIV (1888), 392, 396; *Building News*, XLIV (1883), 668; BoE, *Somerset SW*, 322

THORNHAUGH (Cambs): vicarage
Additions, 1878
Recollections, 162; BoE, 424

UPPER HELLESDON (Norfolk): *see* HELLESDON

UPPINGHAM (Rutland): Uppingham School
New buildings, including headmaster's house and conversion of old house to library, new street frontage, museum and science schools, 1889, 1894-7
Clerks of works, R. Evans and C. Turkentine. Carving by Farmer & Brindley. Founder's statue by George Frampton.
Exhib: RA, 1891, 1898
Recollections, 215, 245, 252; metalwork designs at RA; *Academy Architecture*, I (1889), 65; IV (1892), 17, 169; *Architectural Review*, I (1897), 157; *Architecture*, II (1897), 7, 21; *Builder*, LVIII (1890), 12, LXI (1891), 189; LXIII (1892), 128; LXXIV (1898), 419; *Building News*, LXI (1891), 634; LXXV (1898), 571; BoE, *Leicestershire and Rutland* (1984), 515-6

WALKDEN (Lancs): Ellesmere Memorial
Memorial to the widow of the 1st Earl of Ellesmere, 1867-9
Won in competition, assessed by G.E. Street.
Builder, XXVI (1868), 509-10; BoE, *S Lancs*, 409

WATER EATON (Oxon): Manor House
Restoration, 1880
Subsequently purchased and restored by G.F. Bodley.
Recollections, 179; BoE, 825

WELLS (Som): Cathedral
Drawing of SW tower, 1870
Architecture, II (1897), 86; cf. TGJ's *Modern Gothic Architecture* (1873), 143

WEST CLANDON (Surrey): Church of St Peter & St Paul
Rebuilding of tower and spire, 1913, attributed to TGJ in BoE, 506, but in fact by
W.D. Caröe. However, cf. *Recollections*, 14
Surrey County Record Office PSH/CLW/9/11

WHITCHURCH (Hants): Church of All Hallows
First World War memorial tablet, 1919
Drawing at RA

WIMBLEDON (Surrey): Church of St Augustine
Mentioned in obituary, *Builder*, CXXVII (1924), 753, perhaps in error for the
following

WIMBLEDON (Surrey): Church of St John the Baptist, Spencer Hill
New church, 1872-5; projected tower and spire never built
Font, pulpit and chancel fittings by Farmer & Brindley; carving by Hibbins.
Includes a window of 1914 by Hugh Arnold, a cousin of TGJ.
Exhib: RA, 1889; International Exhibition, Chicago, 1893
ICBS file 7444; *Academy Architecture*, I (1889), 9; *Architect*, XV (1876), 292;
Architecture, II (1897), 23, 93; *Builder*, LVI (1889), 814; LVII (1889), 82, 92-3;
Building News, LVI (1889), 814; *RIBA Journal*, XXXIII (1926), 474-5; BoE,
London 2, 452

WIMBLEDON (Surrey): Church of St Luke, Ryfold Road
New church and parish room, 1908-9
Exhib: RA, 1908
ICBS file 10812; *Builder*, XCIV (1908), 512; BoE, *London 2*, 452

WIMBLEDON (Surrey): Church of St Mary
Monument to Canon H.W. Haygarth, 1904; war memorial chapel, 1922
Exhib: RA, 1922
Drawing at RA; *Builder*, CXXII (1922), 720

WIMBLEDON (Surrey): Eagle House, High Street
Alterations and additions, 1887
Clerk of works, Edwin Long. Eagle House was TGJ's own house, first seen in
1886, where he lived from 1887 until *c.* 1921.
Recollections, 16, 208-9; *Architect*, XLVI (1891), 271; *Architects' Journal*, LX (1924),
763; *Architectural Review*, I (1897), 136; *Builder*, LVIII (1890), 450; CLXXV

(1948), 353-5; *Builders' Journal and Architectural Record*, XII (1900), 431; TGJ, 'Eagle House, Wimbledon', *Surrey Archaeological Society Collections*, X (1891), 151-64; TGJ, 'Eagle House, Wimbledon; its builders and inhabitants', *Wimbledon and Merton Annual*, I (1903), 9-25; T.R. Way & H.B. Wheatley, *Reliques of Old London* (1899), 69; BoE, *London 2*, 455

WIMBLEDON (Surrey): Haygarth Memorial School
New house for girls' training school, 1908
MS Recollections, 1908

WIMBLEDON (Surrey): hospital
Unidentified work, 1911; nurses' hostel, 1920
MS Recollections, 1911; D. Braithwaite, *Building in the Blood* (1981), 134

WIMBLEDON (Surrey): house
Possibly the 'small house for Mr. Walker at Wimbledon', 1893
MS Recollections, 1893; *Architectural Review*, I (1897), 156

WIMBLEDON (Surrey): Keirside, later Stamford House
Alterations, 1885
Probably the house bought by TGJ's cousins, the Arnolds, who moved to Wimbledon from Stamford, and to which TGJ made repairs and added a wing.
MS Recollections, 1885; *Architecture*, II (1897), 92

WIMBLEDON (Surrey): No. 1 Lauriston Road
New house
BoE, *London 2*, 457

WIMBLEDON (Surrey): No. 54 Ridgway
New house, 1908
BoE, *London 2*, 457

WIMBLEDON (Surrey): war memorial, Wimbledon Common
Exhib: RA, 1921

WINCHESTER (Hants): Castle Avenue
Council offices, 1912
BoE, 695

WINCHESTER (Hants): Cathedral
Monument to Col W.G. Byrne, 1886; restoration, including underpinning of foundations and additions of buttresses along S side, 1906-12; Epiphany Chapel, 1906-8, and refitting of chapter room; proposed cloisters, incorporating war memorial, 1918-9
TGJ was appointed Consulting Architect to the Diocese on the death of Sir A.W. Blomfield, 1899. Clerk of works, Edwin Long. Consulting engineer, [Sir] Francis Fox. Glass in Epiphany Chapel by Morris & Co., 1910. In the course of restoration, fragments of the choir screen by Inigo Jones were discovered in the triforium and the central surviving part was incorporated in TGJ's new Museum of Archaeology at Cambridge (q.v.).
Exhib: RA, 1910
MS Recollections, 1908; *Recollections*, 209, 260-73; drawings, specifications and notes at RIBA; drawings, scrapbooks, photographs, notebooks etc in Winchester

Cathedral Library (Jackson and Walker collections); drawings at RA; metalwork designs at RA; slides donated by TGJ to Wimbledon Society Museum; *Architectural Review*, XXIII (1908), 104-7; *Builder*, XCVIII (1910), 524, 696; CIII (1912), 67, 68-72; *Builders' Journal and Architectural Record*, XX (1904, supplement, 28 Dec), 6; XXI (1905, supplement, 27 Dec), 18; *Building News*, CIV (1913), 713; *Journal of the Society of Architects*, V (1912), 362-4 (based on report by TGJ published in *The Times*); *RIBA Journal*, XV (1908), 249-71, 305-6 (article by Fox); *Transactions of the St Paul's Ecclesiological Society*, VI (1906-10), 216-36 (paper by TGJ); BoE, 661, 672; F. Busby, *Winchester Cathedral 1079-1979* (1979), 254-81; J. Fawcett, 'A restoration tragedy: cathedrals in the 18th and 19th centuries', *Ashlar*, I (1979), 15-20; I.T. Henderson & J. Crook, *The Winchester Diver: the Saving of a Great Cathedral* (1984); D. Holbrook, 'The restoration of Winchester Cathedral by Thomas G. Jackson, 1905-1912', *Association for Studies in the Conservation of Historic Buildings*, XI (1986), 48-71

WINCHESTER (Hants): Hospital of St Cross
Alterations to hospital and restoration of chapel, 1910-14; candlesticks, 1918
Clerk of works, Edwin Long.
MS Recollections, 1910; Edwin Long, Notebooks (Winchester Cathedral Library, Jackson Collection D-H); *Recollections*, 270; metalwork designs at RA; *RIBA Journal*, XXXII (1924), 50 (list of works); *Ecclesiology Today*, no. 26 (2001), 2-7

WINCHESTER (Hants): Wolvesey Palace
Repairs to chapel, 1907-8
Clerk of works, Edwin Long.
MS Recollections, 1908; Edwin Long, Notebooks (Winchester Cathedral Library, Jackson Collection D-H); *Recollections*, 268

WINTERBOURNE ABBAS (Dorset)
Mentioned in MS Recollections, 1880 (but as Winterbourne Abbas, Glos)

WONSTON (Hants): Church of the Holy Trinity
Restoration following fire, 1908, attributed to TGJ in BoE, 724, but in fact by Cancellor & Hill
Hampshire County Record Office 21M65/448F/3

WORCESTER: Cathedral
Restoration of Edgar Tower, 1901-3; report on vaulting of choir and nave, 1909, 1911
MS Recollections, 1901, 1903; *RIBA Journal*, XXXII (1924), 50 (list of works); information from B.J. Ashwell, Architect to the Dean and Chapter

WREXHAM (Denbigh): Church of St Giles
Refitting of chancel, 1913-14; fitting up of E end of N aisle as war memorial chapel, 1918-19
Apse windows, 1914, by Powell; chancel fittings include reredos, altar rails and flooring.
MS Recollections, 1913; drawings at RA; Beazley & Howell, *Companion Guide to North Wales* (1975), 65; BoW, *Clwyd*, 300

III. OVERSEAS

CONSTANTINOPLE [ISTANBUL] (Turkey): Church of S. Sophia
Report, for the Ministry of the Efkaf, 1910
Recollections, 269-70; draft of report at RIBA; extracts in TGJ's *Byzantine and Romanesque Architecture*, (1913), vol. 1, 102-5; J. Thomas, 'Sir Thomas Graham Jackson and the church of Hagia Sophia', *Architectural History*, XXV (1982), 98-101

EDMONTON (Canada): Church of St Faith
New church, to replace temporary mission building, 1915
Exhib: RA, 1915
Building News, CVIII (1915), 493, 496; *Builder*, CVIII (1915), 499

JERSEY (Channel Islands): Victoria College
Proposal for school boarding house, *c*. 1897, unexecuted
MS Recollections, 1897

MIDLETON (Cork, Ireland): Church of St John the Baptist
New screen and chancel fittings
Photograph (private collection)

NORFOLK ISLAND (South Pacific): Chapel of St Barnabas
Memorial chapel to Bishop Patteson, 1875-80; sedilia, 1910
Recommended by the Revd Dr Robert Codrington, a college friend. Includes glass by Morris & Co., designed by Burne-Jones. Built from the stones of the old gaol.
MS Recollections, 1910; *Recollections*, 45, 132-3; *Architecture*, II (1897), 23, 93; P. Cox & W. Stacey, *Building Norfolk Island* (Melbourne, 1977), 47-8; R. Nobbs, 'The Melanesian Mission on Norfolk Island', *Church of England Historical Society Journal* (Diocese of Sydney), XXXIV (1989), 49-60

ROME (Italy): Protestant cemetery
Hall-Dare monument, 1877
Drawing at RA

ST PETERSBURG (Russia): Memorial Church
Competition design for a memorial church to Czar Alexander II, 1881
Recollections, 192; *Building News*, XLII (1882), 794; *Builder*, CXXVII, (1924), 753

TASMANIA (Australia): church
Three large lights for a church in Tasmania, 1868
Made by Powell.
Recollections, 116; design sold by Moss Galleries, London

TIPPERARY (Ireland): Town Hall
Town hall and fire station, 1876-7
Commissioned by A.H. Smith Barry of Marbury Hall, Northwich.
Exhib: RA, 1878
Recollections, 138-9; *Architecture*, II (1897), 22; *Building News*, XXXV (1878), 394; *RIBA Journal*, XXXIII (1926), 470; C. Cunningham, *Victorian and Edwardian Town Halls* (1981), 142-3, 279

ZARA [ZADAR] (Dalmatia): Cathedral
Campanile, 1889-93

Exhib: RA, 1889, 1891; International Exhibition, Chicago, 1893
Recollections, 219-21, 239; *Academy Architecture*, I (1889), 16; III (1891), 40; *Architectural Review*, I (1897), 145; *Architecture*, II (1897), 23, 93; *Builder*, LVI (1889), 394, 400-1; LX (1891), 392; *Builder's Journal and Architectural Record*, IV (1897), 167-8; *Building News*, LVI (1889), 814; *Peristil*, no. 25 (1982), 149-58; no. 30 (1987)

IV. MISCELLANEOUS

BOOK COVER
Design for a cover for a book on flutes, 1882
RIBA

BOOKPLATES
For his cousin, C.T. Arnold, 1880; unidentified, 1881, with the arms of the Universities of Cambridge, Oxford, and London; for his wife, Alice Mary Jackson, 1894; for himself, 1894.
His own bookplate includes an aerial view of Oxford with Examination Schools in the foreground.
Exhib: RA, 1894, 1895, 1897 (unspecified)
Ashmolean Museum

CROZIER
For the Bishop of Southwark (Rt Revd Hubert Murray Burge), 1911. Made of oak from the roof of Winchester Cathedral, with silver mounting by Barkentin & Krall and carving by Farmer & Brindley. Given by the boys of Winchester College, presented to the College by Burge's widow in 1925 but stolen in 1983.
Exhib: RA, 1913
Builder, CIV (1913), 499, 713

GLASS
Painted glass ('The Seasons'), 1871, made by Powell
Exhib: International Exhibition, London, 1871
Official Catalogue, Fine Arts Dept, no. 2390

ILLUSTRATIONS
For F. Metcalfe, *The Oxonian in Norway* (London: Hurst & Blackett; 2nd edn, 1857) and *The Oxonian in Thelemarken* (London: Hurst & Blackett, 1858)
Recollections, 44

ILLUSTRATIONS
For F.A. Inderwick (ed.), *A Calendar of the Inner Temple Records* (London: H. Sotheran; vol. 1, 1896; vol. 2, 1898; vol. 3, 1901)
MS Recollections, 1898; designs for headpieces at RIBA

METALWORK
Collection of designs for door furniture, some identified, some made by Hart Son & Peard
RA

METALWORK
Designs for cast-iron grates, including designs used at: Brasenose and Corpus Christi, Oxford; Inner Temple, London; Plonck's Hill, Shamley Green; and Uppingham School
RA

METALWORK
Floor grating, made by Potter of South Molton Street, London
One of his earliest designs, and widely used, including at the Examination Schools, Oxford
Recollections, 73, 142

PIANO *see* LONDON: No. 2 Kensington Court

TABLE GLASS
Various designs, including wine glasses and decanters, for James Powell, *c.* 1868-83. *Recollections*, 116; drawing at RA; *Architectural Review*, VI (1899), 51-5; LXXXIII (1933), 86; B. Morris, 'Aesthetic and Arts and Crafts Glass', in S.M. Wright (ed.), *The Decorative Arts in the Victorian Period* (Society of Antiquaries Occasional Paper XII, 1989), 59; J. Rudoe and H. Coutts, 'The table glass designs of Philip Webb and T.G. Jackson for James Powell & Sons, Whitefriars Glassworks', *Decorative Arts Society Journal*, no. 16 (1992), 24-41; *The Earthly Paradise: Arts and Crafts by William Morris and his Circle in Canadian Collections* (1993), 110; W. Evans, C. Ross and A. Werner, *Whitefriars Glass: James Powell & Sons of London* (1995)

Footnotes

PREFACE

[1] The Delphino is now a pizza parlour

[2] After dining with my wife and me in 1987 Sir Hugh Casson left with an early draft of this edition of T.G. Jackson's 'Recollections' under his arm and wrote us a note saying '…we enjoyed the opportunity of seeing your collection of splendid Jacksonia. I will guard the volumes carefully.' It was, nevertheless, a surprise to find that this story had found its way into *Hugh Casson's Oxford* which was published in the following year!

[3] Reprinted in Canada in 1999

INTRODUCTION

[1] I am particularly indebted to Dr William Whyte of St John's College, Oxford, for his comments on the Introduction and for providing additional references and identifications for the Gazetteer

[2] J. Betjeman, 'Myfanwy at Oxford', from *Old Bats in New Belfries* (1940)

[3] J. Betjeman, *Ghastly Good Taste* (1933, revised edn 1970), 108-9

[4] J. Betjeman, *An Oxford University Chest* (1938, 1979), 122

[5] J. Sherwood and N. Pevsner, *Oxfordshire* (1974), 59. The entries for Oxford itself were written by Pevsner, as the Foreword explains

[6] A.C. Bossom was made a baronet in 1953 and a life peer in 1960, but for his political rather than his architectural achievements. Although Jackson was the first architect actually to be created a baronet, the honour had been offered, and declined, in 1907 – to Norman Shaw (A. Saint, *Richard Norman Shaw* (1976), 394).

[7] Often quoted in studies of Scott and his other pupils, e.g. by G. Stamp in a new edition of Scott's *Personal and Professional Recollections* (1995)

[8] *Recollections*, 99-100

[9] *Modern Gothic Architecture* (1873), 50-1

[10] Ibid., 110

[11] Ibid., 115-6

[12] *Builder*, XXXI (1873), 597

[13] Micklethwaite wrote in his introduction, 'the sections on *Architecture* and *Style* were written, and already in print … before the appearance of Mr. T.G. Jackson's "Modern Gothic Architecture," and the whole of my book was written and revised before I had seen his. Had it not been so, I should probably have said much less than I have done upon those matters of which he has also treated … We have both said some things which

have been said before, but they will have to be repeated yet a great many times before they produce much visible result.' Both works were published by Henry S. King.

[14] *Architect*, IX (1873), 294

[15] Binsted described by Pevsner as 'rough and ready', Slindon as 'shockingly restored … Perhaps he was young and coltish'

[16] Betjeman summed it up admirably in *An Oxford University Chest*, p. 139: 'The interior is exceedingly well planned and the light and depressing rooms have been the scene of much unhappiness'.

[17] Quoted in *Architect*, XV (1876), 364

[18] Ibid., 408

[19] T.G.J., *The Renaissance of Roman Architecture*, part II, England (1922), 68-9

[20] H. Colvin, *Unbuilt Oxford* (1983), 136

[21] Quoted in *Architect*, XXXVIII (1887), 363

[22] Cook & Wedderburn, *Works of John Ruskin* (1908), XXXIII, 363, 476, and XXXVII, 477. The cost was, in fact, under £100,000, generally thought quite reasonable.

[23] *RIBA Journal*, XIX (1912), 698-703. Cf. Pevsner's comment on the Town Hall: 'Hare gave Oxford town what Jackson for fifteen years had been giving Oxford gown … Did Jackson chuckle or foam?' (*Oxfordshire*, 302)

[24] *Recollections*, 163, 178

[25] *Builder*, LXII (1892), 73

[26] *Art Journal* (1892), 94

[27] *Builders' Journal and Architectural Record*, IV (1896), 209-10

[28] *Recollections*, 210

[29] *British Architect*, XXVIII (1887), 5

[30] *Building News*, LXVI (1894), 834

[31] *Builder*, LXVII (1894), 386-7

[32] *Recollections*, 227; *Builder*, LXIV (1893), 162, 264

[33] *Builder*, LXIII (1892), 516

[34] J. Fergusson, *History of the Modern Styles of Architecture* (2nd edn, rev. R. Kerr, 1891), vol 2, 157, 169

[35] *Builder*, LII (1887), 460, LIII (1887), 906

[36] *Architectural Review*, I (1897), 136-60; *Architecture*, II (1897), 3-24, 84-96; *Builders' Journal and Architectural Record*, IV (1897), 355-9

[37] *RIBA Journal*, XVII (1910), 622-3, 627

[38] *Recollections*, 272

[39] *Builder*, CIV (1913), 499

[40] *Builder*, CXII (1917), 24-5

[41] Journal in Bodleian Library, Dept of Western MSS, where it is incorrectly assumed that 'Basil' refers to the architect Champneys

[42] The probate value of his estate was £37,174 15s 5d; cf. *The Times* (9 Jan 1925), 15

[43] *Builder*, CXXVII (1924), 753

[44] *Architects' Journal*, LX (1924), 758-63

[45] Published in *RIBA Journal*, XXXIII (1926), 467-77

[46] H.S. Goodhart-Rendel, *English Architecture since the Regency: an interpretation* (1953), 176-7

[47] *RIBA Journal*, XXXII (1924), 49

[48] H. Colvin, *Unbuilt Oxford* (1983), 136. As examples he cites the High Street front of Brasenose, with its seven oriel windows where a medieval architect might have had one or two, and the entrance to Hertford College, where Jackson uses three Palladian windows instead of the customary one

[49] *Modern Gothic Architecture*, 110

[50] *Architectural Review*, I (1896), 140

[51] J. Sherwood and N. Pevsner, *Oxfordshire* (1974), 59-60, 265-6

[52] Cf. note 22

[53] M. Girouard, *Sweetness and Light: the 'Queen Anne' movement 1860-1900* (1977), 32, 60-1 etc

[54] Jackson's pupils and assistants included J.F.C. Bell, C.B. Bone, E.A. Collett, F.H. Darke, H.L. Goddard, A.J. Grahame, C.R. Harrison, E.A. Hellicar, B.C.P. Heywood, G.H. Kitchin, Henry Ling, E.W. Lockwood, H.E. Mallet, W.C. Marshall, W.H. Nicholls, C.R. Peers, A.E. Perkins, F.E.B. Ravenscroft, S.P. Rees, D. Stewart, G.E.S. Streatfield, Isaac Taylor, and E.L. Warre

[55] J.M. Crook, 'T.G. Jackson and the cult of eclecticism', in H. Searing (ed.), *In Search of Modern Architecture: a tribute to Henry-Russell Hitchcock* (1982), 102-20

[56] A significant exception is the school house at Harrow, demolished to make way for Herbert Baker's War Memorial Building of 1921

[57] See *Building News*, XXXVIII (1880), 237, 340

CHAPTER I

[1] The Grant of Arms is signed by Thos. St.George, Garter and John St. George, Clarenceux. Coincidently in 1931, T.G.Jackson's son, Sir Hugh Jackson married a direct descendant of this family

[2] Duddington Manor continued to be lived in by the Jacksons until 1996, when it passed to members of the Wykeham-Fiennes family who had become relatives

[3] General Paoli (1725-1807) was a Corsican general who in 1768 yielded Corsica to France. Following the execution of Louis XVI he drove the French from Corsica and retired to an estate in England. He is buried in London.

[4] Sir William Beechey (1754-1839), portrait painter to Queen Charlotte, elected RA in 1793

[5] Rear Admiral Frederick William Beechey (1796-1856)

[6] Francis Willis (1718-1807) attended George III in his first attack of madness in 1788

[7] 1905

[8] Clarkson Stanfield (1793-1867) was a marine and landscape painter whose best-known painting is 'The Battle of Trafalgar'

[9] Charles Cockerell (1788-1863) completed the Fitzwilliam Museum, Cambridge and was professor of Architecture to the Royal Academy

[10] Rev. Charles John Heathcote (1796-1874)

[11] Rev. John Gilderdale (1802-1864) held the living of Walthamstow and was principal of the Forest School

CHAPTER 2

[1] Rev. Charles Richmond Tate was curate of West Clandon, 1839-52, and vicar of Send with Ripley, 1852-75

[2] Sir George Gilbert Scott (1811-1878) was always referred to as Gilbert Scott. He was knighted in 1872

[3] Rev. Arthur Macleane, principal of Brighton College (1845-53)

[4] Four small bound volumes of beautifully illustrated translations that T.G.J. made for George Long at the age of 16 are now in the archives at Brighton College

[5] Sir Walter Parratt (1841-1924) was also director of the Royal College of Music and assistant editor of Grove's *Dictionary of Music*

[6] Reginald Edward Thompson (1834-1912), physician at Brompton Hospital, 1880-94; his works include *Therapeutic Value of Drug Smoking*

[7] Dr James Turle (1802-1882) was organist at Westminster Abbey 1831-1882.

[8] Charles Thomas Arnold, second son of Thomas Kirchever Arnold of Lyndon, matriculated at Corpus in 1852

[9] Dr Stephen Elvey (1805-1860),Organist at New College 1830; Mus Doc Oxon 1838; knighted 1871

[10] Samuel Lilckendy Warren was vicar of Kennington, 1865-78, and rector of Esher from 1870. His father Samuel Warren was a barrister and a novelist

[11] Frederick Halcomb (1836-1919) arrived in Australia in 1861, where he became a parliamentary officer, and was clerk of the parliaments and of the Legislative Council, 1901-18

CHAPTER 3

[1] Richard Congreve (1818-1899) founded a positivist community in London (1855) and also studied medicine

[2] The philosopher August Comte (*c.*1795-1852) was a mathematician, who expounded positive philosophy, a doctrine discouraging the belief in anything for which no tangible evidence can be found

[3] Frederic Harrison (1831-1923, president of the English Positivist Committee, 1880-1905, was a Fellow of Wadham 1854-1870, Hon Fellow 1899, and a prolific writer on literary and historical subjects

[4] John Henry Bridges (1832-1906), translator of works by Comte, was a Fellow of Oriel College, 1855-60, and became a doctor. Many years later, T.G.J. was to become a neighbour of his at Wimbledon

[5] Benjamin Parsons Symons (1785-1878) was Warden of Wadham 1831-71, and Vice Chancellor of the University 1844-48

[6] William Tournay was Warden of Wadham 1806-31 and died in 1833

[7] Arthur Steinkopff Thompson became vicar of Arundel, Sussex

[8] John Prescott became a lawyer

[9] Thomas Walter Sale became vicar of Attercliffe, Yorkshire, and later of Skendleby, Lincs

[10] Charles Giles Bridle Daubeny (1795-1867) was Aldrichian Professor of Chemistry, 1822-55, and Sherardian Professor of Botany, 1834-67

[11] George Rawlinson was the Bampton lecturer in 1858, became Camden Professor of Ancient History, 1861, and was also Public Examiner in *literae humaniores*

[12] James Edwin Thorold Rogers (1823-1890), Drummond Professor of Political Economy 1862-7 and 1888, also M.P. for Southwark, 1880-5, and Bermondsey, 1885-6

[13] William More Molyneux, later a lawyer

[14] John Oxenham Bent became vicar of St John the Evangelist, Woolwich, in 1868

[15] Walter Morrison (1836-1921) was a businessman, an MP and a philanthropist. He inherited a large fortune and his benefactions included gifts to northern universities, the Palestine Exploration Fund, Oxford University, the Bodleian Library and Giggleswick School

[16] Arthur Pemberton Heywood-Lonsdale (1835-1897), of Eton and Balliol

[17] Edmond Warre (1837-1920) was later headmaster of Eton, 1884-1905, and Provost, 1909-18

[18] According to the *Oxford University Herald* (1856), 'The bump was disputed but after hearing evidence on both sides the committee allowed the bump'

[19] Sir Maurice Bowra, Warden of Wadham used to tell T.G.J's grandson that Jackson had stroked Wadham to the top of the river fifty years before Dr Hewlett Johnson, later the 'Red Dean' of Canterbury Cathedral, had stroked it to the bottom! In fact the boat was stroked by John Thorley of the university eight

[20] Paul Creed Gwillim Simcoe (died 1875) was the youngest of four brothers at Wadham, where their father Henry Addington Simcoe had also been an undergraduate

[21] Charles Lloyd (1784-1829) became bishop of Oxford in 1827

CHAPTER 4

[1] Richard Pickersgill exhibited at the Royal Academy between 1818 and 1845. His son Frederick William Pickersgill (1820-1900) was a pupil of his maternal uncle William Frederick Witherington (1785-1865) and Richard's brother Henry William (1782-1875) was also an RA and a celebrated portrait painter

[2] Eugène Viollet-le-Duc (1814-1879) restored Notre Dame, Paris, the château of Pierrefonds and the city of Carcassonne. His *Dictionnaire raisonné de l'architecture française du Xe au XVIe siècle* had strong influence on the Gothic Revival

[3] Daniel Auber (1782-1871) wrote nearly 50 operas belonging to the genre of 'opéra comique'. In 1842 he became director of the Paris Conservatoire

[4] This rift permanently severed all connection between the respective families and their descendants until the year 2000, when Sir Nicholas Jackson was contacted by a direct descendant of T.G.J's uncle, John Jackson, whose family had been living in Australia since 1933

[5] Sir John Everett Millais (1829-1896) was elected President of the Royal Academy in the year of his death. 'The Proscribed Royalist' (1853), one of his most celebrated paintings, was set in a wood near Hayes

[6] Clara Novello (1810-1908) was the daughter of Vincent Novello, founder of the music publishers Novello & Co

[7] Willoughby Weiss (1820-1867) was a celebrated opera and oratorio singer who published his own setting of Longfellow's 'The Village Blacksmith' which continued to be a best seller until long after his death

[8] from Andrew Marvell's poem 'The Garden'

[9] George Masters Pyne

[10] Walter Waddington Shirley, fellow of Wadham 1852-4, mathematics lecturer and tutor 1855-63

[11] William Turner 'of Oxford' (1789-1862)

[12] George Wharton was an assistant master and precentor at Radley, 1862-1914 and known to Radleians as 'Dizzy Wharton'

[13] John Hampden (1594-1643) led the opposition to the King's demand for twelve subsidies in exchange for ship money. He moved the resolution giving the control of the militia and the Tower to Parliament.

[14] Adam Storey Farrar, tutor at Wadham 1855-64

[15] Frederick Metcalf (1815-85), fellow of Lincoln 1844-85, and vicar of St Andrew's, Oxford

[16] T.G.J. is incorrect in saying that the second book appeared some years later: it was the following year, 1858

[17] George Gilbert Thomas (later Treherne) was an undergraduate at Balliol 1857-61

18 Probably Dr Charles Thomas Coote, Radcliffe Travelling Fellow of University College 1849-59

CHAPTER 5

1 The house where Scott lived in Hampstead is known as 'The Admiral's House'

2 Sir Edward Coley Burne-Jones (1833-98), Pre-Raphaelite painter, was an undergraduate at Exeter College, 1852, and elected Hon Fellow in 1882

3 This was a current alternative spelling to the more usual 'Pre-Raphaelite'

4 John Ruskin (1819-1900), author of *Modern Painters* (1843-60) and many other works of art history and social reform, was an early champion of the Pre-Raphaelites

5 William Holman Hunt (1827-1910) was another leading member of the Pre-Raphaelite Brotherhood; his most famous painting is perhaps 'The Light of the World' (1854)

6 Rev. Gilbert Nicholas Smith (1796-1878) was rector of Gumfreston from 1837 until his death

7 The part of Pembrokeshire around Tenby is still referred to as 'little England'

8 William Ryton Andrews became rector of Teffont Evias, Wiltshire, in 1873

9 William Burges (1827-81), a leading Gothic Revival architect whose works included Cardiff Castle and Castel Coch, Wales

10 Thomas Garner (1839-1906), in partnership with George Frederick Bodley (1827-1907) 1869-97 won the competition for completing the tower at Christ Church but their design was never fully carried out. Both were pupils of Scott, whose brother married Bodley's sister

11 Augustus Welby Northmore Pugin (1812-1852), perhaps the most influential architect and designer to promote the Gothic Revival, who worked with Sir Charles Barry on the new Houses of Parliament. *Contrasts* was published in 1836

12 At St. David's, Scott removed the Perpendicular East window and replaced it with an Early English style one of his own design.

13 Andrea Palladio (1508-1580), Italian architect and author of *Quattro Libri dell' Architettura* (1570) which became the standard work of reference on Classical architecture and formed the foundation of the English Palladian style

14 John Burlison (1810-68) was Scott's principal assistant and surveyor for over twenty-five years

15 George Edmund Street (1824-81), worked for Scott 1844-9. His works include the Law Courts in the Strand, 1874-82

16 George Frederick Bodley (1827-1907) built many churches including Holy Trinity, Prince Consort Road and Washington Cathedral, U.S.A.

17 William Henry Crossland (died 1909) practised in Yorkshire before moving to London. As well as Holloway College he also built the Holloway Sanatorium at Virginia Water

18 George Gilbert Scott junior (1839-1897) was a church architect of great originality and promise but succumbed to madness. John Oldrid Scott (1841-1913) succeeded to his father's practice.

19 Charles Hodgson Fowler (1840-1910) was architect to Rochester and Lincoln cathedrals as well as being Diocesan Architect to York and Durham

20 John James Stevenson (1831-1908) was best known for his designs for the London Schools Board

21 Somers Clarke (1841-1926) was Surveyor to St Paul's Cathedral 1896-1906. He was in partnership with John Thomas Micklethwaite (1843-1906), 1876-92, author of *Modern Parish Churches* (1874)

22 Richard Coad (1825-1900) was Scott's clerk 1847-64

23 James Thomas Irvine (1825-1900) worked for Scott from 1854 and, after Scott's death, for J.L.Pearson

24 John Lewis (1805-1876) specialised in Italian, Spanish and oriental subjects

25 Paul Naftel (1817-1876) was a native of Guernsey who came to London in 1870

CHAPTER 6

1 'Some grave antiquaries will have it that so far from this being a new university in the time of Edward III it was the revival of an old one. 'Bladud who built Stamford and made it an University, reigned in England in the yeare of the world's creation 3066. He, coming from Athens before the birth of Christ 863 yeares, then built this towne, and to compleat the same as an University, he placed here four philosophers which he brought with him from Athens.''

2 Alfred J. Butler (1850-1936) was elected Fellow of Brasenose in 1877, Bursar 1881-1920

3 'The property was knocked down for £1,950, much less than it sold for eleven years previously, and, as the local paper says, "It transpired that Mr. Moore had bought the property on behalf of the Fellows of Brasenose College, Oxford, whose principal object it appears was to obtain possession of the famous knocker which formed part of and parcel of the premises: and he had been instructed, so we are informed, not to come away without it." Alfred Butler attended the sale and carried the knocker away with him.

4 This later became the Victoria and Albert Museum

5 This drawing is reproduced in colour as an illustration in *Gothic Architecture in France, England and Italy,* vol. 1, plate lxxx

6 John Cooper, Fellow of Wadham 1848-82

7 This refers to the Foreign Office

8 'An admirable letter appeared in *The Times* advocating Gothic as a better and more convenient style for use than Classic. It concluded thus: "Gothic then is National; it is constructively real; it is equally adapted to all sorts of buildings; it is convenient; it is cheap. In none of these respects does Italian surpass it; in most of them it is very inferior to it. If then Gothic is less adapted to a Foreign-office than Italian, the fault is with Foreign-offices and not with Gothic Architecture." The letter was signed E.A.F., initials not then so readily recognised as afterwards. Next day appeared a letter from Ruskin expressing a wish to know who E.A.F. was and to be acquainted with the author of so valuable and exhaustive a view of the subject. The editor, I suppose, gave Ruskin Freeman's name, for a day or two later appeared a raving letter from Freeman accusing the editor of a breach of confidence, abusing Ruskin and all his works, and scorning his offer of intimacy. "You see," said J Dasent, the editor, to Scott, "what we get by helping our friends"; and from that time the columns of *The Times* were closed against any more correspondence on the subject and Scott lost the best champion of his cause".

9 It is now a garden-centre

10 Local south Pembrokeshire name for puffin, guillemot, and razorbill

CHAPTER 7

1 '*The Times* said: "We cannot disguise from ourselves the fact that Louis Napoleon is secretly, and no less energetically than darkly, working against our supremacy in India. What Russia is effecting from the North, France is attempting from the West and South. The eagerness with which the Suez Canal scheme has been pushed forward is but a small proof in comparison with the unremitting and colossal efforts she is making in Abyssinia and elsewhere. In the Red Sea her exertions have of late been astounding. From Zelya to Zanzibar she has been endeavouring indefinitely to establish her influence so that she may thwart the peaceful policy of Great Britain."'

[2] William Slater

[3] See letter from Sir Gilbert Scott to the author on completion of his pupilage 1861 (page xv)

[4] Since replaced by offices

[5] John Newton, elected Associate of the RIBA in 1863

[6] Giacomo Meyerbeer (1791-1864) was, at that time, enjoying success as an operatic composer

[7] Charles Keene (1823-1891) worked for *Punch* from 1851, and the *Illustrated London News*

[8] [K—] Probably Henry King, elected Fellow of Wadham 1844, called to the Bar in the same year; Bursar of Wadham 1850-1

[9] Benjamin Robert Haydon (1786-1846) was a historical painter. Landseer was among his pupils

[10] Charles Douglas Ross was Fellow of Wadham 1848-82

CHAPTER 8

[1] A house belonging to Twining the banker and tea merchant

[2] Which John Scott spells 'vallés de plas.' It is assumed he meant *valets* , i.e. servants

[3] Robert Biscoe Tritton, vicar of Otford 1845-77

[4] James Charles Herbert Welbore Ellis Agar, 3rd Earl of Normanton and 1st Baron Normanton of Somerley (1818-1896)

CHAPTER 9

[1] Samuel Lover (1797-1868)

[2] Alice was twenty-seven years younger than her eldest brother Multon Lambarde

[3] Beechmont was bombed during World War II

[4] The hospital today is an aftercare home for the elderly called 'Emily Jackson'

[5] Henry Sidebottom, rector of Sevenoaks 1861-74

[6] James Crofts Powell (1847-1914). The 'o' in Powell was pronounced as in 'go' rather than in 'now'

[7] At Vézelay there is what is claimed to be the earliest example of a pointed arch

[8] Godfrey Thring became rector of Alford in 1858 and prebendary of Wells in 1876

[9] Julius Paul David (1840-1932) was music master at Uppingham for forty years. Brahms' friend, the violinist Joachim, had been taught by his father

[10] Edward Thring (1821-1887) was headmaster of Uppingham from 1853 until his death

[11] Multon Lambarde became T.G.J's brother-in-law, following his marriage in 1880

[12]*Modern Gothic Architecture*

[13] Richard Norman Shaw (1831-1912) built New Scotland Yard, many studios for artists and some large country houses

CHAPTER 10

[1] John Griffiths (1806-1885), elected fellow of Wadham 1830, sub-warden 1837-54, warden 1871-81

[2] Sir Maurice Bowra used to joke that T.G.J's first Oxford work was the design of a conservatory in his lodgings facing north!

[3] Henry John Stephen Smith (1826-1883), fellow of Balliol 1850-74 and 1882-3, himself a mathematician

[4] Richard Charles Hussey (1806-1887), church architect, partner of Thomas Rickman and then of his pupil and Rickman's son, Thomas Miller Rickman

[5] Basil Champneys (1842-1935), architect of the Indian Institute (1883-96), the Rhodes Building of Oriel College (1908-11), and other Oxford buildings in the manner established by T.G.J.

[6] Henry Wentworth Acland (1815-1900), Regius Professsor of Medicine 1858-94, knighted in1884.

[7] Vincent Benedetti (1817-1900), French ambassador in Berlin at the outbreak of the Franco-Prussian war

[8] By General Sir G. T. Chesney. It was first published in *Blackwood's Magazine*, May 1871

[9] Written in 1904

[10] John Coleridge Patteson (1827-71), bishop of Melanesia from 1861 until his murder in 1871

[11] Robert Henry Codrington (1830-1922), elected fellow of Wadham in 1855, head of the Melanesian Mission 1871-77, vicar of Wadhurst, Sussex, 1888-93, Prebendary of Wightring in Chichester Cathedral 1895-1921

[12] Thomas Newenham Deane (1828-99) designed the Meadow Building for Christ Church, 1862-65. His father was the architect (with Benjamin Woodward) of the University Museum, 1855-60

[13] George Earlham Thorley (1830-1904), fellow of Wadham from 1854, sub-warden 1868-81, warden from 1881 until his death

[14] 'I did do something like these ceilings afterwards over the great staircase'

CHAPTER II

[1] Rev. James Edwards Sewell (1810-1903), elected warden of New College 1860, vice-chancellor 1874-78

[2] Rt Rev. Henry George Liddell (1811-98), dean of Christ Church 1855-91, vice-chancellor 1870-74

[3] Rev. Thomas Vere Bayne, elected a student of Christ Church in 1849

[4] James Allen (1802-97) was dean of St Davids 1878-95

[5] Sir Leopold Cust, 2nd Bt (1831-78), survived his father by only seven weeks

[6] George Rolleston (1829-81), fellow of Merton College, Linacre Professor of Human and Comparative Anatomy 1860-81

[7] William Cecil Marshall (born 1849) worked for both T.G.J. and Basil Champneys before setting up his own practice in 1876; elected fellow of the RIBA in 1906

[8] Probably A.S. Gulston, who exhibited at the Grosvenor Gallery in 1883

[9] His son Basil Jackson took his nephew (Nicholas Jackson) to stay at the Delphino in 1949

[10] Sir Nicholas Jackson and his wife also stayed at the Delphino on Isola Bella in 1976 where they found one of Contini's descendants working as a guide in the Palace

CHAPTER I2

[1] Henry Willis (1821-1901) played the organ and the double bass. He built fine instruments in many cathedrals and churches. Examples of his work are to be found in the Royal Albert Hall, St Paul's Cathedral, Winchester Cathedral, Gloucester Cathedral, St Davids Cathedral etc.

[2] These pipes have since been removed, so that the case is now as originally envisaged.

[3] James Alexander Moore (died 1916) was principal of St Edmund Hall 1864-1913

[4] James Alexander Cruikshank, assistant master at Harrow from 1866 and housemaster 1870-91. The house has since been demolished

[5] James John Hooper was a fellow of Oriel, 1848-84, and recorder of South Molton 1877-84

[6] Il était un roi d'Yvetot
  Peu connu dans l'histoire;
  Se levant tard, se couchant tôt,
  Dormant fort bien sans gloire,
  Et couronné par Jeanneton
  D'un simple bonnet de coton,
  Dit-on – Oh! oh! oh oh! ah! ah! ah! ah!
  Quel bon petit roi c'était là! – Là, là.
  Pierre-Jean de Beranger, 1812
  T.G.J. knew Thackeray's daughter at Wimbledon so may have known her father's translation of this rhyme:
  There was a king of Yvetot,
  Of whom renown hath little said,
  Who let all thoughts of glory go,
  And dawdled half his days in bed;
  And every night, as night came round,
  By Jenny, with a nightcap crowned,
  Slept very sound:
  Sing ho, ho, ho! and he, he, he!
  That's the kind of king for me.

[7] *Modern Gothic Architecture* in which T.G.J. says that if, 'a man of educated taste were walking down the streets of London … the only buildings which he would find to admire are those built before the Gothic Revival was even thought of … barely one in a hundred will seem to him even decently tolerable.'

[8] Mendelssohn's diaries relate a similar experience, only when he exclaimed to his companion 'Did you ever see a bearded castrato before?' a stout lady behind him protested, 'Castrato indeed, I will have you know that that great artist is none other than my husband and the father of my five children'

[9] Metastasio (real name Pietro Trepassi) (1698-1782) wrote librettos for the operas of Gluck, Handel, Haydn and Mozart. In fact T.G.J. is misinformed here as it was not Metastasio but his father who was born at Assisi

[10] Domenico Cimaroso (1749-1801). When his 'Il matrimonio segreto' was performed in Vienna, the Emperor ordered supper for the performers and then told them to go through it all over again

[11] Fernando Paer (1771-1839) wrote over forty operas and was musical director at the court of Napoleon Bonaparte

[12] Giovanni Paesiello (1740-1816) composed one hundred operas and was about the courts of Joseph Bonaparte and Catherine the Great

[13] Francis John Jayne (1845-1921), principal of St David's College, Lampeter, 1879-86, bishop of Chester 1889-1919

[14] Bonamy Price (1807-88) was Drummond Professor of Political Economy 1868-88

CHAPTER 13

[1] On September 11th 1879 Alice Lambarde had written to him turning down his proposal of marriage

  Sevenoaks, Sept 11th, 1879

  Dear Mr. Jackson,

  I have been … thinking most seriously over your proposal … I really cannot say yes not having the affection to justify such a step … I never imagined it was me you cared for … I will always remain yrs sincerely

  A. M. Lambarde

[2] William Basil Tickell Jones (1822-97) was a fellow of University College 1851-57, and became bishop of St Davids in 1874

[3] Prince Leopold, Duke of Clarence (1854-1884) was the fourth and youngest son of Queen Victoria

[4] The clerk of works

[5] Albert Estcourt, of Gloucester, was contractor for a number of T.G.J.'s buildings, including the Examination Schools, Radley College, and Eagle House

[6] Sir Augustus Berkeley Paget (1823-96) was envoy extraordinary and minister plenipotentiary to King Victor Emmanuel of Italy, 1867-76, and ambassador 1876-83, and ambassador at Vienna in 1884-93

[7] Edward Augustus Freeman (1823-92), fellow of Trinity and Regius Professor of Modern History 1884-92

CHAPTER 14

[1] Madeleine Septimia Shaw Lefevre (1835-1914), principal of Somerville 1879-89

[2] Arthur Edward Perkins (1854-1904) worked with Sir Gilbert Scott and J.O.Scott and was chief assistant to T.G.J. for eleven years before setting up his own practice in 1885

[3] Mrs. Elizabeth Montagu (1720-1800), the original 'blue stocking'

[4] Harry Ellis Wooldridge (1845-1917), Slade Professor of Fine Art 1895-1904

[5] Mountague Bernard (1820-1882), fellow of All Souls' and Chichele Professor of International Law, 1859-74

[6] Nicholas Hawksmoor (1661-1736) designed buidings for Queen's College and All Souls'

[7] Sir John Soane (1753-1837), founder of the Soane Museum; rebuilt the Bank of England; RA., 1802

[8] Philip Hardwick (1792-1870), whose works include buildings for Lincoln's Inn

[9] Rev. Albert Watson, fellow of Brasenose 1852 and principal 1886

[10] Robinson Ellis (1834-1914), fellow of Trinity 1858, Corpus Professor of Latin Literature from 1893

[11] Rev. Henry George Woods (1842-1915), fellow of Trinity 1865, President 1887-97, Master of the Temple from 1904

[12] Benjamin Jowett (1817-1893) was Master of Balliol College from 1870-1893

[13] John Callcott Horsley (1817-1903) was treasurer of the Royal Academy 1882-1897

[14] Thomas Webster R.A. (1800-1886) A painter and etcher who was also a chorister at St George's Chapel, Windsor

[15] William Frith R.A. (1819-1909). Studied art at the Royal Academy Schools where he exhibited from 1840. His works include 'Derby Day', 1858 (now in the Tate Gallery), 'The Railway Station', 1862, and 'Ramsgate Sands', 1853. C.V.O., 1908

[16] Sir George Frampton R.A. (1860-1928). His works include the statue of 'Peter Pan' in Kensington Gardens

[17] Thomas George Baring, 1st Earl of Northbrook (1826-1904)

[18] Alexander Hugh Baring, 4th Baron Ashburton (1835-89)

[19] Alfred Stowe, fellow of Wadham 1962, dean 1870, bursar of Corpus Christi 1873-74

[20] Robert Scott (1811-87), dean of Rochester 1870-87, collaborated with H.G.Liddell on their *Greek-English Lexicon*, first published in 1843

[21] Stephen Parkinson (1823-1889), elected fellow of St John's in 1845 and President in 1865

CHAPTER 15

[1] Robert Browning (1812-1889), poet

[2] Oliver Wendell Holmes (1809-94), poet, essayist and anatomist

CHAPTER 16

[1] a one-horse vehicle

[2] Rudolf von Eitelberger published *Die mittelalterlichen Kunstdenkmäle Dalmatiens* in 1884

[3] E.A. Freeman's *Sketches from the Subject and Neighbour Lands of Venice* was published in 1881

[4] Pula was, at that time, a garrison town

[5] Geffroy de Villehardouin (*c* 1150-1218) took part in the Fourth Crusade and wrote a chronicle of it

[6] Professor Eitelberger of Vienna published the second edition of his book on the medieval art of Dalmatia in 1884

[7] Unfortunately T.G.J's efforts to save these buildings were ultimately of no avail, as can be seen in photos taken from the same viewpoint as his sketch in many travel brochures of Hvar (Lesina)

[8] Following his visit to Korčula in 2002 Sir Nicholas Jackson received a letter from Ms Stanka Kraljevic in which she wrote, 'My niece who runs the Town Museum says your Grandfather initiated the museum. He bought three late Gothic windows (monophora and biphora), which were moved from ruined façades and set in other buildings of the town. He also was the first to make drawings of the Cathedral'

[9] *Dalmatia, the Quarnero and Istria* contains 66 plates, 135 illustrations in the text and 22 copies of inscriptions

CHAPTER 17

[1] Eagle House has now been acquired by Sheikh Ahmed Yemani where it houses the Al-Furqun Islamic Heritage Foundation

[2] William Wyndham Grenville (1755-1846). Created peer 1790. Speaker 1789. Home Secretary 1789-90. Foreign Secretary 1789-90. Chancellor of Oxford 1809.

[3] Anne Ritchie, later Lady Ritchie (1837-1919) was the daughter of William Makepeace Thackeray. She was a novelist and woman of letters. She married Richmond Ritchie who was knighted in 1907

[4] Robert Rowand Anderson (1834-1921) worked for Scott, was knighted in 1902 and awarded the Royal Gold Medal for Architecture in 1916

[5] Sir Aston Webb R.A. (1849-1930) designed the Victoria & Albert Museum and Christ's Hospital School, and was P.R.A. 1919-1924

[6] Edward Ingress Bell (1837-1914) was in partnership with Aston Webb

[7] Thomas Edward Collcutt (1840-1924) worked in Street's office before setting up in 1873. Other buildings by him include the Savoy Hotel

[8] Alfred Waterhouse R.A. (1861-1905). His buildings include the Natural History Museum, the Prudential Assurance Office, Holborn and Balliol College ,Oxford. He possessed great personal charm and his smile was said to be worth £10,000 a year. [Sir Hugh Casson's *Oxford*]

[9] Charles Barry junior (1823-1900), son of Sir Charles Barry; his works include Dulwich College and the Piccadilly frontage of Burlington House

[10] William Henry White (1838-96) was appointed secretary of the RIBA in 1878

[11] Sir Arthur Blomfield R.A. (1829-1899) His works include Sion College on the Thames Embankment

[12] Rev. Sir John Henry Fludyer (1803-96), 4th Bt

[13] The interior of the chapel had been remodelled by S.S.Teulon, *c.* 1850 and completed by David Brandon *c.* 1870. T.G.J's design for an organ case in the chapel was never realised

[14] Athelstan Riley (1858-1945), Seigneur de la Trinité and one of the founders of the Alcuin Club

[15] Now part of the Milestone Hotel

[16] C.H. Bessant, cabinet maker

[17] Philip Webb (1831-1915) designed many houses including 'Red House' at Bexleyheath for William Morris with whom he was a co-founder of the Society for the Protection of Ancient Buildings

[18] James Brett's (1831-1902) Pre-Raphaelite pictures were admired by Ruskin.

[19] Sir Francis Dicksee (1853-1928) was a fashionable portrait painter

[20] Sir William Richmond (1842-1921) did the mosaic decorations for St Paul's Cathedral

[21] Onslow Ford (1852-1901), sculptor

[22] Walter Crane (1845-1915) was the first president of the Art Workers' Guild and Principal of the Royal College of Art in 1890

[23] Selwyn Image (1849-1930) was Slade professor of fine art at Oxford 1910-1916

[24] Joseph Batchelor, of Little Chart, Ashford, Kent

[25] Sir William Wyndham Portal, 2nd Bt (1850-1931)

[26] James Clarke Hook (1819-1907), elected RA in 1861. In 1890 he exhibited 'A Dutch Pedlar'

CHAPTER 18

[1] William Arnold was also responsible for Montacute House, Dunster Castle and Cranborne House

[2] Rev. Joseph Haythorne Edgar

[3] Sir William Temple (1628-1699), statesman and author, settled at Sheen in 1663. After 1680 he lived at Moor Park, Surrey, where Jonathan Swift (1667-1745), author of *Gulliver's Travels*, was his secretary from 1689

[4] Carl Krall and his partner Jes Barkentin (Barkentin & Krall) were among the best metalworkers of the time

[5] Thomas Case (1844-1925) was elected fellow of Corpus Christi in 1882 and was President, 1904-24; Professor of Moral and Metaphysical Philosophy, 1889-1910

[6] Adam Sedgwick (1785-1873) was Woodwardian Professor of Geology 1818-73

[7] Thomas McKenny Hughes was Sedgwick's successor as Professor of Geology, until his death in 1917

[8] John Chessell Buckler (1793-1894), who designed buildings for Magdalen and Jesus Colleges

[9] Sir William Blake Richmond (1842-1921) was elected RA in 1885 and knighted in 1897; Slade Professor at Oxford, 1878-83

CHAPTER 19

[1] Unfortunately the gold medal was wrongly inscribed with his initials as T.E. Jackson

[2] Later donated to the Victoria and Albert Museum.

[3] In doubt

[4] Good joke.

[5] The bridge at Mostar which was destroyed in 1993, during the Croat–Bosnian war. Restoration is under way.

[6] 'The marble tablet placed on the first floor of the Campanile of which we have the honour to enclose six photographs will hand down to posterity the revered memory of the intelligent

and gifted architect who designed the building and the name of the Englishman Mr. T. G. Jackson will always be remembered in this city with respect, veneration and gratitude'

CHAPTER 20

[1] Rev. Charles Halford Hawkins (1838-1900), chaplain of Winchester College from 1863, housemaster from 1869

[2] Lorina, wife of Henry George Liddell (1811-1898), dean of Christ Church

[3] Georgina Adelaide, wife of Friedrich Max-Müller (1823-1900), Corpus Professor of Comparative Philology from 1868

[4] Sir Henry Acland's wife Sarah had died in 1878

[5] William Stubbs (1825-1901) was bishop of Oxford from 1889

[6] Sir James Paget (1814-99) was Surgeon to the Prince of Wales from 1863 and Serjeant-Surgeon to Queen Victoria from 1877. He was created a baronet in 1871

[7] The organ has since been removed to make more room for boys in the gallery

[8] His son Hugh was also present being given the day off from Winchester

[9] 'H' Social

[10] At the service for the centenary of the Chapel in 1995 his grandson, an OR, read the lesson

[11] Sir Thomas Brock (1847-1922) was the sculptor responsible for the memorial to Queen Victoria in front of Buckingham Palace done in conjunction with Sir Aston Webb

[12] John Singer Sargent (1856-1925), best known as a portrait painter, was elected RA in 1897

[13] John William North (1841-1924), elected ARA in 1893

[14] William Butterfield (1814-1900) designed Keble College , Oxford and All Saints' Margaret Street

[15] Ernest Crofts (1847-1911) was a historical painter, mainly of Napoleonic subjects

[16] Philip Hermogenes Calderon (1833-98), elected RA in 1867, was Keeper of the Royal Academy from 1887

[17] Sir Edward Poynter Bt (1836-1919) was the first Slade professor of fine art in London

[18] Archbishop George Benson (1829-1896), who vigorously opposed the disestablishment of The Church in Wales, became archbishop in 1882

[19] Rev. Henry Boyd (1831-1922), principal of Hertford, 1877-1922, vice-chancellor 1890, master of the Drapers' Company 1896-7; commissioned T.G.J. to enlarge and partly rebuild Hertford College. He was an accomplished watercolourist

[20] Burlison and Grylls was a leading firm of stained glass makers, founded in 1868 at the instigation of Bodley and Garner. John Burlison (1843-91) was the son of Scott's assistant of the same name; his partner was Thomas Grylls. (1845-1913)

[21] James W.R. Linton, figure painter, flourished between 1890 and 1909; not to be confused with the painter Sir James Linton (1840-1916)

[22] William Henry Nichols (1875-1949), articled to T.G.J. 1896-99, assistant 1900-04, later worked for Sir Edwin Lutyens

[23] Douglas Stewart (1874-1934), student at the Architectural Association, later designed Brooke Hall and other buildings for his old school, Charterhouse

[24] 1905

[25] George William Kitchin (1827-1912) was dean of Durham from 1894

[26] John Loughborough Pearson R.A. (1817-1897) designed Truro Cathedral and restored the north transept of Westminster Abbey.

CHAPTER 21

[1] Sir Fred Eaton (1838–1913), Secretary to the Royal Academy, was knighted in 1911

[2] Sir Hubert von Herkomer (1849-1914) was elected RA in 1890 and knighted in 1907

[3] Now 'Tate Britain'

[4] Lord Charles Beresford became an admiral in 1906 and from 1907 to 1910 was commander-in-chief of the Channel fleet

[5] Edmond Lancelot Warre was articled to T.G.J. He worked in the War Office after being wounded in the First World War and later designed the Organ Room at Glynebourne

[6] Organist at St. George's Chapel, Windsor

[7] William Frederick Yeames RA (1835-1918) was curator of the Painted Hall at Greenwich Hospital and librarian of the Royal Academy

[8] Sir Lawrence Alma-Tadema R.A., O.M. (1836-1912)

[9] Andrew Carrick Gow (1848-1920), elected RA in 1891, was Keeper of the Royal Academy from 1911

[10] Joseph Solomon R.A., (1860-1927)

[11] Phil May (1846-1903) made a reputation as a comic artist in the *Daily Graphic* and other illustrated papers

[12] Sir Howard Grubb (1844-1931), was an astronomical instrument maker and contractor to the British and a number of other governments

[13] Hugh Riviere (1849-1956), portrait painter

[13] Bernard Jules Minssen was French master at Harrow. In December 1891 the 16-year-old Winston Churchill had also gone to stay for a month with Professor Minssen and his family at 18 Rue de Provence Versailles, and had been far from pleased about being sent there instead of going home for Christmas.

[14] They stayed at the Hôtel Grand Monarque. 100 years later T.G.J.'s grandson and his wife stayed at the same hotel when making a recording on the organ at Chartres Cathedral.

[15] Arthur Hill, second son of the distinguished organ builder William Hill, who had succeeded his brother as head of the firm in 1893

[16] Augustus Spencer (1860-1924) was Principal of the Royal College of Art, 1900-20

[17] Gerald Moira (died 1959) was an artist who specialised in mural decorations

[18] William Lethaby (1857-1931), architect and author of *Architecture, Mysticism and Myth* (1891) and *Architecture, and the Art of Building*

CHAPTER 22

[1] Sir Frank Cavendish Lascelles (1841-1920) was Ambassador to Germany, 1895-1908

[2] Hugh Gough, 3rd Viscount Gough (1849-1919) was Secretary of Embassy at Berlin, 1896-1901

[3] See Appendix III

[4] Sir Francis Fox (1844-1927), whose other engineering feats included the construction of the Simplon Tunnel, Switzerland

CHAPTER 23

[1] Another example of Jackson/Warre humour was the motto (a rowing man's joke) which was affixed to T.G.J.'s cricket pavilion at Eton, which may be translated 'Go out slowly – come back quickly'

[2] Lord Curzon (1859-1925), following his time as Viceroy of India, had become Chancellor of Oxford University in 1907

[3] Sir Robert Forsyth Scott (1849-1933) was Master of St John's College, Cambridge, from 1908 and Vice-Chancellor of the University 1910-1912

[4] William Waldegrave Palmer, 2nd Earl of Selborne (1859-1942), had recently completed his term of office as Governor of Transvaal and High Commissioner for South Africa

[5] Syeed Ameer-Ali (1849-1928), Indian judge, was a member of the Judicial Committee of the Privy Council

[6] Arthur James Mason (1851-1928) was Master of Pembroke College, Cambridge, 1903-12, and a canon of Canterbury

[7] Rev. Patrick Arkley Wright-Henderson (1841-1922), warden of Wadham 1903-13

[8] T.G.J. was joined by his son Basil on October 4th

CHAPTER 24

[1] 'Most Oxford of artists, who by combining all styles of architecture have shown to this generation a new form of beauty, I by my authority and that of the whole University admit you to the honorary degree of Doctor of Civil Law'

[2] Herbert Henry Asquith (1852-1928), Prime Minister 1908-16, created 1st Earl of Oxford and Asquith in 1925

[3] Mary St Helier (died 1931), widow of Lord St Helier, described herself in *Who's Who* as 'indefatigable in service of the poor, and in Society … famed for her brilliant art of entertaining'

CONCLUSION

[1] In 1964 T.G.J.'s grandson dined in the precincts of Westminster Abbey with Canon Adam Fox, who as Warden of Radley had commissioned the archway. 'I tried to tell him that those arches were too small for modern traffic,' said Fox, 'but he wouldn't listen!'

[2] Sir Maurice Bowra (1898-1971) who was Warden of Wadham from 1938 to 1970 and had been a fellow since 1922

[3] Frederic Harrison is also referred to on page 33. In Maurice Bowra's *Memories* he relates the story of Harrison's father appearing in his six-year-old son's nursery to inform him of the death of King William IV, which prompted the young Harrison to inquire as to who would be the new king. On being told that they were not going to have a king but were now going to have a queen instead, Frederic Harrison maintained that he replied 'Oh, it's come to that, has it'; and went on playing with his bricks!

Bibliography

I PUBLICATIONS BY T.G.J.

Address as President of the Section of Architecture, National Association for the Advancement of Science, Birmingham, *Builder*, LIX (1890), 364-6, 383-5; cf. *Builder*, LXI (1891), 76-9

Address to the students of the Durham School of Art (3 Mar 1898). Issued as pamphlet

Architecture (London: Macmillan, 1925; reissued 1932; reprinted New York, 1972). Cf. *Recollections*, 275

'Architecture', in A. Tilley (ed.), *Medieval France: a companion to French studies* (Cambridge: University Press, 1922), 331-87

Architecture a profession or an art: thirteen short essays on the qualification and training of architects, edited by R.N. Shaw and T.G.J. (London: John Murray, 1892). Essays by T.G.J., Shaw, J.T. Micklethwaite, Reginald Blomfield, G.F. Bodley, Mervyn Macartney, Ernest Newton, E.S. Prior, J.R. Clayton, Basil Champneys, W.R. Lethaby, W.B. Richmond, and G.C. Horsley. Reviewed in *Builder*, LXIII (1892), 312-4; letter by Cole Adams, 359, response by T.G.J., 382

'Architecture in relation to the crafts'. Paper read to the Architectural Association (2 Oct 1897), *Builder*, LXXII (1897), 334-9

'The Architecture of Dalmatia'. Paper read to the RIBA, *RIBA Transactions*, III (1886-7), 161-78

'The Art of Dalmatia'. Paper read to the RIBA, *RIBA Transactions*, III (1886-7), 358-67, 388; *Builder*, LII (1897), 917-20

'Avallon and the French Portals', *Country Life*, XXXIX (1916), 736-8

Byzantine and Romanesque Architecture (Cambridge: University Press, 1913; 2nd edn, 1920; reprinted New York 1975). 2 vols.

'Byzantine Architecture'. Lecture given at Carpenters' Hall (30 Jan 1918), *Architect and Contract Reporter*, XCIX (1918), 86

The Church of St Mary the Virgin Oxford (Oxford: Clarendon Press, 1897). Press mark designed by T.G.J. for his history of Wadham College, 1893. Reviewed in *Architectural Review*, IV (1898), 1-8, 50-3, 109-14; *Building News*, LXXIII (1897), 391-2

'The Churches of Serbia', *Proceedings of the Society of Antiquaries of London*, XXX (1917-18), 10-17

'The Commonplace of Architecture'. Paper to the Leeds and Yorkshire Architectural Society (9 Mar 1885), *Builder*, XLVIII (1885), 407-10

Dalmatia the Quarnero and Istria with Cettigne in Montenegro and the Island of Grado (Oxford: Clarendon Press, 1887). 3 vols. Reviewed in *British Architect*, XXVIII (1887), 169-70; *Builder*, LIII (1887), 259-62, 270; *Building News*, LIII (1887), 123-6; *Edinburgh Review*, CLXVII (1888), 81-108. Cf. *Recollections*, 207; T.G.J.'s notes at RIBA; *Architectural Review*, I (1897), 144; *Building News*, LIII (1887), 454; *Building Design*, no. 828 (1987 Mar 20), 28-9

'Eagle House, Wimbledon', *Surrey Archaeological Society Collections*, X (1891), 151-64

'Eagle House, Wimbledon; its builders and inhabitants', *Wimbledon and Merton Annual*, I (1903), 9-25

Gothic Architecture in France, England, and Italy (Cambridge: University Press, 1915; reprinted New York 1975). 2 vols. Reviewed in *Architectural Record*, XL (1916), 282-4. Cf. *Recollections*, 269-70

'The High Street of Oxford, and Brasenose College', *Magazine of Art*, VIII (1889), 332-40

A Holiday in Umbria, with an account of Urbino and the Cortegiano of Castiglione (London: John Murray, 1917). Reviewed in *Builder*, CXII (1917), 226-7. Cf. *Recollections*, 200-1

'Individuality in art': summary of speech made at the Birmingham Municipal School of Art (18 Feb 1897), *Builders' Journal and Architectural Record*, V (1897), 62; also issued as pamphlet

'Intarsia and inlaid wood-work', Arts & Crafts Exhibition Society, *Catalogue of the third Exhibition* (1890), 67-77; *Arts and Crafts Essays, by Members of the Arts and Crafts Exhibition Society* (London: The Society, 1893), 330-44

'The L.C.C. new street: Holborn to the Strand', *Architectural Review*, VII (1900), 156-62

'The Libraries of the Middle Ages'. Paper read to the RIBA, *RIBA Journal*, V (1898), 365-85

Memories of Travel (Cambridge: University Press, 1923)

'A Modern Cathedral', *Guardian* (1902), 155

Modern Gothic Architecture (London: Henry S. King, 1873). Reviewed in *Architect*, IX (1873), 294; *Builder*, XXXI (1873), 597-8; *see also Recollections*, 121-2, 142, 153, 218; *Architectural Review*, I (1897), 139-40

'Obstacles opposed to the advancement of architecture by architects themselves'. Paper read to the First Congress of the National Association for the Advancement of Art, Liverpool (5 Dec 1888), *Transactions of the National Association … * (1888), 193-202; *Builder*, LVI (1889), 47-9

'The Proposal to make architects a close profession by imposing the test of examination and registration'. Paper read to the Architectural Association (16 Dec 1887), *Builder*, LII (1887), 873-6; discussion, 869, 894-7; cf. *RIBA Journal*, IV (1887-8), 82, 207-9, 222-4, 242, *AA Notes*, I (1887), 190, 214, and *Builder* (1888), 260

'Pyrford Church', *Surrey Archaeological Society Collections*, VII (1869), 57-60

'Ragusa. Il palazzo rettorale; il duomo; il reliquario del teschio de S. Biagio', *Annuario Dalmatico*, Zara, II (1885)

Reason in Architecture: lectures delivered at the Royal Academy of Arts in the year 1906 (London: John Murray, 1906). Cf. Recollections, 264

Recollections of Thomas Graham Jackson, arranged and edited by Basil H. Jackson (Oxford: University Press, 1950). Reviewed in *Architectural Review*, CIX (1951), 324; *New*

Statesman and Nation, XL (1950), 329 (by John Summerson); *Time and Tide* (26 Aug 1950) (by John Betjeman)

The Renaissance of Roman Architecture (Cambridge: University Press, 1921-3; reprinted New York, 1975). 3 vols: part 1, Italy (1921); part 2, England (1922); part 3, France (1923). Cf. *Recollections*, 182, 275

'Serbian Church Architecture', in M.I. Pupin (ed.), *Serbian Orthodox Church* (South Slav Monuments. 1; London: John Murray, 1918), 7-23

Six Ghost Stories (London: John Murray, 1919; reprinted with introduction by Richard Dalby, Ashcroft, B.C., 1999)

'Some account of St Mary's, the Parish Church of Wimbledon', *Surrey Archaeological Collections*, XXXIV (1921), 1-14

'Some account of Slindon Church', *Sussex Archaeological Collections*, XIX (1867), 126-33

'Some thoughts on the training of architects'. Paper delivered at the opening of the Liverpool School of Architecture and Applied Arts (10 May 1895), *Builder*, LXVIII (1895), 370, 375-6; *Building News*, LXVIII (1895), 687; *RIBA Journal*, II (1895), 636-42; also issued as a pamphlet. Cf. Q. Hughes, 'Before the Bauhaus: the experiment of the Liverpool School of Architecture and Applied Arts', *Architectural History*, XXV (1982), 102-13

'Street architecture'. Paper read to the Applied Art Section of the Society of Arts (Dec 1904), *American Architect and Building News*, LXXXVII (1905), 30-2, 51-2; *Architect and Contract Reporter*, LXXII (1904), 425-9; *Builder*, LXXXVII (1904), 653, 661-3; *Builders' Journal and Architectural Record*, XX (1904), 340; *Journal of the Society of Arts*, LIII (1904), 107-23

'The training of architects to the pursuit of architecture: some suggestions for the practical education of an architect'. Paper read to the Architectural Association (11 Dec 1891), *Builder*, LXI (1891), 460-3 (discussion, 468-71, leading article, 455-6, correspondence (including letter by T.G.J.), 488-9, editorial comment 477-8); letter by T.G.J. in *AA Notes*, VI (1891-2), 161, cf. 178-80, 186-91

'Winchester Cathedral. An account of the building and of the repairs now in progress'. Paper read to the St Paul's Ecclesiogical Society (16 Feb 1910), *Transactions*, VI (1906-10), 216-36

Wadham College, Oxford: its foundation, architecture and history, with an account of the family of Wadham and their seats in Somerset and Devon (Oxford: Clarendon Press, 1893). Press mark designed by T.G.J. Cf. *Recollections*, 229; papers in Wadham College Library

II WRITINGS ABOUT T.G.J.

See also references in the list of works, especially under Oxford

Obituaries: *Architect*, CXII (1924), 301; *Architects' Journal*, LX (1924), 756, 758-63 (by A.T. Bolton); *Builder*, CXXVII (1924), 748, 753 (by Beresford Pite), 926; *RIBA Journal*, XXXII (1924), 49-50 (by Reginald Blomfield); *The Times* (8 Nov 1924), 7; (10 Nov 1924), 8; (18 Nov 1924), 20; *Wadham College Gazette*, no. 76 (1924), 154-7 (by Joseph Wells)

Anon. 'Contemporary British architects', *Building News*, LVIII (1890), 221

Anon. [Profile on election as ARA], *Art Journal* (1892), 94

Anon. [Profile on election as RA], *Builders' Journal and Architectural Record*, IV (1896), 209-10

Anon. 'T.G. Jackson RA and his work', *Architecture*, II (1897), 3-24, 84-96

Anon. 'Men who build, no. 48: The Collegiate Work of T.G. Jackson, RA', *Builders' Journal and Architectural Record*, IV (1897), 355-9

Anon. [Profiles on the occasion of baronetcy], *Architects' and Builders' Journal*, XXXVII (1913), 51-2; *Building News*, CIX (1913), 5

Crook, J.M. 'T.G. Jackson and the cult of eclecticism' in H. Searing (ed.), *In Search of Modern Architecture: a tribute to Henry-Russell Hitchcock* (1982), 102-20

George, E. [Royal Gold Medal presentation], *RIBA Journal*, XVII (1910), 621-9

Goodhart-Rendel, H.S. 'The Work of Sir Thomas Graham Jackson, R.A., Royal Gold Medallist', *RIBA Journal*, XXXIII (1926), 467-78; cf. *Architect & Building News*, CXV (1926), 618-20

Goodhart-Rendel, H.S. 'Jackson, Sir Thomas Graham', *Dictionary of National Biography* (1937)

Latham, Ian, 'Thomas Jackson – baronet architect', *Building Design*, no. 665 (11 Nov 1983), 10

Mallows, C.E., 'The Complete Work of Thomas Graham Jackson', *Architectural Review*, I (1897) 136-60

W. Whyte, 'Oxford Jackson: architecture, education, status and style' (DPhil thesis, Oxford, 2002)

Index

Note: *Italic* type indicates references to captions; **bold** type indicates specific references to places in the gazetteer and general references to the appendices.

Abbeville, France 40, 225, 252
Abergwili, Carmarthen 143
Acland, Dr (Sir) Henry Wentworth 106, 267, 309, 314
Acland, Lady Sarah 220, 267, 314
Adelaide International Exhibition (TGJ prize) 7
Agram (*now* Zagreb) 175
Aix-les-Bains, France 130
Albano 227–8
Albany, Duchess of 228
Aldenham, Herts 157, **274**
Aldershot, Hants **274**
Alexander II of Russia 159, 298
Alford, Som 137, **274**
Al-Furqun Islamic Heritage Foundation (at Eagle House) 312
Alibranti, Canonico 183, 184
Allen, James (Dean of St. David's) xii, 118, 143, 202, 222, 309
Alma-Tadema, Sir Lawrence 235, 245, 261, 263, 316
Ameer-Ali, Syeed 245, 315
Amiens, France 40, 97–8, 225, 252
Ancona, Italy (*Plate 27*), 163
Anderson, Robert Rowand 189, 262, 312
Andrews, William Ryton 54, 306
'Anglo-Jackson' style xii, 1, 2, 9
Annesley, Notts 4, 100, *100*, **274**
Aquileja 173
Arbe (*now* Rab) (*Plate 33*) *178*
Architect 4
Architects' Journal 9
Architectural Exhibition Society 101
Architectural Record 9
Architectural Review 9, 13
Architecture 9
Architecture – a profession or an art (TGJ and Shaw) 7
Architecture (TGJ) 255
Arles, France 80, 87

Armstead, H. 263
Arnold, Charles Thomas (TGJ's cousin) 30–1, 51, 59, 70, 76, 106, 129, 133, 185, 296, 299
Arnold, Elizabeth (*later* Jackson; TGJ's mother) *see* Jackson, Elizabeth
Arnold, Hugh (TGJ's cousin) 295
Arnold, John 199
Arnold, Thomas Kirchever 304
Arnold, Dr Thomas (TGJ's grandfather) 18
Arnold, Dr Thomas (TGJ's great-grandfather) 18
Arnold, Tom (TGJ's uncle) 25
Arnold, William (architect of Wadham) 199, 313
Arnold, William (TGJ's uncle) 18–19
Arthur, Prince of Connaught 252
Art Journal 7
Arts and Crafts Exhibitions 196
Arts and Crafts Society 103
Art Workers' Guild 103, 195–6, 202, 224, 236
Ash, Kent 224, **274**
Ashbourne, Derbys **274**
Ashburton, Lady 158
Ashburton, Lord (Alexander Hugh Baring, 4th Baron) 158, 290, 311
Asquith, Herbert Henry 250, 316
Assisi, Italy 133–7, *133, 135*
Auber, Daniel 42, 305
Audley End, Essex 189
Auvergne peasants 78, *78*
Auxerre, France 96

Badsey, Worcs **274**
Baker, Herbert 303
Bale, Charles Sackville 161
Banbury, Oxon **274**
Baring, family 280, 281, 290
Baring, Alexander Hugh, 4th Baron Ashburton 158, 290, 311
Baring, T.C. 270
Baring, Thomas George, 1st Earl Northbrook 158, 280, 311

Barkentin, Jes 313
Barnet, Herts **274–5**
Barry, Charles (son) 190, 191, 312
Barry, Sir Charles 306, 312
Barton St. David, Som **275**
Basingstoke, Hants **275**
Batchelor, Joseph 196, 223, 313
Bath, Som **275**
Bathurst, Dr 153
Battle of Dorking, The (Chesney) 108, 309
Bayeux, France 252
Bayne, Rev. Thomas Vere 117–18, 309
Beauchamp, Augusta and Alice 130
Beauvais, France 40, 225
Becket, Edmund, Lord Grimthorpe 9, 263
Beechey, Anne (*later* Jackson) 18
Beechey, Charlotte (*later* Lady Grantly) 18, 25
Beechey, Rear Admiral Frederick William 18, 19,
   303
Beechey, Sir William 18, 19, 22, 303
Begna, Conte 211
Bell, Alice 186
Bell, Edward Ingress 189, 312
Bell, J.F.C. 303
Bell, Robert 186
Benedetti, Vincent 108, 309
Benko, Baron 214
Benson, Archbishop George 228, 236, 278, 314
Benson, W.A.S. 267, 277
Bent, John Oxenham 36, 304
Bentley, John 262
Beresford, Lord Charles 233, 315
Beresford-Peirse, Lady viii, xiii
Berlin 241
Bernard, Dr. Mountague 152, 267, 311
Bessant, C.H. 194, 275, 313
Béthune, France (*Plate 16*), 129
Betjeman, John xii, 1, 301, 302
Bignold, John 58
Billinge, Lancs **275**
Binstead, West Sussex 4, 88, **275**, 302
Birkenhead, Lord 255
Bishops Waltham, Hants **275**
Blagaj 216
Blenheim Palace, Oxon 192, *193*, 195, **275–6**
Blois, France (*Plate 18*), xiii, 98, 99, 237
Blomfield, Sir Arthur William 191, 192, 242,
   261-2, 271, 296, 312
Blomfield, Reginald 12
Bodley, G.F. 4, 5, 14, 58, 105, 110, 111, 120,
   190, 262, 267, 295, 306
Bologna, Italy 133
Bolton, Arthur T. 12
Bone, C.B. 303
Borth, Wales (Uppingham School at) 101
Bosheston, Pembroke 67, 68
Bosnia 213, 214

Bossom, A.C. 301
Boswell, James, *Life of Johnson* 18
Bothamley, Rev. Hilton 275
Botley, Hants **276**
Bottisham, Cambs **276**
Boulton & Sons 274
Bournemouth, Hants **276**
Bourton-on-the-Water, Glos **276**
Bowra, Sir Maurice xii, 255, 305, 308, 316
Boyd, Rev. Henry (Principal of Hertford) 229,
   234, 314
Branby (musician) 73
Brandon, David 312
Branscombe church, Devon 199
Brassington (joiner) 231
Brett, James 196, 313
Brett, John 263
Bridges, John Henry 33, 304
Brighton, East Sussex
   Brighton College *28*, **276–7**
   TGJ buildings at 2, 9, 157
   TGJ pupil at 2, 4, 27–9, 31
   Church of St. Augustine **277**
Brindley *see* Farmer & Brindley
Brioude 248
British Architect 8
Broadwood & Sons 192, *193*, 287
Brock, Sir Thomas 224, 228, 235, 241, 263, 278,
   314
Bromley, Kent
   Church of St. Peter and St. Paul **277**
   Plonck's Hill *see* Shamley Green
Browning, Robert 161, 311
Brown, Ford Maddox 263
Brudenell-Carter (oculist) 143
Bruges 198
Brydon, J.M. 262
Brympton 148
Buckler, John Chessell 205, 225, 313
Builder 2, 3–4, 7, 8, 9, 11
Builders' Journal 9
Burge, Rt Rev. Hubert Murray 299
Burges, William 55, 128, 306
Burgess, J.B. 263
Burghley House, Lincs 120
Burlison, John (stained glass maker) 57, 230, 282,
   291, 306, 314
Burne-Jones, Edward 51, 53, 110, 194, 223, 261,
   263, 280, 287, 289, 298, 306
Burns, John 251
Burpham, West Sussex 88, **277**
Burrell, Mr. 281
Burroni, Fra 134, 136
Burton, Decimus 50
Butler, Alfred 62, 307
Butterfield, William viii, 225, 249, 262, 267,
   291, 314

Byzantine and Romanesque Architecture (TGJ) 9, 11, 245, 248, 255

Caen, France, Abbaye aux hommes 40, *41*
Cairns, Johnny 29, 46
Calderon, Philip Hermogenes 226, 314
Cambridge 160, 204–5, 244, 245, 252
    King's College 160, 204, 236, 252, **277**
    Newnham College 160
    Senate House **277**
    Trinity College 204, 252
    University Buildings (Sedgwick Museum, etc.: Downing Street, Downing Place and Tennis Court Road) 9, 204, 205, 235–6, **277–8**, 296
Cancellor & Hill, 297
Canterbury, Kent 95, 96, 228, **278**
Carlisle, Lord 242
Carlstadt, Croatia (*now* Karlovac) 174, *176*
Caroë, W.D. 262, 295
Carter, I. 286
Carter, T. 282
Case, Thomas 203, 207, 313
Casson, Sir Hugh xiii, 301
Castel Gandolfo 227
Castelnuovo, silver plate from *171*
Castle Ashby, Northants **278**
Caterham, Surrey **278**
Cattaro 174
Catton Hall, Derbys **278**
Cecil, Lord Robert (*later* Lord Salisbury) 62
Cettigne, Montenegro 174
Chambord, France 98–9, 238
Champneys, Basil 5, 13, 105, 110, 249, 262, 302, 309
Charles I 162
Charlotte, Queen 18, 303
Chartres Cathedral, France (*Plate 17*), 78, 236, 315
Chauvigny 248
Cheam, Surrey 88, **278**
Chertsey, Surrey **278**
Cheshunt, Herts **278**
Chesney, General Sir G.T., *The Battle of Dorking* 108, 309
Chessington, Surrey 88, **278**
Chichester Cathedral, East Sussex 70–1
Childs (of Farmer & Brindley) 236, 273, 285
Choisy-le-Roi, Paris, glass factory 150–1
Christchurch, Hants 9, **278**
Christ's Hospital, Horsham (TGJ design) 8, 284
Churchill, Winston 315
Cimarosa, Domenico 136, 310
Clarendon Press 184
Clarke, Somers 58, 262, 306
Clayton, John R. 263
Clewer, Berks **278**
Coad, Richard 58, 307
Coblenz, Germany 108

Cockerell, Charles 25, 303
Codd, Frederick 14
Codrington, Robert 110, 298, 309
Collcutt, Thomas Edward 189, 312
Collett, E.A. 303
Colley, Bennet (carpenter) 128
Cologne 248
    Cathedral 106, 225
Colvin, Sir Howard 5, 12–13
Como, Italy (*Plate 22*), 173
Compton Martin, Som **279**
Comte, August 33, 304
Congreve, Dr Richard 33, 304
Constable, John 22, 25, 30
Constantine Porphyrogenitus 173
Constantinople (Istanbul), Turkey 245, 246, **298**
Contini, Giovanni 125, 131, 132–3, 163, 309
Cooper, John 64, 90, 307
Coote, Dr Charles Thomas 48, 306
Cordangan, Ireland 118
Corhampton, Hants **279**
Corsica 303
Cortina 165
Council for Art 239
Coutances, France 252
Coventry, Warwicks 255, **279**
Cowley, Oxon *see* Military College *under* Oxford
Cox, Miss Fanny 86
Cozzi, Signor (Pompeii) 226
Craddock, E.H. 267
Cranbook, Kent 157, 158, **279**
Crane, Walter 196, 240, 263, 313
Crofts, Ernest 226, 314
Crook, J. Mordaunt 14
Crossland, William Henry 58, 306
Cruikshank, James Alexander 127, 137, 283, 309
Crystal Palace, Sydenham, Kent 43, 51
Curdridge, Hants 159, **279**
Curzola (*now* Korčula) (*Plate 29*), 180–3, *181*, 184, 312
Curzon, Lord 245, 249, 315
Cust, Sir Leopold 118, 119, 309

Dalmatia xiv, 166, 167, 174–84, 208–18, 226
    TGJ's book on xiii, 7, 184, 190, 197, 312
Danby Hall, Yorks **279**
Danube, River 173
Darke, F.H. 303
Daubeny, Professor Charles Giles Bridle 35–6, 304
David, Julius Paul 101, 308
Deane, Thomas Newenham 5, 110, 189, 309
de Beranger, Pierre-Jean 310
Dedham, Essex **279**
Delphino Hotel, Isola Bella, Lake Maggiore viii, 123–5, 309
Desenzano, Italy 116

de Villehardouin, Jeffroi 173, 312
Devonshire, Duke of 231
Dicksee, Sir Francis 196, 313
Dictionary of National Biography 12
Dodgson, Charles ('Lewis Carroll') 163
Dolomites 165–6
Dorking, Surrey **279**
Dotheboys Hall (in *Nicholas Nickleby*) 231
Douglas, John 262
Doulton 270, 287
Drapers' Company 9, 229, 269, 272, 277
Doullens 129
Drioli, Salghetti 168, 200, 208, 209, 210, 218
Dubrovnik (*now* Ragusa) (*Plates 31, 32*), 170-1,
    174, 211–13, *212, 213, 214,* 215–16, *215*
Duddington, Northants 15–16, *16,* **279–80,** 303
Dudley Gallery 129
Dürer, Albert 107
Durham 231, **280**
Dursley, Glos 89, **280**

Earl Soham, Suffolk **280**
East Bergholt, Suffolk **280**
Eastbourne, East Sussex 207
East Clandon, Surrey 27, **280**
Easthampstead, Berks **280**
Eastrop, Hants *see* Basingstoke
East Stratton, Hants 158, **280**
Eaton, Sir Fred 232, 315
Edgar, Rev. Joseph Haythorne 200, 283, 313
Edge Hill, Battle of 127
Edge House, Devon 199
Edmonton, Canada 9, **298**
Edward VI 282
Edward VII 274
Edwards, Robert 119, 269, 277, 287
Egham, Surrey, Holloway College 58, 306
Ehrenburg Castle, Germany 106–7, *107*
Eilgugs (puffins, guillemots and razorbills) 67, 307
Eitelberger, Rudolf von 169, 173, 312
Elizabeth I, interview with Lambarde 93, **257–9**
Ellesmere, 1st Earl of 295
Ellingham, Hants 89, 137, **281**
Ellis, Robinson 153–4, 311
Elstow, Beds **281**
Eltham Palace, Kent 65, **281**
Elvey, Sir George 31
Elvey, Dr. Stephen 31, 304
Elz Castle, Germany 107
Ems, Germany 108
English Architecture since the Regency (Goodhart-
    Rendel) 12
Erith, Raymond 285
Esher, Surrey **281**
Estcourt, Albert 144, 186, 291, 311
Eton College, Berks 157, 220, 244, **281,** 315
Etty, William 197

Evans, R. (clerk of works) 231, 282, 294
Evans, Herbert 30
Evercreech House, Som **281**
Ewell, Surrey, Pit House, TGJ's parents at 65–7,
    66
Exeter, Lord 62
Exeter, Devon 200, **281**

Faccini, Dr (of Zara) 208, 210
Fairthorn House, Hants **281**
Farmer & Brindley 120, 146, 228, 236, 267, 269,
    270, 271, 272, 273, 276, 277, 280, 285, 286,
    287, 289, 290, 291, 293, 294, 295, 299
Farnham, Surrey **281**
Farrar, Adam Storey 46, 305
Fawcett, W.M. 262
Fenny Compton, Warwicks 127, 137, **281**
Ferguson, Charles 262
Field, Horace 263
Field of the Cloth of Gold 129
Filippi, Signor 208, 209, 210
Fioravanti (outlaw) 228
Fiume (*now* Rijeka) 175, *176*
Fladgate, Young & Jackson 18
Flaxman, John 159
Flore, Northants **282**
Florence, Italy 13, 80, 133, 248
Fludyer, Sir John Henry 192, 312
Font-Couvert, France 130
Ford, Onslow 196, 240, 263, 277, 313
Forest School, Snaresbrook 26, 30
Fourville, France 121–2
Fowler, Charles Hodgson 58, 262, 306
Fox, Canon Adam 316
Fox, Francis 11, 243, 250, 265, 296, 315
Framlingham, Suffolk **282**
Frampton, Sir George 158, 268, 276, 282, 286,
    287, 291, 294, 311
France, TGJ visits 40-2, 74, 78–80, 96–100, 121–
    3, 128-9, 130, 225, 248, 252
Francesconi, Dr. 248
Franco-Prussian War 99–100, 106, 108
Frankfurt, Germany 165
Freeling, Rev. G.K. 271
Freeman, Edward Augustus 5–6, 148, 169, 307,
    312
Frith, William 158, 311
Fryern Barnet Church 60
Furnes, France (*Plate 15*), 128–9

Garibaldi, Giuseppe 145
Garner, Thomas 5, 56, 58, 263, 267, 306
Garrard, F. 263
Gelcich, Professor 180, 209, 211, 212–13, 214,
    216
Genoa, Italy 80, 87, 145, 225
George, Ernest 10

George III 18, 303
George V 11, 250, 274
George (Wadham porter) 47
George, Mr. (modeller) 273
German, Major 293
Germany, TGJ visits 106–8, 165
Ghetaldi-Gondola, Baron di 214, 215
Gibbon, Edward 64, 164
Giggleswick, Yorks 9, 37, 230–1, *230*, 241, 267, **282**
Gilbert, Alfred 263
Gilderdale, Rev. John 25–6, 303
Gillhüber (architect in Zara) 208, 209, 211
Gladstone, W.E. 131
Glastonbury, Som, St. John's 158
Goddard, H.L. 303
Godwin of Lugwardine 293
Goodhart-Rendel, H.S. 12, 272
Gordon, Rev. Osborne 280
Gothic Architecture (TGJ) 11, 250
Gough, Lord (Hugh, 3rd Viscount) 241, 315
Gow, Andrew Carrick 235, 315
Goxhenen, Switzerland 109
Grado 173
Grahame, A.J. 303
Grande Chartreuse, France 121
Grange, The (school in Folkstone) xi
Grantly, Lady (*née* Charlotte Beechey) 18, 25
Grantly, Lord 18
Great Exhibition (1851) 29
Great Malvern, Worcs *see* Malvern
Greenhams (English merchants at Trieste) 166, 208, 218
Grenville, William Wyndham 189, 312
Gresford, Denbigh **282**
Greta Bridge, Yorks, Mr. Simpson's Academy 231
Griffith, J.R. 273
Griffiths, Rev. John 104–5, 144, 147, 155–6, 273, 308
Grimsby, Lincs **282**
Grimthorpe, Lord *see* Becket, Edmund 9, 263
Grocers' Company 9
Grove Place, Hants **282**
Grubb, Sir Howard 236, 315
Grylls, Thomas 230, 282, 286, 291, 314
Guippana 216
Gulston, Alan 123, 124, 163, 309
Gumfreston, Pembroke 51, 52, 53, 89, **282**

Haddon Hall, Derbys 121
Hadfield, Charles 262
Hagley, Worcs **283**
Halcomb, Frederick 32, 37, 74, 148, 242, 304
Hall (boat builder) 44, 148
Hale-Dare family 298
Hambleton 17–18, *17*

Hamersley, Mr. and Mrs (Oxford friends) 45–6, 49
Hamilton, Lady 189
Hampden, John 45
Hampstead *see under* London
Hampton Court 23
Hampton Gay, Oxon **283**
Handel, George Frederic 43, 126
Hansen, Professor 197
Hardwick, Philip 152, 311
Hardwick Hall, Derbys 121
Hare, Henry T. 6, 13, 302
Hargreaves, A.K. & L.R. 289
Harpenden, Herts **283**
Harrison, C.R. 303
Harrison, Frederic 33, 255, 304, 316
Harrison, N.W. & G.A. 272
Harrow, Middx 127–8, *127*, 137, 157, 283, 303
Hart, Son & Peard 299
Hatfield, Yorks 89, **283**
Hawkins, Rev. Charles Halford 220, 314
Hawksmoor, Nicholas 152, 311
Haydon, Benjamin Robert 75, 308
Hayes, Kent **283**
Haygarth, Canon H.W. 295
Heathcote, Rev. Charles John 25, 303
Helfurt, Baron 197
Hellesdon, Norfolk **283**
Hellicar, E.A. 277, 303
Henderson, Rev. Patrick Arkley Wright 245, 316
Henley Regatta, Wadham boat at 35, 234–5
Henson, G.F. 278
Hereford **283**
Herkomer, Sir Hubert von 233, 263, 315
Hersham, Surrey **283**
Herzegovina 213, 214
Hesdin 129
Hewlett Johnson, Dr 305
Heywood, B.C.P. 303
Heywood-Lonsdale, Arthur Pemberton 37, 304
Hibbins (carver) 295
Hicks (rector of Fenny Compton) 127
Hilder, Tom (college scout) 47
Hill, Arthur 238, 315
Hill, William 315
Hingston (foreman) 291
Hippisley, Tobias 17
History of the Modern Styles of Architecture (Fergusson) 9
Hitchins (Pembroke farmer) 67–8
Holiday, Henry 275
Holman Hunt, William 51, 59, 242, 263, 306
Holmes, Madame Oliver 195
Holmes, Oliver Wendell 161, 311
Hook, James Clark 198, 313
Hooper, James John 128, 137, 148, 160, 294, 309
Hoorn, Holland (*Plate 9*), 198

Hornblotton, Som 4, 100, 148, **283**
Horsham, West Sussex **284**
Horsley, G.C. 262
Horsley, John Callcott 157–8, 311
Hughes, Professor Thomas McKenny 204, 313
Hungary 174
Huntingford, Dr. 185, 186
Hunton, Kent **284**
Hurst, Miss (and Brasenose knocker) 62
Hussey, Richard Charles 105, 308
Hvar (*formerly* Lesina) (*Plates 28, 30*), 179, 184, 312
Hyde, Hants **284**
Hyman, Orlando Haydon Bridgeman 75

Ilminster, Som 199, 236, **284**
Ilton, Som 199
Image, Selwyn 196, 263, 313
Imperial Institute 189–90
Inderwick, F.A. 263, 299
Indian Mutiny 46
Innsbruck 165
International Trust for Croatian Monuments xiii-xiv
Ipsden, Oxon **284**
Ireland, TGJ visits 118–19
Iron Acton, Glos 127, 137, **284**
Irvine, James Thomas 58–9, 307
Isola Bella, Lake Maggiore, Italy (*Plate 23*) 123–5, *123*, *124*, *125*, 131, 163, 173, 309
Isola Piscatore, Lake Maggiore (*Plate 24*)
Issoire 248
Istria 167
Istrian peasants *172*
Italy, TGJ visits 3, 77, 80–8, 106, 109, 123–5, 131–7, 163–4, 165–6, 225–8
    honeymoon 144, 145–7

Jackson, Alice (*née* Lambarde; TGJ's wife) (*Plate 8*), 6, 93, 143-149, 160, *189*, 191, 201, 239, 240, 274, 299, 308, 310
    diary entries 165, 167–9, 183–4, 210–11, 212–14, 226, 236, 237, 238
Jackson, Annie (TGJ's sister; *later* Arnold) 76, 106
Jackson, Basil (TGJ's brother) 23, 185
Jackson, Basil (TGJ's son) xi, xii, xiii, 11, 185, 206–7, 223, 233–4, 236–7, 238, 239, 241, 248, 250-55, 273, 292, 294, 309, 316
Jackson, Elizabeth (*née* Arnold; TGJ's mother) 18, 19, 20, 22, 29, 67, 129, 144
Jackson, Emily (TGJ's sister) 20, 93, 106, 292
Jackson, Hugh (TGJ's father) 17, 18, 19–20, 31–2, 40, 42, 49, 77, 92, 95, 130, 234, 249, 287, 293
    cartoon letter 95
Jackson, Sir Hugh (TGJ's son) xiii, 7, 149, 200–1, 220, 224, 236, 238, 239, 241, 250, 252, 254, 303, 314

letters to (*Plates 9, 10*)
Jackson, Rev. Jeremiah (18th century) 18, 192
Jackson, John (TGJ's uncle) 18, 19, 42, 305
Jackson, Nicholas (17th century) 15
Jackson, Sir Nicholas (TGJ's grandson) 305, 309, 312
Jackson, T.G.
    birth 2, 20
    bookplate design *202*
    cartoons by *200*, *201*
    chess playing with mother *68*
    death 11, 255
    education (Oxford) *see under* Oxford, Wadham College
    education (school) 2, 25–32
    engagement 143, 310
    gazetteer of designs and works by **266–300**
    glass designs 3, *95*
    honours 1–2, 10–11, 245, 249, 250, 255–6, 316
    piano by *193*
    picture letters (*Plates 9, 10*), *222*
    portrayed (*Plate 1*), *68*, *233*, *237*, *243*
    publications listed 317–19
    wedding 144
    writings about 319–20
Jackson, Thomas (17th century) 16
Jackson, Thomas John 281
Jackson, Tom (TGJ's uncle) 22
Jackson, William 15–16
Jackson, William Goddard 280
Jayne, Francis John 137, 310
Jeffroi de Villehardouin 173, 312
Jersey, Channel Islands **298**
Joachim (violinist) 101, 308
Johnson (architect, pupil of Scott) 58
Jones, Adrian 288
Jones, Inigo 277, 296
Jones, Bishop William Basil Tickell 143, 311
Jowett, Dr. Benjamin 154, 161–2, 271, 311

Kallay, Count 214
Karlovac (*formerly* Carlstadt), Croatia 174, *176*
Kauffmann, Angelica 236
Keene, Charles 73, 308
Kelmscott, Glos 223
Kempe, C.E.R. & Co. 279
Kemsing, Kent 89, **284**
Kenilworth Castle 25
Kent Thomas, R. 5, 269
Kerr, Robert 9
Ketton, Rutland 72, 74, 88, **284**
King, Henry ('K—') 74–5, 308
King Ina's palace 148
Kippington, Kent **284**
Kirby, Edmund 262
Kirby Hall, Northants 5, 6, 13, 111, 120
Kitchin, Dean George William and Mrs. 231, 314

Kitchin, G.H. 303
Knole, Kent 92, 101, 120, 121, 233
Korčula (*formerly* Curzola) (*Plate 29*), 180–3, *181*, 184, 312
Kraljevic, Stanka 312
Krall, Carl 202, 299, 313
Kupka, Herr 197, 245–6

La Berarde, France 122
Lake Como, Italy 112, 173
Lake Maggiore, Italy *see* Delphino Hotel; Isola Bella
Lambarde, Alice (TGJ's wife) *see* Jackson, Alice
Lambarde, Charles James (TGJ's brother-in-law) 224, 274
Lambarde, Charlotte (Alice's cousin) 163
Lambarde, Frank (TGJ's brother-in-law) 152
Lambarde, Harriet (TGJ's sister-in-law) 93, 224
Lambarde, Mr (founder of church at Sevenoaks Weald) 89
Lambarde, Multon (TGJ's brother-in-law) 93, 102, 130, 161, 308
Lambarde, William (Elizabeth I's record keeper) 93, **257–9**
Lambarde, William (TGJ's father-in-law) 93
Lampeter, Cardigan 137, 143, **284–5**
Landseer, Sir Edwin 308
Lantana, Conte 210
Laon, France (*Plate 14*), 98
L'Ariccia 227
Lascelles, Sir Frank Cavendish 241, 315
Lausanne, Switzerland 112
Laverstoke, Hants **285**
Lawes-Wittewronge, Sir Charles 283
Lawrenny, Pembroke 117, 118, **285**
Law Society 191
Lazzari, M. 246
Lee, Stirling 263
Leghorn, Italy 80
Leighton, Sir Frederic 224, 226
Leiper, William 262
Leopold, Prince, Duke of Clarence 144, 145, 311
Le Puy, France 78–9, *79*, 248
Les Ecrins, France 122
Lesina (*now* Hvar) (*Plates 28, 30*), 179, 180, 184, 312
Leslie, Henry (choir of) 72–3
Lethaby, William Richard 239, 263, 315
Lewis, John 60, 307
Liddell, Henry (son) 159
Liddell, Rt Rev. (Dean) Henry George 117, 159, 309, 311
Liddell, Mrs. Lorina 220, 314
Lincoln 160
Ling, Henry 303
Linton, Sir James W.R. 230, 282, 314
Lisle, Dame Alice 89

Little Bromley, Essex **285**
'Little England', Pembroke 51, 306
Llandrindod Wells, Radnor 72, **285**
Lloyd, Dr Charles 39, 305
Loches, France (*Plates 19, 20*), 238, 239
Lockwood, E.W. 303
London
    see also Barnet; Bromley; Cheam; Chessington; Eltham Palace; Harrow; Hayes; Malden; Wimbledon
    Admiralty and War Office buildings, Whitehall 8, **285**
    Albemarle Street **285**
    Arkwright Road and Finchley Road, Hampstead (library) 8, **285**
    Brompton Museum (*later* Victoria and Albert Museum) 63, 307
    Buckingham Street (TGJ's office) 197–8, **285**
    Burlington House, Piccadilly (Royal Academy) 236, **285–6**
        see also main heading Royal Academy
    Church of All Saints, Margaret Street viii
    Church of St. Barnabas **286**
    Cock Inn 101
    County Hall 8, 286
    Devereux Chambers/Court (TGJ's office) 77, 101, **286**
    Dover Street **286**
    Drapers' Hall 9, 228, 229, *229*, **286**
    Evelyn Gardens **286**
    Foreign Office building (Scott) 2, 64–5, 72, 307
    Gallery of British Art, Millbank (*now* Tate Britain) 233, 315
    Greenwich, Royal Naval Hospital 244, 288
    Greenwich Palace 235
    Grocers' Hall 9, 229, **286**
    Hampstead
        artisan houses by TGJ's father 31–2
        Church of St. John the Baptist **286**
        Heath Street 20–2, *21*
        New Court, Streatley Place, Hampstead **287**
        public library (Arkwright Road and Finchley Road 8, **285**, 293
        TGJ's parents at 19–22, 23–5
        Upper Terrace 23–4, *23*
    Hare Court, Inner Temple 9, **286–7**
    Houses of Parliament 55
    Hungerford Market and Wharf 59
    Imperial Institute 8, **287**
    Inner Temple (TGJ) 9, 286–7, 299
    Kensington Court 10, 192, *193*, *194*, **287**
    King's College Hospital 287
    Little Dean's Yard *see* Westminster School
    Mall (TGJ design) 8
    Marlborough House 235
    New Court, Streatley Place, Hampstead **287**, 293

Newgate Prison 197
Nottingham Place, Marylebone (TGJ's home
   and office) 7, 146, **287**
Prince Consort Memorial Hall (unbuilt) 72
Queen Victoria Memorial 8, 241, **287–8**
Royal Marines Memorial **288**
Royal Naval Hospital, Greenwich 244, **288**
St. Pancras Station xii
St. Paul's Cathedral 29, 230
Salisbury Street (TGJ's office) 72, **288**
School Board Offices, Embankment 5, 58, 111
South Kensington Museum 8, 50, 263, **288**
Strand 195, **288**
Victoria and Albert Museum 8, 50, 63, 263,
   288, 307
Victoria monument 8, 241, **287–8**
Westminster Abbey 63, 129
Westminster School 157, 219–20, **288**
Whitefriars Glassworks 94–96, 151, 157, **288**
Whitehall: Admiralty and War Office
   buildings 8, **285**
Whitehall: Foreign Office 2, 64–5, 72, 307
Winchester House 59
London Scottish Volunteers, TGJ joins 70
Long, Edwin 186, 268, 269, 270, 271, 272, 273,
   275, 279, 291, 293, 295, 296, 297
Longfellow, Henry Wadsworth 305
Long, George 28–9, 304
Longleat, Wilts **288**
Lonsdale, Arthur Pemberton Heywood
   (Heywood-Lonsdale) 37, 304
Lottisham, Som 117, 137, **288**
Louis Napoleon (Napoleon III) 70, 307
Louis XV 42
Lover, Samuel 92, 308
Lucas, Thomas 267
Lucca, Italy 80, 87, *247*, 248
Lucerne, Switzerland 108, 248
Lutyens, Sir Edwin 314
Lyndhurst, Hants **289**
Lyndon, Rutland 88, 94, **289**
Lyons, France 248

Macartney, Mervyn 261–2
Mackmurdo, A.H. 262
Macleane, Rev. Arthur 27–8, 303
Madden, F. 157
Madehurst, West Sussex 74, 88, **289**
Malden, Surrey 74, 88, **289**
Mallet, H.E. 303
Malvern, Worcs **289**
Manners, Lord John 64
Maples (carver from Farmer & Brindley) 120,
   269
Marden, Kent **289**
Marlborough, Duke of 192, 194
Marshall, Herbert 263

Marshall, William Cecil 120, 128, 129, 262, 277,
   303, 309
Marten, A.G. 287
Martin Chuzzlewit (Dickens) 148
Marvell, Andrew (poem quoted) 43, 305
Maskelyne, A.M.S. 290
Mason, Canon Arthur James 245, 316
Maupas, Monsignor 209
Max-Müller, Friedrich 314
Max-Müller, Mrs. Georgina Adelaide 220, 314
May, E.J. 262
May, Phil 235, 315
Mazzioli 173
Mecca, Grand Shereef of 236
Mee, Howard 196
Melida 216
Mendelssohn, Felix 310
Metastasio (Pietro Trepassi) 136, 310
Metcalf, Frederick 46, 299, 305
Meyerbeer, Giacomo 73, 308
Micklethwaite, J.T. 58, 262, 306
   Modern Parish Churches 3, 301–2, 306
Middleton, J. Henry 262
Midleton, Cork, Ireland **298**
Milan 109, 133, 146, 173, 248
Miles, C.T. & Son 276
Millais, Sir John Everett 43, 51, 60, 224, 226,
   235, 250, 305
Milton-under-Wychwood, Oxon **289**
Minssen, Professor Bernard Jules 236, 315
Misetic, Dr. 212
Mitchell, Sidney 262
Mittrowski, Count 86
Mockford (clerk of works) 267, 270, 271, 273
Modena 80
Modern Gothic Architecture (TGJ) 3–4, 102–3,
   130, 310
Modern Parish Churches (Micklethwaite) 3, 301–2,
   306
Moira, Gerald 239, 315
Mold, Flint **289**
Molyneux, William More 36, 304
Mondragon (Spanish Captain) 198
Montacute, Som 148, **289**
Montagu, Elizabeth 151, 311
Mont Cenis tunnel 86
Monte Carlo 80
Monte Cristello 166
Moore, H.W. 14
Moore, Dr James Alexander 126, 127, 309
Morris & Co, stained glass 10, 110, 280, 287,
   296, 298
Morris, William 195, 196, 206–7, 223, 263, 313
Morrison, Walter 37, 229, 230, 231, 249, 304
Moselkern, Germany 107–8
Mostar, Herzigovina (*Plate 34*), 214, 216–17
Mozac, France 78

Murray, George 196, 282
Murray, John 285, 286

Naftel, Paul 60, 123, 124, 163, 307
Naples, Italy 226–7, *227*, 252
Napoleon III (Louis Napoleon) 70, 307
Narberth, Pembroke 53, 137, **289**
Nelson, Lord 18, 189
Newton, Ernest 262
Newton, John 72, 288, 308
Nicholls, Rev. Henry 289
Nicholls, William Henry 230, 303, 314
Nicolson, Harold xi
Nimes, France (*Plate 21*) 80, 87
Nineteenth Century (Becket) 9
Norfolk Island, South Pacific 110, **298**
Normanton, Lord (James Charles Herbert
　Welbore Ellis Agar) 89, 137, 281, 308
North, John William 224, 314
Northamptonshire **290**
Northbrook, Lord (Thomas George Baring,
　1st Earl) 158, 280, 311
Northcote, Sir Stafford 62
Northington, Hants 9, 11, 158, **290**
Norwich, John Julius xi
Norwich, Norfolk 96, **290**
Nottingham Castle **290**
Novello, Clara 43, 305
Novello, Vincent 305
Noyon, France 55, 98
Nuremberg, Germany 165

O'Brien (Scott's senior pupil) 54, 58
Ockham, Surrey 290
Oiyac, Jean (gendarme) 80
Omarini (landlord of Delphino) 125, 163
Ossero *179*
Otford, Kent 89, 290
Otway, Mr (Lambarde ancestor) 161
Overton, Hants **290**
Oxford
　Acland Home 220, 228, **267**
　All Souls' College 152, **267**
　Balliol College 249–50, **267**
　　('King's Mound') 6, 162, 205, **271**
　'Bathurst' building 153–4
　Bodleian Library 5, 110, 120, 137, 148, 150,
　　157, **267**
　Botanic Garden **267**
　Brasenose College xiii, 6, 148, 152–3, *153*,
　　192, 204, 244–5, **267**, 299, 303
　　and Stamford 62–3, 307
　　see also Frewen Hall *below*
　Carfax Tower 229
　Christ Church
　　bridge over Cherwell 6, 151–2, **268**
　　Wolsey's tower 4, 105–6, *105*, 110, 118, **267**

Church of All Saints 220, 229, **268**
Church of St. Martin, Carfax 220, 229, **268**
Church of St. Mary-at-the-Wall *see* Hertford
　College *below*
Church of St. Mary the Virgin 9, 205, 206,
　219, 224–5, **268**
　TGJ book on 7, 219, 223
Church of St. Peter-in-the-East 147, **268**
Clarendon Laboratory *see* Electrical
　Laboratory *below*
Clarendon Press **268**
Corpus Christi College xiii, 137, *151*, 152,
　268–9, 299
　barge *206*
　TGJ commoner at 2, 31, 32
　TGJ sits for scholarship 30
Cricket Pavilion, Parks 5, 151, **269**
Divinity Schools 13
Electrical Laboratory 6, 245, **269**
Examination Schools (*Plates 2, 3*), 4–5, 6, 7, 9,
　12, 13, 110, *111*, 116, 117, 119–20, 137,
　148, 150, 152, 154, 173, 186, **269–70**
Frewen Hall **270**
Hertford College
　Bridge ('Bridge of Sighs') xii-xiii, 6, *251*, 251
　buildings ix, 6, 157, 244, **270**, 303
　Church of St. Mary-at-the-Wall **270**
　staircase xiii, 146, *156*
　TGJ portrait ix
High School for Boys 6, 14, 137, *138*, 144,
　145, 150, 205, **270**
High School for Girls 6, 13, 137, 148, 150, **270**
Keble College xii
King's Mound 6, 162, 204, **271**
Lincoln College 148, 151, **271**
　see also Church of All Saints *above*
Magdalen College 6
　School **271**
Martyrs' Memorial 5
Merton College 152, **271**
Military College, Cowley 6, 120, 137, 148,
　150, **271**
New College 6, 137
Old Ashmolean Museum **271**
Oriel College 152, **271–2**
　barge 6, 205, *205*
Queen's College **272**
Radcliffe Camera **272**
Radcliffe Infirmary **272**
Radcliffe Observatory 236, **272**
Radcliffe Science Library 6, 229, 236, **272**
St. Basil's Home **272**
Schools of Rural Economy and Forestry **272**
Sheldonian Theatre (*Plate 4*), 120, 126–7,
　272–3
Somerville College 151, **273**
Taylor Galleries 6, 47

Town Hall 6, 13, 302
Trinity College 6, 148, 152, 153–4, *154*, **273**
University College, Master's Lodgings 5
University Commissions 32, 64, 90, 144
Wadham College
  see also Bourton-on-the-Water; Hampton
    Gay; Ilminster; Little Bromley
  Henley Regatta (1849) 35, 234–5
  TGJ architectural and other work for xiii, 4,
    5, 105, 156–7, *155*, **273**
  TGJ book on 7, 199
  TGJ in bumps (1856) 37, 160, 230, 233, 305
  TGJ elected Bursar 4, 7
  TGJ fellowship at 2, 3, 4, 7, 64, 74–6, 90,
    143, 160
  TGJ portrait xii, xiii, 236, *237*
  TGJ scholar at 2, 32–9, 74
Oxford Almanack (1883), TGJ buildings 5
Oxonian in Norway, The; *Oxonian in Thelemarken,*
  The (Metcalf), TGJ illustrations for 46, 299

Padua, Italy 173
Paer, Fernando 136, 310
Paesiello, Giovanni 136, 310
Paget, Sir Augustus Berkeley 145, 197, 311
Paget, Sir James 220, 314
Paget, Misses 275
Palermo, Italy 251
Palestine 230
Palladio, Andrea 56, 306
Palmerston, Lord 64–5, 70
Palmer, William Waldegrave (Lord Selborne)
  245, 316
Paoli, General 18, 303
Parenzo (*now* Poreč) *174, 175*
Paris 173, 225, 247, 250
  International Exhibition (TGJ prize/exhibit) 7,
    130, 131
  Siege of 99–100
Parkinson, Dr. Stephen 160, 311
Parma, Italy 81
Parratt, Sir Walter 29, 233, 304
Patteson, John Coleridge 110, 298, 309
Pavia, Italy, Certosa of 109
Pearson, John Loughborough 231, 307, 314
Peek, Sir Cuthbert Edgar 291
Peers, C.R. 303
Pegram, Henry 277, 286
Pembrokeshire, TGJ visits 51–3, 67–9
Peper Harrow, Surrey 127, **290**
Pepys, Samuel 197
Perkins, Arthur Edward 151, 303, 311
Perugia, Italy 146
Pesaro, Italy 163
Peterborough *see* Northamptonshire
Peter the Great 198
Petersfield, Hants, Castle House 160

Pevsner, Nikolaus xii, 1, 13, 301, 302
Pickersgill, Frederick Richard 40, 305
Pickersgill, Frederick William 305
Pickersgill, Henry William 305
Pieve di Cadore, Italy 166
Pilgrim's Progress, A, TGJ's illustrations xiii
Pisa, Italy 80, 87, 251
Pistoja 80
Pite, A. Beresford 11–12, 262
Pitt, William, the Younger 186, 189
Plymouth 70
Poitiers, France (*Plate 13*), 238, 248
Pola (*now* Pula) 166, 173, 312
Polignac 248
Pompeii, Italy 226
Poreč (*formerly* Parenzo) 173, *174, 175*
Portal, Sir William Wyndham 196, 313
Portsmouth, Hants 70, **290**
Potter of South Molton Street 65
Powell, James Crofts 3, 94–99, 101, 106, 128,
  129, 131, 150, 151, 152, 163, 196, 230, 263,
  271, 274, 275, 282, 284, 288, 289, 290, 293,
  297, 298, 299
Poynter, Sir Edward 226, 235, 314
Prance, Reginald 274
Pre-Raphaelites 51, 60, 64, 195, 306
Prescott, Jack (John) 34, 304
Price, Bonamy 137, 310
Prior, Edward S. 261
Pugin, Augustus Welby Northmore, *Contrasts* 56,
  306
Pula (*formerly* Pola) 166, 173, 312
Purchon, W.S. 6
Purton, Wilts **290**
Pyne, George Masters 43–4, 305
Pyrford, Surrey 88, **291**
Pyrton Manor, Oxon 45

Quarnero islands 174, 175, 177

Rab (*formerly* Arbe) (*Plate 33*), *178*
Radley College, Berks xii, 9, 157, 220, *221*, 244,
  255, **291**
Ragusa (*now* Dubrovnik) (*Plates 31, 32*), 170, 172,
  174, 211–13, *212, 213, 214*, 214, 215–16, *215*
Raicevich, Monsignor 209, 210–11, 216
Ravenna, Italy (*Plate 26*), 81, 88, 133
Ravenscroft, F.E.B. 303
Rawlinson, George 36, 46, 47–8, 304
Reason in Architecture (TGJ) 242
'Recollections', history of xi–xii, xiii
Rees, S.P. 303
registration of architects 7, 10, 14, 190–1, **260–3**
Reid, Sir John 67
Renaissance of Roman Architecture, The (TGJ) 11,
  255
Reynolds, Sir Joshua 60, 73, 159, 161, 285

Rheims, France 98
Rhine, River 173
RIBA *see* Royal Institute of British Architects
Ricardo, H. 262
Richmond, Sir William Blake 196, 206–7, 239, 240, 263, 313
Rickarby, Alfred 72, 89
Rickmansworth, Herts 72, **291**
Rickman, Thomas 308
Rickman, Thomas Miller 308
Riggi, Signor 145
Rijeka (*formerly* Fiume) 174, *176*
Riley, Athelstan 10, 192, 195, 287, 313
Riom, France 78
Ripley, Surrey 88, **291**
Ripon, Yorks **291**
Ritchie, Anne (*née* Thackeray) 189, 242, 310, 312
Ritchie, Richmond 189, 312
Riviere, Hugh 236, *237*, 315
Riviere, Briton 263
Robeston Wathen, Pembroke 53, 89, 118, **291**
Robson, E.R. 14
Rochester, Kent 95, 160, 233
Rogers, James Edwin Thorold 36, 48, 110, 304
Rolleston, Professor George 119, 309
Rome, Italy 144, 145–6, *146*, 225–28, 251, **298**
Rosa, Commandatore 145
Ross, Charles Douglas 75–6, 308
Rossini, Gioacchino 136
Rothamsted Manor *see* Harpenden
Rouen, France 42, 252
Rousdon, Devon **291**
Royal Academy
  Burlington House 236, **285–6**
  Council portrait (1907) *233*
  TGJ elected Associate 7, 103, 158, 191, 202–3
  TGJ elected full Academician 7, 226, 232–3
  TGJ elected Treasurer 241
Royal College of Art 239–40
Royal Institute of British Architects
  Goodhart-Rendel talk on TGJ 12
  registration of architects 7, 10, 14, 190–1, **260–3**
  TGJ's Royal Gold Medal 10
Royal Institution 190
Rugby School, Warwicks 9, 157, 225, 244, **291**
Rushton Hall, Northants **292**
Ruskin, John 6, 44, 51, 63–4, 73, 120, 162–3, 280, 306, 307, 313
Rye, East Sussex **292**

St. Blaise (S. Biagio) 171–2
St. Bruno 121
S(ta) Caterina, Lake Maggiore, Italy 132, *132*
St. David's, Pembroke 67, 69, 118, 220, *222*, 222–3
  Cathedral (*Plates 6, 11*), xii, 69, 202, 222, **292**, 306
St. Denis, France 248
St. George, Thomas and John 303
St. Helier, Mary (Lady) 252, 316
St. John the Baptist, Community of 272
St. Louis International Exhibition (TGJ prize) 7
St. Paul 216, 227
St. Petersburg, Russia 7, 159, **298**
St. Pol 129
St. Quentin, France 98
St. Vincent, Lord 18
Sale, Thomas Walter 35, 304
Salisbury, Lord (*formerly* Lord Robert Cecil) 62, 74, 143
Salisbury, Wilts **292**
Salona 183–4
Salonica, Greece 246–7
Salter Bros. 272
Sanderson, Lt Col R.M. 291
Sandwich, Kent 157, **292**
Sarajevo 217, 218
Sargent, John Singer 224, 245, 314
Schönbrunn palace, Vienna 245–6
Scott, C.M.O. 276
Scott, Sir (George) Gilbert xii, 2, 5, 27, 50–1, 53–4, 56, 57, 63, 64–5, 72, 77–8, 96, 98, 105, 109, 129–30, 303, 284, 306, 307, 308
  letter to Jackson xv
Scott, George Gilbert (junior) 14, 58, 63, 71, 263, 306
Scott, John Oldrid 5, 58, 71, 78, 80–2, 96, 110, 117, 236, 262, 276, 306
Scott, Dean Robert 160, 311
Scott, Sir Robert Forsyth 245, 316
Scott, Sir Walter 61
Scott, Walter (clerk of works) 271
Sebenico (*now* Sibenik) 168–9, *170*, *171*
Sedding, John D. 261-2
Seddon, J.P. 294
Sedgwick, Professor Adam 204, 277, 313
Selborne, Lord (William Waldegrave Palmer, 2nd Earl) 245, 315
Send, Surrey 4, 72, 73–4, **292**
Sevenoaks, Kent
  Board School **292**
  Church of St. Nicholas **292**
  Cottage hospital (hospital for hip disease) 93, *93*, *94*, **292**
  Emily Jackson Wing Hospital **292**, 308
  Granville Road **293**
  Lime Tree Walk 10, 130, 137–9, *139*, 287, **293**
  Maywood House (private house) **293**
  St. Julian's (private house) 4, **293**
  Vine Cottage (TGJ's parents at) 92
  Woodlands (private house) 4, 89, **293**
Sevenoaks Weald, Kent, Church of St. George 89, **293**
Sewell, Rev. James Edwards 117, 309
Shamley Green, Surrey **293**

Shaw, (Richard) Norman 7, 10, 14, 103, 158, 190, 191, 195, 202–3, 225, 239, 249, 260-3, 301, 308
Shaw Lefevre, Madeleine Septimia 151, 162, 311
Sheering, Essex **293**
Sheerness 70
Sherrin, George 262
Shirley, Walter Waddington 43, 305
Sibenik (*formerly* Sebenico) 168–69, *170*, *171*
Sidebottom, Henry 94, 308
Siena, Italy (*Plate 25*), 80, 87, 145, 251
Simcoe, Henry Addington 305
Simcoe, Paul Creed Gwillim 39, 305
Simonds, George 263
Simpson, F.M. 262
Sirmio, Italy 116
Slater, William 308
Slater, S.S. **293**
Slindon, West Sussex 4, 88, **293**, 302
Smirnoff, Dr 159
Smith, Henry John Stephen 105, 130–1, 308
Smith, James & Sons 272
Smith, Miss (mathematician) 105
Smith, Mr. Bowden (Rugby School master) 225
Smith, Prof. Roger 263
Smith, Rev. Gilbert Nicholas 51–3, 89, 306
Smith Barry, A.H. 298
Smyth, Bishop 63
Soane, Sir John 152, 311
Society for the Protection of Ancient Buildings 9, 205, 313
Soissons, France 98, *99*
Solomon, Joseph 235, 236, 315
Somerley, Hants 281
Southwell, Notts 160
Spalato (*now* Split) 168, *168*, *169*
Spencer, Augustus 239, 315
Spiers, R. Phene 262
Split (*formerly* Spalato) 168, *168*, *169*
Squire, Miss (Cambridge benefactor) 235
Stacey, Mrs (housekeeper) 72
Stamford, Lincs 61–3
   Browne's Hospital **293**
   Church of All Saints 88–9, 294
   Church of St. Mary **294**
   St. Martin's, Stamford Baron 18, 22
   St. Mary's Street, Tom Jackson's house 22
   University 62, 307
Stanfield, Clarkson 25, 303
Stapleford, Notts **294**
Stefarroni (mason) 145
Stevenson, John James 14, 58, 262, 306
Stewart, Douglas 230, 282, 303, 314
Stoppini family, Assisi 137
Stowe, Alfred 160, 311
Strasbourg 108, 248
Stratton (East Stratton), Hants 158

Streatfield, G.E.S. 277, 303
Street, A.E. 262
Street, George Edmund 58, 110, 191, 225, 295, 306
Stresa, Italy 112, 123, 131
Stubbs, Bishop William 220, 314
Sumner, Heywood 196, 263
Sundridge, Kent 89, **294**
Sutton, Sir Richard 63
Sutton, Rev. F.H. 284
Swain, R. 293
Swift, Jonathan 200, 313
Switzerland, TGJ visits 108–9, 241
Sydenham, Kent, TGJ's parents in 42–3
Sydney International Exhibition (TGJ prize) 7
Symons, Dr Benjamin Parsons ('Big Ben'; Warden of Wadham) 33–5, 38, 39, 45, 46–7, 76, 90, 104, 105, 304
Symons, Lydia 33, 34–5

Taroiseau, France *97*
Tasmania, Australia 96, **298**
Tate, Rev. Charles Richmond 4, 27, 31, 32, 72, 73, 291, 292, 303
Taylor, Isaac 303
Taylor, Mat (boat builder) 44
Temple, Sir William 200, 313
Temple Grove, East Sheen 200–1
Tenby, Pembroke (*Plate 5*) 51, 53, 67, **294**
Teulon, S.S. 312
Thackeray, Anne (*later*) Ritchie 189, 242, 310, 312
Thackeray, William Makepeace 310, 312
Thomas, George Gilbert (*later* Treherne) 47, 305
Thomas, R. Kent 5, 269
Thompson, Arthur Steinkopff 34, 304
Thompson, Reginald Edward 30, 97, 98, 304
Thorley, George Earlham 74, 110, 117, 144, 309
Thorley, John 305
Thorne House, Yeovil, Som 128, *128*, 137, 148, 160, **294**
Thornhaugh, Cambs 137, **294**
Thornycroft, Hamo 263
Thring, Edward 100–1, 192, 274, 283, 288, 293, 308
Thring, Godfrey 100, 117, 148, 308
Tiberius, Emperor 151
Tiburzi (outlaw) 228
Tichborne trial 250
Tipperary, Ireland 118, **298**
Tournay, Dr William 33, 304
Tours 248
Trau (*now* Trogir) 174, *177*
Traylen, H.F. 294
Trevenen, Mrs. 31, 36
Trieste, Italy 166, 173, 177–9, 208, 218
Tritton, Robert Biscoe 89, 290, 308

Trogir (*formerly* Trau) 174, *177*
Turkentine, C. 294
Turle, Dr James 30, 304
Turner, E. Page 286
Turner, J.M.W. 60
Turner, William (Turner of Oxford) xiii, 44–5, 305
Twining (banker and tea merchant) 308

Upper Hellesdon, Norfolk *see* Hellesdon
Uppingham School, Rutland 9, 18, 100–1, 157, 192, 228, **294**, 299
Urbino 163

Valaresso, Archbishop of Zara 196
Van Alen, J.J. 292
Venice, Italy 81, 82–6, *82*, *83*, *84*, *85*, 112–16, *112*, *113*, *114*, *115*, *116*, 146, *182*, 183, *183*, *217*, 218
    'Bridge of Sighs' xii-xiii, 83
    Doge's Palace 83
    St. Mark's 83, 88
Verona, Italy 116, 146
Vesuvius 226
Vézelay, France 96, *97*, 308
Victoria, Queen 8, 241, 274, 282, 287–8
Vienna 245–6
Viollet-le-Duc, Eugène 42, 55, 56, 98, 305
Vitruvius 11
volunteers, TGJ joins 70, 101–2

Wadham, Nicholas and Dorothy (Founders of Wadham College) 199, 284
Wales, Prince of (*later* Edward VII) 119, 150, 189, 224, 228, 235
Wales, Prince of (*later* George IV) 18
Walkden, Lancs, Ellesmere Memorial 2–3, **295**
Walker, Mr. 296
Walker, William 11
Warre, Dr Edmond 37, 151, 233, 241, 242, 244, 245, 305
Warre, Edmond Lancelot 233, 303, 315
Warren, E. Prioleau 263
Warren, Samuel 304
Warren, Samuel Lilckendy 32, 74, 304
Warwick 25
Water Eaton, Oxon 148, **295**
Waterford, Ireland 118
Waterhouse, Alfred 8, 189–90, 263, 312
Watson, Rev. Albert 152, 311
Watts & Co. 273, 290
Webb, Sir Aston 189, 241, 312, 263, 314
Webb, Philip 3, 195, 263, 313
Webster, Thomas 158, 311
Weiss, Willoughby 43, 305
Wellington, Duke of, TGJ at funeral of 29–30
Wells, Som **295**
West Clandon, Surrey 27, **295**

Westbury, Lord 273
Wharton, George 45, 305
Whitby, Yorks, TGJ's accident at 141–3
Whitchurch, Hants **295**
Whitefriars Glassworks *see under* London
White, William Henry 191, 263, 312
Whyte, Dr William 301
Wilde, Spencer 278
Wilkinson, William 14
William, King of Prussia 108
Williams, W.J. 293
Willis, Dr Francis 18, 303
Willis, Henry ('Father Willis') 126, 230, 272, 273, 293, 309
Wimbledon, Surrey 304
    Church of St. Augustine **295**
    Church of St. John the Baptist **295**
    Church of St. Luke **295**
    Church of St. Mary **295**
    Eagle House (*Plate 7*), 29, 185–9, *187*, *188*, *189*, 201–2, **295–6**
    Haygarth Memorial School **296**
    hospital **296**
    house **296**
    Keirside (*later* Stamford House) **296**
    Lauriston Road **296**
    Ridgway **296**
    war memorial **296**
Wimbledon Society xiii
Winchester, Hants
    Castle Avenue **296**
    Cathedral 9, 10–11, 186, 242–3, *243*, 250, 264–5, **296–7**
    Hospital of St. Cross **297**
    Winchester College **220**
    Wolvesey Palace 244, **297**
Windsor, Berks 233
Winterbourne Abbas, Dorset **297**
Wisbech Grammar School 18
Witherington, William Frederick 305
Wolsey, Cardinal, and Christ Church Oxford tower 4, 105, *105*
    see also Oxford, Christ Church
Wolvesey Palace Chapel, Winchester, Hants 244, **297**
Wonston, Hants 297
Woods, Rev. Henry George 154, 311
Woodward, Benjamin 309
Wooldridge, Harry Ellis 152, 271, 286, 290, 311
Worcester **297**
Worms 248
Wrexham, Denbigh **297**
Wright-Henderson, Rev. Patrick Arkley 245, 316
Wykeham-Fiennes family 303

Yeames, William Frederick 235, 315
Yemani, Sheikh Ahmed 312

Young, Sir Charles 29
Ypres 129
Yvetot, king of (poem about) 129, 310

Zadar (*formerly* Zara), Dalmatia 164, 166, 167–8,
    167, 174, 177, *180*, 183, 208–11, 218
    Cathedral 9, 196–7, 208–10, *209*, 211, 218,
        298–9, 313
Zagreb (*formerly* Agram) 174
Zara (*now* Zadar) *see* Zadar
Zierichsee 198
Zola, Emile 162